Vol. 1.
p. 106.
A Beaver 26 inches long from the head to the tail
wild Beeves
A beeve catch'd by y^e horns with ropes
Crocodile going to devour a little calf
A beeve attack'd with Spears
A Savage springing upon a beeve
Savages drying their meat

NEW VOYAGES

TO

NORTH-AMERICA

BY THE

BARON DE LAHONTAN

Reprinted from the English edition of 1703, with facsimiles of original title-pages, maps, and illustrations, and the addition of Introduction, Notes, and Index

By Reuben Gold Thwaites, LL.D.

Editor of "The Jesuit Relations and Allied Documents," Hennepin's "New Discovery," etc.

In Two Volumes

VOLUME I

CHICAGO
A. C. McCLURG & CO.
1905

Published February 25, 1905

Composition by The Dial Press, Chicago.
Presswork by The University Press, Cambridge.

CONTENTS—VOLUME I

PAGE

INTRODUCTION—*The Editor* ix

LAHONTON BIBLIOGRAPHY—*Victor Hugo Paltsits* . . li

LAHONTAN'S "NEW VOYAGES TO NORTH-AMERICA"—
Volume I.

Title-page (facsimile of original) 1
Dedication to the Duke of Devonshire . . . 3
Preface 5
Contents of Letters, Memoirs, Discourses, Dialogue, etc., in both Volumes 13
Letters I (November 8, 1683)-XXV (January 31, 1694) 25
Memoirs of North-America; containing a Geographical Defcription of that vaft Continent; the Cuftoms and Commerce of the Inhabitants, &c.
Introductory Remarks 299
A ſhort Defcription of Canada 301
A Lift of the Savage Nations of Canada . . 339
A Lift of the Animals of Canada 343
A Defcription of fuch Animals or Beafts, as are not mention'd in the Letters 345
A Lift of the Fowl or Birds that frequent the South Countries of Canada 350
The Birds of the North Countries of Canada . 351

PAGE

A Defcription of fuch Birds as are not accounted for in my Letters 353
A Defcription of the Infects of Canada . . 357
The Names of the Fifh in the River of St. Laurence, from its Mouth to the Lakes of Canada . 358
The Fifh that are found in the Lakes of Canada, and in the Rivers that fall into 'em . . . 359
The Fifh found in the River of Miffifipi . . 359
A Defcription of the Fifh that are not mention'd in the Letters 360
The Trees and Fruits of the South Countries of Canada 364
The Trees and Fruits of the North Countries of Canada 364
A Defcription of the above-mention'd Trees and Fruits 366
A Defcription of the Trees and Fruits of the Northern Countries 370
A General view of the Commerce of Canada . 373
The Names of the Skins given in exchange, with their Rates 379
An Account of the Government of Canada in General 381
A Difcourfe of the Intereft of the French, and of the Englifh, in North-America 394
A Table explaining fome Terms made ufe of in both Volumes 401

ILLUSTRATIONS—VOLUME I

(FACSIMILES OF ORIGINALS)

	PAGE
A beaver; the hunting of buffaloes; savages drying their meat	*Frontispiece*
Map of the Great Lakes	*Facing* 1
Map of the straits of Mackinac	„ 36
"Canows made of Birch-bark"—sketches and plans	„ 80
"Mr. De la Barre's camp"	„ 124
"A General Map of New France, Com̃. call'd Canada"	„ 156
"The curiofity of the Rackets, and the way of hunting Elks"	„ 188
"The Hunting of divers Animals"	„ 220
"The Difcovery of an Ambufcade"	„ 254
"A Map of ye Long River and of fome others that fall into that fmall part of ye Great River of Miffifipi which is here laid down"—with sketch-plans of a house, a vessel, and a medal	„ 284
"The Attack of Quebec"	„ 316
"The Great bay of Placentia"	„ 344
Map of Newfoundland	„ 384

INTRODUCTION

Village of Lahontan.

IN the frontier department of the Basse-Pyrenées, once a part of the ancient province of Béarn, on gently-undulating hillsides which occupy middle ground between the broad-stretching pastures and marshes of the Landes and the over-topping escarpments of the Pyrenées, lies the pleasant little village of Lahontan. A community of twelve hundred souls, it boasts of an interesting history, but is now almost unknown in its dreamy isolation, save that the scholar may remember that it was once the fief of the illustrious Montaigne.

Lahontan's father.

About the middle of the seventeenth century, Lahontan was erected into a barony, of which Isaac de Lom, Sieur d'Arce, the father of our author, was the second baron. The Sieur d'Arce was famous as a civil engineer, having made the port of Bayonne navigable for sea-going vessels (1630–48). As a recompense for this and certain military services, Louis XIV granted to him and his heirs forever (1658) a monopoly of navigation and transportation in the harbor of Bayonne, and a pension of three thousand livres per annum for a dozen years; in later years, he was made reformer-general of Béarn, a councillor of the parlement of Navarre, a chevalier of St. Michel, and a bourgeois of Bayonne.

His first wife (Jeanne Guérin), with whom he had lived for fifteen years, having died in 1663 without issue, he contracted in his old age a second marriage, this time with Jeanne-Françoise le Fascheux de Couttes. To them was born at Lahontan, the ninth of June, 1666, Louis-Armand, whose book of adventurous travel in the heart of North America we are here reprinting. The infant was presented at the baptismal font by no less personages than the Comte de Guiche, then governor of Béarn, and his sister, the Marquise de Lons,—a distinguished welcome to the stage of life, in strong contrast to the experiences incident to his departure.

Birth of our author.

When young Louis was but eight years old, his father died at the age of eighty. Honors and wealth had accompanied Baron Isaac until about the time of his son's birth; thereafter, he became involved in the toils of obligations incurred by his great engineering operations, and of the lawsuits incidental thereto. The son inherited the title of Le Baron de Lahontan et Heslèche (to-day, d'Esleich), and a shattered estate which went from bad to worse. It is small wonder that one of the characteristic features of his *Voyages* is an unquenchable bitterness against lawyers and legal processes.

A shattered estate.

After the fashion of the times, the third baron had from his cradle been destined for the army; and while still a child, family influence secured for him a cadetship in the famous Bourbon regiment. Later, in the effort to secure for the young nobleman a more rapid advancement, he was entered as a "garde" in the marine corps—the Department of the Marine being then entrusted with the

Dedicated to the army.

care of colonies. From earliest boyhood, Louis had heard much of Canada. From a neighboring seignory had gone forth the Baron de St. Castin, famous in the annals of Maine; the land of the Basques, on both the Spanish and the French slopes of the Pyrenées, had for nearly two centuries been a recruiting ground for adventurers to the New World; and Louis's relative, Claude Bragelonne, a high official in the French army, had been one of the Company of the Hundred Associates, whose monopoly long exploited the commerce of the king's ambitious colony over seas. Lefebvre de la Barre had but just succeeded Count Frontenac as governor of New France. His petition to the court for eight hundred regular troops to be used in proposed chastisements of the death-dealing Iroquois, had been in part met by sending to his assistance three companies of French marines in the autumn of 1683. Enrolled among the members of this detachment—exactly in what official capacity, we do not know—was Louis-Armand de Lom d'Arce, the youthful Baron de Lahontan, then seventeen years of age.

Lahontan's outlook on a life of reverses had thus early made of him a cynic. The first Letter in his *Voyages*, describing the trip to America, contains premonitory symptoms of that caustic humor which was soon to be characteristic of his pen; here, as later, description is freely mingled with scoffing, and information with persiflage. The season was late when the frigate left Rochelle; it was already November, with drift ice in the St. Lawrence and its rugged shores white with snow, when Quebec was reached after a

Arrival in New France.

tempestuous voyage. "I cannot," Lahontan tells his anonymous correspondent, "as yet give you any account of the Country, excepting that 'tis mortally cold." The day following the arrival of the troops, the great La Salle left the little wilderness capital on his voyage to France, whence he was to embark for the Gulf of Mexico upon his final, fateful enterprise.

The marines at once went into winter quarters "in ſome Villages or Cantons adjacent." It fell to Lahontan's share to be billeted among the habitants of Beaupré, some seventeen miles down the river from Quebec. There, he declares, "the boors of thoſe Manors live with more eaſe and conveniency than an infinity of the Gentlemen in France;" and he has many pleasant words for this "free ſort of People," every one of whom "lives in a good and a well furniſh'd House." He remarks the vast fire-places, and the enormous quantities of wood consumed, "by reaſon of the prodigious Fires they make to guard themſelves from the Cold, which is there beyond all meaſure, from the month of December, to that of April." Despite the nipping and protracted frost, the lad appears to have been contented with his lot. Hunting in company with the Indians, acquiring the dialects of the tribesmen, and visiting their villages in sledges and upon snow-shoes, with a few official duties intermingled, and now and then a gay assembly at the little colonial court on the hill-top in neighboring Quebec, furnished agreeable diversity of occupation. His letters give us a pleasing picture of life among the easy-going habitants in the suburbs; and from

A winter at Beaupré.

them we also obtain a vivid notion of the aspect of the little frontier capital, in this hey-day of New France.

In the spring (1684), Lahontan proceeded under orders to Montreal. Along the way, during a leisurely progress, he picked up odds and ends of information, and in brief phrase cleverly described what he saw. Late in June, he accompanied an expedition which Governor La Barre undertook against the recalcitrant Iroquois, and on the eleventh of the following month arrived with the advance party at Fort Frontenac, where they awaited the main body of the army; but owing to the delays incident to such enterprises under primitive conditions, it was some five weeks later before a start could be made. Crossing Lake Ontario the little column took up a position near Famine River, being there so wasted by malarial fever that La Barre was forced to an ignominious peace, which soon led to his recall from the colony. The story of this unfortunate expedition is skilfully told by Lahontan, who gives the speeches of the governor and of the Iroquois envoys in phrases which have become classic examples of Indian oratory and diplomacy.

An Iroquois campaign.

The following winter, the young baron passed in garrison at Montreal. With the opening of spring (1685) he was sent with a detachment to the frontier fort of Chambly, where the summer was spent in the congenial occupation of accompanying the neighboring habitants and tribesmen upon their hunting and fishing parties, which he describes with the gusto of a true sportsman and a close observer of nature. In September he was ordered to

Hunting and fishing expeditions.

Boucherville, to be quartered on the habitants for the space of a year and a half—a protracted sojourn, but without ennui, for he was given his fill of sport, especially of elk hunting, at one time being absent upon such an excursion for three months in mid-winter. On another occasion, he spent an autumn month "in a Canow upon ſeveral Rivers, Marſhes, and Pools, that diſembogue in the Champlain Lake, being accompany'd with thirty or forty of the Savages that are very expert in Shooting and Hunting, and perfectly well acquainted with the proper places for finding Water-foul, Deer, and other fallow Beaſts." He gives us careful reports not only of the methods of the chase, but of the habits of the birds and animals, spiced with much humor and keen comment on men and things.

Dearly as the baron loved sport, he appears to have devoted much of his spare time, even when in forest camps amid rude wood-rangers and savages, to study and to mental growth. "Beſides the pleaſure of ſo many different ſorts of Diverſion," he writes, "I was likewiſe entertain'd in the Woods with the company of the honeſt old Gentlemen that liv'd in former Ages. Honeſt Homer, the amiable Anacreon, and my dear Lucian, were my inſeperable Companions. Ariſtotle too deſir'd paſſionately to go along with us, but my Canow was too little to hold his bulky Equipage of Peripatetick Silogiſms: So that he was e'en fain to trudge back to the Jeſuits, who vouchſaf'd him a very honourable Reception." We doubtless obtain here a glimpse of the source of the Dialogues with Adario, which occupy so

A student of the classics.

large a share of the second volume; Lucian apparently furnished the model for those caustic satires on the Christianity and civilization of the seventeenth century.

The studies and pleasures of this interesting young man-at-arms were occasionally interfered with by the austerities of the priests about him. He indignantly relates that when stationed in Montreal he was "inrag'd at the impertinent Zeal of the Curate of this City." Seeking his room in his absence, this over-zealous ecclesiastic "finding the Romance of the Adventures of Petronius upon my Table, he fell upon it with an unimaginable fury, and tore out almoſt all the Leaves. This Book I valued more than my Life, becauſe 'twas not caſtrated; and indeed I was ſo provok'd when I saw it all in wrack, that if my Landlord had not held me, I had gone immediately to that turbulent Paſtor's House, and would have pluck'd out the Hairs of his Beard with as little mercy as he did the Leaves of my Book."

Lahontan's second Iroquois campaign.

In the spring of 1687 all was bustling confusion in the settlements on the St. Lawrence. Denonville, the new governor, was about to try his hand at subduing the irrepressible Iroquois, whom Champlain had unwittingly converted into sworn enemies of the French. The largest expedition yet projected was fitted out by the soldier-governor, and rendezvoused at the island of St. Helen, opposite Montreal. Eight hundred regulars had been sent over from France, doubling the number already in the colony. With the new troops came an order from the ministry to allow the return of young Lahontan, whose tangled affairs were sadly in need of his presence in Paris; his relatives had secured his furlough by the exercise of much personal influence. But the governor, needing all his useful men, deferred compliance, promising it for the close of the campaign, and Lahontan had no alternative but to advance a second time into the country of the Iroquois.

This campaign, while more fruitful than the preceding, effected nothing further than an invasion of the land of the Seneca, the laying waste of their villages and harvests, and the construction at Niagara of a fort designed to check their aggressions. It was upon this expedition that the few friendly Iroquois, who had, under missionary tutelage, settled around Fort Frontenac, were captured by the French and sent prisoners to France to serve in the royal galleys—a piece of arrant treachery, which the wretched and misguided colony was to expiate two years later in the fire and blood of the massacre at Lachine. Lahontan's sympathies were so keenly aroused by the unmerited sufferings of these innocent prisoners at Fort Frontenac, that he stood in close danger of falling a victim to the wrath of the Algonkin allies, who, in their savage fashion, delighted in maltreating the ill-fated Iroquois, whom the missionaries had segregated from the care of their own people. The baron had soundly thrashed some of the young tormentors, but was immediately set upon by the infuriated band, who "flew to their Fuſees, in order to kill me." He was saved only by the interposition of the Canadians, who "aſſur'd 'em I was drunk (Among the Savages, drunken Perſons are always excus'd: for, the Bottle attones for all Crimes), that all the French were prohibited to give me either Wine or Brandy, and that I ſhould certainly be impriſon'd as ſoon as the Campaign were over."

The campaign finished, Lahontan hoped to be allowed to return to France, but before having an opportunity of reminding Denonville of his promise of a furlough, the luckless officer was summoned to the great man's presence and informed that because of his knowledge of native languages and his skill in forest diplomacy, he was detailed forthwith to the command of a detachment destined to the upper lakes, in response to the request of the wily Huron and Ottawa of Lake Huron, who wished to "ſee a Fort ſo conveniently plac'd, which might favour their retreat upon any Expedition againſt the Iroqueſe . . . At the ſame time he aſſur'd me, he would inform the Court of the Reaſons that mov'd him to detain me in Canada, notwithſtanding that he had orders to give me leave to go home. You may eaſily gueſs, Sir, that I was thunderſtruck with theſe News, when I had fed myſelf all along with the hopes of returning to France, and promoting my Intereſt, which is now ſo much thwarted."

Ordered to the Upper Lakes.

The commands of the governor were not to be questioned by a subordinate, so the disappointed Lahontan, smothering his grief with reflections upon his professional advancement, once more turned his back on home, and hastily made preparations for his journey into the vast and almost unknown region of the Northwest. "The Men of my Detachment," he writes, "are brisk proper fellows, and my Canows are both

b

new and large. I am to go along with Mr. Dulhut, a Lions Gentleman, who is a Perſon of great Merit, and has done his king and his Country very conſiderable Services. M. de Tonti makes another of our Company; and a Company of Savages is to follow us."

Among the motley war-party which Denonville had led to his assault on the insolent Iroquois, was a band of the "far Indians" brought by their commandant, La Durantaye, from the distant post of Mackinac. Sweeping down in a flotilla of birch-bark canoes, La Durantaye had halted his savage forces at the head of the strait leading from Lake Huron to Lake St. Clair; and there, on "the seventh of June, 1687, in the presence of the reverend Father Angeleran, superior of the mission of the Outaouas at Michilimachinac, of Ste. Marie du Sault, of the Miamis, of the Illinois, of the Baie des Puans and of the Sioux, of M. de la Forest, late commandant of the fort at St. Louis at the Illinois, and of M. de Beauvais, our lieutenant of the fort of St. Joseph at the strait of Lakes Huron and Erie," had erected the arms of France and taken formal possession of this vast region in the name of the king.[1]

Fort St. Joseph.

The little fort of St. Joseph was a bastioned block-house of logs, built the previous year by Duluth upon the orders of the governor — one of the long chain of French posts designed to keep English negotiants from the fur country,

[1] *Prise de possession* (vol. x, fol. 206, Archives du Canada, at Paris), quoted in Roy's excellent paper on "Le Baron de Lahontan," in Can. Roy. Soc. *Proceedings*, 1894, sec. i, p. 79, note.

and to control the vagrant *coureurs des bois.* This important vantage point, refounded (1701) some miles below by La Mothe de la Cadillac, was the place to which the young Gascon was designated, and for whose command he was required to abandon the gayeties of Paris, and the more important business regarding his estates. Setting forth from Fort Niagara on the third of August, Lahontan and his companions proceeded westward as fast as the crude transportation facilities of their day would permit. The first stage was the long Niagara portage, "being oblig'd to tranſport our Canows from a League and a half below the great Fall of Niagara, to half a League above it. Before we got at any beaten or level Path, we were forc'd to climb up three Mountains, upon which an hundred Iroqueſe might have knock'd us all on the head with Stones." Frequently attacked by these "cruel Fellows," Lahontan was naturally much alarmed at the danger of falling into the hands of such expert torturers, declaring that "To die is nothing but to live in the midſt of Fire is too much." This constant fear apparently paralyzed our author's usual powers of description, for he dismisses with a scant paragraph the "fearful Cataract," which nine years before the garrulous Friar Hennepin had so carefully pictured with both pen and pencil.

The journey out.

The little company of whites and savages "coaſted along the North-Coaſt of the Lake of Erie," feasting abundantly on fish and wild turkeys, and arrived at the mouth of Lake Huron on the fourteenth of September. "You cannot imagine," he assures his correspondent, "the pleaſant proſpect of this Streight, and of the little Lake [of St. Clair]; for their banks are cover'd with all ſorts of wild Fruit-Trees." The garrison of the little log fortress "surrendered their Poſt very chearfully" to the newcomers and, being now relieved from duty, in the way of their kind at once turned fur-traders, and quickly scattered throughout the distant camps of the savages.

Duluth and Tonty tarried for a few days, the former having left some supplies at this station and being interested in a crop of Indian corn which he had sown the previous spring. Charmed with the beauty and free life of the country, the youthful commandant passed the autumn agreeably enough, occupied with the chase, to which he had become passionately devoted, and dallying with parties of tribesmen that passed up and down bent on war, plunder, or hunting. But the ensuing winter was rigorous to a degree that restricted hunting, and the consequent short commons is suggested by Lahontan's sly remark that the Jesuit Father Claude Aveneau, who arrived towards the end of November to serve as chaplain, "found no occaſion to trouble himſelf with preaching Abſtinance from Meat in the time of Lent."

Life at Fort St. Joseph.

By the first of April (1688), the restless commander, no doubt intensely wearied by the long and inactive winter, sought excuse in his lack of provisions to set out with the majority of his force — a small garrison being left at the fort — for the little French military and trading station then on the north shore of the strait of Mackinac, to "buy up Corn from the Hurons and Outaouans." Soon after his

Departure for Mackinac.

arrival at that distant outpost, there appeared there Abbé Cavelier, La Salle's austere brother, and the other survivors of the lost Texan colony of that ill-fated explorer.

At Mackinac Lahontan learned also that his own affairs in France were in desperate straits. From the "fagg end of the World" he thereupon addressed a letter to the Marquis de Seignelay, then powerful at court, craving his protection for the "Son of a Gentleman that ſpent three hundred Crowns in deepening the Water of the two Gaves of Bearn . . . rendering the Bar of Bayonne paſſable by a fifty Gun Ship, whereas in former times a Frigot of ten Guns durſt not venture over it . . . and the bringing down of Maſts and Yards from the Pyrenean Mountains, which could never have been effected, if he had not by his Care, and by the disburſing of immenſe Sums, enlarged the quantity of Water in the Gave of Oleron to a double proportion." Not only, pleads our petitioner, had the entailed privileges and fees been cut off at his father's death, but the son had been denied several high political positions, "all which were mine by Inheritance"; and now there followed "an unjuſt Seizure that ſome pretended Creditors have made of the Barony of la Hontan, of a piece of Ground that lies contiguous to it, and of a hundred thouſand Livres that lay in the hands of the Chamber of Bayonne." He is confident that his absence in the American wilds is the sole justification of his creditors, and asks for "Leave to come home the next Year," that he may confront and rout them.

An appeal for protection.

The wander lust strong within his veins, the adventurous

lieutenant roved as far afield as Sault Ste. Marie and the neighboring regions, and in July joined a party of Chippewa on an inglorious raid into the Iroquois country, east of Lake Huron, stopping at his fort only to land a few sacks of corn. It was upon this excursion, far removed from his field of duty, that Lahontan was accompanied by the Huron chief, The Rat, whom he has idealized and immortalized in his *Voyages*, under the title "Adario."

Rovings in the Northwest.

Late in the summer he returned to Fort St. Joseph, but found the situation now untenable. Parties of Indians who had stopped at the post for the usual parleying and present-begging, brought news of the reduction of the garrison at Niagara by disease and destitution, of its probable abandonment, also of the peace which Denonville was "clapping up" with their common foe, the Iroquois. Lahontan reasoned that all this rendered his fort of no value, that he had an accumulation of scarce two months' provisions, and having received neither orders nor supplies from the governor, was thus thrown upon his own discretion. He therefore abandoned his command, burned the block-house and its stockade, and on the twenty-seventh of August embarked with all his men for Mackinac, where he arrived on the tenth of the following month. In the French edition of his work, the commandant elaborately argues that while the abandonment of his post would be a misdemeanor in an officer in Europe, it was in the far interior of America an example of military sagacity. Whatever may be one's judgment on this question, there is no evidence that Lahontan

Fort St. Joseph abandoned.

because of this action was either reprimanded or degraded in rank. Doubless Fort St. Joseph was valueless at this juncture of affairs, and its destruction certainly resulted in no disadvantage to New France.

Upon reaching Mackinac with his detachment, the baron found advices to the effect that he had been relieved, and ordered to return with his men to Quebec, provided "the Seafon and other Circumftances permit; or to tarry here till the Spring if I forefee unfurmountable Difficulties in the Paffage." But the convoys for that year had returned to the lower country, and the commandant at Mackinac and the savages united in representing to him the difficulties of the journey, the rapids to be run, the hazardous portages to be made. With comparatively inexperienced soldiers this was all but impossible, and they must perforce content themselves in the upper country until the arrival of spring.

Ordered to Quebec.

Thus far Lahontan himself has been our guide; his accounts of his own adventures and shortcomings have been recorded in the letters with a *naïveté* and a wealth of detail that bear the stamp of verity. But we now come to that apochryphal relation in the *Voyages*, which for many years has caused the entire work to be rejected by historians as fiction—the alleged journey to the River Long. Writing to his friend under date of September 18, he announces his intention "to travel through the Southern Countries that I have fo often heard of," for "I cannot mew my felf up here all this Winter." The following May he gives

Expedition to the River Long.

to his correspondent a particularized and highly readable account of the tour which he pretends to have made, accompanied by "my own Detachment and five good Huntsmen of the Outaouas," later supplemented by Fox (Outagami) guides.

Leaving Mackinac on the twenty-fourth of September, the story goes, the explorers coasted along the northwest shore of Lake Michigan, visited the Sauk, Potawatomi, and Menominee villages on Green Bay, ascended Fox River, made the mile-and-a-half swampy portage to the Wisconsin (October 16–19), and arrived at the Mississippi four days later. Working their way up that river, the party reached the mouth of the River Long on the second of November. This the baron claims to have ascended for many leagues, visiting upon its banks the wonderful nations of the Eokoros, Esanapes, and Gnacsitares, from whom he gathered information concerning the Mozeemlek and Tahuglauk beyond; also of a river in the far West that emptied itself into a salt lake of three hundred leagues in circumference. At the western limit of this voyage, Lahontan, as was the custom of French explorers in that day, set up a long pole, bearing the "Arms of France done upon a Plate of Lead."

Upon the twenty-sixth of January (1689), the adventurers set out upon the return, reaching the Mississippi on the second of March. Continuing their trip as far down stream as the mouth of the Ohio, they returned to Illinois River, by means of which and the Chicago portage they entered Lake Michigan, finally arriving at Mackinac the twenty-second of May. Two weeks later, in the company of twelve Ottawa

Indians, in two canoes, our author set out for Montreal by the Ottawa River route, after an absence of two years in the wilderness and among the savages of the Northwest.

"July the 9th I arriv'd at Montreal, after venturing down ſeveral fearful Cataracts in the River of the Outaouas, and enduring the hardſhips of fifteen or twenty Land-carriages, ſome of which are above a League in length." Nearing Montreal, his canoe overturned in the Sault St. Louis, but he was saved by the adroitness of the Chevalier de Vaudreuil—"The only time I was in danger," he exclaims, "through the whole courſe of my Voyages." He found the colony calmly watching the departure of the unpopular Governor Denonville, but eagerly awaiting the return of the Count de Frontenac, "for that Governour drew Eſteem and Veneration, not only from the French, but from all the Nations of this vaſt Continent, who look'd upon him as their Guardian Angel."

The return to Quebec.

But when the new governor came on the fifteenth of October, he "countermanded the leave I had to go for France, and has offer'd me a free acceſs to his Pocket and his Table . . . and ſo I am bound to obey." Frontenac made of the penniless and now disconsolate baron a companion on his journeyings, and, because of his wide experience at the farthest outposts, and his close studies of the aborigines, took counsel of him in regard to remedies for the desperate condition of New France. In the spring (1690), the governor offered to send his *protegé* on an embassy to the Iroquois; but having no wish again to place his head within

The friend of Frontenac.

the lion's jaws, Lahontan skilfully obtained an excuse from the mission. He records with self-gratulation that the Chevalier d'Aux, going in his stead, was seized, bound, and sent to a long imprisonment at Boston.

Lahontan, meanwhile following the governor's train, was at Montreal when news came of the English invasion under Phips. Hurrying to the capital with his chief, he was in time to witness the withdrawal of the discomfited English admiral (October), and to be chosen by Frontenac to carry the glad tidings to the king and court. Thus, after seven years of life upon the frontiers of civilization, the bronzed young officer reappeared at the social capital of the world, a solicitor of favors at the court of the great Louis. Unfortunately his protector Seignelay was now dead, and the new ministers, the Messrs. Pontchartrain, looked with slight favor upon the nonchalant adventurer from America. They coldly made answer to his petitions for redress, that he could have but the summer to regulate his affairs, for in the autumn he must embark once more for Quebec. However, by way of reward for the welcome news he had brought, Lahontan was promoted to a captaincy in his corps, and created a chevalier of the order of Notre Dame of Mont-Carmel and of St. Lazarre. With his customary cynicism the recipient, who had paid roundly in fees for this last empty title, declares that "The Ceremony of that Inſtalment was perform'd in Mr. de Louvois his Chamber, and did not laſt ſo long as the telling of the Money." The new chevalier had entertained hopes that his uncle, the generous Abbé des Couttes, might bestow

At the French court.

upon him some simple benefice; but a scruple of conscience stood in the way of granting church money to one who, like Lahontan, scoffed at religion and its priests, and the infidel applicant was sent away empty-handed. With parting jibes at the venality and favoritism prevalent at the court, the young captain left Versailles, and, with no apparent reluctance, for his estate was now beyond resuscitation, started for La Rochelle, where he again embarked for Canada.

The eighteenth of September, 1691, found captain the Baron de Lahontan, now in his twenty-fifth year, once more climbing the steep and winding roadway which ascends the cliff of Quebec, and meeting at the chateau of his friend Frontenac the same generous hospitality which had previously been his, and that of many another luckless gentleman of that day. The winter was exceptionally gay at the governor's little court. Balls and theatricals were much in vogue among the official class and the fur-trade and rustic aristocracy; but the Jesuits vigorously condemned these practices, and declaimed publicly against the satellites who hung about the head of the colony. The anti-clerical Lahontan was no doubt spurred thereby into a still more active participation in the sports and vices of the capital.

Again in Canada.

To this period probably belongs his experience with Mlle. Geneviève d'Amours, a romance which he relates under an easily-penetrated disguise. No doubt the young people met freely during the winter's amusements, since the lady was a god-daughter of the governor, and belonged to the family of one of the royal councillors. Her

Lahontan's romance.

brothers were, as well, prominent young Canadians, whose attachment for the life of the woods, common to the young gentlemen of New France, had tempted them to the wilderness of Pentagoët and the picturesque River St. John, where among the Abenaki savages they had encountered a pleasant English gentleman from Boston, who traded thither. The fortunes of war had brought this trader a prisoner to Quebec, where the genial Frontenac treated him with marked courtesy, and releasing him on parole made him a participant in the pleasures of the court. All of these friends conspired in making a match between our baron and the brilliant young beauty. On his part, the governor promised licenses to the sum of seven to eight thousand livres; the English guest requested leave to add a thousand more — this, with the dowry of a thousand already possessed by the lady, would have recuperated the ruined baron's fortunes; and, basking as they did in the governor's favor, might have started the couple on the high road to prosperity. But suddenly the negotiations came to a standstill; the young cynic proved stubborn, and would not sign the contract. He requested two months in which to consider, then two months more — which causes one to wonder at the young woman's patience; but no doubt Lahontan was a handsome fellow, with many social graces, and considered a most eligible parti. At last he found his liberty more precious than an establishment in life, and repented of having desired to make her as unhappy as himself. "They were far from expecting any ſuch retracta-tion; ſo the poor reform'd Captain ſuffer'd for it, for ſome time after Mr. de Frontenac did him a piece of Injuſtice, in beſtowing a vacant Company over his Head, upon Madame de Pontchartrain's Nephew, notwithſtanding that the Court had ſent orders on his behalf."

Our author's nonchalance, however, did not forsake him; it was not long before he presented a memorial concerning the defences of the upper country against the ravaging Iroquois, in which plan the forgiving Frontenac discovered so much merit that it pleased him to order Lahontan to go in person to present his project to the ministry. In the summer of 1692, therefore, the captain once more started for the Old World, again bearing the governor's despatches to the court at Versailles.

Again despatched to France.

Putting in at Plaisance (the Placentia of our day), a new French post upon the southeastern peninsula of Newfoundland, the frigate which bore him awaited the fishing fleet which it was, according to custom, to convoy to France. Just as they were about weighing anchor, in the third week of September, a fisherman arrived at the fort with the startling news that five English frigates were bearing up the bay. Governor de Brouillon, despite his deficient fortifications and scarcity of ammunition, made immediate arrangements for a vigorous defense. Lahontan was sent with sixty habitants to repulse the landing of the English marines. This being skilfully achieved, the English offered to parley, whereupon Lahontan and a companion were chosen to go aboard the admiral's ship, where they were received with much courtesy. Negotiations failing, the governor

The defense of Plaisance.

pushed the defenses with such vigor that the English were obliged to withdraw, after firing two thousand cannon shots at the fort and burning some neighboring fishing villages and their drying scaffolds.

At Versailles.

A second time the fortune befell Lahontan to be the bearer of good tidings to the royal ear, again to tell of the repulse of a powerful English fleet by a handful of defenders better equipped with courage and energy than with assistance and powder. Armed with this pleasing message, the captain arrived in France after a comparatively brief voyage of seventeen days, and shortly after presented himself at Versailles. The court, however, was more ready to receive agreeable news than to furnish the sinews of war for the far-away colony. Lahontan's ingenious project for the defense of the upper lake region smacked of large expenditures, hence was dismissed with scant ceremony; but he himself was rewarded with the command of an independent company of a hundred men, and the highly honorable position of lieutenant of the king for Newfoundland and Acadia. Our author correctly ascribes his good fortune to no other patron than good chance, remarking at the same time: "I ſhould have been better pleas'd if I could have put the abovemention'd Project in execution, for a ſolitary Life is moſt grateful to me, and the manners of the Savages are perfectly agreeable to my Palate." The free, roving life of the Great West of his day was vastly superior, in the opinion of this man of spirit, to immolation upon the storm-swept fjords of gloomy

Newfoundland, second in command to a governor of suspicious habits and capricious temper.

His new honors proved the undoing of our unfortunate adventurer. The coming upon the scene of a royal lieutenant sadly disarranged De Brouillon's plans for his own emolument and the advancement of his family. Lahontan was received at Plaisance with grudging welcome, and soon an open feud broke out between the new official and his chief. It was not soothing to the irascible governor's spirits, that the inhabitants took the part of the subordinate who would not become his puppet; that the ready pen and caustic wit of the latter made lampoons concerning his superior, which were sung publicly in the taverns of Plaisance; and that even the Recollect friars protected the young gallant in his escapades, and spoke in his behalf.

Royal lieutenant in Newfoundland.

After the autumnal departure of the ships for France, carrying to the court De Brouillon's accusations against his lieutenant, the former began more freely to show his temper. One evening Lahontan was entertaining some of the residents, when his door was suddenly burst open, the governor and his train of serving men entered masked, and began to break the glass and windows, handle the furniture roughly, and destroy all else that came beneath their hands. By the time the baron could load his pistols, the intruders were gone; but only to fall upon his servants the next morning, and give them an unmerciful drubbing.

De Brouillon's persecution of Lahontan

The lieutenant, alleging fear for his own life, determined

to escape. The skipper of a small fishing boat that lay in the harbor accepted the offer of a thousand livres to carry the fugitive to Europe; and thus, a second time deserting his post of duty, he fled from the hateful situation — an unwise step, which brought a sweet revenge for De Brouillon, for it wrought the gallant young officer's downfall. It was the fourteenth of December, nearly always a boisterous month off the dread coast of wreck-strewn Newfoundland; but the risk was taken, several "terrible Storms" were encountered, and once they were shot at by a French privateer — at last, however, the little vessel landed her passenger safely in a harbor of Portugal, for he dared not attempt to seek shelter in France, where the only welcome he might expect was disgrace and the Bastille.

An unwise escape.

By slow stages the unfortunate runaway now journeyed into Holland, the home of refugees who were "awaiting patiently till it pleafes God that M. de Pontchartrain fhould either remove to Paradife or do Juftice" to the wronged. From Holland he visited Hamburg, whence (June 19, 1694), he sent a letter which was intended to fall under the notice of the French court, containing an account of the survivors of La Salle's last expedition, whom he claimed to have met in that city. The ministry at once authorized investigation, only to find that Lahontan had invented the tale out of whole cloth. in the vain hope of winning favor at court.[1]

Wanderings of the refugee.

[1] Margry, *Découvertes et établissements des Français* (Paris, 1876–85), iv, pp. 6–8.

Meanwhile, our author had proceeded to Copenhagen, where he ingratiated himself with the French ambassador, De Bonrépaux, who sent him to Versailles with favorable letters designed to secure his pardon and re-instatement in the king's favor; but his majesty, ever a severe disciplinarian, declined to receive the justification of an officer who had transgressed against his superior, and Lahontan had no recourse but to betake himself in disgrace to his native province, where, his barony having long since been confiscated, he found himself an unwelcome guest. An order having gone forth for his arrest, he avoided it in the nick of time by escaping across the border into Spain, whence emanated the last of his Letters, dated at Saragossa, October 8, 1695.

Last days at the court of Hanover.

Thence, until the initial publication of his book in Holland (1703), we have no details concerning the whereabouts of the poor fugitive. In the prefaces of the various editions, one may trace his wanderings from the Low Countries to Denmark, thence to Hanover, whence he visited England, until the year 1710 finds him at the court of the Elector of Hanover, recognized as an accomplished man beset by ill fortune, and maintained as the friend and companion of the philosopher Leibnitz. The unfortunate officer had then, according to the latter,[1] a number of works prepared which he would give to the press, if his now impaired health should improve. He appears to have died soon after this, apparently in 1715, but the actual date of his decease is not known. A year or so later, Leibnitz published a

[1] Leibnitz, *Epistol. ad diversos* (Berlin, 1710), iv, p. 22.

posthumous essay by Lahontan, under the title, *Réponse à la lettre d'un particulier opposée au manifeste de S. M. le roi de la Grande-Bretagne contre la Suède*, proving that he followed the increasing fortunes of his protector, the Elector of Hanover, and was ready to aid that ruler's cause with his pamphleteering pen. Parkman also cites[1] a *Memoir on the Fur-trade of Canada*, written in the English interest, which was once in the library of the poet Southey.

Lahontan's *Voyages to North America* was avowedly printed as a last resource on the part of the bankrupt fugitive. We have seen that every vestige of hope regarding the resuscitation of his estate had vanished, and all appeals to the court for reinstatement had proved futile; in this crisis, the Letters, which in the event of his monarch's favor might have been consigned to the flames, were brought forth from their obscurity and given to the world — his distress thus proving our gain. While these now classic epistles were printing in Holland, Lahontan passed over to England, where he secured the patronage of the powerful Duke of Devonshire, and put out an English translation of his work, which in some respects is preferable to the original French.

Voyages published in revenge.

The vogue of the baron's book was immediate and widespread, and must have soon replenished his slender purse. In simple sentences, easily read and comprehended by the masses, Lahontan recounted not only his own adventures and the important events that occurred beneath his eyes in the much-talked-of region of New France, but

Their popularity.

[1] *La Salle and the Discovery of the Great West* (Boston, 1879), p. 169.

drew a picture of the simple delights of life in the wilderness, more graphic than had yet been presented to the European world. His idyllic account of manners and customs among the savages who dwelt in the heart of the American forest, or whose rude huts of bark or skin or matted reeds nestled by the banks of its far-reaching waterways, was a picture which fascinated the "average reader" in that romantic age, eager to learn of new lands and strange peoples. In the pages of Lahontan the child of nature was depicted as a creature of rare beauty of form, a rational being thinking deep thoughts on great subjects, but freed from the trammels and frets of civilization, bound by none of its restrictions, obedient only to the will and caprice of his own nature. In this American Arcady were no courts, laws, police, ministers of state, or other hampering paraphernalia of government; each man was a law unto himself, and did what seemed good in his own eyes. Here were no monks and priests, with their strictures and asceticisms, but a natural, sweetly-reasonable religion. Here no vulgar love of money pursued the peaceful native in his leafy home; without distinction of property, the rich man was he who might give most generously. Aboriginal marriage was no fettering life-covenant, but an arrangement pleasing the convenience of the contracting parties. Man, innocent and unadorned, passed his life in the pleasures of the chase, warring only in the cause of the nation, scorning the supposititious benefits of civilization, and free from its diseases, misery, sycophancy, and oppression.

An American Arcady.

In short, the American wilderness was the seat of serenity and noble philosophy.

Europeans weary of courts and their futile ambitions, found in all this a delightful representation. Moreover, the keenest curiosity had been aroused among them regarding the New World — a land so enormous that its breadth had as yet been scarcely half-spanned by the most adventurous of the roving coureurs de bois; a region of great rivers and amazing cataracts, of lakes like inland oceans, and vast unknown stretches wherein roamed mysterious beasts of prey, and animals clad in furs which might be envied by a monarch. All statements from such a realm were to be accepted as a matter of course. The *Relations* of the Jesuits had been read with absorbing interest by people with a turn for piety. Those more liberal in their thinking turned with amused tolerance to the books of the garrulous and worldly Recollect, Friar Hennepin, or found keen but perhaps not too open enjoyment in the neatly-printed volumes of the audacious and cynical Baron de Lahontan, with their numerous flings at the polity and teachings of the Canadian Jesuits, and many a well-considered thrust at king and ministry also. A glance at Mr. Paltsits's Bibliography is sufficient to prove the demand for Lahontan's *Voyages* — a taste lasting well into the middle of the eighteenth century.

European curiosity regarding the New World.

In estimating the historical value of this work, it is well to bear in mind what we believe to be its double purpose — that of a satire upon European life and civilization, and a narration of the author's adventures in new and unknown realms. The first understood and allowed for, the book becomes of great utility to the student of life and conditions in the forests and hamlets of New France. Here is no rambling journal-writer, like Father Hennepin, puffed up by inordinate vanity. Lahontan relates in a clear, straightforward manner all that came before his eyes. With vivid strokes, he pictures the thinly diffused colony of New France — fishing hamlets fringing the fog-drenched fjords of spruce-mantled Newfoundland; the fur-trade rendezvous at gloomy Tadoussac; habitants nestled upon the billowy shores of the St. Lawrence, or on waving meadows at the mouths of its tributaries, which come swiftly coursing from out the dark forests hanging on its rugged rim; the capital, perched defiantly on the steep cliff of Quebec, overlooking hillsides and rolling plains, in his day becoming well-dotted with the whitewashed stone cabins of a thrifty peasantry; Three Rivers, the centre of a widespread commerce; ecclesiastical Montreal, shadowed by its mountain, and ever alert against the crouching Iroquois; and beyond that — up the stately Ottawa or along the far-reaching waters of the upper lakes, and still farther beyond upon the interlocking drainage systems of the continental interior — the isolated camps of coureurs de bois, and little log fortresses, like that of St. Joseph, seeking to hold the wilderness trade against all comers.

Practical utility to the scholar.

A participant in some of the most stirring campaigns in the brilliant epoch of Frontenac's government, Lahontan presents to us admirable reports of these events. We have also in his pages first-hand accounts of the political institutions of the colony — its officials, courts, and local government, combined with incisive characterizations of the respective governors, intendants, and official noblesse. The strutting functionary, the zealous Jesuit who balks at no hazard, the gay soldier, the hardy habitant, the roving coureur de bois, and the naked savage, all stand out in bold relief upon his pages. Even the birds and animals, the plants, and the minerals of this strange land do not escape our observer's eye. Thus not only in history, but in topography, geography, ethnology, and natural history, all of it the record of personal knowledge, Lahontan's work stands as one of the important sources for the intimate study of New France.

Investigations as to the River Long.

The frequent neglect of Lahontan by scientific and historical students, has not been justified by the lack of material in his pages. As already intimated, it is in large measure due to the spurious character of the alleged discovery of the River Long, described in the sixteenth Letter. Investigators have, from this one chapter, rejected all. The geographers of the time, eager for information regarding heretofore unknown regions in North America, were easily deceived by the circumstantial character of our author's fluent description, and especially by his map of the mythical waterway; and in consequence the river was incorporated in several maps published early in the eighteenth century, persisting even down to that of Vaugondy, corrected to 1783. But doubts soon arose in the minds of some. Hennepin had omitted to mention such a stream, or the peoples that Lahontan had placed upon its banks. The miner and trader Le Sueur, a colleague of Iberville, who ascended the Mississippi nearly to its source and passed two years (1700–02) upon its upper waters, reported neither the Long nor its tribes. Perrot and Duluth, eminent forest rangers of the period, knew no such river — but they were not authors; and it was probably not until Charlevoix visited the country (1721) and published his *Journal historique*, that the spurious nature of Lahontan's pretended discovery fully dawned upon the European world. In 1728 a French expedition built a fort upon Lake Pepin, in the upper Mississippi — one of the chain which was to further the discovery of a route to the Pacific. Its officers found the Issati of Hennepin and the Scioux of Le Sueur, but no traces of the Eokoros, Esanapes, Gnacsitares, and Mozeemleks of Lahontan. Scepticism now succeeded to faith in the author's verity, and neglect to the former vogue of his works.

Many hypotheses have been advanced, to account for Lahontan's wilful tale. The theory of interpolation, sometimes applied to Hennepin, has been suggested in this case; but the style of the baron's story of his far Western tour is quite in keeping with that of the entire work — Letters and Dialogue carry, throughout, the evidence of coming from one and the same hand. Others have seen in the narrative of the journey only exaggeration of possible facts, and have sought to identify the fabulous waterway with the St. Peter's (present Minnesota), whose latitude somewhat closely corresponds with Lahontan's River Long. The late

Hypotheses advanced.

Elliot Coues followed the suggestion of the explorer Nicollet, that the St. Peter's, with its principal affluent the Cannon, may be of sufficient length to justify the baron's description; and that this southward tributary being the last to freeze, might account for the journey thither in the dead of winter. Still others have seen in the Moingona (present Des Moines) a river whose long, straight stretch from the West may be identical with Lahontan's famous stream. Those who have studied the subject more carefully — such as the baron's latest biographer, Edmond Roy — point out the impossibility of reconciling the pretended voyage with the rest of the author's descriptions. They note that upon leaving Mackinac for the West, the traveller, formerly giving precise and detailed information as to dates and routes, becomes indistinct. The daily occurrences and episodes of a journey, that give it an air of verisimilitude, are now forced and betray invention; the tribes encountered do not speak with the same certain ring as the Iroquois and Algonquian savages whom the author meets elsewhere in his travels, but have an air of posing, while their customs, manners, mode of government, and diplomacy is that of imaginary rather than of real beings; finally, by careful calculation and comparison there is not found available time for so extensive a voyage in birch-bark canoes.

In Roy's opinion, the impecunious fugitive, eager for quick returns, doubtless thought the unvarnished record of a simple officer now in disgrace, would attract few buyers for the volume; he must, in order to secure patronage and readers, pose as a discoverer, and imitate the achievements of

Marquette and La Salle. Possibly he may have entertained a distant hope of being again despatched to his beloved wilderness, on a mission of further exploration and discovery. In the interior of America he had spent many days with Perrot and Duluth, who knew the West as probably no other white men did. Out of their reports, the published accounts of Membré, La Salle, Marquette, and Hennepin, and chance information received from the Indians, he may have obtained the material for the tale of his marvellous journey, and imposed it upon the public for the sake of gain. That he was not incapable of such a feat, his letter on the survivors of La Salle's ill-fated colony, already cited, is sufficient proof.

There remains to be accounted for, his disposition of the time claimed to have been spent upon this voyage of discovery. We have seen that having abandoned Fort St. Joseph, he arrived at Mackinac in the second week of September, 1688. It is hardly probable that this uneasy spirit remained cooped up at that frontier post until his descent to the colony the following summer. With his habits of forest ranging, his fondness for the chase, his delight in savage comrades, it is not difficult to see how he might have spent the few months of this interval. What more probable than that he joined a band of Wisconsin tribesmen — probably Foxes (Outagami), from his choice of them as guides for his pretended expedition — returning from a trading venture at Mackinac, and after a winter in their villages and hunting camps returned to the French outpost in time to descend with the

What he did with his winter.

A journey to Wisconsin suggested.

season's convoy to Montreal? This would readily explain his apparent familiarity with the northwest shores of Lake Michigan, with Green Bay, and the Fox River, and his subsequent vagueness in regard to the Wisconsin and the Mississippi.

Again, may not the entire account of the voyage to the River Long, and of the savage Arcady which he found established upon its banks, be deliberately part and parcel of his satire upon European customs and manners — a cynical rebuke to the credulity of the reading world, and a parody upon the avidity of the explorers of his day to find a route through the continent of America to the land of the great khan of Tartary? May one not see in this an anticipation of Swift, in his more famous *Gulliver's Travels*, and recognize in Lahontan's fantastic Eokoros, Esanapes, etc., the predecessors if not the prototypes of Liliputians and Brobdignagians?

A satire on others' discoveries.

It fell to the lot of this unfortunate man, possessed of keen powers of observation, a biting wit, a passion for justice, and an independence of mind and temper verging upon license, to see his patrimony stolen through the chicanery of the law; to plead in vain for justice, at the doors of partial and corrupt ministers; to be bound to military service in the remote quarters of the world, and thus for years deprived of opportunity to meet the harpies who were sapping his inheritance; to suffer indignities at the hands of his superior, and injudiciously flying the scene to become the victim of still greater injustice; to be refused redress of every sort at the court of the most powerful mon-

An unfortunate career.

arch of his time, and to be driven from one court to another an exile and fugitive, seeking patronage which was grudgingly granted. It is not surprising that even in his earlier years his wit turned caustic, his independence became caprice, his observation developed into satire, his reason became cynicism. Add to all this an inconstant habit of mind, easily overcome by ennui, and a tendency to seek diversion in fantastic amusements, in coarse and sensual pleasures, in familiar contact with social inferiors and with savages, and the secret of both Lahontan's success and failure is laid bare.

During his protracted sea-voyages, unending days in wilderness garrisons, and long months of campaigning in gloomy forests, Lahontan brooded upon the blemishes of civilization, contrasting it caustically with the simplicity of barbarism, and erecting an ideal system of savage perfection, which he used as a whip to lash the vices of his time. With the European passion for money, he compares the communal life of the North American aborigine who seeks to satisfy only his immediate needs, and shares his possessions with whoever needs them; over against the servile caste spirit of the courtier, he places the proud independence of each Indian warrior; with the rigid bonds of the married state, he contrasts the easy libertinism of the barbarian; with the elaborate ritual and dogmas of the Church, the primitive nature myths of the sons of the forest. Both the legal and medical professions stand for their share of sarcasm — the flaws in French jurisprudence are ruthlessly thrust forth to view, the ignorance and malpractice of European

Brooding on the blemishes of civilization.

physicians denounced. The comforts and luxuries of civilization are ridiculed, while the hardships and paucity of wilderness life are minimized. In short, to quote the words of his marvellous Huronian, Adario, "The Great Spirit has vouchſaf'd us an honeſt Mould, while Wickedneſs neſtles in yours; and that he ſends you into our Country, in order to have an opportunity of Correcting your Faults, and following our Example."

Lahontan's scorn of civilization and exaltation of savagery, culminate in the famous Dialogue between him and Adario — a bit of clever satire modelled on the Dialogues of Lucian, whom we have seen was one of our author's favorite classics. With vision as keen as his Latin prototype, he scoffs at the hypocrisies, shams, corruptions, and other deformities of the world of the seventeenth century, in a manner as bold and with a wit as incisive as his fellow satirist of the second. Nor do the *Voyages* lack Lucian's obscenity and occasional indecency — indeed, this is of so gross a character that some critics have thought Lahontan, the gentleman, scholar, and officer, could hardly be guilty of it; deeming it not unlikely that these touches were either the additions of the English translator — the Dialogue is much more extended in the English than in other editions — or the emendations of a certain unfrocked and ribald French friar, Nicolas Gueudeville, also a refugee in Holland, and well known as a political and religious satirist, as well as a writer on geographical discoveries.[1] Indeed, some authorities have credited to

The Dialogue with Adario.

[1] Nicolas Gueudeville, the son of a Rouen physician, was born about 1650 or 1654 — authorities differ. Becoming a Benedictine friar, he finally abjured Catholicism, which necessitated his fleeing at once and taking refuge in Holland, where about 1690

Gueudeville the entire book popularly attributed to Lahontan. We are not, however, inclined to this sweeping judgment, believing that the work bears throughout unmistakable evidence of Lahontan's hand — the philosophy of the satire frequently crops out through the most sober narrative, and the historical facts and ethnological information are clearly the product of a man of accurate observation thoroughly conversant with the facts. While it is of course quite possible that Gueudeville may have assisted in sharpening the weapon, we have no direct evidence of this fact; and there is no doubt that the Dialogue is quite in accord with the spirit of Lahontan, hence may properly be treated as substantially the latter's production.

Two suggestions made by our author deserve more than passing remark, as showing still further what manner of man he was, and how the colony of New France might have benefited from the adoption of his plans. The first concerns the project of garrisoning the upper lakes, in order to prevent Iroquois incursions and British trading ventures. The astute Frontenac thought his young friend's plan of sufficient importance to send the author to

Lahontan's plans of defense.

he married. His publications were numerous. For several years he edited at the Hague a journal of political satire, *L'Esprit des cours de l'Europe*, in which the French government was violently attacked. Suppressed on the instigation of that power, Gueudeville revived the sheet under a slight change of title, and it enjoyed a large circulation. In 1704 he republished Lahontan's *Dialogue*, at Amsterdam; in 1705, he issued at Leyden a five-volume encyclopædia of universal history; in Amsterdam, 1713–21, there appeared his seven-volume *Atlas historique*, in which figured Lahontan's River Long. His translations of Plautus, Erasmus, etc., were mediocre, showing a pen inferior to that of Lahontan, who had quite caught the classical style. Gueudeville appears to have died about 1721.

propose it at Versailles. Had it been carried out — the important portages guarded, and the trade concentrated in competent hands — it is fair to presume that the subsequent ruinous Fox wars in Wisconsin might have been averted, the integrity of New France preserved, and the English defied. La Mothe Cadillac, developing one portion of the plan, secured the upper country for New France for nearly sixty years.

Lahontan's other project was, to people the sparsely-settled colony with the Huguenot heretics, whose energy, industry, and steadfastness went to the building up of the rivals and enemies of France. The short-sighted Louis would have greatly strengthened his hold upon America, had his Protestant population, expelled from the mother land through the revocation of the edict of Nantes, been permitted to turn their steps toward Canada. Lahontan's vision was in this regard, however, in advance of his contemporaries.

A plea for Huguenot settlement.

There remains but to notice a few of the lesser points in which Lahontan shows his sagacity, foresight, and purely modern spirit. In an age of cruel punishments, he was humane beyond his time. He had no patience with the torture and cruelty of savage warfare, and its imitation by the half-barbarized frontiersmen of New France. The inquisition, as studied by him in Portugal, he denounced rather for its cruelties than its intolerance. He makes the savage Adario inveigh against taking testimony by means of the rack. In all this sensitiveness to physical suffering he

Lahontan's qualities.

shows the fineness of his spirit, and the delicacy of his organization. Moreover, while railing at the prevalent beliefs of his time, he is not himself intolerant; he has erected no counter system of philosophy before which his contemporaries must bow; he sees good in various systems of religion, laws, and government, even while he satirizes their deformities and extravances.

In many ways Lahontan was a precursor of some of the great thinkers of the Revolutionary period in France. His was not the spirit of his own age — the devout worshiping of supreme power as vested in Louis XIV, and of supreme authority as resting in the church of Rome. By nature, Lahontan was an investigator and a critic. No institution, no custom, no mode of thought was by him accepted on faith or by tradition — each must run the gauntlet of his reasoning powers, and show its worth in the light of cold rationalism. His mind was passionately just; in the midst of his cynicism he is fair — even the Jesuits receive from him their meed of praise: he admits their chastity and good works, while despising what he deems their prudery and bigotry. Taking him as a whole, Lahontan was a generation in advance of his age. The *Zeitgeist* from the hills of the future descended upon him. In his hatred and scorn of the current ecclesiasticism and despotism, he anticipated Rousseau; his cynical criticism of existing institutions foreshadowed Voltaire; his exaltation of the virtues and blessings of the savage state, preluded the Encyclopedists. In the *Discours sur l'Origine et les Fondements de l'Inégalité parmi*

Lahontan's philosophy in advance of his time.

les ommes, Rousseau apparently borrows many ideas from Lahontan's Dialogue; Chateaubriand's gentle barbarian Atala is brother to the astute and charming Adario.

We have sought to reproduce the old text as closely as possible, with its typographic and orthographic peculiarities, our wish being to preserve the "atmosphere" of the original.

Exact reproduction.

It has, however, been found advisable here and there to make a few minor mechanical changes; these consist almost wholly of palpable blemishes, the result of negligent proof-reading in the edition followed—such as turned letters, transposed letters, slipped letters, and misspacings. Such corrections have been made without specific mention; but in some instances the original errors have been retained, and in juxtaposition the correction given within brackets. Throughout, we indicate the pagination of the old edition which we are reprinting, by inclosing within brackets the number of each page at its beginning, e. g. [75]; in the one instance, in the second volume, where a page was, as the fruit of carelessness in make-up, misnumbered in the original, we have given the incorrect as well as the correct figure, thus: [276, i. e. 279].

In the preparation for the press of this reprint of the original London edition of 1703, the Editor has had throughout the valued coöperation of Louise Phelps Kellogg, Ph. D.,

Aid acknowledged.

his editorial assistant on the staff of the Wisconsin Historical Society. He is also under especial obligations to Victor Hugo Paltsits, of the Lenox Branch of the New York Public Library, whose careful and scientifically constructed Bibliography of Lahontan was prepared for the present publication. As in the case of Hennepin, a year ago, Mr. Paltsits has here given us the first accurate Bibliography of this difficult subject thus far issued.

R. G. T.

MADISON, WIS., October, 1904.

LAHONTAN BIBLIOGRAPHY

By Victor Hugo Paltsits

The path trodden by the bibliographer who undertakes a critical study of the various editions of the voyages of the Baron de Lahontan is beset with innumerable stumbling-blocks. Vagaries in the books themselves; imperfections of extant or available copies in libraries; and the fact that no complete series exists in the libraries of any single city — all these conditions he encounters in his investigations. He discovers also, by the most painstaking analysis, that others who have dealt with the subject have tabulated editions as extant which never existed; and that numerous errors have been perpetuated by the shirking of independent research.

The bibliography presented herewith has been made from the books themselves — generally by testing the collations by several copies. Only by this method has it been possible to present an almost definitive work. Yet, after all the care bestowed, it is not unlikely, on account of the difficulty of finding immaculate copies of certain editions, that some plates or maps are not here recorded. The books of Lahontan have not been collected with that avidity which we find elsewhere evident in this collecting age.

The present bibliography differs from all of its predecessors, in that it gives an analysis of each volume by its component parts, by its pagination, by its signatures, and by the location of its plates and maps. This is, to coin a new term, anatomical bibliography, and follows an idea which I have sought, in several similar monographic studies, to introduce as a more scholarly method in American bibliography. Only by such means can the librarian, scholar, or collector ascertain whether his books are perfect, or wherein they lack completeness. The mere lumping of pagination or plates falls far short of usefulness; it is, indeed, a source of irritation and annoyance.

In Henry Harrisse's *Notes sur la Nouvelle France* (Paris, 1872), nos. 795–803, a brief summary of a few editions of Lahontan's work was given, devoid of collations or other bibliographical data. Joseph Sabin, in his *Dictionary of Books relating to America*, vol. x. (1878), pp. 27–32, gave the fullest record which was printed up to his time; but he read into his work non-extant editions, and distorted the facts. Justin Winsor presented "A bibliographical and critical note" to his *Narrative and Critical History of America*, vol. iv. (1884), pp. 257–262; it is, however, a more or less inaccurate and incomplete summary. James Constantine Pilling was the first bibliographer to get at all a proper grasp of the subject, in his *Bibliography of the Algonquian Languages* (Washington, 1891), pp. 288–295, with seven facsimile title-pages of the 1703 French editions. He made some mistakes, which reappeared in Roy and Dionne, who drew almost bodily from him. J. Edmond Roy appended a bibliography to his otherwise very important work on "Le Baron de Lahontan," published in the *Proceedings and Transactions* of the Royal Society of Canada for 1894, section i. His monograph is divided into the following divisions: "Avant-propos," pp. 63–64; genealogy and biography of Lahontan, pp. 64–109; examination and critique of Lahontan's book, pp. 109–165; "Piéces Justificatives" (documents), pp. 166–179; "Notes sur les diverses Editions des Ouvrages de Lahontan," pp. 179–192. There is also a separate issue of his work from the "Proceedings," with its own printed wrapper. Philéas Gagnon, in his *Essai de Bibliographie Canadienne* (Quebec, 1895), item 1922, summarized the bibliography of Lahontan in about ten lines. Narcisse E. Dionne is the latest bibliographer of the subject, in *Le Courrier du Livre* (Quebec: Raoul Renault, 1899), vol. iii, pp. 313–326. His work is merely a compilation from former bibliographies and sale-catalogues, presents nothing original, and is uncritical.

In the present account, the abbreviated designation for the location of copies is explained by the following key:

B = Boston Public Library.
BA = Boston Athenæum.
BE = Bureau of Ethnology, Washington, D. C.
BM = British Museum, London.
BN = Bibliothèque Nationale, Paris.
C = Library of Congress, Washington, D. C.
HC = Harvard College Library, Cambridge, Mass.
JCB = John Carter Brown Library, Providence, R. I.
LLQ = Legislative Library, Quebec.
LP = Library of Parliament, Ottawa.
LU = Laval University, Quebec.
MHS = Massachusetts Historical Society, Boston.
NL = New York Public Library (Lenox Library Building).
NYHS = New York Historical Society, New York City.
WHS = Wisconsin Historical Society, Madison.

The arrangement pursued is chronological, by the imprint date of each volume; when the volumes of an edition bear the same date they are placed sequentially under that particular year. Each volume, in fact, has for identification its own earmarks.

It is a pleasure to acknowledge the special facilities afforded by librarians in the prosecution of this work, and particularly to Mr. George Parker Winship, librarian of the Carter Brown Library, and Dr. Herbert Putnam, Librarian of Congress.

1703 — FRENCH: *Angel issue* — VOL. I.

Nouveaux | Voyages | de | Mr. le Baron de Lahontan, | dans | l'Amerique | Septentrionale, | Qui contiennent une rélation des différens Peuples | qui y habitent; la nature de leur Gouvernement; leur | Commerce, leurs Coutumes, leur Religion, & | leur maniére de faire la Guerre. | L'intérêt des François & des Anglois dans le Com- | merce qu'ils font avec ces Nations; l'avantage que | l'Angleterre peut retirer dans ce Païs, étant | en Guerre avec la France. | Le tout enrichi de Cartes & de Figures. | Tome Premier. | [*Emblematic circular cut of Angel, etc., with inscription underneath*] |

A La Haye, | Chez les Fréres l'Honoré, Marchands Libraires. | M. D C C III. |

Collation. — 12mo; title, verso blank; "A sa Majesté Frederic IV," pp. (4); "Preface," pp. (7); "Table des Lettres du Tome I," pp. (9); "Voyages" or text, pp. 1–266; "Explication de quelques Termes qui se trouvent dans le premier tome," pp. 267–279; verso of p. 279 blank. No mispaging. The 2d, 4th, 6th, 8th, 12th, and 17th lines and place and date of imprint printed in red.

Plates. — Opposite pp. 34, 46, 72, 85, 98, 116, 141, 174, 211, 226, and 242; three frontispieces, namely, a globe and bird in a circle, an Indian in an oval with superscription "Et leges et sceptra terit," and a small "Carte generale de Canada a petit point;" also a large folded "Carte que le Gnacsitares ont dessiné," etc., found sometimes opp. p. 1, but intended for p. 136. In the preface of this volume the following note appears: "La Carte mise à la tête du premier Volume doit se raporter à la 16. Lettre du même Volume."

Signatures. — * in eleven, A—L in twelves, M in eight. Sig. I5 printed correctly.

Copies. — BM, JCB (the Globe and Indian frontispieces mounted),

NL (two, one in perfect condition, and one lacking Globe and Indian frontispieces; both copies bound in contemporary hogskin), NYHS (imperfect and otherwise a poor copy).

1703 — FRENCH: *Angel issue* — VOL. 2.

Memoires | de | l'Amerique | Septentrionale, | ou la Suite | des Voyages de Mr. le | Baron de Lahontan. | Qui contiennent la Defcription d'une grande éten- | duë de Païs de ce Continent, l'interêt des François & des | Anglois, leurs Commerces, leurs Navigations, | les Mœurs & les Coutumes des Sauvages &c. | Avec un petit Dictionaire de la Langue du Païs. | Le tout enrichi de Cartes & de Figures. | Tome Second. | [*Same cut as in first volume*] |

A La Haye, | Chez les Fréres l'Honoré, Marchands Libraires. | M. DCCIII. |

Collation. — 12mo; title, verso blank; "Memoires," pp. 3–194; half-title: "Petit | Dictionaire | de la Langue | des Sauvages," on p. [195]; p. [196] blank; "Petit Dictionaire," pp. 197–220; "Table des Matieres contenues dans les deux tomes," pp. (16). P. 219 is mispaged 29. The 1st, 3d, 6th, 7th, 12th, and 14th lines and place and date of imprint printed in red.

Plates. — Opposite pp. 95, 125, 133, 148, 155, 160, 185, 187, 188, 189, and 191; a large folded "Carte generale de Canada Dediée au roy. de Danemark," opp. p. 3; two frontispieces, namely, a globe and bird in a circle, and an Indian in an oval, exactly like these two cuts in the first volume of this issue.

Signatures. — A—I in twelves, K in ten.

Copies. — BM, JCB (the Globe and Indian frontispieces mounted), NL (two, one in perfect condition, and one lacking Globe and Indian frontispieces), NYHS (imperfect and otherwise a poor copy).

1703 — French: *Angel issue* — Vol. 3.

Suple'ment | aux Voyages | du | Baron de Lahontan, | Où l'on trouve des Dialogues curieux | entre | l'Auteur | et | un Sauvage | De bon ſens qui a voyagé. | L'on y voit auſſi pluſieurs Obſervations faites par le même | Auteur, dans ſes Voyages en Portugal, en Eſpagne, | en Hollande, & en Dannemarck, &c. | Tome Troisie'me. | Avec Figures. | [*Same cut as in vols. 1 and 2 of Angel issue*] |

A La Haye, | Chez les Frères l'Honoré, Marchands Libraires. | M. DCC. III. |

Collation. — 12mo; title, verso blank; "Preface," pp. (12); "Avis De l'Auteur, Au Lecteur," pp. (2); "Dialogues Ou Entretiens entre un Sauvages, Et le Baron de Lahontan," pp. 1–103; p. [104] blank; half-title: "Voyages | Du | Baron de Lahontan | En | Portugal, | Et en | Danemarc," on p. [105]; p. [106] blank; "Voyages De Portugal, Et de Danemarc," pp. 107–222. P. 86 is mispaged 89. Title-page printed wholly in black.

Plates. — Folded plates at pp. 1, 118, 149, and 155; folded maps of Portugal and Denmark, by N. de Fer, opp. pp. 107 and 145, respectively.

Signatures. — * in eight, A—I in twelves, K in three (some copies have a blank leaf to complete the last signature in four).

Copies. — BM, JCB, LP.

1703 — French: *Ornament issue* — Vol. 1.

Nouveaux | Voyages | de | M[r] le Baron de Lahontan, | dans | l'Amerique | Septentrionale, | Qui contiennent une Relation des differens | Peuples qui y habitent; la nature de leur | Gouvernement; leur Commerce, leurs Coû- | tumes, leur Religion, & leur maniére de | faire la Guerre. | L'intérêt des François & des Anglois dans le Commer- | ce qu'ils font avec ces Nations; l'avantage que | l'Angleterre peut retirer dans ce Païs, étant | en Guerre avec la France. | Le tout enrichi de Cartes & de Figures. | Tome Premier. | [*Ornament*] |

A La Haye, | Chez les Fréres l'Honoré, Marchands Libraires. | M. DCIII. |

Collation. — 12mo; title, verso blank; "A sa Majesté Frederic IV," pp. (4); "Preface," pp. (7); "Table des Lettres du Tome I," pp. (11); "Voyages" or text, pp. 1–266; "Explication de quelques Termes qui se trouvent dans le premier tome," pp. 267–279; verso of p. 279 blank. Pp. 35, 82, 98, 123, 128, 177, 241, and 242 are mispaged 34, 84, 78, 133, 126, 176, 242, and 142, respectively. The 2d, 4th, 6th, 8th to 12th, and 18th lines and place and date of imprint printed in red.

Plates. — Frontispiece and opposite pp. 14, 34, 47, 72, 85, 98, 116, 141, 155 (really belongs in second volume at that page), 174, 225, and 242; a small "Carte generale du Canada en petit point," opp. p. 9, and folded "Carte que les Gnacsitares ont Dessine," etc., at p. 136.

Signatures. — * in twelve, A—L in twelves, M in eight. Sig. I5 is misprinted I3.

Copies. — B, BA, JCB, MHS.

1703 — French: *Ornament issue* — Vol. 2.

Memoires | de | l'Amerique | Septentrionale, | ou la Suite des Voyages | de | M^r^ le Baron de Lahontan. | Qui contiennent la Defcription d'une grande | étenduë de Païs de ce Continent, l'intérêt | des François & des Anglois, leurs Com- | merces, leurs Navigations, les Mœurs & | les Coûtumes des Sauvages &c. | Avec un petit Dictionnaire de la Langue du Païs. | Le tout enrichi de Cartes & de Figures. | Tome Second. | [*Ornament*] |

A La Haye, | Chez les Fréres l'Honoré, Marchands Libraires. | M. DCCIII. |

Collation. — 12mo; title, verso blank; "Memoires," pp. 3-194 (mispaged 164); half-title: "Petit | Dictionaire | de la Langue | des Sauvages," on p. [195]; p. [196] blank; "Petit Dictionaire," pp. 197-220; 'Table des Matieres contenues dans les deux tomes," pp. (17), verso of last leaf blank; one blank leaf to complete sig. K. Pp. 167, 169, 175, 194 and 219 are mispaged 761, 269, 375, 164, and 26, respectively. The 1st, 3d, 5th, 7th, 13th, and 15th lines and place and date of imprint printed in red.

Plates. — Opposite pp. 55, 95, 101, 125, 130, 151, 174, 189, 190, and 191; a "Carte generale de Canada," opp. p. 5.

Signatures. — A—K in twelves, the last leaf blank. D3 is printed in small cap., and F3 is misprinted F2. The small printer's ornament, or *fleuron*, differs in size from that of the first volume of this issue.

Copies. — B, BA, JCB, MHS.

1703 — FRENCH: *Globe issue* — VOL. I.

Nouveaux | Voyages | de | M^r le Baron de Lahontan, | dans | l'Amerique | Septentrionale, | Qui contiennent une relation des differens Peuples | qui y habitent; la nature de leur Gouvernement; | leur Commerce, leur Coutumes, leur Reli- | gion, & leur maniere de faire la Guerre. | L'intérêt des François & des Anglois dans le Commer- | ce qu'ils font avec ces Nations; l'avantage que | l'Angleterre peut retirer dans ce Païs, étant | en Guerre avec la France. | Le tout enrichi de Cartes & de Figures. | Tome Premier. | [*Cut of a globe*] |

A La Haye, | Chez les Fréres l'Honoré. Marchands Libraire [*sic*] | M. DCCIII. |

Collation. — 12mo; collation the same as the "Ornament" issue of the same year, with similar mispaging and signatures.

Plate. — The plate for p. 155 is sometimes found in this volume, but really belongs in the second volume. The title-pages of both volumes of this "Globe" issue are printed entirely in black ink, and the plates are superior to those in the "Ornament" issue. The "Globe" issue has corrections in the place-nomenclature on the maps, and some additions of places on these maps have also been noticed. The "Ornament" issue has fancy initial letters, head and tail pieces, while the "Globe" issue is simpler in this respect; but the two issues agree typographically as to text, even in broken letters and singular mispaging.

Copies. — BA, C, LLQ, LU, NL.

1703 — FRENCH: *Globe issue* — VOL. 2.

Memoires | de | l'Amerique | Septentrionale, | ou la Suite des Voyages | de | M^r le Baron de Lahontan. | Qui contiennent la Defcription d'une grande étenduë de | Païs de ce Continent, interêt des François & des | Anglois, leurs Commerces, leurs Navigations, les | Mœurs & les Coutumes des Sauvages, &c. | Avec un petit Dictionnaire de la Langue du Païs. | Le tout enrichi de Cartes & de Figures. | Tome Second. | [*Cut of a globe*] |

A La Haye, | Chez les Fréres l'Honoré, Marchand [*sic*] Libraires. | M. DCCIII. |

Collation. — 12mo. The plate which is found in the "Ornament" issue of this volume opposite p. 55 is properly placed at p. 155 in this "Globe" issue.

Plates. — "Lac des Outagamis" and another plate containing a bow, hatchet, etc., and scenes in Indian warfare and cruelty, are not found similarly located in several copies examined; the former appears to belong opp. p. 165, and the latter opp. p. 174.

Signatures. — Some copies have p. 218 misprinted 418, and the signature mark D3 is not printed in small caps, as in the "Ornament" issue, but sig. F3 is misprinted F2.

Copies. — BA, C, LLQ, LU, NL.

1703 — ENGLISH — VOL. 1.[1]

New | Voyages | to | North-America. | Containing | An Account of the ſeveral Nations of that vaſt Con- | tinent; their Cuſtoms, Commerce, and Way of | Navigation upon the Lakes and Rivers; the ſeve- | ral Attempts of the Engliſh and French to diſpoſſeſs | one another; with the Reaſons of the Miſcarriage | of the former; and the various Adventures be- | tween the French, and the Iroqueſe Confederates of | England, from 1683 to 1694. | A Geographical Deſcription of Canada, and a Natu- | ral Hiſtory of the Country, with Remarks upon | their Government, and the Intereſt of the Engliſh | and French in their Commerce. | Alſo a Dialogue between the Author and a General of the | Savages, giving a full View of the Religion and ſtrange | Opinions of thoſe People: With an Account of the Au- | thors Retreat to Portugal and Denmark and his Remarks | on thoſe Courts. | To which is added, | A Dictionary of the Algonkine Language, which is generally | ſpoke in North-America. | Illuſtrated with Twenty Three Mapps and Cutts. | Written in French | By the Baron Lahontan, Lord Lievtenant | of the French Colony at Placentia in New- | foundland, now in England. | Done into Engliſh. | In Two Volumes. | A great part of which never Printed in the Original. |

London: Printed for H. Bonwicke in St. Paul's Church-yard; | T. Goodwin, M. Wotton, B. Tooke, in Fleetſtreet; and S. Manſhip | in Cornhil, 1703. |

Collation. — 8vo; title, verso blank; "To His Grace William Duke of Devonshire," pp. (2); "The Preface," pp. (8); "The Contents," pp. (12); "Some New Voyages" pp. 1–202; "Memoirs of North-America," pp. 203–274; "A Table explaining some Terms made use of in both Volumes," pp. 275–280; "Books lately Printed,

[1] This is the original English edition which is herewith reprinted.

&c.," p. (1); one blank page. No mispaging. The "Table" ends in the midst of the letter "T" on p. 280, and there is a superfluous catch-word "THE" at the foot of that page.

Plates.— Opposite pp. 26, 43, 55, 65, 75, 89, 106, 160, 184 and 225 (map of Newfoundland); a small full-page map of Canada to face the title-page, and two large folded maps to face p. 1, as follows: (A) "A General Map of New France Com̃, call'd Canada," (B) "A Map drawn upon Stag-skins by y[e] Gnacſitares," etc.

Signatures. — A in eight. *a* in four, B—S in eights, T in four, and one advertisement leaf.

Copies.—B, HC, JCB, MHS, NL (three), WHS.

The following extract from the preface of this volume is worthy of notice here:

> While my Book was a Printing in Holland, I was in England; and as soon as it appear'd, several English Gentlemen of a distinguishing Merit, who understand the French as well as their Mother Tongue, gave me to know, that they would be glad to see a more ample Relation of the Manners and Customs of the People of that Continent, whom we call by the name of Savages. This oblig'd me to communicate to these Gentlemen, the substance of the several Conferences I had in that Country with a certain Huron, whom the French call Rat. While I stay'd at that American's Village, I imploy'd my time very agreeably in making a careful Collection of all his Arguments and Opinions; and as soon as I return'd from my Voyage upon the Lakes of Canada, I shew'd my Manuscript to Count Frontenac, who was so pleas'd with it, that he took the pains to assist me in digesting the Dialogues, and bringing them into the order they now appear in: For before that, they were abrupt Conferences without Connexion. Upon the Solicitation of these English Gentlemen, I've put these Dialogues into the hands of the Person who translated my Letters and Memoirs: And if it had not been for their pressing Instances, they had never seen the light; for there are but few in the World that will judge impartially, and without prepossession, of some things contained in 'em.
>
> I have likewise intrusted the same Translator with some Remarks that I made in Portugal, and Denmark, when I fled thither from Newfound-Land. There the Reader will meet with a description of Lisbon and Copenhagen, and of the capital City of Arragon.
>
> To the Translation of my first Volume, I have added an exact Map of Newfound-Land, which was not in the Original. I have likewise corrected almost all the Cuts

of the Holland Impression, for the Dutch Gravers had murder'd 'em, by not understanding their Explications, which were all in French. They have grav'd Women for Men, and Men for Women ; naked Persons for those that are cloath'd, and è Contra. As for the Maps, the Reader will find 'em very exact; And I have taken care to have the Tracts of my Voyages more nicely delineated, than in the Original.

1703 — English — Vol. 2.

New | Voyages | to | North-America. | Giving a full Account of the Cuftoms, | Commerce, Religion, and ftrange O- | pinions of the Savages of that Country. | With | Political Remarks upon the Courts | of Portugal and Denmark, and the Prefent | State of the Commerce of thofe Countries. | Never Printed before. | Written | By the Baron Lahontan, Lord | Lieutenant of the French Colony at | Placentia in Newfoundland: Now in | England. | Vol. II. |

London: | Printed for H. Bonwicke in St. Paul's Church-yard; T. Goodwin, | M. Wotton, B. Tooke in Fleetftreet; and S. Manfhip in Cornhil, | 1703. |

Collation. — 8vo; title, verso blank; "A Discourse," pp. 1–89; "A Conference or Dialogue," pp. 90–183; p. [184] blank; "An Appendix, Containing Some New Voyages to Portugal and Denmark," pp. 185–286; "A Short Dictionary Of the most Universal Language of the Savages," pp. 287–302; "The Index," pp. (13); one blank page. The second figure of the paging of p. 43 is inverted and p. 279 is misprinted 276. Sets of this edition are usually very much mixed up in the arrangement of the preliminary and end leaves, and the majority of copies examined lacked the frontispiece to the second volume.

Plates. — Frontispiece containing an Indian within an oval, having the superscription "Et Leges et Sceptra terit"; and opposite pp. 5, 29, 36, 51, 59 (two), 80, 82, 84 and 86.

Signatures. — Title-page, Aa—Sf in eights, Tt in seven, Vv in seven.

Copies. — B (with frontispiece), HC (lacks front.), JCB (with front.), MHS (lacks front.), NL (two, both lack front.), WHS (lacks front.).

1704 — FRENCH — VOL. 1.

Nouveaux | Voyages | de Mr le Baron | de Lahontan | dans | l'Amerique | Septentrionale. | Qui contiennent une relation des differens Peu- | ples qui y habitent, la nature de leur Gouver- | nement, leur Commerce, leur Coûtume, leur | Religion, & leur maniere de faire la Guerre. | L'interêt des François & des Anglois dans le | Commerce qu'ils font avec ces Nations, l'a- | vantage que l'Angleterre peut retirer dans ce | Païs, étant en Guerre avec la France. | Le tout enrichi de Cartes & de Figures. | Tome Premier. | [*Small ornament*] |

A La Haye, | Chez les Freres LHONORE', Marchands Libraires. | M. DCCIV. |

Collation. — 12mo; title, verso blank; "A sa Majesté Frederic IV," pp. (2); "Preface," pp. (5); "Table des Lettres du I. Tome," pp. (9); "Voyages," pp. 1–266; "Explication de quelques Termes," pp. 267–280. P. 82 is misprinted 84. The title-page printed wholly in black.

Plates. — Frontispiece of an Indian in an oval, and opposite pp. 14, 34, 47, 72, 85, 98, 116, 141, 174, 225 and 242; a small "Carte générale du Canada en petit point" opp. p. 1 of the text; a folded map opp. p. 136, entitled: "Carte que les Gnacsitares ont Dessine," etc.

Signatures. — A—M in twelves, N in six (the last leaf blank). Sig. E5 is misprinted E6.

Copies. — JCB, LP.

1704 — FRENCH — VOL. 2.

Memoires | de | l'Amerique | Septentrionale, | ou | la Suite des Voyages | de | Mr le Baron de Lahontan. | Qui contiennent la Deſcription d'une | grande étenduë de païs de ce Conti- | nent, l'interêt des François & des An- | glois, leurs Commerces, leurs Na- | vigations, les Mœurs & les Coûtu- | mes des Sauvages, &c. | Avec un petit Dictionnaire de la Langue du Païs. | Le tout enrichi de Cartes & de Figures. | Et augmenté dans ce ſecond Tome de la ma- | niere dont les Sauvages ſe régalent. | [*Small ornament, same as in vol. 1*] |

A La Haye, | Chez les Freres LHONORE', Marchands Libraires. | M. DCCIV. |

Collation. — 8vo; title, verso blank; "Memoires," pp. 3-198; "Petit Dictionaire," pp. 199-222; "Table des Matieres," pp. (18). Pagination of p. 101 imperfectly printed 10. Title-page printed wholly in black.

Plates. — Opposite pp. 95, 98, 101, 125, 130, 151, 155, 167, 185, 189, 190, and 191; a folded "Carte generale de Canada" opp. p. 5.

Signatures. — A—K in twelves.

Copies. — JCB, LP.

1704 — FRENCH — VOL. 3.

Suite | Du | Voyage, | De l'Amerique, | Ou Dialogues | De Monſieur le | Baron de Lahontan | Et d'un | Sauvage, | Dans l'Amerique. Contenant une deſcription | exacte des mœurs & des coutumes de ces | Peuples Sauvages. | Avec les Voyages du même en Portgugal & en | Danemarc, dans leſquels on trouve des parti- | cularitez trés curieuſes, & qu'on n'avoit | point encore remarquées. | Le tout enrichi de Cartes & de Figures. | [*Small scrolled ornament*] |

A Amsterdam, | Chez la Veuve de Boeteman, | Et ſe vend | A Londres, chez David Mortier, Li- | braire dans le Strand, à l'Enſeigne d'Eraſme. | M. DCCIV. |

Collation. — 12mo; title, verso blank; "Preface," pp. (12); "Avis

De l'Auteur Au Lecteur," pp. (2); "Dialogues," pp. 1–103; p. [104] blank; half-title: "Voyages | Du | Baron de Lahontan | En Portugal, | Et en | Danemarc," on p. [105]; p. [106] blank; text of "Voyages," pp. 107–222. P. 86 is mispaged 89. The 1st, 3d, 5th, 7th, and 9th lines and place of imprint printed in red.

Plates. — Opposite pp. 1, 118, 149, and 155; a map of Portugal at p. 107, and a map of Denmark at p. 145.

Signatures. — * in eight, A—I in twelves, K in three. This volume is merely a reissue of the original sheets of the 1703 edition of the *Suplément*, with a new title-page. We have seen sets of the "Angel issue" of vols. 1 and 2 accompanied by the 1703 edition of the *Suplément;* by the 1704 *Suite*, and by the issue of 1704 called *Dialogues* (*vide* next item).

Copies. — LLQ, NL.

1704 — French: *Dialogues issue* — Vol. 3.

Dialogues | De Monſieur le | Baron de Lahontan | Et d'un | Sauvage, | Dans l'Amerique. | Contenant une deſcription exacte des mœurs | & des coutumes de ces Peuples Sauvages. | Avec les Voyages du même en Portugal & en | Danemarc, dans leſquels on trouve des parti- | cularitez trés curieuses, & qu'on n'avoit | point encore remarquées. | Le tout enrichi de Cartes & de Figures. | [*Cut, a vase of flowers*]

A Amsterdam, | Chez la Veuve de Boeteman, | Et ſe vend | A Londres, chez David Mortier, Li- | braire dans le Strand, à l' Enſeigne d' Eraſme. | M. DCCIV. |

Collation. — This is a separate issue of the *Suite Du Voyage* of this year, which as already shown *in loco* is merely the sheets of the 1703 original with a new title-page.

Copies. — BM, C, JCB, NL (two).

1705 — FRENCH: *Jonas l'Honoré* — VOL. 1.

Voyages | du Baron | de La Hontan | dans | l'Amerique | Septentrionale, | Qui contiennent une Rélation des différens Peuples | qui y habitent; la nature de leur Gouvernement; leur | Commerce, leur Coûtumes, leur Religion, & | leur maniére de faire la Guerre: | L'Intérêt des François & des Anglois dans le Com- | merce qu'ils font avec ces Nations; l'avantage que | l'Angleterre peut retirer de ce Païs, étant | en Guerre avec la France. | Le tout enrichi de Cartes & de Figures. | Tome Premier. | Seconde Edition, revuë, corrigée, & augmentée. | [*Cut, with emblematic scene, globe, pillar and figures*] |

A La Haye, | Chez Jonas l'Honoré, & Compagnie. | MDCCV. |

Collation. — 12mo; engraved frontispiece, with title: "Nouveaux | Voyages | du Barron | de Lahontan"; title, verso blank; "Préface," pp. (8); "Table des Lettres du Tome Premier," pp. (8); "Voyages" or text, pp. [1]–364; "Explication de quelques Termes," pp. 365–376. No mispaging. The 1st, 3d, 5th, 6th, 11th to 14th, and 16th lines and place and date of imprint printed in red. In some copies, if not indeed in all, the paper of signatures N—P (pp. 289–360) is browned.

Plates. — Opposite pp. 1, 38, 53, 82, 91, 118, 127, 174, 244, 303, 324, and 340; a folded "Carte que les Gnacsitares ont dessiné," etc., opp. p. 1. The only characteristic variation between the Jonas and François l'Honoré issues of this year seems to be their title-pages.

Signatures. — * in nine, A—P in twelves, Q in eight.

Copies. — BM, JCB, NL, NYHS (imperfect).

1705 — FRENCH: *Jonas l'Honoré* — VOL. 2.

Memoires | de | l'Amerique | Septentrionale, | ou la Suite | des Voyages de Mr. le | Baron de La Hontan: | Qui contiennent la Description d'une grande étenduë | de Païs de ce Continent, l'intérêt des François & des | Anglois, leurs Commerces, leurs Navigations, | les

Mœurs & les Coutumes des Sauvages, &c. | Avec un petit Dictionaire de la Langue du Païs. | Le tout enrichi de Cartes & de Figures. | Tome Second. | Seconde Edition, augmentée des Conversations de | l'Auteur avec un Sauvage diftingué. | [*Same cut as in first volume*] |

A Amsterdam, | Pour Jonas l'Honoré à la Haye. | M DCC V. |

Collation. — 12mo; title, verso blank; "Memoires," pp. 5-196; "Conversations de l'Auteur de ces Voyages avec Adario," pp. 197-310; half-title: "Dictionaire | de la Langue | des Sauvages," on p. [311]; p. [312] blank; "Dictionaire," pp. 313-336; "Table Des Matieres principales contenues dans ce II Volume," pp. (2). No mispaging. The 1st, 3d, 6th, 7th, 12th, and 14th lines and place and date of imprint printed in red.

Plates.— Opposite pp. 95, 104, 125, 129, 133, 148, 155, 160, 185, 187, 189, and 191; frontispiece "Carte Generale de Canada a petit point," and a large folded "Carte Generale de Canada" opp. p. 5.

Signatures. — Title-page, A3—[A12], B—O in twelves, P in one.

Copies. —BM, JCB, NL.

1705—FRENCH: *François l'Honoré*—VOL. I.

Voyages | du Baron | de La Hontan | dans | l'Amerique | Septentrionale, | Qui contiennent une Rélation des différens Peuples | qui y habitent; la nature de leur Gouvernement; leur | Commerce, leurs Coûtumes, leur Religion, & | leur maniére de faire la Guerre: | L'Intérêt des François & des Anglois dans le Com- | merce qu'ils font avec ces Nations; l'avantage que | l'Angleterre peut retirer de ce Païs, étant | en Guerre avec la France. | Le tout enrichi de Cartes & de Figures. | Tome Premier. | Seconde Edition, revuê, corrigée, & augmentée. | [*Emblematic cut, a globe with five figures seated near a column*] |

A Amsterdam, | Chez François l'Honoré vis-à-vis de la Bourfe. | M D CC V. |

Collation. — 12mo; engraved frontispiece, with title: "Nouveaux | Voyages | du Barron | de Lahontan"; title, verso blank; "Preface," pp. (8); "Table des Lettres du Tome Premier," pp. (8); "Voyages" or text, pp. [1]—364; "Explication de quelques Termes," pp. 365–376. No mispaging. The 1st, 3d, 5th, 6th, 11th to 14th, and 16th lines and place and date of imprint printed in red.

Plates. — Opposite pp. 1, 38, 53, 82 (corrected from 72), 91, 118, 127, 174, 244, 303, 324, and 340; a folded "Carte que les Gnacsitares ont dessiné," etc., opp. p. 1, but often found at some other location in the volume. The only characteristic variation between the François and Jonas l'Honoré issues of this year seems to be their title-pages.

Signatures. — * in nine, A—P in twelves, Q in eight.

Copies. — B, BM, C, HC.

1705 — French: *François l'Honoré* — Vol. 2.

Memoires | de | l'Amerique | Septentrionale, | ou la suite | des Voyages de Mr. le Baron de La Hontan: | Qui contiennent la Defcription d'une grande étenduë | de Païs de ce Continent, l'intérêt des François & des | Anglois, leurs Commerces, leurs Navigations, | les Mœurs & les Coutumes des Sauvages, &c. | Avec un petit Dictionaire de la Langue du Païs. | Le tout enrichi de Cartes & de Figures. | Tome Second. | Seconde Edition, augmentée des Conversations de | l'Auteur avec un Sauvage diftingué. | [*Same cut as in first volume*] |

A Amsterdam, | Chez François l'Honoré & Compagnie.| M DCC V. |

Collation. — 12mo; title, verso blank; "Memoires," pp. 5–196; "Conversations," pp. 197–310; half-title: Dictionare | de la Langue | des Sauvages," on p. [311]; p. [312] blank; "Dictionaire," pp. 313–336; "Table Des Matieres principales contenues dans ce II Volume," pp. (2). No mispaging. The 1st, 3d, 6th, 7th, 12th, and 14th lines and place and date of imprint printed in red.

Plates. — Opposite pp. 95, 104, 125, 129, 133, 148, 155, 160, 185, 187, 189, and 191; frontispiece "Carte Generale de Canada a petit point," and large folded "Carte generale du Canada" opp. p. 5, but having the location mark "Pag: 1" engraved upon it.

Signatures. — A—O in twelves, P in one.

Copies. — B, BM, C, HC (lacks large map).

1705 — English: *Extract.*

A Voyage to North America. Or a Geographical Defcription of Canada. By the Baron La Hontan, Lord Lieutenant of the French Colony at Placentia in Newfound-Land.

The above title is the heading of chap. xvi of the original folio edition of John Harris's *Navigantium atque Itinerantium Bibliotheca: Or, a Compleat Collection of Voyages and Travels: . . . Volume II.* (London: Printed for Thomas Bennet . . . MDCCV). The complete extract from Lahontan is embraced by Harris's chapters xvi–xxvi, or pp. 915–928.

The revised editions of Harris (edited by J. Campbell), published in 1744–1748 and 1764, do not contain these excerpts.

1706 — French — Vol. 1.

Voyages | du Baron | de La Hontan | dans | l'Amerique | Septentrionale, | Qui contiennent une Rélation des differens Peuples | qui y habitent; la nature de leur Gouvernement; leur | Commerce, leurs Coûtumes, leur Religion; & | leur maniére de faire la Guerre: | L'Interêt des François & des Anglois dans le Com- | merce qu'ils font avec ces Nations; l'avantage que | l'Angleterre peut retirer de ce Païs, étant | en Guerre avec la France. | Le tout enrichi de Cartes & de Figures. | Tome Premier. | Seconde Edition, revuë, corrigé, & augmentée. | [*Cut of three cherubs*] |

A La Haye, | Chez Charles Delo, ſur le Singel. | MDCCVI. |

This edition is merely a reissue from the same sheets of the two 1705 issues of François and Jonas l'Honoré, with which it agrees in collation; even the paper of signatures N—P is browned as in them, and all typographical peculiarities are repeated in the body of both volumes.

Copies. — BA (lacks many plates and the large map), JCB, NL.

1706 — French — Vol. 2.

Memoires | de | l'Amerique | Septentrionale, | ou la Suite | des Voyages de Mr. le | Baron de La Hontan: | Qui contiennent la Deſcription d'une grande étenduë | de Païs de ce continent, l'interêt des François & des | Anglois, leurs Commerces, leurs Navigations, | les Mœurs & les Coutumes des Sauvages, &c. | Avec un petit Dictionaire de la Langue du Païs. | Tome Second. | Seconde Edition, augmenté des Conversations | de l'Auteur avec un Sauvage diſtingué. | [*Cut of two cherubs bearing the host*] |

A La Haye, | Chez Charles Delo, ſur le Singel. | MDCCVI. |

This edition is merely a reissue from the same sheets of the two 1705 issues of François and Jonas l'Honoré, with which it agrees in collation.

Copies. — BA *(lacks many plates and the large map)*, JCB, NL.

1707 — French — Vol. 1.

Nouveaux | Voyages | de Monsieur | le Baron de Lahontan, | dans | l'Amerique | Septentrionale, | Qui contiennent une Relation des diffe- | rens Peuples qui y habitent, la nature | de leur Gouvernement, leur Commerce, | leurs Coûtumes, leur Religion, & leur | maniere de faire la Guerre. | L'interêt des François & des Anglois dans le | Commerce qu'ils font avec ces Nations; | l'avantage que la France, peut retirer dans ce | Païs, étant en Guerre avec l'Angleterre. | Le tout enrichi de Cartes & de Figures. | Tome Premier. | [*Floral cut*] |

A La Haye, | Chez Isaac Delorme, Libraire. | M. DCCVII. |

Collation. — 12mo; title, verso blank; "A sa Majesté Frederic IV," pp. (4); "Preface," pp. (6); "Table des Lettres du tome I," pp. (6); "Voyages," pp. 1–342; "Explication de quelques Termes qui se trouvent dans le premier Tome," pp. 343–354; "Table des Matieres contenues dans le premier Tome," pp. (12). Pp. 22, 190, 191, 193, 218, 282, and 283 are mispaged 72, 192, 193, 195, 198, 284, and 285, respectively. Title-page printed wholly in black.

Plates. — The copy in the Library of Congress, the only one I have been able to examine, evidently lacks six plates and two maps. It has a frontispiece of an Indian in an oval, and plates opposite pp. 47, 101, 119, 161, and 313. Two leaves from sig. E (pp. 107–110) are also wanting in that copy.

Signatures. — Title, a in eight, A—B in sixes, b in twelve, C—P in twelves, Q in four (last leaf blank). F5 printed Fv; I4 printed Iiiij; I5 printed Iv.

Copies. — C (imperfect).

1708 — FRENCH — VOL. 2.

Memoires | de | l'Amerique | Septentrionale, | ou la Suite des Voyages | de Monsieur | le Baron de Lahontan, | qui contiennent | La Deſcription d'une grande étenduë de | Païs de ce Continent, l'interêt des | François & des Anglois, leurs Com- | merces, leurs Navigations, les Mœurs | & les Coutumes des Sauvages &c. | Avec un Dictionnaire de la Langue du Païs. | Le tout enrichi de Cartes & de Figures. | Tome Seconde. | [*Cut, a pot of flowers*] |

A La Haye, | Chez Isaac Delorme, Libraire. | M. DCCVIII. |

Collation. — 12mo; title, verso blank; "Memoires," pp. 1–215;

p. [216] blank; "Petit Dictionaire de la Langue des Sauvages," pp. 217–239; verso of p. 239 blank. Pp. 38, 39, 40, 44, 105, 116, 150, and 160 are mispaged 36, 37, 38, 48, 89, 115, 250, and 60, respectively. The title-page printed wholly in black.

Plates. — The copy in the Library of Congress, the only one I have been able to examine, evidently lacks five plates and perhaps a small map of Canada. It has plates opposite pp. 97, 104, 132, 136, 155, 166, and 211; and a "Carte generale de Canada" opp. p. 3.

Signatures. — Title, A—K in twelves. Sig. A3 is printed Aiij; C5 printed Cv; E5 printed Ev; K2 printed Kij.

Copies. — C (imperfect).

1708 — FRENCH — VOL. 3.

Dialogues | de Monsieur | le Baron de Lahontan, | et d'un | Sauvage, | dans l'Amerique. | Contenant | Une deſcription exacte des mœurs | & des coutumes de ces Peuples | Sauvages. | Avec les Voyages du même en Portugal | & en Danemarc, dans leſquels on | trouve des particularitez très-curieuſes, | & qu'on n'a point encore remarquées. | Le tout enrichi de Cartes & de Figures. | Tome Troisieme. | [*Same floral cut as in vol. 1*] |

A La Haye, | Chez Isaac Delorme, Libraire. | M. DCCVIII. |

Collation. — 12mo; title, verso blank; "Preface," pp. (13); "Avis de l'Auteur au Lecteur," pp. (3); "Dialogues," pp. 1–174; one blank leaf for pp. [175] and [176]; half-title: "Voyages | de | Portugal | et de | Danemarc," on p. [177; p. [178] blank; "Voyages," pp. 179–374. Pp. 265, 268, 269, 272, 273, 276, 277, 280, 281, 284, 285, and 288 are mispaged 269, 272, 273, 276, 277, 280, 281, 284, 285, 288, 289, and 290, respectively. Title-page printed wholly in black.

Plates. — The copy in the Library of Congress, the only one I have been able to examine, evidently lacks three plates and two maps, of Portugal and Denmark. It has one plate opposite p. 1.

Signatures. — a in five, b in four, A—P in twelves, Q in eight (last leaf blank). Sig. H4 is a blank leaf.

Copies. — C (imperfect).

1709 — French — Vol. 1.

Nouveaux | Voyages | de Mr le Baron | de Lahontan, | dans | l'Amerique | Septentrionale. | Qui contiennent une relation des differens Peu- | ples qui y habitent, la nature de leur Gouver- | nement, leur Commerce, leur Coûtume, leur | Religion, & leur maniere de faire la Guerre. | L'intetêt des François & des Anglois dans le | Commerce qu'ils font avec ces Nations, l'a- | vantage que l'Angleterre peut retirer dans | ce Païs, étant en Guerre avec la France. | Le tout enrichi de Cartes & de Figures. | Tome Premier. | [*Small ornament*] |

A La Haye, | Chez les Freres L Honoré, Marchands | Libraires. | M. DCCIX.

Collation. — 12mo; title, verso blank; "A sa Majesté Frederic IV," pp. (3); "Preface," pp. (5); "Table des Lettres du I. tome," pp. (8); "Voyages," pp. 1–266; "Explication de quelques Termes," pp. 267–280. Pp. 229 and 274 are misprinted 129 and 174, respectively. Title-page printed entirely in black.

Plates. — Frontispiece of an Indian and opposite pp. 14, 34, 47, 72, 85, 98, 116, 141, 174, 225, and 242; small "Carte generale du Canada en petit point" opp. p. 1, and a small folded " Carte que les Gnacsitares ont Dessine" opp. p. 136.

Signatures. — A—M in twelves, N in six (the last leaf blank).

Copies. — HC (two), JCB.

1709 — FRENCH — VOL. 2.

Memoires | de | l'Amerique | Septentrionale, | ou | la Suite des Voyages | de | Mr le Baron de Lahontan. | Qui contiennent la Deſcription d'une | grande étenduë de païs de ce Con- | tinent, l'interêt des François & des | Anglois, leurs Commerces, leurs | Navigations, les Mœurs & les Coû | tumes des Sauvages, &c. | Avec un petit Dictionnaire de la Langue du Païs. | Le tout enrichi de Cartes & de Figures. | Et augmenté dans ce ſecond Tome de la ma- | niere dont les Sauvages ſe régalent. | [*Same small ornament as in vol. 1*] |

A La Haye, | Chez les freres L Honoré, Marchands Libraires. | M. DCCIX. |

Collation. — 12mo; title, verso blank; "Memoires," pp. 3–198; "Petit Dictionaire de la Langue des Sauvages," pp. 199–222; "Table des Matieres contenues dans les deux Tomes," pp. (18). Pp. 200 and 220 are mispaged 220 and 120, respectively. Title-page printed entirely in black.

Plates. — Opposite pp. 95, 101, 125, 130, 151, 155, 167, 185, 189, 190, and 191; a folded "Carte generale de Canada" opp. p. 5.

Signatures. — A—K in twelves. Sig. K4 is misprinted K3.

Copies. — HC (two), JCB.

1709 — GERMAN: *Abridgment.*

Des berühmten | Herrn | Baron De Lahontan | Neueste Reisen | Nach | Nord-Indien/ | Oder dem | Mitternächtischen America, | Mit vielen besondern und bey keinem Scribenten | befindlichen | Curiositæten. | Aus dem Frantzösischen übersetzet | Von | M. Vischer. |

Hamburg und Leipzig/ | Im Reumannischen Verlag/MDCCIX. |

Collation. — 12mo; doublepage title, with reverse blank; "Geneigter Leser!", signed by the translator and dated at "Hamburg d. 15. April: 1709," pp. (8); text with heading: "Des Herrn Baron de la Hontan Nord-Indien," pp. 1-252; half-title of second part: "Der | Historischen | Nachrichten | Des | Herrn Baron de la | Hontan, | Von | Nord-Indien/ | Zweyter Theil," on p. 253; text of same, pp. 254-432; "Anhang eines Wörter-Buchs von der Wilden Sprache," pp. 433-454; "Register," pp. 455-459; verso of p. 459 blank. Pp. 127, 373, 376, 377, and 380 are mispaged 107, 343, 347, 358, and 339, respectively. Title-page printed wholly in black.

Plates. — No plates, but small folded "General Carte von Canada" before the title-page.

Signatures. —)(in six (of which the folded title-page is a part), a—t in twelves, u in two. The signature mark of b6 is on the verso of that leaf, and that of d4 is wanting.

Copies. — BM, C, JCB.

1710 — DUTCH: *Extract.*

Van den oorspronk en de kracht der Vooroordeelen, Door J. T. Als mede een koort Uyttreksel Uyt de Aanteykeninge van de Baron de Lahontan, rakende de Zeden, 't Geloof, en't verstant van de Wilden tot Canada, en de lof der hedendaagse Eeuw, in vergelykinge, van de voorgaande Eeuwen. En dat er zoo veele Atheisten niet zyn als men doorgaans gelooft, Door J. de Klerk. Amsterdam: Jan Blum. 1710. 12mo.

This title is copied from Joseph Sabin's *Dictionary of Books Relating to America*, item 38048. A distorted title of the same is given in Frederik Muller's *Catalogue of Books, Maps, Plates on America. Part I.* (Amsterdam, 1872), item 317. I have not seen this extract. See another edition, under 1723.

1711 — GERMAN.

Des berühmten | Herrn | Baron De Lahontan | Neueste Reisen | Nach | Nord-Indien/ | Oder dem | Mitternächtischen America | Mit vielen besondern und bey keinem Scribenten befindlichen | Curiositæten. | Auch bey dieser andern Auflage mit | Seiner Reise nach Portugall/Dennemarck und | Spanien/vermehret. | Aus dem Frantzösischen übersetzet | Von M. Vischer. |

Hamburg und Leipzig/ | Im Reumannischen Verlag/MDCCXI. |

Collation. — 12mo; doublepage title, with reverse blank; "Vorrede. An den verständigen Leser," dated at end "Hamburg, d. 20. Novemb. 1710," pp. (19); one blank page; text headed: "Des Herrn Baron de la Hontan Nord-Indien," pp. 1–316; half-title: "Der | Historischen | Nachrichten | Des | Herrn Baron de la | Hontan, | Von | Nord-Indien/ | Zweyter Theil," on p. [317]; text of same, pp. 318–563; "Anhang eines Wörter-Buchs von der Wilden Sprache," pp. 563–590; "Des Berühmten Herrn Baron de la Hontan Reise nach Portugall und Dennemarck," pp. 591–747; "Register," pp. 748–753; verso of p. 753 blank. Pp. 51, 212, and 359 are mispaged 24, 112, and 395, respectively; there is also an elision of pp. 254 and 255. Title-page wholly in black.

Plates. — No plates, but a "General-Carte von Canada," folded, to precede p. 1.

Signatures. —)(in twelve (of which the folded title-page forms a part), A—Hh in twelves, Ii in four. Signature mark R4 is wanting. The translator calls this the "Zweite Auflage" in German.

Copies. — JCB.

1715 — FRENCH — VOL. 1.

Nouveaux | Voyages | de Mr. le Baron | de Lahontan, | dans | l'Amerique | Septentrionale. | Qui contient une relation des differens Peuples | qui y habitent, la nature de leur Gouverne- | ment, leur

Commerce, leur Coûtume, leur | Religion, & leur maniere de faire la Guerre. | L'intérêt des François & des Anglois dans le Com- | merce qu'ils font avec ces Nations, l'avantage | que l'Angleterre peut retirer dans ce Païs, | étant en Guerre avee la France. | Le tout enrichi de Cartes & de Figures. | Tome Premier. | [*Small ornament*] |

A La Haye, | Chez les Freres L Honoré, Marchands Libraires. | M. DCCXV. |

Collation. — 12mo; title, verso blank; "A sa Majesté Frederic IV," pp. (3); "Preface," pp. (5); "Table des Lettres du I. tome," pp. (8); "Voyages" or text, pp. 1–266; "Explication de quelques Termes," pp. 267–280. Pp. 130, 141, and 274 are misprinted 180, 411, and 174, respectively, and the paging of 131 is broken. Title-page printed entirely in black.

Plates.— Frontispiece and opposite pp. 14, 34, 47, 72, 85, 98, 116, 141, 155, 174, 225, and 242; a small "Carte generale du Canada en petit point" opp. p. 9, and a folded "Carte que les Gnacsitares ont Dessiné, etc., opp. p. 136.

Signatures. — A—M in twelves, N in six (the last leaf blank). Sig. M6 is misprinted H6.

Copies. — BN, HC, LU.

1715 — French — Vol. 2.

Memoires | de | l'Amerique | Septentrionale, | ou | la Suite des Voyages | de | Mr le Baron de Lahontan. | Qui contient la Defcription d'une gran- | de étenduë de Païs de ce Continent, | l'interêt des François & des Anglois, | leurs Commerces, leurs Navigations, | leur Mœurs & les Coûtumes des Sau- | vages, &c. | Avec un petit Dictionnaire de la Langue du Païs. | Le tout enrichi de Cartes & de Figures. | Et augmenté dans fe Second Tome de la maniere | dont les Sauvages fe régalent. | [*Same ornament as vol. 1*] |

A La Haye, | Chez les Freres L Honoré, Marchands Libraires. | M. DCCXV. |

Collation.—12mo; title, verso blank; "Memoires," pp. 1 [*i.e.* 3]–198; "Petit Dictionnaire de la Langue des Sauvages," pp. 199–222; "Table des Matieres," pp. (18). Pp. 3, 100, 200, and 220 are misprinted 1, 1, 220, and 122, respectively.

Plates.—Opposite pp. 55, 95, 101, 125, 130, 151, 174, 189, 190, and 191; a large folded "Carte generale de Canada," without page location, but opposite the title-page in Harvard copy.

Signatures.—A—K in twelves. Sig. F3 and K4 misprinted F5 and C3, respectively.

Copies.—BN, HC, LU.

1723—DUTCH: *Extract.*

Den Oorſpronk en de kracht | der | Vooroordeelen; | klaar vertoont in een brief door J. T. | Als mede | In de zeden, 't geloof, en 't verſtant | der Wilden te | Kanada, | getrokken uit de Aantekeningen van | den Baron de | La Hontan. | Waar by gevoegt is | Den lof der hedensdaagſche Eeuw, in | vergelyking met de voorgaande Eeuwen. | Door | J. De Klerk. | [*Floral ornament*] |

Gedrukt in 't Jaar 1723. |

Collation.—Small 8vo; title, verso blank; "Den oorspronk en de kracht der Vooroordeelen," pp. 3–11; "Een kort Uyttreksel Uyt de Memoires de l'Amerique Septentrionale van Mr. le Baron de Lahontan, Tome Second," pp. 12–26; "Een kort Extract Uyt de beschryvinge van 't Eyland Formosa," pp. 27–29; "Den lof der hedendaagze Eeuw," etc., pp. 29–39; verso of p. 39 blank. No mispaging. Title wholly in black.

Signatures.—A—B in eights, C in four.

Copies.—JCB.

1728 — FRENCH — VOL. I.

Voyages | du Baron | de Lahontan | dans | l'Amerique | Septentrionale, | Qui contiennent une Rélation des différens | Peuples qui y habitent ; la nature de leur | Gouvernement ; leur Commerce, leurs | Coûtumes, leur Religion, & leur maniére | de faire la Guerre : | L'Intérêt des François & des Anglois dans le | Commerce qu'ils font avec ces Nations ; l'a- | vantage que l'Angleterre peut retirer de ce | Païs, étant en Guerre avec la France. | Le tout enrichi de Cartes & de Figures. | Tome Premier. | Seconde Edition, revuë, corrigée, & augmentée. | [*Cut with two flower vases*] |

A Amsterdam, | Chez François l'Honoré, vis-à-vis de la Bourſe. | M. DCC. XXVIII. |

Collation. — 12mo ; title, verso blank ; "Préface," pp. (8) ; "Table des Lettres du tome premier," pp. (8) ; "Voiages" or text, pp. 1–398 ; "Explication de quelques Termes," pp. 399–408. No mispaging. The 1st, 3d, 5th, 6th, 12th to 15th, and 17th lines and place and date of imprint printed in red.

Plates. — Frontispiece and opposite pp. 17, 40, 56, 90, 91, 97, 129, 136, 188, 216, 351, and 358 ; a small "Carte génerale du Canada en petit point" opp. p. 105, and folded "Carte que les Gnacsitares ont Dessine," etc., opp. p. 162.

Signatures. — Title-page, * in eight, A—R in twelves.

Copies. — B (two), BA, BM, BN, C, HC (lacks a map), JCB, LLQ, LP, LU, NL, WHS.

1728 — FRENCH — VOL. 2.

Memoires | de | l'Amerique | Septentrionale, | ou la Suite | des Voyages de Mr. le | Baron de Lahontan : | Qui contiennent la Deſcription d'une grande etenduë | de Païs de ce Continent, l'intérêt des François | & des Anglois, leurs Commerces, leurs Naviga- | tions, les

Mœurs & les Coûtumes des Sauvages, | &c. | Avec un petit Dictionaire de la Langue du Païs. | Le tout enrichi de Cartes & de Figures. | Tome Second. | Second Edition, augmentée de la maniére dont les | Sauvages ſe régalent. | [*Cut with two flower vases*] |

A Amsterdam, | Chez François l'Honoré & Compagnie. | M. DCC. XXVIII. |

Collation.—12mo; title, verso blank; "Memoires," pp. 1–219; "Dictionaire de la Langue des Sauvages," pp. 220–238. Pp. 161 and 185 are misprinted 151 and 158, respectively. The 1st, 3d, 6th, 7th, 13th, and 15th lines and place and date of imprint printed in red.

Plates.—Opposite pp. 98, 109, 142, 158, plate of "Lac des Outagamis" variously placed (but incorrectly engraved "Tom. 2 Pag. 358"), plate of sun-dance variously placed (but incorrectly engraved "Tom. 2. Pag. 267"), 178, 189, 193, and 209; a folded "Carte generale de Canada" opp. p. 5.

Signatures.—Title-page, A—L in twelves (last three leaves blank), but often found without the final blank leaves.

Copies.—B (two), BA, BM, BN, C, JCB, LLQ, LP, LU, NL (lacks a map), WHS.

1728—French—Vol. 3.

Suite | du | Voyage | de l'Amerique | ou Dialogues | de Monsieur | le Baron de Lahontan | et d'un | Sauvage, | de l'Amerique. | Contenant une deſcription exacte des mœurs | & des coûtumes de ces Peuples Sauvages. | Avec les Voiages du méme en Portugal & en Dane- | marc dans leſquels on trouve des particularitez | très-curieuſes, & qu'on n'avoit point encore re- | marquées. | Le tout enrichi de Cartes & de Figures. | [*Small ornament*] |

A Amsterdam. | Chez la Veuve de Boeteman. | M. DCC. XXVIII. |

Collation.—12mo; title, verso blank; "Préface," pp. (10); "Avis de l'Auteur au Lecteur," pp. (2); "Dialogues," pp. 15–128; "Voiages de Portugal et de Danemarc," pp. 129–257, with verso of p. 257 blank. Pp. 84, 206, 207, and 209 are misprinted 48, 106, 107, and 109, respectively. The 1st, 3d, 5th, 7th, 9th, and 17th lines and place and date of imprint printed in red; in the Harvard and Carter-Brown copies the 11th and 12th lines are also printed in red.

Plates. — Opposite pp. 15, 136, 176, and 182; maps of Portugal and Denmark at pp. 129 and 171, respectively. All the plates are marked for "Tom. III."

Signatures. — A—L in twelves (the last three leaves blank).

Copies. — B (two, one of which lacks the maps), BA, BM, BN, C, HC, JCB, LLQ, LP, LU, NL, WHS.

? 1731 — French — Vols. 1 and 2.

Voyages du Baron de Lahontan.

In Charles Leclerc's *Bibliotheca Americana* (Paris: Maisonneuve & Cie, 1867), p. 193, item 825, the following description appears:

825. — Le même ouvrage. Amsterdam, Fr. L'Honoré, 1731, 2 vol. in —12, mar. chocolat, d. s. t.

Vol. i. 4 fnc., 188 pp., 2 fnc., front. gravé, 8 pl. et cartes. — Vol. ii. 2 fnc., 220 pp., 6 pl. et cartes.

I believe no such edition exists, and that the date was mistaken for M. DCC. XXXXI, for the collation agrees with vol. i and vol. ii (called *Suite*) of the 1741 edition. This vagary has misled every bibliographer who has had recourse to Leclerc's title.

? 1731 — French — Vols. 1 and 2.

Nouveaux Voyages * * * dans l'Amerique Septentrionale * * * . La Haye, Chez les Frères l'Honoré. MDCCXXXI. 2 vols., 12mo, pp. (8), 188, (4); (4), 220. 14 Plates and Maps.

f

This title appears in Joseph Sabin's *Dictionary of Books relating to America*, no. 38640. It is merely a repetition of Leclerc's erroneous title (*q. v.* preceding title), in which Sabin has rearranged the material of Leclerc and mistaken the "Fr." as "Frères," instead of "François," and changed the place of imprint to the common "La Haye" of the earlier editions by "les Frères l'Honoré." I believe that no such edition exists. This vagary has misled every bibliographer who has had recourse to Sabin for this subject.

1735 — ENGLISH: *J. and J. Bonwicke*, etc. — VOL. I.

New | Voyages | to | North-America. | Containing | An Account of the ſeveral Nations of that vaſt Con- | tinent; their Cuſtoms, Commerce, and Way of Naviga- | tion upon the Lakes and Rivers; the ſeveral Attempts of | the Engliſh and French to diſpoſſeſs one another; with the | Reaſons of the Miſcarriage of the former; and the various | Adventures between the French, and the Iroqueſe Confe- | derates of England, from 1683 to 1694. | A Geographical Deſcription of Canada, and a | Natural Hiſtory of the Country, with Remarks upon their | Government, and the Intereſt of the Engliſh and French | in their Commerce. | Alſo a Dialogue between the Author and a General of the | Savages, giving a full View of the Religion and ſtrange Opi- | nions of thoſe People: With an Account of the Author's Retreat | to Portugal and Denmark, and his Remarks on thoſe Courts. | To which is added, | A Dictionary of the Algonkine Language, which is | generally ſpoke in North-America. | Illuſtrated with Twenty-Three Maps and Cuts. | Written in French | By the Baron Lahontan, | Lord Lieutenant of the French Colony at Placentia | in Newfoundland, at that Time in England. | Done into Engliſh. The Second Edition. | In Two Volumes. | A great Part of which never Printed in the Original. | Vol. I. |

London: | Printed for J. and J. Bonwicke, R. Wilkin, S. Birt, T. Ward, | E. Wicksteed; and J. Osborn. M, DCC, XXXV. |

Collation. — 8vo; title, verso blank; "To His Grace William Duke of Devonshire," pp. (2); "The Preface," pp. (8); "The Contents," pp. (12); "Some New Voyages," pp. [1]–202; "Memoirs of North-America," pp. 203–274; "A Table explaining some Terms made use of in both Volumes," pp. 275–280. No mispaging.

Plates. — Opposite pp. 26, 43, 55, 65, 75, 89, 106, 160, 184, and 225; small full-page map of Canada opp. the title-page, and two large folded maps, marked *A* and *B*, opp. p. 1, as follows: "A General Map of New France Com̃, call'd Canada," and "A Map drawn upon Stag-skins by ye Gnacſitares," etc.

Signatures. — A in eight, a in four, B—S in eights, T in four.

Copies. — BA, C.

1735 — ENGLISH: *Osborn issue* — VOL. I.

New | Voyages | to | North-America. | Containing | An Account of the ſeveral Nations of that vaſt Con- | tinent; their Cuſtoms, Commerce, and Way of Naviga- | tion upon the Lakes and Rivers; the ſeveral Attempts of | the Engliſh and French to diſpoſſeſs one another; with the | Reaſons of the Miſcarriage of the former; and the various | Adventures between the French, and the Iroqueſe Confe- | derates of England, from 1683 to 1694. | A Geographical Deſcription of Canada, and a | Natural Hiſtory of the Country, with Remarks upon their | Government, and the Intereſt of the Engliſh and French | in their Commerce. | Alſo a Dialogue between the Author and a General of the | Savages, giving a full View of the Religion and ſtrange Opi- | nions of thoſe People: With an Account of the Author's Retreat | to Portugal and Denmark, and his Remarks on thoſe Courts. | To which is added, | A Dictionary of the Algonkine Language, which is | generally ſpoke in North-America. | Illuſtrated with Twenty-Three Maps and Cuts. | Written in French | By the Baron Lahontan, | Lord Lieutenant of the French Colony at Placentia | in Newfoundland, at that Time in England. | Done into Engliſh. The Second Edition. | In Two Volumes. | A great Part of which never Printed in the Original. | Vol. I. |

London: | Printed for J. Osborn, at the Golden-Ball, in Pater-noſter-Row. | M, DCC, XXXV. |

Collation.—8vo; title, verso blank; "To His Grace William," pp. (2); "The Preface," pp. (8); "The Contents," pp. (12); "Some New Voyages to North-America," pp. [1]–202; "Memoirs of North-America," pp. 203–274; "A Table explaining some Terms made use of in both Volumes," pp. 275–280. No mispaging.

Plates.—Opposite pp. 26, 43, 55, 65, 75, 89, 106, 160, and 184; a small map of Canada to face the title-page; two large folded maps to face p. 1 of text, as follows: (A) "A General Map of New France, Com̃, call'd Canada," and (B) "A Map drawn upon Stag-skins by ye Gnacſitares," etc.; map of Newfoundland opp. p. 225.

Signatures.—A in eight, a in four, B—S in eights, T in four.

Copies.—BM, MHS, NL (two, one imperfect).

1735—ENGLISH: *J. Walthoe*, etc.—VOL. 2.

New | Voyages | to | North-America. | Giving a full Account of the Cuſtoms, | Commerce, Religion, and ſtrange Opinions | of the Savages of that Country. | With | Political Remarks upon the Courts | of Portugal and Denmark, and the Preſent State of | the Commerce of thoſe Countries. | The Second Edition. | Written | By the Baron Lahontan, Lord-Lieutenant of | the French Colony at Placentia in New- | foundland: Now in England. | Vol. II. |

London : | Printed for J. Walthoe, R. Wilkin, J. and J. Bonwicke, | J. Osborn, S. Birt, T. Ward and E. Wickſteed. 1735. |

Collation. — 8vo ; title, verso blank ; "A Discourse," pp. 3–91 ; "A Conference," pp. 92–185 ; p. [186] blank ; "An Appendix," pp. 187–288 ; "A Short Dictionary," pp. 289–304. No mispaging.

Plates. — Frontispiece, and opposite pp. 5, 29, 36, 59 (two), 80, 82, 84, and 86.

Signatures. — Aa—Tt in eights. Sig. Tt3 is misprinted Tt4.

Copies. — BA (lacks plates), C, MHS, NL (two, one of which lacks last leaf).

1735 — ENGLISH : *Brindley issue* — VOL. I.

New | Voyages | to | North-America. | Containing | An Account of the ſeveral Nations of that vaſt Con- | tinent ; their Cuſtoms, Commerce, and Way of Naviga- | tion upon the Lakes and Rivers ; the ſeveral Attempts of | the Engliſh and French to diſpoſſeſs one another ; with the | Reaſons of the Miſcarriage of the former ; and the various | Adventures between the French, and the Iroqueſe Confe- | derates of England, from 1683 to 1694. | A Geographical Deſcription of Canada, and a | Natural Hiſtory of the Country, with Remarks upon | their Government, and the Intereſt of the Engliſh and | French in their Commerce. | Alſo a Dialogue between the Author and a General | of the Savages, giving a full View of the Religion and | ſtrange Opinions of thoſe People : With an Account of | the Author's Retreat to Portugal and Denmark, and his | Remarks on thoſe Courts. | To which is added, | A Dictionary of the Algonkine Language, which is | generally ſpoke in North-America. | Illuſtrated with Twenty-Three Maps and Cuts. | Written in French | By the Baron Lahontan, | Lord Lieutenant of the French Colony at Placentia | in Newfoundland, at that Time in England. | Done into Englifh. The Second Edition. | In Two Volumes. | A great Part of which never Printed in the Original. | Vol. I. |

London: | Printed for John Brindley, Bookfeller, at the King's-Arms | in New-bond-ftreet, Bookbinder to her Majefty, and his | Royal Highnefs the Prince of Wales; and Charles | Corbett, at Addifon's-head, Temple-bar. 1735. |

Collation. — 8vo; title, verso blank; dedication "To His Grace William Duke of Devonshire," pp. (2). "The Preface," pp. (8); "The Contents," pp. (12); "Some New Voyages to North-America," pp. [1]-202; "Memoirs," pp. 203-274; "A Table explaining some Terms made use of in both Volumes," pp. 275-280. No mispaging. The Carter Brown copy, the only one I have examined, has the following plates, etc.:

Plates. — Opposite pp. 26, 43, 65, 75, 89, and 106; a small map of Canada to face the title-page; a map of Newfoundland at p. 225; and two large folded maps to precede p. 1 of the text, as follows: (A) "A General Map of New France Com̃, call'd Canada," (B) "A Map drawn upon Stag-skins by ye Gnacfitares," etc. The copy examined apparently lacks plates opposite pp. 55, 160, and 184.

Signatures. — A in eight, a in four, B—S in eights, T in four.

Copies. — C, JCB.

1735 — ENGLISH: *Brindley issue* — VOL. 2.

New | Voyages | to | North-America. | Giving a full Account of the Cu- | ftoms, Commerce, Religion, and ftrange | Opinions of the Savages of that Country. | With | Political Remarks upon the Courts | of Portugal and Denmark, and the Prefent | State of the Commerce of thofe Countries. | The Second Edition. | Written | By the Baron Lahontan, Lord Lieutenant | of the French Colony at Placentia in New- | foundland: Now in England. | Vol. II. |

London: | Printed for J. Brindley, Bookfeller, at the King's | Arms in New-bond-ftreet, Bookbinder to her Ma- | jefty, and his Royal Highnefs the Prince of Wales; | and C. Corbett, at Addifon's-head, Temple-bar. | M D. CC. XXXV. |

Collation. — 8vo; title, verso blank; "A Discourse," pp. 3-91; "A Conference or Dialogue," pp. 92-185; p. [186] blank; "An Appendix," pp. 187-288; "A Short Dictionary," pp. 289-304. No mispaging.

Plates. — Opposite pp. 5, 29, 36, 59 (two), 80, 82, 84, and 86, perhaps also a plate on healing sick and burying the dead at p. 51 (not found in the Carter Brown copy), and a frontispiece of an Indian in an oval.

Signatures. — Aa—Tt in eights.

Copies. — C, JCB.

1739 — DUTCH — VOL. I.

Reizen | van den Baron | van La Hontan | in het | Noordelyk | Amerika, | Vervattende een Verhaal van verfcheide Volke- | ren die het bewoonen; den aart hunner Re- | geering, hun Koophandel, hun Ge- | woontens, hun Godsdienft, en | hun wys van Oorloogen. | Neevens het Belang der Franfchen en der Engel- | fchen in hun Koophandel met die Volkeren; en | 't voordeel dat Engeland, met Vrankryk in | Oorlog zynde, van dat Land kan trekken. | Alles met verfcheide Aanteekeningen vermeer- | dert en opgeheldert, en met Kaarten en | Plaaten verciert. | Eerste Deel. | Vertaalt door | Gerard Westerwyk. | [*Ornament*] |

In's Gravenhage, | By Isaac Beauregard. 1739. |

Collation. — 8vo; title, verso blank; "Voorbericht van den Vertaaler," pp. (3); "Korte Inhouden," pp. (7); "Reizen," pp. [1]-280, an insert map-key of four pages at this location, and 281-582. Pp. 58,

59, 62, 298, 305, and 445 are mispaged 59, 60, 64, 498, 30, and 447 respectively; there are no pp. 191 and 192. The 1st, 3d, 6th, 12th to 15th and 21st lines and place of imprint printed in red.

Plates. — Opposite pp. 1, 65, 190 (plate marked 192), 297, 398, 488, and 544; a large folded "Carte que les Gnacsitares ont dessiné," etc., between pp. 280 and 281.

Signatures. — * in six, A—Nn in eights, Oo in two, with an insert of two leaves between S3 and S4.

Copies — C, JCB, NL, WHS.

1739 — Dutch — Vol. 2.

Gedenkschriften | van het | Noordelyk | Amerika, | of het vervolg der | Reizen van den | Baron van La Hontan. | Vervattende de Beſchryving van een groote | ſtreek Land van dat Weerelddeel; het Belang | der Franſchen en der Engelſchen in 't zelve; | hun Koophandel, hun Schipvaart, en de | Zeeden en Gewoontens der Wil- | den, &c. Alles met Aanteekeningen | vermeerdert en opgeheldert. | Neevens de Zaamenſpraaken van den Schryver met | een Wilden, en een Woordenboek | van de Taal dier Volkeren. | Met Kaarten en Plaaten Verciert. | Tweede Deel. | Vertaalt door | Gerard Westerwyk. | [*Ornament*] |

In's Gravenhage, | By Isaac Beauregard, 1739. |

Collation. — 8vo; title, verso blank; "Gedenkschriften," pp. [1]–358; half-title: "Saamenspraaken | van den | Schryver dezer Reizen | met | Adario | een Wilden van Aanzien," etc., on p. [359]; p. [360] blank; text of same, pp. [362]–523; "Woordenboek van de Taal der Wilden," pp. 524–552. Pp. 91, 327, and 427 are misprinted 19, 227, and 527, respectively. The 1st, 4th, 7th, 15th to 17th, and 21st lines and place of imprint printed in red.

Plates.— Opposite pp. 178, 190, 239, 273, 297, 352, 357, 358 (long narrow cut not numbered), and 390; a "Carte generale de Canada" opp. p. 5 (marked on plate "Tom: 2. P: 1"), which has three pages of text to accompany it — the whole intended to be bound between pp. 4 and 5 of the text.

Signatures. — Title, A—Ll in eights, Mm in four, with two insert leaves between A2 and A3.

Copies. — C, JCB, NL, WHS.

1741 — FRENCH — VOL. I.

Voyages | du Baron | de Lahontan | dans | l'Amerique | Septentrionale, | Qui contiennent une Relation des diffé- | rens Peuples qui y habitent; la nature | de leur Gouvernement; leur Commer- | ce, leurs Coûtumes, leur Religion, & | leur maniére de faire la Guerre: | L'Intérêt des François & des Anglois dans le | Commerce qu'ils font avec ces Nations, l'a- | vantage que l'Angleterre peut retirer de ce | Païs, étant en Guerre avec la France. | Le tout enrichi de Cartes & de Figures. | Tome Pemier [*sic*] | Seconde Edition, revûë, corrigée, & augmentée. | [*Ornament*] |

A Amsterdam, | Chez François L'Honoré, vis-à-vis de la Bourſe. | M. DCC. XXXXI. |

Collation. — 12mo; title, verso blank; "Préface," pp. (8); "Voyages" or text, pp. 1–188; "Table des Lettres," pp. (4). P. 82 is mispaged 28. The 1st, 3d, 5th, 6th, 12th to 15th, and 17th lines and place and date of imprint printed in red.

Plates. — Opposite pp. 14, 25, 38, 56, 87, 97, 129, and 156, and frontispiece of an Indian in an oval; a small "Carte general du Canada en petit point" opp. p. 10.

Signatures. — Title-page, * in four, A—H in twelves.

Copies. — BE, C, JCB, WHS.

1741 — French — Vol. 2 (called Vol. 3).

Memoires | de | l'Amerique | Septentrionale, | ou la Suite | des Voyages de Mr le | Baron de Lahontan : | Qui contiennent la Defcription d'une grande | étenduë de Païs de ce Continent, l'intérêt des | François & des Anglois, leurs Commerces, | leurs Navigations, les Mœurs & les Coûtu | tumes [*sic*] des Sauvages, &c. | Avec un petit Dictionaire de la langue du Païs. | Le tout enrichi de Cartes & de Figures. | Tome Troisieme. | Seconde Edition, augmentée de la maniére dont | les Sauvages fe régalent. | [*Cut, a double cornucopia*] |

A Amsterdam, | Chez François l'Honoré & Compagnie. | M. DCC. XXXXI. |

Collation. — 12mo; title, verso blank; "Memoires," pp. 1–218; "Dictionnaire de la Langue des Sauvages," pp. 219–237, with verso of p. 237 blank. No mispaging. The 1st, 3d, 6th 7th, 13th, and 15th lines and place and date of imprint printed in red.

Plates. — Opposite pp. 51, 103, 110, 137, 142, 166, 191, 208, 209, and 210; a large folded "Carte generale de Canada" opp. p. 1.

Signatures. — Title, A—K in twelves (the last leaf blank).

Copies. — BE, C, HC, JCB, WHS.

1741 — French — Vol. 3 (called Vol. 2).

Suite | des Voyages | du Baron | de Lahontan | dans | l'Amerique | Septentrionale, | Qui contiennent une Relation des diffé- | rens Peuples qui y habitent; la nature | de leur Gouvernement; leur Commer- | ce leurs Coûtumes, leur Religion, & | leur maniére de faire la Guerre: L'Intérêt des François & des Anglois dans le | Commerce qu'ils font avec ces Nations, l'a- | vantage que l'Angleterre peut retirer de ce | Païs, étant en Guerre avec la France. | Le tout enrichi de Cartes & de Figures. | Tome Second. | Seconde Edition, revûë, corrigée, & augmentée. | [*Ornament*] |

A Amsterdam, | Chez François l'Honoré, vis-à-vis de la Bourſe. | M. DCC. XXXXI. |

Collation. — 12mo; title, verso blank; "Table des Lettres du Tome Second," pp. (4); "Suite," pp. 1–210; "Explication de quelques Termes," pp. 211–220. No mispaging. The 2d, 4th, 6th, 7th, 13th to 16th, and 18th lines and place and date of imprint printed in red.

Plates. — Opposite pp. 23, 38, 172, and 175; a "Carte que les Gnacsitares ont Dessiné," etc. opp. p. 1.

Signatures. — Title and two leaves, A—I in twelves, K in two

Copies. — BE, C, JCB, WHS.

1757 — FRENCH: *Extract.*

Voiage du Baron de la Hontan sur la Riviere Longue.

The above marginal title belongs to a short extract in the original quarto edition of *Histoire Général des Voiages, ou Nouvelle Collection de toutes les Relations de Voiages*, edited by Antoine François Prevost d'Exiles. It is found in vol. xiv *(Paris: Chez Didot*, 1757), pp. 719–729.

This French collection of voyages was also issued in duodecimo — *Paris: Chez Didot*, 1749–1789, 80 vols. of text; in quarto — *A La Haye: Chez Pierre De Hondt*, 1747–1780, 25 vols. It appeared in Dutch — *In's Gravenhage: By Pieter de Hondt*, 1747–1767, 21 vols., quarto; in German — *Leipzig: Arkstee und Merkus*, 1747–1774, 21 vols., quarto; and in Spanish — *En Madrid: En la Imprenta de Don Juan Antonio Lozano*, 1763–1791, 28 vols., quarto.

1758 — GERMAN: *Extract.*

Reiſe des Barons de la Hontan auf dem langen Fluſſe. |

This is the heading of an extract in vol. 16 of the "Allgemeine Hiſtorie | der Reiſen zu Waſſer und Lande; | oder | Sammlung | aller | Reiſebeſchreibungen, | [*etc.*] Leipzig, bey Arkſtee und Merkus.

1758. | " This is the German translation of Prevost's collection, *q. v.* under 1757. The German editor was Johann Joachim Schwabe. Lahontan begins the fourth "Abschnitt" of the twelfth chapter, on p. 694. Described from a copy in BA.

1812 — ENGLISH: *Abridgment.*

Travels in Canada; | by the Baron Lahontan. |

Such is the heading of this abridgment in John Pinkerton's "A General Collection of the best and most interesting Voyages and Travels in all Parts of the World; * * * Volume the thirteenth. * * * London: Printed for Longman, Hurst, Rees, Orme, and Brown, Paternoster-Row; and Cadell and Davies, in the Strand. 1812." A foot-note shows that the English edition (London, 1735) was used as the source of the text. It extends from pp. 254–373. Good illustrations are included as follows: "Coffer of Perotte," opp. p. 266; double plate, "On the River St. Lawrence" and "Characteristic Scenery of the Hudson River," opp. p. 271; "Falls of Niagara," which is "Engraved by G. Cooke, from an Original Drawing," opp. p. 296.

1831 — ITALIAN — VOLS. 1 AND 2.

Viaggi | del | Barone di Lahontan | nell'America Settentrionale | Tradotti dal Francese | dal già Capitano Italiano | A. F. | Volume Primo [Secondo] |

Milano | Per G. Truffi e Comp. | 1831 |

Collation. — 2 vols.; small 8vo; Vol. 1: Half-title: "Viaggi | del | Barone di Lahontan," verso blank; title, verso blank; "Viaggi" or text (Letters I–XV), pp. [5]–215; "Indice," on verso of p. 215. No plates or maps.

Signatures. — Two unmarked signatures in eights, 2–12 in eights, 13 in four.

Vol. 2: Half-title, verso blank; title, verso blank; text (Letters XVI–XXV), pp. [5]–201; "Indice," p. 202. No plates or maps.

Signatures. — [1] in four, 2–12 in eights, 13 in four, 13* in six (last leaf blank).

Printed paper covers, with cut of a globe on a stand; that of vol. 2 is dated "M. DCCC. XXXII." This is a translation of the first volume of the French work, or series of twenty-five letters. The only copy I have seen is in the Library of Congress.

1900 — French.

Un Outre-Mer | au xviie Siècle | Voyages au Canada | Du Baron de La Hontan | publiés | Avec une Introduction et des Notes | par | M. François de Nion | [*Printers' mark*] |

Paris | Librairie Plon | Plon-Nourrit et Cie, Imprimeurs-Editeurs | Rue Garancière, 8 | 1900 | Tous droits réservés |

Collation. — 8vo; cover-title, verso blank; half-title, with list of works by the same editor, etc., on verso; title, verso blank; "Introduction," pp. [v]–xix; one blank page; text pp. [1]–331; p. [332] blank; "Table des Matières," pp. [333]–338; colophon, with verso blank; list of publications by the same publishing house, on last cover, with recto blank. No mispaging.

Signatures. — Cover-title, half-title, title, *a* in eight, 1—21 in eights, 22 in two, last cover. This work is arranged under twenty-five letters. It is not a full reprint of Lahontan, but presents parts of his work, with interpretations in the narrative. There are no maps or plates, and the editorial notes are sparse.

Described from a copy in NL.

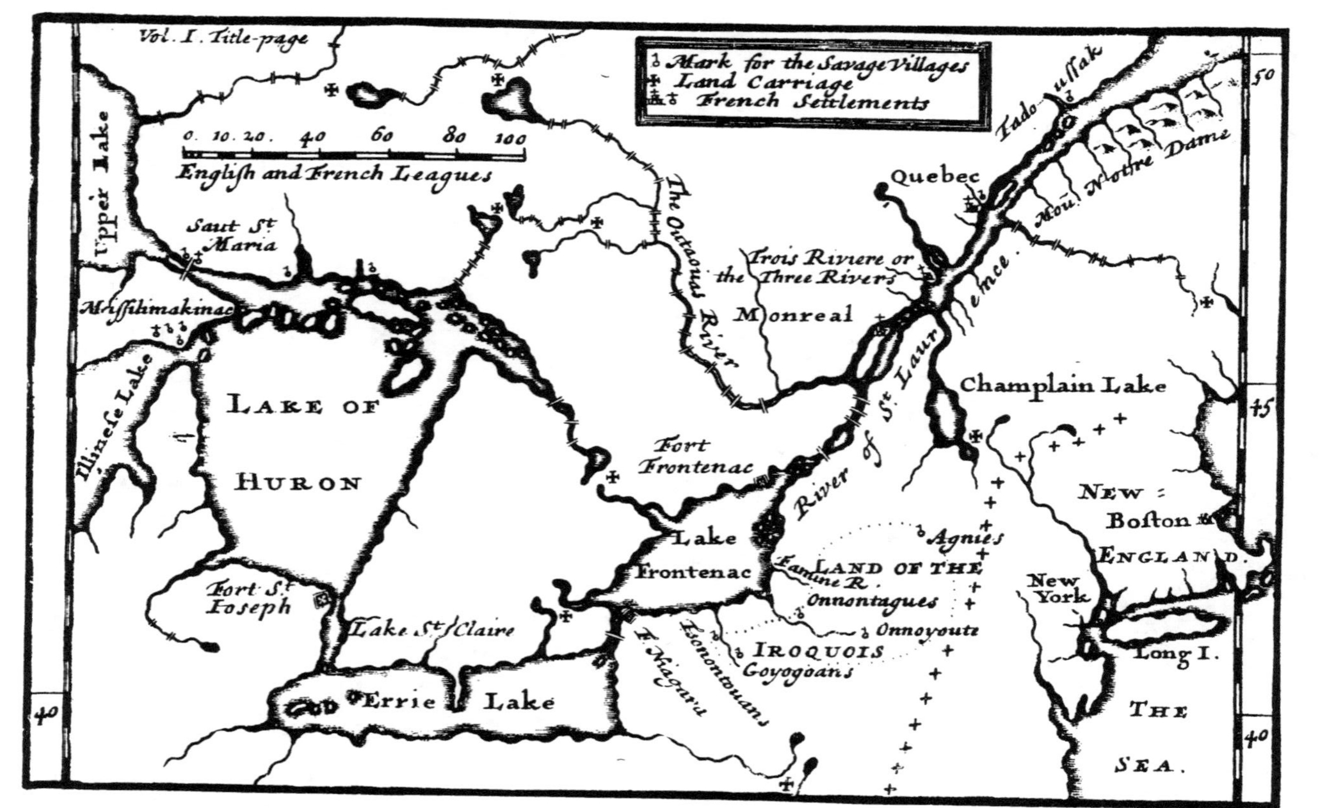

Vol. I. Title-page
Mark for the Savage Villages
Land Carriage
French Settlements
0. 10. 20. 40 60 80 100
English and French Leagues
Upper Lake
Saut St Maria
Missilimakinac
Illinese Lake
Lake of Huron
Fort St Joseph
Lake St Claire
Errie Lake
The Outaouas River
Fort Frontenac
Lake Frontenac
F. Niagara
Isonontouans
Trois Riviere or the Three Rivers
Monreal
Quebec
Tadoussak
Mou. Notre Dame
River of St Laurence
Champlain Lake
Agnies
Land of the Iroquois
Famine R.
Onnontagues
Onnoyoutz
Goyogoans
New England
Boston
New York
Long I.
The Sea.
50
45
40
40

NEW VOYAGES TO North-America.

CONTAINING

An Account of the ſeveral Nations of that vaſt Continent; their Cuſtoms, Commerce, and Way of Navigation upon the Lakes and Rivers; the ſeveral Attempts of the *Engliſh* and *French* to diſpoſſeſs one another; with the Reaſons of the Miſcarriage of the former; and the various Adventures between the *French*, and the *Iroqueſe* Confederates of *England*, from 1683 to 1694.

A Geographical Deſcription of *Canada*, and a Natural Hiſtory of the Country, with Remarks upon their Government, and the Intereſt of the *Engliſh* and *French* in their Commerce.

Alſo a Dialogue between the Author and a General of the Savages, giving a full View of the Religion and ſtrange Opinions of thoſe People: With an Account of the Authors Retreat to *Portugal* and *Denmark*, and his Remarks on thoſe Courts.

To which is added,

A Dictionary of the *Algonkine* Language, which is generally ſpoke in *North-America*.

Illuſtrated with Twenty Three Mapps and Cutts.

Written in *French*

By the Baron LAHONTAN, Lord Lievtenant of the *French* Colony at *Placentia* in *Newfoundland*, now in *England*.

Done into *Engliſh*.

In Two VOLUMES.

A great part of which never Printed in the Original.

LONDON; Printed for *H. Bonwicke* in St. *Paul's* Church-yard; *T. Goodwin*, *M. Wotton*, *B. Tooke*, in *Fleetſtreet*; and *S. Manſhip* in *Cornhil*, 1703.

To His Grace

WILLIAM

Duke of *Devonſhire*,

Lord Steward of Her Majeſties Houſehold, Lord Lieutenant of the County of Derby, *Chief Juſtice in Eyre of all Her Majeſties Forreſts, Chaſes, Parks,* &c. Trent-North; *One of the Lords of Her Majeſties Moſt Honourable Privy Council, and Knight of the Moſt Honourable Order of the Garter.*[1]

My Lord,

SINCE I had the Honour to preſent the King of *Denmark* with the firſt part of this Book, I preſume to make a Preſent of the Latter to your Grace.[2] In making the firſt Dedication, I had no other inducement, than a due regard to

[1] Unlike Hennepin, Lahontan did not present his book directly to the ruler of England, but chose rather as patron one of the great Whig lords, who was distinguished for his taste in art and letters, and was a critic of some note. William Cavendish, duke of Devonshire, had been active in politics since the reign of Charles II. A private quarrel, as well as public wrongs, had estranged him from James II; he was one of the chief supporters of the Revolution of 1688, and high in favor at the courts both of William III and of Anne. Next to the English ruler, Lahontan could have applied to no more popular or more powerful patron. — ED.

[2] Frederick IV, one of the best-known princes of his day, was also a savant and connoisseur. He had received Lahontan at his court, and protected him in need. Lahontan refers here to the first edition, rather than the "first part" of his book—the edition which appeared at the Hague (in French) early in 1703. — ED.

the benefits I receiv'd from His Majeſties favour; and the ſame Motive with reference to your Grace, has prompted me to make this acknowledgment of the undeſerved Favours you kindly vouchſaf'd me.

I did not dare to launch out into the praiſe of His *Daniſh* Majeſty, who has a juſt Title to all ſorts of Encomiums; by reaſon that the little *French* I had, has been forgot among a ſort of People, that take Panegyricks to be Affronts. 'Tis with the ſame view, My Lord, that I decline the pleaſure of publiſhing thoſe diſtinguiſhing Qualities, that place Your Lordſhip at the Head of the Moſt Accompliſh'd Grandees of the World, and the Moſt Zealous Patriots of their Country.

I am with all Gratitude and Veneration,

My Lord,

Your Grace's,

Moſt Humble, and Moſt

Obedient Servant.

Lahontan.

THE PREFACE.

H*AVING flatter'd my ſelf with the vain hopes of retrieving the King of* France's *favour, before the Declaration of this War;*[1] *I was ſo far from thinking to put theſe Letters, and Memoirs, to the Preſs; that I deſign'd to have committed 'em to the flames, if that Monarch had done me the honour of reinſtating me in my former Places, with the good leave of Meſſieurs* de Pontchartrain,* *the Father and the Son.*[2] *'Twas with that view that I neglected to put 'em in ſuch a dreſs as might now be wiſh'd for, for the ſatisfaction of the Reader that gives himſelf the trouble to peruſe 'em.*

* *The one Chancellor of* France, *and the other Secretary of State: Both of 'em vaſtly rich.*

[1] The reference is to the War of the Spanish Succession (in America, called Queen Anne's War), which began in 1703 between France and Spain on the one hand, and England, Austria, and Holland on the other, involving in its course most European powers. It was terminated by the treaty of Utrecht (1713). — Ed.

[2] After the able ministers who served during the vigor of his reign, those chosen by Louis XIV during his old age were mediocre in talent. The two Counts of Pontchartrain belonged to this latter class. Louis Phelypeaux the elder was born in 1643, and early entered the public service; in 1689 he became comptroller-general of finance, and the following year minister of the marine, with charge of colonial affairs. His son Jérome (born in 1674) became secretary of state in 1693, and upon his father's promotion to the chancellorship (1699), succeeded to the latter's offices. Thus during the latter years of Louis XIV the Pontchartrains were the most powerful ministers of the court. Both lost their offices upon the demise of the king (1715), the elder dying in 1727, the younger in 1717. — Ed.

Between the fifteenth and ſixteenth year of my Age I went to Canada, *and there took care to keep up a conſtant Correſpondence by Letters with an old Relation, who had required of me a Narrative of the Occurrences of that Country, upon the account of the yearly aſſiſtance he gave me. 'Tis theſe very Letters that make the greateſt part of the firſt Volum. They contain an account of all that paſs'd between the* Engliſh, *the* French, *the* Iroqueſe, *and the other Savage Nations, from the year* 1683, *to* 1694. *Together with a great many curious Remarks, that may be of uſe to thoſe who have any knowledge of the* Engliſh *or* French *Colonies.*

The whole is writ with a great deal of Fidelity; for I repreſent things juſt as they are. I neither flatter nor ſpare any Perſon whatſoever; I attribute to the *Iroqueſe, *the glory they have purchaſed on ſeveral occaſions, tho' at the ſame time I hate that Raſcally People, as much as Horns and Law-Suits. Notwithſtanding the Veneration I have for the Clergy, I impute to them all the miſchief the* Iroqueſe *have done to the* French *Colonies, in the courſe of a War that had never been undertaken, if it had not been for the Counſels of theſe pious Church-Men.*

* *Call'd by the* Engliſh *in* New-York, *Mahak.*

The Reader is deſir'd to take notice that the Towns of New-York, *are known to the* French *by their old Names only, and for that reaſon I was oblig'd to make uſe of the ſame in my Letters, as well as my Mapps. They give the name of* New-York *to all that Country, that reaches from the Source of its River to the Mouth, that is, to the Iſland, upon which there ſtands a City call'd in the time of the* Dutch Manathe, *and now by the* Engliſh, New-York.

In like manner the Plantation of Albany, *that lies towards the head of the River, is call'd by the* French, Orange.

Farther; I would not have the Reader to take it amiss, that the thoughts of the Savages are set forth in an European *Dress. The occasion of that choice proceeded from the Relation I Corresponded with; for that honest Gentleman ridiculed the Metaphorical Harangue of the* * Grangula; *and intreated me not to make a literal Translation of a Language that was so stuff'd with Fictions and Savage Hyperboles. 'Tis for this reason that all the Discourses and Arguments of those Nations, are here accommodated to the* European *Style and way of Speaking; for having comply'd with my Friend's Request, I contented my self in keeping only a Copy of the Letters I writ to him, during my Pilgrimage in the Country of these naked Philosophers.*

* *See Letter* 7th.

'Twill not be improper to acquaint the Reader by the bye, that those who know my faults, do as little justice to these People, as they do to me, in alledging I am a Savage my self, and that that *makes me speak so favourably of my Fellow-Savages. These Observators do me a great deal of Honour, as long as they do not explain themselves, so as to make me directly of the same Character with that which is tack'd to the word* Savage *by the* Europeans *in their way of thinking: For in saying only that I am of the same temper with the Savages, they give me without design, the Character of the honestest Man in the World. 'Tis an uncontested truth, that the Nations which are not debauch'd by the Neighbourhood of the* Europeans, *are strangers to the Measures of* Meum *and* Tuum, *and to all Laws, Judges, and Priests. This can't be call'd in question, since*

all Travellers that have viſited thoſe Countries, vouch for its truth; and a great many of different Profeſſions, have given the World repeated aſſurances that 'tis ſo. Now this being granted, we ought not to ſcruple to believe, that theſe are ſuch wiſe and reaſonable People. I take it, a Man muſt be quite blind, who do's not ſee that the property of Goods (I do not ſpeak of the ingroſſing of Women) is the only Source of all the Diſorders that perplex the European *Societies. Upon that Conſideration 'twill be eaſie to perceive, that I have not ſpoke wide in deſcribing that Wiſdom and Acuteneſs which ſhines through the Words and Actions of theſe poor* Americans. *If all the World had acceſs to the Books of Voyages, that are found in ſome well ſtock'd Libraries, they would find in above a hundred Deſcriptions of* Canada, *an infinity of Diſcourſes and Arguments offer'd by the Savages, which are incomparably ſtronger, and more nervous than thoſe I've inſerted in my Memoirs.*

As for ſuch as doubt of the Inſtinct and wonderful capacity of Beavers, they need only to caſt their Eyes upon the Great Map of America, *drawn by the Sieur* de Fer, *and grav'd at* Paris *in the year* 1698.[1] *Where they will meet with ſeveral ſurpriſing things, relating to theſe Animals.*

While my Book was a Printing in Holland, *I was in* England; *and as ſoon as it appear'd, ſeveral* Engliſh *Gentlemen of a diſtinguiſhing Merit, who underſtand the* French *as well as their Mother Tongue, gave me to know, that they would be glad to ſee a more*

[1] Nicolas de Fer (1646–1720) was a well-known cartographer of his time, bearing the title of royal geographer of Belgium (1701–16). His maps were more noted for the adornment of their borders, and their picturesque appearance, than for accuracy. Lahontan doubtless refers to engravings of beavers which ornament the margin of the chart here cited. — Ed.

ample Relation of the Manners and Cuſtoms of the People of that Continent, whom we call by the name of Savages. This oblig'd me to communicate to theſe Gentlemen, the ſubſtance of the ſeveral Conferences I had in that Country with a certain Huron, *whom the* French *call* Rat. *While I ſtay'd at that* American's *Village, I imploy'd my time very agreeably in making a careful Collection of all his Arguments and Opinions; and as ſoon as I return'd from my Voyage upon the Lakes of* Canada, *I ſhew'd my Manuſcript to Count* Frontenac, *who was ſo pleas'd with it, that he took the pains to aſſiſt me in digeſting the Dialogues, and bringing them into the order they now appear in*[1]*: For before that, they were abrupt Conferences without Connexion. Upon the Solicitation of theſe* Engliſh *Gentlemen, I've put theſe Dialogues into the hands of the Perſon who tranſlated my Letters and Memoirs: And if it had not been for their preſſing Inſtances, they had never ſeen the light; for there are but few in the World that will judge impartially, and without prepoſſeſſion, of ſome things contain'd in 'em.*

I have likewiſe intruſted the ſame Tranſlator with ſome Remarks *that I made in* Portugal, *and* Denmark, *when I fled thither from* Newfound-Land. *There the Reader will meet with a deſcription of* Lisbon *and* Copenhagen, *and of the capital City of* Arragon.

To the Tranſlation of my firſt Volume, I have added an exact Map of Newfound-Land, *which was not in the Original. I have likewiſe corrected almoſt all the Cuts of the* Holland *Impreſſion, for*

[1] Frontenac's responsibility for the famous dialogue between Lahontan and the Huron has been much discussed. Without doubt, the governor of Canada permitted himself liberties in religious thought, and enjoyed Lahontan's clever flings against the Jesuits; but it can hardly be held that all the sentiments expressed by the traveller accorded with his own. — Ed.

the Dutch *Gravers had murder'd 'em, by not underſtanding their Explications, which were all in* French. *They have grav'd Women for Men, and Men for Women; naked Perſons for thoſe that are cloath'd, and* è Contra. *As for the Maps, the Reader will find 'em very exact; And I have taken care to have the Tracts of my Voyages more nicely delineated, than in the Original.*

I underſtand by Letters from Paris, *that the two Meſſieurs* de Pontchartrain *indeavour by all means to be reveng'd upon me for the affront they say I have given 'em in publiſhing ſome triffling Stories in my Book, that ought to have been conceal'd. I am likewiſe inform'd, that I have reaſon to be apprehenſive of the Reſentment of ſeveral Eccleſiaſticks, who pretend I have inſulted God in cenſuring their Conduct. But ſince I expected nothing leſs than the furious Reſentment both of the one and the other, when I put this Book to the Preſs; I had time enough to arm myſelf from top to toe, in order to make head againſt 'em. 'Tis my comfort, that I have writ nothing but what I make good by Authentick proofs; beſides, that I could not have ſaid leſs of 'em than I have done; for if I had not tied my ſelf up to the direct thread of my Diſcourſe, I could have made Digreſſions, in which the Conduct both of the one and the other, would have appear'd to be prejudicial to the repoſe of the Society, and the publick Good. I had provocation enough to have treated 'em in that manner; but my Letters being addreſs'd to an old Bigotted Relation of mine, who fed upon Devotion, and dreaded the influence of the Court; he ſtill beſeech'd me to write nothing to him that might diſoblige the Clergy or the Courtiers, for fear of the intercepting of my Letters. However, I have advice from* Paris, *that ſome Pedants are ſet at work to laſh me in writing; and ſo I muſt prepare to ſtand the brunt of a ſhower of affronts, that will be pour'd upon me in a few days. But 'tis no matter; I am ſo good a Conjurer, that I can ward off any ſtorm from the ſide of* Paris. *I laugh at their Threats; and ſince I can't make uſe of my Sword, I'll wage War with my Pen.*

This I only mention by the bye, in this my Preface to the Reader, whom I pray the Heavens to Crown with Proſperity, in preſerving him from having any buſineſs to adjuſt with moſt of the Miniſters of State, and Prieſts; for let them be never ſo faulty, they'll ſtill be ſaid to be in the right, till ſuch time as Anarchy be introduc'd amongſt us, as well as the Americans, *among whom the ſorryeſt fellow thinks himſelf a better Man, than a Chancellor of* France. *Theſe People are happy in being ſcreen'd from the tricks and ſhifts of Miniſters, who are always Maſters where-ever they come. I envy the ſtate of a poor Savage, who tramples upon Laws, and pays Homage to no Scepter. I wiſh I could ſpend the reſt of my Life in his Hutt, and ſo be no longer expos'd to the chagrin of bending the knee to a ſet of Men, that ſacrifice the publick good to their private intereſt, and are born to plague honeſt Men. The two Miniſters of State I have to do with, have been ſolicited in vain, by the Ducheſs of* Lude, *Cardinal* Bouillon, *Count* Guiſcar, *Mr.* de Quiros, *and Count* d' Avaux[1]: *Nothing could prevail, tho' all that is laid to my charge, conſiſts only in not bearing the affronts of a Governour, whom they protect; at a time when a hundred other Officers, who*

[1] These patrons who spoke on behalf of Lahontan were among the eminent personages of the court of Louis XIV. The Count de Lude was grand master of artillery, his wife a friend of Madame de Frontenac. Cardinal Bouillon was the younger son of the great Turenne, a prominent supporter of Fenelon; at this time he was in a sort of honorable exile in Holland, as was likewise Count Guiscard, a diplomat and

live under the imputation of Crimes, infinitely greater than mine, are excus'd for three Months abſence from Court.[1] *Now the Reaſon is, that they give leſs quarter to thoſe who have the misfortune to diſpleaſe the two Meſſieurs* de Ponchartrain. *than to ſuch as act contrary to the King's Orders.*

But after all my Misfortunes, I have this to ſolace me, that I injoy in England *a ſort of Liberty, that is not met with elſewhere: For one may juſtly ſay, that of all the Countries inhabited by civil-is'd People, this alone affords the greateſt perfection of Liberty. Nay, I do not except the liberty of the Mind, for I am convinc'd, that the* Engliſh *maintain it with a great deal of tenderneſs: So true it is, that all degrees of Slavery are abhorr'd by this People, who ſhew their Wiſdom in the precautions they take to prevent their ſinking into a fatal Servitude.*

---

politician of some fame. Don Francesco Bernardo de Quiros was Spanish ambassador at the Hague; and Count d'Avaux had long been French minister at the same court, retiring upon William III's invasion of England (1688), and again upon the outbreak of the War of Spanish Succession (1703). It was he who accompanied James II (1689) to Ireland, as representative of Louis XIV. — Ed.

[1] Lahontan here refers to his disagreement with Brouillan, governor of Newfoundland, and his own departure thence without leave. — Ed.

THE

CONTENTS.

VOL. I.

[Original pagination retained.]

LETTER I.

Dated at *Quebec Nov.* 8. 1683.

C*ONTAINING a Deſcription of the Paſſage from* France *to* Canada; *with ſome Remarks upon the Coaſts, Channels,* &c. *and the variation of the Needle.* p. 1.

LETTER II.

Dated at the Canton of *Beauprè May* 2. 1684.

Containing a Deſcription of the Plantations of Canada, *and the manner in which they were firſt form'd: As alſo an Account of the Tranſportation of Whores from* France *to that Country; together with a view of its Climate and Soil.* p. 7.

LETTER. III.

Dated at *Quebec May* 15. 1684.

Containing an ample Deſcription of the City of Quebec, *and of the Iſland of St.* Laurence. p. 11.

LETTER. IV.

Dated at *Monreal June* 14. 1684.

Containing a brief Description of the Habitations of the Savages in the Neighbourhood of Quebec; *of the River of St.* Laurence, *as far up as* Monreal; *of a curious way of fishing Eels; and of the Cities of* Trois Rivieres, *and* Monreal: *Together with an account of the Conduct of the Forrest-Rangers or Pedlers.* p. 16.

LETTER. V.

Dated at *Monreal June* 18. 1684.

In which is contain'd a short account of the Iroquese, *with a view of the War and Peace they made with the* French, *and of the means by which it was brought about.* p. 22.

LETTER. VI.

Dated at *Monreal June* 20. 1684.

Being an ample Description of the Canows made of Birch Bark, in which the Canadans *perform all their Voyages; with an Account of the manner in which they are made and manag'd.* p. 26.

LETTER. VII.

Dated at *Monreal Novemb.* 2. 1684.

Describing the River of St. Laurence, *from* Monreal *to the first great Lake of* Canada, *with the Water-falls, Cataracts, and Navigation of that River: As also Fort* Frontenac, *and the advantages that accrue from it. Together with a Circumstan-*

tial account of the Expedition of Mr. de la Barre, *the Governour General, against the* Iroquese; *the Speeches he made, the Replies he receiv'd, and the final Accommodation of the difference.* p. 29.

LETTER. VIII.

Dated at *Monreal June* 28. 1685.

Representing the Fortifications of Monreal, *and the indiscreet zeal of the Priests, who are Lords of that Town: With a Description of* Chambli, *and of the Commerce of the Savages upon the great Lakes.* p. 45.

LETTER. IX.

Dated at *Boucherville Oct.* 2. 1685.

Being an Account of the Commerce and Trade of Monreal: *Of the Arrival of the Marquis of* Denonville *with some Troops; and of the recalling of Mr.* de la Barre. *With a curious Description of certain Licenses for trading in Beaver-Skins in the remote Countries.* p. 51.

LETTER. X.

Dated at *Boucherville July* 8. 1686.

Relating the Arrival of Mr. de Champigni, *in the room of Mr.* de Meules, *who is recall'd to* France; *the arrival of the Troops that came along with him, the curiosity of the Rackets, and the way of hunting Elks; with a Description of that Animal.* p. 55.

LETTER. XI.

Dated at *Boucherville May* 28. 1687.

Being a curious Deſcription of the Hunting of divers Animals. p. 60.

LETTER. XII.

Dated at St. *Helens* over againſt *Monreal June* 8. 1687.

The Chevalier de Vaudreuil *arrives in* Canada *with ſome Troops. Both the Regular Troops and the Militia are poſted at St.* Helens, *in a readineſs to march againſt the* Iroqueſe. p. 68.

LETTER. XIII.

Dated at *Niagara Aug.* 2. 1687.

Repreſenting the unfavourable Iſſue of the Campaign, made in the Iroqueſe *Country; the diſcovery of an Ambuſcade, and the iſſuing of Orders for the Author to march with a Detachment to the great Lakes.* p. 70.

LETTER. XIV.

Dated at *Miſſilimakinac May* 26. 1688.

The Author leaves Nagara, *and has an Incounter with the* Iroqueſe *at the end of the Land-Carriage. The after-part of his Voyage. A Deſcription of the Country. He arrives at Fort St.* Joſeph *in the Mouth of the Lake of* Hurons. *A Detachment of the* Hurons *arrive at the ſame place. After an Ingagement, they ſet out for* Miſſilimakinac. *A ſtrange Adventure of Mr.* de la Salle's *Brother.* Miſſilimakinac *deſcrib'd.* p. 80.

LETTER. XV.

Dated at *Miſſilimakinac Sept.* 18. 1688.

Deſcribing the Fall call'd Saut St. Marie, *where the Author perſwades the Inhabitants to joyn the* Outaouas, *and march againſt the* Iroqueſe. *And containing an account of the Occurrences of the Voyage between that Place and* Miſſilimakinac. p. 92.

LETTER. XVI.

Dated at *Miſſilimakinac May* 28. 1689.

Containing an Account of the Author's Departure from, and Return to, Miſſilimakinac. *A Deſcription of the Bay of* Puants, *and its Villages. An ample Deſcription of the Beavers, follow'd by the Journal of a remarkable Voyage upon the Long River, and a Map of the adjacent Country.* p. 104.

LETTER. XVII.

Dated at *Quebec Sep.* 28. 1689.

The Author ſets out from Miſſilimakinac *to the Colony, and deſcribes the Country, Rivers, and Paſſes that he ſaw by the way. The* Iroqueſe *make a fatal incurſion into the Iſland of* Monreal: *Fort* Frontenac *is abandon'd; Count* Frontenac *is ſent to* Canada, *and the Marquis of* Denonville *is recall'd.* p. 142.

LETTER. XVIII.

Dated at *Quebec Nov.* 15. 1689.

Giving an Account of Mr. de Frontenac's *Arrival, his Reception, his Voyage to* Monreal, *and the repairing of Fort* Frontenac. p. 151.

LETTER. XIX.

Dated at *Monreal October* 2. 1690.

Relating the Attempts upon New-England *and* New-York; *a fatal Embaſſy ſent by the* French *to the* Iroqueſe, *and an ill-concerted Enterpriſe of the* Engliſh *and the* Iroqueſe, *in marching by Land to attack the* French *Colony.* p. 155.

LETTER. XX.

Dated at *Rochel January* 12. 1691.

Being a Relation of a ſecond and very important Expedition of the Engliſh *by Sea; in which is contain'd a Letter written by the* Engliſh *Admiral to Count* Frontenac, *with the Governour's Verbal Anſwer. As alſo an account of the Author's departure for* France. p. 159.

LETTER. XXI.

Dated at *Rochel July* 26. 1691.

Containing a Deſcription of the Courts or Offices of the Miniſters of State, and a view of ſome Services that are ill rewarded at Court. p. 166.

LETTER. XXII.

Dated at *Quebec Nov.* 10. 1691.

Which contains an account of the Author's departure from Rochel *to* Quebec, *of his Voyage to the mouth of the River St.* Laurence, *of a Rencounter with an* Engliſh *Ship which he fought; of the ſtranding of his Ship; of his ſailing thro' the River St.* Laurence; *of the news he receiv'd that a party of the* Engliſh *and* Iroqueſe, *had defeated a Body of the* French *Troops.* p. 171.

LETTER. XXIII.

Dated at *Nants Octob.* 25. 1692.

Containing an Account of the taking of ſome Engliſh *Veſſels, of defeating a Party of the* Iroqueſe, *of an* Iroqueſe *burnt alive at* Quebec; *of another Party of theſe Barbarians, who having ſurpris'd ſome* Coureurs de Bois, *were afterwards ſurpris'd themſelves. Of the Project of an Enterprize propos'd by Mr.* Frontenac *to the Author. Of the Author's departure in a Frigat for* France, *and his ſtopping at* Placentia, *which was then attack'd by the* Engliſh *Fleet that came to take that Poſt from us. How the* Engliſh *fail'd in their Deſign, and the Author purſu'd his Voyage.* p. 175.

LETTER. XXIV.

Dated at *Nants May* 10. 1693.

Containing an Account of Mr. Frontenac's *Project, which was rejected at Court, and the reaſon why it was rejected. The King gives the Author the Lieutenancy of* Newfound Land, &c. *together with the Independent Company.* p. 187.

LETTER. XXV.

Dated at *Viana* in *Portugal Jan.* 31. 1694.

The Author's departure from France *to* Placentia. *A Fleet of* 30 Engliſh *Ships came to ſeize upon that place; but is diſappointed, and Sheers off. The reaſon why the* Engliſh *have bad ſucceſs in all their Enterpriſes beyond Sea. The Author's Adventure with the Governour of* Placentia. *His departure for* Portugal. *An Engagement with a* Fluſhing *Privateer.* p. 193.

Memoirs of *North-America.*

Containing a Geographical Defcription of that vaft Continent; the Cuftoms and Commerce of the Inhabitants, &c. p. 203.
A fhort Defcription of Canada. p. 205.
A Lift of the Savage Nations of Canada. p. 230.
A Lift of the Animals of Canada. p. 232.
A Defcription of fuch Animals or Beafts as are not mention'd in the Letters. p. 233.
A Lift of the Fowl or Birds of Canada. p. 237.
A Defcription of fuch Birds as are not accounted for in the Letters. p. 239.
A Defcription of the Infects of Canada. p. 242.
The Names of the Fifh of Canada. p. 243.
A Defcription of the Fifh that are not mention'd in the Letters p. 244.
The Trees and Fruits of Canada. p. 247.
A Defcription of the above-mention'd Trees. p. 248.
A General view of the Commerce of Canada. p. 254.
The Commodities truck'd to and again between the French *and the Savages.* p. 257.
An Account of the Government of Canada *in General.* p. 260.
A Difcourfe of the Intereft of the French *and* Englifh *in* North-America. p. 260.
A Table Explaining fome uncommon Terms. p. 276.

The Contents of the Second Volume.

A *Difcourfe of the Habit, Houfes, Complexion and Temperament of the Savages of* North-America. P. 1. Vol. 2.

A fhort view of the Humours and Cuftoms of the Savages. p. 7.

The Belief of the Savages, and the Obftacles of their Converfion. p. 19.

The way of Worfhip us'd by the Savages. p. 29.

An Account of the Amours and Marriages of the Savages. p. 34.

A View of the Difeafes and Remedies of the Savages. p. 45.

The Diverfions of Hunting and Shooting ufual among the Savages. p. 55.

The Military Art of the Savages. p. 71.

A View of the Heraldy and the Coats of Arms of the Savages. p. 84.

An Explication of the Savage Hieroglyphicks. p. 86.

A Conference or Dialogue between the Author and *Adario*, a noted Man among the Savages.

Containing a Circumftantial view of the Cuftoms and Humours of that People. p. 90.

An *APPENDIX*, Containing ſome New Voyages to *Portugal* and *Denmark;* after the Author's Retirement from *Canada*.

LETTER. I.

Dated at *Lisbon April* 20. 1694.

Containing a Deſcription of Viana, Porto a Porto, Aveiro, Coimbra, Lisbon; *together with a View of the Court of* Portugal; *and an Account of the Government, Laws, Cuſtoms, and Humours of the* Portugueſe. p. 185.

LETTER. II.

Dated at *Travemunde* 1694.

Containing an Account of the Author's Voyage from Lisbon *to* Garnſey; *his Adventure with an* Engliſh *Man of War, and an* Engliſh *Privateer: A Deſcription of* Rotterdam *and* Amſterdam; *the Author's Voyage to* Hamburgh; *the Dimenſions of a* Flemiſh *Sloop; a Deſcription of the City of* Hamburg; *the Author's Journey from thence to* Lubeck, *and a Deſcription of that City.* p. 211.

LETTER. III.

Dated at *Copenhagen Sept.* 12. 1694.

Containing a Deſcription of the Port and City of Copenhagen, *a view of the* Daniſh *Court, and of the Humours, Cuſtoms, Commerce, Forces,* &c. *of the* Danes. p. 226.

LETTER. IV.

Dated at *Paris Decemb.* 29. 1694.

Containing a Journal of the Author's Travels from Copenhagen *to* Paris. p. 244.

LETTER. V.

Dated at *Erleich July* 4. 1694.

Giving a view of the Superstition and Ignorance of the People of Bearn; *their addictedness to the notions of Witchcraft, Apparitions,* &c. *And the Author's Arguments against that Delusion.* p. 255.

LETTER. VI.

Dated at *Huesia July* 11. 1695.

Containing an Account of the Author's escape and journey to Spain; *his being taken up for a* Huguenot, *and the Ignorance and Bigotry of the Curates and People of* Bearn *in* France. p. 268.

LETTER. VII.

Dated at *Saragoza Octob.* 8. 1695.

Containing a Description of Saragoza; *a View of the Government of* Arragon, *and an Account of the Customs of the People.* p. 274.

A short Dictionary of the Language of the Savages. p. 287.

Some New

VOYAGES

TO

North-*America*.

TOME I.

LETTER I.

Dated at the Port of *Quebec*, *Nov*. 8. 1683.

Containing a Deſcription of the Paſſage from France *to* Canada; *with ſome Remarks upon the Coaſts, Channels,* &c. *and the Variation of the Needle.*

SIR,

I AM ſurpris'd to find that a Voyage to the New World is ſo formidable to thoſe who are oblig'd to undertake it; for I ſolemnly proteſt that 'tis far from being what the World commonly takes it for. 'Tis true, the Paſſage is in ſome meaſure long; but then the hopes of viewing an unknown Country, attones for the tedioufneſs of the Voyage. When we broke ground from *Rochel*, I acquainted you with the Reaſons that mov'd Mr. *le Fevre de la Barre*, Governor General of *Canada*, to ſend the *Sieur Mahu*, a *Canadeſe*, to *France*[1]; and at the ſame time gave you to know, that he [2] had reſolv'd upon the utter deſtruction of the *Iroqueſe*, who are a very Warlike and Savage People.[2] Theſe Barbarians befriend the *Engliſh*, upon the account of the Succours they receive from 'em; but they are enemies to us, upon the apprehenſion of being deſtroy'd by us ſome time or other. The General I ſpoke of but now, expected that the King would ſend him ſeven or eight hundred Men; but when we ſet out from *Rochel* the ſeaſon was ſo far advanc'd, that our three Companies of Marines were reckon'd a ſufficient Venture.

---

[1] Le Fêbre de la Barre was in 1682 appointed governor of New France, to supersede Frontenac. He was an officer of experience, having seen service in the West Indies, been governor of Cayenne (1664–66), and defeated an English fleet and recovered Antigua, Montserrat, and Nevis for the French. In early life he had been a lawyer and government official in France. Upon his arrival in the colony (1682), he determined upon war with the Iroquois, and dispatched to the king urgent requests for regular troops, of whom the colony was bereft. In the spring of 1683, the Iroquois again harassed the colony, and the governor impressed a small vessel lying at Quebec to send news thereof to France. This would appear to have been the ship of one Jean Paul Meheu, seigneur of a fief of La Rivière Maheu. Some years previous, a Canadian of the same name is noted as bearing letters to France. — Thwaites, *Jesuit Relations* (Cleveland, 1896–1901), xlvi, p. 179. When this urgent request reached the court, the king determined to at once send to New France three companies of soldiers. See *Collection de Manuscrits relatifs à la Nouvelle France* (Quebec, 1883), i, p. 310. The transport was named the "Tempest," commanded by Sieur Pingo. It departed from La Rochelle Aug. 29, 1683; among the officers was Lahontan, this being his first venture across seas. — Ed.

[2] The Iroquois had long been the scourge of Canada; taking advantage of their strategic position between the English and Dutch of New York and the French of the St. Lawrence, they were attempting to control the fur-trade of the interior in the interest of the English, bringing disaster upon the colony of New France. They made war upon the Indian allies of the French on the Upper Lakes, and had recently (1680–82) inflicted a heavy blow upon the Illinois, among whom La Salle was endeavoring to found a colony. — Ed.

I met with nothing in our Paſſage that was diſagreeable, abating for a Storm that alarm'd us for ſome days, upon the precipice of the bank of *Newfound-Land*, where the Waves ſwell prodigiouſly, even when the Winds are low. In that Storm our Frigat receiv'd ſome rude ſhocks from the Sea; but in regard that ſuch accidents are uſual in that Voyage, they made no impreſſion upon the old ſeaſon'd Sailors. As for my part, I could not pretend to that pitch of indifference; for having never made ſuch a Voyage before, I was ſo alarm'd in ſeeing the Waves mount up to the Clouds, that I made more vows to *Neptune*, than the brave *Idomenæus* did in his return from the Wars of *Troy*. After we made the bank, the Waves ſunk, and the Wind dwindled, and the Sea became ſo ſmooth and eaſie, that we could not work our Ship. You can ſcarce imagine what quantities of Cod-fiſh were catch'd there by our Seamen, in the ſpace of a quarter of an hour; for though we had thirty two fathom Water, yet the Hook was no ſooner at the bottom, than the Fiſh was catch'd; ſo that they had nothing to do but to throw in, and take up without interruption: But after all, ſuch is the misfortune of this Fiſhery, that it do's not ſucceed but upon certain banks, which are commonly paſt over without ſtopping. However, as we were plentifully [3] entertain'd at the coſt of theſe Fiſhes, ſo ſuch of 'em as continued in the Sea, made ſufficient repriſals upon the Corps of a Captain, and of ſeveral Soldiers, who dy'd of the Scurvy, and were thrown over-board three or four days after.

In the mean time the Wind veering to the Weſt-North-Weſt, we were oblig'd to lye bye for five or ſix days; but after that it chop'd to the North, and ſo we happily made Cape *Raſe*, tho' indeed our Pilots were at a loſs to know where we were, by reaſon that they could not take the Latitude for ten or twelve days before.[1] You may eaſily imagine, that 'was with great joy that we heard one of our Sailors call from the Top-Maſt, *Land*, *Land*, juſt as St. *Paul* did when he approach'd to *Maltha*, Γῆν ὁρῶ, γῆν ὁρῶ: For you muſt know that when the Pilots reckon they approach to Land, they uſe the precaution of ſending up Sailors to the Top-Maſt, in order to ſome diſcovery; and theſe Sailors are reliev'd every two hours till Night comes, at which time they furl their Sails if the Land is not yet deſcry'd: So that in the Night-time they ſcarce make any way. From this it appears how important it is to know the Coaſt, before you approach to it; nay, the Paſſengers put ſuch a value upon the diſcovery, that they preſent the firſt diſcoverer with ſome Piſtoles. In the mean time, you'll be pleas'd to obſerve, that the Needle of the Compaſs, which naturally points to the North, turns upon the bank of *Newfound-Land*, twenty three Degrees towards the North-Weſt; that is, it points there a degree nearer to the Weſt, than North-North-Weſt. This remark we made by our Compaſs of Variation.

We deſcry'd the Cape about Noon; and in order to confirm the Diſcovery, ſtood in upon it with all ſails aloft. At

[1] The name Race, applied to the southeastern extremity of Newfoundland, is first met under the form "Cap Rogo," on a map of about the year 1500. The name seems to have been given from the French word "ras," bare or flat. See Harrisse, *Découverte et Evolution cartographique de Terre-Neuve* (Paris, 1900), p. 43. — Ed.

laſt, being aſſur'd that 'twas the Promontory we look'd for, an univerſal joy was [4] ſpread throughout the Ship, and the fate of the wretches that we had thrown over-board, was quite forgot. Then the Sailors ſet about the Chriſtening of thoſe who had never made the Voyage before, and indeed they had done it ſooner, if it had not been for the death of our above-mention'd Companions. The Chriſtening I ſpeak of, is an impertinent Ceremony, practis'd by Sea-faring Men, whoſe humours are as ſtrange and extravagant, as the Element it ſelf, upon which they fooliſhly truſt themſelves. By vertue of a Cuſtom of old ſtanding, they profane the Sacrament of Baptiſm in an unaccountable manner. Upon that occaſion, the old Sailors being blacken'd all over, and diſguis'd with Rags and Ropes, force the greener ſort that have never paſs'd ſome certain degrees of Latitude before, to fall down on their Knees, and to ſwear upon a Book of Sea Charts, that upon all occaſions they will practiſe upon others, the ſame Ceremony that is then made uſe of towards them. After the adminiſtring of this ridiculous Oath, they throw fifty Buckets full of Water upon their Head, Belly, and Thighs, and indeed all over their Body, without any regard to times or ſeaſons. This piece of folly is chiefly practis'd under the Æquator, under the Tropicks, under the Polar Circles, upon the bank of *Newfound-Land;* and in the Streights of *Gibraltar*, the *Sund*, and the *Dardanelloes.* As for Perſons of Note or Character, they are exempted from the Ceremony, at the expence of five or ſix bottles of Brandy for the Ships Crew.

Three or four days after the performance of this Solemnity, we difcover'd Cape *Raye*,[1] and fo made up to St. *Laurence Bay*, in the Mouth of which we were becalm'd for a little while; and during that Calm, we had a clearer and pleafanter day, than any we had feen in the Paffage. It look'd as if that day had been vouchfaf'd us by way of recompence [5] for the Rains, Foggs, and high Winds, that we incounter'd by the way. There we faw an Engagement between a Whale and a * Sword-Fifh, at the diftance of a Gunfhot from our Frigat. We were perfectly charm'd when we faw the Sword-Fifh jump out of the water in order to dart its Spear into the Body of the Whale, when oblig'd to take breath. This entertaining fhow lafted at leaft two hours, fometimes to the Starboard, and fometimes to the Larboard of the Ship. The Sailors, among whom Superftition prevails as much as among the *Egyptians*, took this for a prefage of fome mighty Storm; but the Prophecy ended in two or three days of contrary Winds, during which time we travers'd between the Ifland of *Newfound-Land*, and that of Cape *Breton*. Two days after we came in fight of the Ifland of Fowls, by the help of a North-Eaft Wind; which drove us from the Mouth of St. *Laurence* Bay, to the Ifle of *Anticofti*, upon the bank of which, we thought to have been caft

* Efpadon, *a Fifh between* 10 *and* 15 *Foot long, being four Foot in circumference, and having in its Snout a fort of Saw which is four Foot long, four Inches broad, and fix Lines thick.*

[1] Cape Ray is at the southwestern extremity of Newfoundland; the name first appeared on a map of 1600. Harrisse, *op. cit.*, p. 285. — Ed.

away, by nearing it too much. In the Mouth of that River we fell into a ſecond calm, which was follow'd by a contrary Wind, that oblig'd us to lye bye for ſome days. At laſt we made *Tadouſſac*, by gradual approaches, and there came to an Anchor.[1]

This River is four Leagues broad where we then rode, and twenty two at its Mouth; but it contracts it ſelf gradually, as it approaches to its ſource. Two days after, the Wind ſtanding Eaſt, we weigh'd Anchor; and being favor'd by the Tyde, got ſafe through the Channel of the Red Iſland, in which the Currents are apt to turn a Veſſel on one ſide, as well as at the Iſland of *Coudres*, which lies ſome Leagues higher.[2] But upon the Coaſt of the laſt [6] Iſland, we had certainly ſtruck upon the Rocks, if we had not drop'd an Anchor. Had the Ship been caſt away at that place, we might eaſily have ſav'd our

---

[1] The Island of Fowls is probably the group still known as Bird Rocks, in St. Lawrence Gulf, north of Magdalen Islands.

Anticosti is a large island one hundred and forty miles long by about twenty-seven in average breadth. It lies in the mouth of St. Lawrence River, and three years before this voyage of Lahontan had been granted as a seigniory of Louis Jolliet, the Mississippi explorer.

Tadoussac, at the entrance of Saguenay River, is one of the oldest towns in Canada, having been founded before Quebec. It was the favorite resort of the Montagnais Indians, and the centre of a thriving fur-trade and fishery. The Récollects said mass here as early as 1617; and here the hostile English fleet, under Admiral Sir David Kirk, anchored in July, 1628. The Jesuits began a mission at Tadoussac before 1642, and one of their early churches (built 1647-50) is still to be seen.— Ed.

[2] Red Island is that now known as Isle Rouge, in the St. Lawrence opposite Tadoussac. It was early noted for its seal fishing. See *Jesuit Relations*, xxxii, p. 93.

Isle aux Coudres was so designated for the hazelnut bushes with which it abounded, and appears to have been so named by Cartier. The early voyagers speak of the number of elk to be found on this island. — Ed.

ſelves: But it prov'd ſo, that we were more affraid than hurt. Next Morning we weighed with a freſh gale from the Eaſt, and the next day after came to an Anchor over againſt Cape *Tourmente*, where we had not above two Leagues over, tho' at the ſame time 'tis a dangerous place to thoſe who are unacquainted with the Channel.[1] From thence we had but ſeven Leagues ſailing to the Port of *Quebec*, where we now ride at Anchor. In our Paſſage from the red Iſland to this place, we ſaw ſuch floats of Ice, and ſo much Snow upon the Land, that we were upon the point of turning back for *France*, tho' we were not then above thirty Leagues off our deſired Port. We were affraid of being ſtop'd by the Ice, and ſo loſt; but thank God we 'ſcap'd.

We have receiv'd advice, that the Governor has mark'd out Quarters for our Troops in ſome Villages or Cantons adjacent to this City; ſo that I am oblig'd to prepare to go aſhore, and therefore muſt make an end of this Letter. I cannot as yet give you any account of the Country, excepting that 'tis already mortally cold. As to the River, I mean to give you a more ample deſcription of it, when I come to know it better. We are informed that Mr. *de la Salle* is juſt return'd from his Travels, which he undertook upon the diſcovery of a great River that falls into the Gulf of *Mexico;* and that he

---

[1] Cape Tourmente is a lofty promontory on the St. Lawrence, about twenty miles below Quebec, towering nineteen hundred feet above the meadows (Beaupré) at its base. It was so named by Champlain (1608), who noted that "however little wind may blow the sea there is as if it were high tide. At this place the water begins to be fresh." — ED.

imbarques to morrow for *France*.[1] He is perfectly well acquainted with *Canada*, and for that reason you ought to visit him, if you go to *Paris* this Winter. I am,

SIR,

Yours, &c.

---

[1] Réné Robert Cavelier, Sieur de la Salle, had just returned from his successful journey into the interior, where he had explored the Mississippi and in Illinois founded the colony of St. Louis. Frontenac, his patron, had been replaced, and the new governor gave a ready ear to La Salle's detractors. The fortunes of the explorer were desperate, and he was about to embark for France to seek redress at court. This was his farewell to Canada, his final voyage being made to the Gulf of Mexico, upon whose waters he was assassinated (March 18, 1687).— Ed.

LETTER II.

Dated at the Canton of *Beauprè*,[1] *May* 2. 1684.

Containing a Deſcription of the Plantations of Canada, *and the manner in which they were firſt form'd: As alſo an account of the Tranſportation of Whores from* France *to that Country; together with a view of its Climate and Soil.*

SIR,

AS ſoon as we landed laſt year, Mr. *de la Barre* lodg'd our three Companies in ſome Cantons or Quarters in the Neighbourhood of *Quebec*. The Planters call theſe places *Cotes*, which in *France* ſignifies no more than the Sea-Coaſt; tho' in this Country where the names of *Town* and *Village* are unknown, that word is made uſe of to expreſs a Seignory or Manour, the Houſes of which lie at the diſtance of two or three hundred Paces one from another, and are ſeated on the brink of the River of St. *Laurence*.[2] In earneſt, Sir, the Boors of thoſe

---

[1] The three companies were quartered at villages in the vicinity of Quebec. It fell to Lahontan's lot to pass the winter in the seigniory of Beaupré, which stretched for six leagues along the river and embraced more than the present county of Montmorency. Beaupré was early settled, and as a Jesuit seigniory received much attention. At this time it was considered the most orderly and thrifty settlement in the colony. — ED.

[2] Feudalism was established in New France by the act of Richelieu, in his grant to the Company of One Hundred Associates (1627). Seigniorial tenure was not abolished in Lower Canada (Province of Quebec) until 1854. On the influence of this system see Parkman, *Old Regime in Canada* (Boston, 1874), chap. xv; Weir, *Administration of the Old Regime in Canada* (Montreal, 1896–97). — ED.

Manors live with more eaſe and conveniency, than an infinity of the Gentlemen in *France*. I am out indeed in calling 'em Boors, for that name is as little known here as in *Spain;* whether it be that they pay no Taxes, and injoy the liberty of Hunting and Fiſhing; or that the eaſineſs of their Life, puts 'em upon a level with the Nobility. The pooreſt of them have four †*Arpents* of Ground in front, and thirty or forty in depth: The whole Country being a continued Forreſt of lofty Trees, the ſtumps
[8] of which muſt be grub'd up, before they can make uſe of a Plough. 'Tis true, this is a troubleſom and chargeable task at firſt; but in a ſhort time after they make up their Loſſes; for when the Virgin ground is capable of receiving Seed, it yields an increaſe to the rate of an hundred fold. Corn is there ſown in *May*, and reap'd about the middle of *September*. Inſtead of threſhing the Sheafs in the Field, they convey 'em to Barns, where they lie till the coldeſt ſeaſon of the Winter, at which time the Grain is more eaſily diſengag'd from the Ear. In this Country they likewiſe ſow Peaſe, which are much eſteem'd in *France*. All ſorts of Grain are very cheap here, as well as Butchers Meat and Fowl. The price of Wood is almoſt nothing, in compariſon with the charge of its carriage, which after all is very inconſiderable.

† *An* Arpent *is a ſpot of ground containing* 100 *Perches ſquare, each of which is eighteen Foot long.*

Moſt of the Inhabitants are a free ſort of People that remov'd hither from *France*, and brought with 'em but little Money to ſet up withal: The reſt are thoſe who were Soldiers about thirty or forty years ago, at which time the Regiment of *Carignan* was broke, and they exchang'd a Military Poſt, for the Trade of *Agriculture*.[1] Neither the one nor the other pay'd any thing for the grounds they poſſeſs, no more than the Officers of theſe Troops, who mark'd out to themſelves, certain portions of unmanur'd and woody Lands; for this vaſt Continent is nothing elſe than one continued Forreſt. The Governours General allow'd the Officers three or four Leagues of ground in front, with as much depth as they pleas'd; and at the ſame time the Officers gave the Soldiers as much ground as they pleas'd, upon the condition of the payment of a Crown *per Arpent*, by way of Fief.

After the reform of theſe Troops, ſeveral Ships were ſent hither from *France*, with a Cargoe of Women of an ordinary Reputation, under the direction [9] of ſome old ſtale Nuns, who rang'd 'em in three Claſſes. The Veſtal Virgins were heap'd up, (if I may ſo ſpeak) one above another, in three different Apartments, where the Bridegrooms ſingled out their Brides, juſt as a Butcher do's an Ewe from amongſt a Flock of Sheep. In theſe three *Seraglio's*, there was ſuch variety and change of Diet, as could ſatisfie the moſt whimſical Appetites; for here was ſome big ſome little, ſome fair ſome brown, ſome fat and ſome meagre. In fine, there was ſuch Accommodation,

[1] Lahontan's chronology is quite inaccurate; scarcely twenty years had passed since the regiment of Carignan-Salières, the first regular troops in New France, was ordered to America. This command had seen service in France and against the Turks. Coming to Canada in 1665, the soldiers were effectively employed against the Iroquois. A few years later several companies were disbanded, and urged to become colonists. Rewards in money and land were given those who married and settled in the province, and the descendants of these soldiers were among the most able and prominent citizens of the colony. See Sulte, "Le Regiment de Carignan," in Canadian Royal Society *Proceedings*, 2d series, viii, pp. 25–95. — Ed.

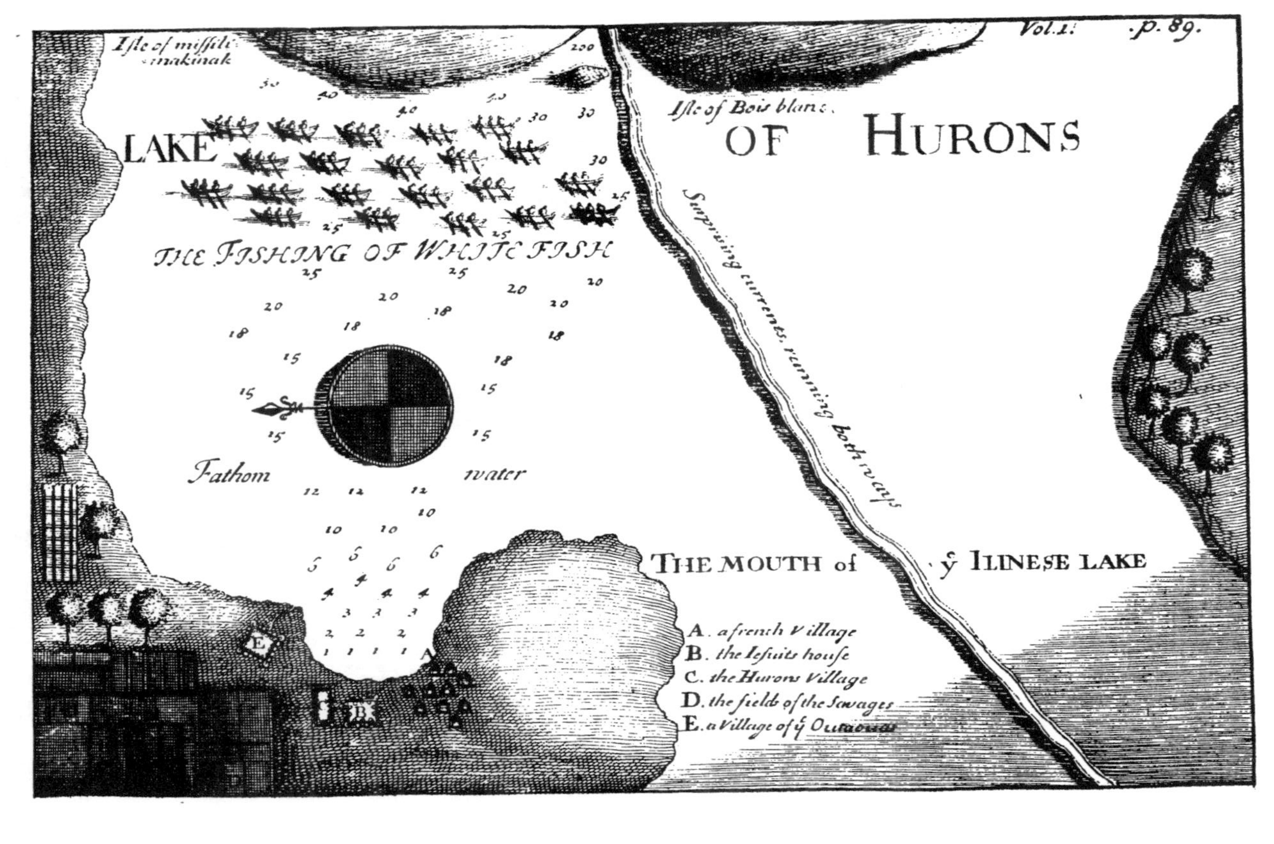

Vol.1. p. 89.
Isle of missili-makinak
Isle of Bois blanc
LAKE OF HURONS
THE FISHING OF WHITE FISH
Fathom water
Surprising currents, running both ways
THE MOUTH of ye ILINESE LAKE
A. a french Village
B. the Iesuits house
C. the Hurons Village
D. the fields of the Savages
E. a Village of ye Outaouas

that every one might be fitted to his Mind: And indeed the Market had ſuch a run, that in fifteen days time, they were all diſpos'd of. I am told, that the fatteſt went off beſt, upon the apprehenſion that theſe being leſs active, would keep truer to their Ingagements, and hold out better againſt the nipping cold of the Winter: But after all, a great many of the He-Adventurers found themſelves miſtaken in their meaſures. However, let that be as it will, it affords a very curious Remark; namely, That in ſome parts of the World, to which the vicious *European* Women are tranſported, the Mob of thoſe Countries do's ſeriouſly believe, that their Sins are ſo defac'd by the ridiculous Chriſtening, I took notice of before, that they are look'd upon ever after as Ladies of Vertue, of Honour, and of an untarniſh'd conduct of Life. The Sparks that wanted to be married, made their Addreſſes to the above-mention'd Governeſſes, to whom they were oblig'd to give an account of their Goods and Eſtates, before they were allow'd to make their choice in the three *Seraglio's*. After the choice was determin'd, the Marriage was concluded upon the ſpot, in the preſence of a Prieſt, and a publick Notary; and the next day the Governor-General beſtow'd upon the married Couple, a Bull, a Cow, a Hog, a Sow, a Cock, a Hen, two Barrels of ſalt Meat, and eleven Crowns; together with [10] a certain Coat of Arms call'd by the *Greeks* || *κέρατα*.[1]

|| *Horns*

[1] This slanderous and apparently malicious account of the mothers of the Canadian population has brought much obloquy upon our author. For a refutation from contemporary documents, see Parkman, *Old Regime*, pp. 221–230; Roy, "Le Baron de Lahontan," *Can. Roy. Soc. Proc.*, 1894, sec. 1, pp. 150–162; Sulte, "Pretendues Origines des Canadiens français," in Id., 1885, sec. 1, pp. 13–26. — ED.

The Officers having a nicer tafte than the Soldiers, made their Application to the Daughters of the ancient Gentlemen of the Country, or thofe of the richer fort of Inhabitants; for you know that *Canada* has been poffefs'd by the *French* above an hundred years.

In this Country every one lives in a good and a well furnifh'd Houfe; and moft of the Houfes are of Wood, and two Stories high. Their Chimnies are very large, by reafon of the prodigious Fires they make to guard themfelves from the Cold, which is there beyond all meafure, from the Month of *December*, to that of *April*. During that fpace of time, the River is always frozen over, notwithftanding the flowing and ebbing of the Sea; and the Snow upon the ground, is three or four foot deep; which is very ftrange in a Country that lies in the Latitude of forty feven Degrees, and fome odd Minutes. Moft People impute the extraordinary Snow to the number of Mountains, with which this vaft Continent is replenifh'd. Whatever is in that matter, I muft take notice of one thing, that feems very ftrange, namely, that the Summer days are longer here than at *Paris*. The Weather is then fo clear and ferene, that in three Weeks time you fhall not fee a Cloud in the *Horizon*. I hope to go to *Quebec* with the firft opportunity; for I have orders to be in a readinefs to imbarque within fifteen days for *Monreal*, which is the City of this Country, that lies fartheft up towards the Head of the River.

I am,

SIR,

Yours, &c.

[11] LETTER III.

Dated at *Quebec May* 15. 1684.

Containing an ample Defcription of the City of Quebec, *and of the Ifland of* Orleans.

SIR,

BEFORE I fet out for *Monreal,* I had the curiofity to view the Ifland of *Orleans*, which is feven Leagues in length, and three in breadth: It extends from over againft Cape *Tourmente*, to within a League and a half of *Quebec*, at which place the River divides it felf into two branches. The Ships fail through the South Channel; for the North Channel is fo foul with Shelves and Rocks, that the fmall Boats can only pafs that way. The Ifland belongs to a General Farmer of *France*, who would make out of it a thoufand Crowns of yearly Rent, if himfelf had the management of it. 'Tis furrounded with Plantations, that produce all forts of Grain.[1]

Quebec is the Metropolitan of New-*France*, being almoft a League in Circumference; It lies in the Latitude of 47 Degrees, and 12 Minutes. The Longitude of this place is uncer-

[1] The island of Orleans, which lies in the St. Lawrence near Quebec, is twenty-one miles long by about five in width. It was named by Cartier (1535) Isle of Bacchus, but subsequently given its present appellation by the same explorer. This island was granted as a fief in 1636. At the time of Lahontan it was a fief-noble in the possession of the family of Berthelot. See Bois, *L'Isle d'Orleans* (Quebec, 1895). — ED.

tain,[1] as well as that of ſeveral other Countries, with the leave of the Geographers, that reckon you up 1200 Leagues from *Rochel* to *Quebec*, without taking the pains to meaſure the Courſe: However, I am ſure that it lies but at too great a diſtance from *France*, for the Ships that are bound hither; For their paſſage commonly laſts for two Months and a half, whereas the homeward bound Ships may in 30 or 40 days ſailing, eaſily make the *Belle* Iſle, which is the ſureſt [12] and moſt uſual Land, that a Ship makes upon a long Voyage. The reaſon of this difference, is, that the Winds are Eaſterly for 100 days of the year, and Weſterly for 260.

Quebec is divided into the upper and the lower City. The Merchants live in the latter, for the conveniency of the Harbor; upon which they have built very fine Houſes, three Story high, of a ſort of Stone that's as hard as Marble. The upper or high City is full as populous, and as well adorn'd as the lower. Both Cities are commanded by a Caſtle, that ſtands upon the higheſt Ground. This Caſtle is the Reſidence of the Governours, and affords them not only convenient Apartments, but the nobleſt and moſt extenſive Proſpect in the World. *Quebec* wants two eſſential things, namely, a Key and Fortifications; though both the one and the other might be eaſily made, conſidering the conveniency of Stones lying upon the ſpot.[2] 'Tis incompaſs'd with ſeveral Springs, of the

---

[1] The true latitude of Quebec is 46° 49′ north; the longitude, 71° 13′ west of Greenwich. — Ed.

[2] Champlain began the fortifications of Quebec by the founding of Fort St. Louis on the citadel rock. This building was replaced in stone by his successor Montmagny, who also laid the foundations for the first Chateau St. Louis, which was

beſt freſh Water in the World, which the Inhabitants draw out of Wells; for they are ſo ignorant of the Hydroſtaticks, that not one of 'em knows how to convey the Water to certain Baſins, in order to raiſe either flat or ſpouting Fountains. Thoſe who live on the River ſide, in the lower City, are not half ſo much pinch'd with the Cold, as the Inhabitants of the upper; beſides that the former have a peculiar conveniency of tranſporting in Boats, Corn, Wood, and other Neceſſaries, to the very Doors of their Houſes: But as the latter are more expoſs'd to the injuries of the Cold, ſo they injoy the benefit and pleaſure of a cooler Summer. The way which leads from the one City to the other is pretty broad, and adorn'd with Houſes on each ſide; only 'tis a little ſteep. *Quebec* ſtands upon a very uneven Ground; and its Houſes are not uniform.[1] The Intendant lives in a [13] bottom, at ſome ſmall diſtance from the ſide of a little River, which by joyning the River of St. *Laurence*, coops up the City in a right Angle. His Houſe is the Palace in which the Soveraign Council aſſembles four times a Week[2]; and on one ſide of which, we ſee great Magazines

---

demolished in 1694 to make way for tne finer structure which Frontenac constructed during his last years. See Gagnon, *Le Fort et le Chateau St. Louis* (Quebec, 1895). Quebec's walls were not built until the latter years of Frontenac; again, in 1720, Chassegros de Léry made great improvements in the circumvallation, and enlarged the area contained therein. Repairs and improvements were maintained throughout the French régime. See Doughty and Dionne, *Quebec under Two Flags* (Quebec, 1903), pp. 101–145. — ED.

[1] For a plan of Quebec at this period, see that of J. B. Franquelin (1683), in Sulte, *Histoire des Canadiens français*, ii, p. 32; and another of 1700 in the same work, p. 49. — ED.

[2] The sovereign council was established by the king upon the retrocession of the colony by the Company of New France (1663). It was first composed of the governor,

of Ammunition and Provifions. There are fix Churches in the High City: The Cathedral confifts of a Bifhop, and twelve Prebendaries, who live in common in the Chapter-Houfe, the Magnificence and Architecture of which is truly wonderful. Thefe poor Priefts are a very good fort of People; they content themfelves with bare Neceffaries, and meddle with nothing but the Affairs of the Church, where the Service is perform'd after the *Roman* way.[1] The fecond Church is that of the Jefuits, which ftands in the Center of the City; and is a fair, ftately, and well lighted Edifice. The great Altar of the Jefuits

---

bishop, and five appointed councillors. Later, the intendant was added to the council, and the number gradually increased to twelve. Its functions were mainly judicial, but it likewise took cognizance of civil and financial affairs. Its records have been published.

At first the council met in the ante-room of the governor's palace, but upon the complaint of the intendant the ministry ordered the purchase of the site of a brewery formerly erected by Talon upon St. Charles River. Here the intendant's palace was begun. This was burned in 1713, being rebuilt upon a scale of splendor. The site is once more occupied by a brewery. — Ed.

[1] The cathedral of Notre Dame, now called the "Basilica," was long the only parish church of Quebec. Begun in 1647, the first mass was said therein three years later; it was consecrated by Bishop Laval in 1666. In the early eighteenth century its size was found inadequate, and it was rebuilt after the plans of the chief engineer of New France, Chaussegros de Léry (1747-48). The building suffered much during the English siege (1759), all the wooden parts being burned. Repairs were instituted in 1769-71, since when only minor changes have been made. The chapter house, or Seminary, which had been begun in 1678, was considered one of the finest buildings in the country. See Têtu, *Histoire du palais episcopal de Quebec* (Quebec, 1896). The Seminary priests officiated as secular parish curés. Lahontan's enconiums are the more remarkable, that his sympathies were seldom with ecclesiastics. It appears that the altar and its columns was a superfluous invention upon his part. The Jesuit historian Charlevoix, writing of this church in 1720 (*Journal Historique*, letter iii), indicates that there was no such ornament, and indulgently remarks: "One would voluntarily pardon that author [Lahontan] if he disfigured the truth only to give lustre to churches." — Ed.

Church, is adorn'd with four great Cylindrical Columns of one Stone; The Stone being a ſort of *Canada* Porphyry, and black as Jet, without either Spots or Veins. Theſe Fathers have very convenient and large Apartments, beautify'd with pleaſant Gardens, and ſeveral rows of Trees, which are ſo thick and buſhy, that in Summer one might take their Walks for an Ice-Houſe: And indeed we may ſay without ſtretching, that there is Ice not far from 'em, for the good Fathers are never without a reſerve in two or three places, for the cooling of their Drink. Their College is ſo ſmall, that at the beſt they have ſcarce fifty Scholars at a time.[1] The third Church is that of the Recollects, who, through the interceſſion of Count *Frontenac*, obtain'd leave of the King to build a little Chappel (which I call a Church;) notwithſtanding the Remonſtrances of Mr. *de Laval* our Biſhop, who, in concert with the Jeſuits, us'd his utmoſt Efforts for ten years together to hinder it.[2] Before the building [14] of this Chappel, they liv'd in a

[1] The Jesuits came to Canada in 1625, and thereafter played a prominent part in the development of the colony. Their college was founded in 1635, a year before that of Harvard, making it the oldest institution of learning on the North American continent. The church occupied the northeast angle of the college, on the site of the present Jesuit barracks. The city hall now covers the larger portion of the site of the college and its gardens. At the time of Lahontan's visit, the Jesuit church was in size and decoration far superior to the cathedral. — Ed.

[2] François de Montmorency-Laval, first bishop of Canada, was born in 1623 and educated in a Jesuit seminary. Upon the death of his brothers, he became heir of a seigniory in France, but renounced it for the service of the church. In 1658 he was made bishop of Petræa and sent as vicar apostolic to New France. In 1674 Quebec was raised to a bishopric, and Laval made first bishop thereof, a position which he resigned in 1684. Four years later he returned to spend the remainder of his days in Canada, where he died in 1708. He supported the Jesuits, and was opposed to the re-introduction of the Recollects. — Ed.

little Hofpital that the Bifhop had order'd to be built for 'em; and fome of 'em continue there ftill.[1] The fourth Church is that of the *Urfelines*, which has been burn'd down two or three times, and ftill rebuilt to the Advantage. The fifth is that of the Hofpital-Order, who take a particular Care of the Sick, tho' themfelves are poor, and but ill lodg'd.[2]

The Soveraign Council is held at *Quebec*. It confifts of twelve Counfellors of * *Capa y de fpada*, who are the fupreme Judicature, and decide all Caufes without Appeal. The Intendant claims a Right of being Prefident to the Council; but in the Juftice-Hall the Governour-General places himfelf fo as to face him, the Judges being fet on both fides of them; fo that one would think they are both Prefidents. While *Monfieur de Fron-*

See the Explication Table.

[1] The Recollects (a branch of the Franciscans) were the first ecclesiastics to enter New France, coming over in 1615. During their first occupation they had a small convent called Notre Dame des Anges, on St. Charles River, where the General Hospital of Quebec is now situated. After the capture of Quebec by the English (1628), the friars were sent back to France; and the order did not return to this field until 1670, when they were sent out as a counterpoise to the Jesuits. Frontenac favored this order, and gave them a concession of land facing the governor's palace, where they built the chapel here mentioned by Lahontan, although some of the brothers were still living at their suburban convent, Notre Dame des Anges. This church of the Recollects was one of the finest in New France, being finished in 1681. Charlevoix said in the next century, that it was "worthy of Versailles." In 1796 it was burned, the site now being occupied by the Anglican cathedral of Quebec; the court house occupies a portion of the convent grounds. — Ed.

[2] The Ursulines were the first order of nuns to come to New France (1639), which they did under the patronage of Madame de la Peltrie. Two years later they began their convent, which still occupies the original site, although the buildings have several times been burned, and recently much enlarged.

The Hospitalières came over at the same time as the Ursulines, and founded Hôtel Dieu, a great hospital which still exists on the same site where the corner stone was laid in 1654. — Ed.

tenac was in *Canada*, he laugh'd at the pretended Precedency of the Intendants; nay he ufed the Members of that Affembly as roughly as *Cromwell* did the Parliament of *England.* At this Court every one pleads his own Caufe, for Sollicitors or Barrifters never appear there; by which means it comes to pafs, that Law-Suits are quickly brought to a Period, without demanding Court Fees or any other Charges from the contending Parties. The Judges, who have but four hundred Livers a Year from the King, have a Difpenfation of not wearing the Robe and the Cap. Befides this Tribunal, we have in this Country a Lieutenant-General, both Civil and Military, an Attorney-General, the Great Provoft, and a Chief Juftice in Eyre.[1]

The way of travelling in the Winter, whether in Town or Country, is that of Sledges drawn by Horfes; who are fo infenfible of the Cold, that I have feen fifty or fixty of 'em in *January* and *February* ftand in the Snow up to their Breaft, in the [15] midft of a Wood, without ever offering to go near their Owner's Houfe. In the Winter-time they travel from *Quebec* to *Monreal* upon the Ice, the River being then frozen over; and upon that occafion thefe Sledges will run you fifteen Leagues a day. Others have their Sledges drawn by two Maftiff Dogs, but then they are longer by the way. As for their way of travelling in Summer, I fhall tranfmit you an Account of it, when I come to be better inform'd. I am told that the People

[1] One of the chief causes of dissension between Frontenac and the intendant, was the presidency of the supreme council. See Parkman, *Frontenac*, pp. 47–71. On the officers of justice, see Weir, *Administration of Old Regime*, pp. 63–67. — Ed.

of this Country will go a thouſand Leagues in Canows of Bark; a Deſcription of which you may expect, as ſoon as I have made uſe of 'em. The Eaſterly Winds prevail here commonly in the Spring and Autumn; and the Weſterly have the Aſcendant in Winter and Summer. Adieu Sir: I muſt now make an end of my Letter, for my Matter begins to run ſhort. All I can ſay, is, that as ſoon as I am better inſtructed in what relates to the Commerce, and the Civil and Eccleſiaſtical Government of the Country, I'll tranſmit you ſuch exact Memoirs of the ſame, as ſhall give you full ſatisfaction. Theſe you may expect with the firſt Opportunity; for in all Appearance our Troops will return after the Concluſion of the Campaign that we are now going to make in the Country of the *Iroqueſe*, under the Command of *Monſieur de la Barre.* In ſeven or eight Days time I mean to imbark for *Monreal;* and in the mean time am going to make a Progreſs to the Villages of *Scilleri*, of *Saut de la Chaudiere*, and of *Lorete*, which are inhabited by the *Abenakis* and the *Hurons.* Theſe Places are not above three or four Leagues off; ſo that I may return with eaſe next Week. As for the Manners of the People, I cannot pretend to deſcribe 'em ſo ſoon; for a juſt Obſervation and Knowledge of theſe things cannot be compaſs'd without time. I have been this Winter at hunting with thirty or [16] forty young *Algonkins*, who were well made clever Fellows. My Deſign in accompanying them, was, to learn their Language, which is mightily eſteem'd in this Country; for all the other Nations for a thouſand Leagues round (excepting the *Iroqueſe* and the *Hurons*) underſtand it perfectly well; nay, all their refpective Tongues come as near to this, as the *Portuguefe* does to the *Spanifh*.[1] I have already made my felf Mafter of fome Words with a great deal of Facility; and they being mightily pleafed in feeing a Stranger ftudy their Tongue take all imaginable pains to inftruct me. I am,

SIR,

Yours, &c.

---

[1] The Algonquian language was the most wide-spread of the Indian dialects of North America, being used by most of the tribes east of the Mississippi and south of Hudson Bay. The Huron-Iroquois stock were aliens in their midst. See Powell, "Linguistic Families of North America," in U. S. Bureau of Ethnology *Report*, 1885–86.

The Algonkins proper were a tribe whose original home was in the province of Quebec. See *Jesuit Relations*, index. — Ed.

LETTER IV.

Dated at *Monreal*, *June* 14. 1684.

Containing a brief Deſcription of the Habitations of the Savages in the Neighbourhood of Quebec; *Of the River of St.* Lawrence, *&c. as far up as* Monreal; *Of a curious way of fiſhing Eels; and of the Cities of* Trois Rivieres *and* Monreal: *Together with an Account of the Conduct of the * Forreſt Rangers or Pedlers.*

* Coureurs de Bois. *See the Explication Table.*

SIR,

BEFORE my Departure from *Quebec*, I viſited the adjacent Villages inhabited by the Savages. The Village of *Lorete* is peopled by two hundred Families [17] of *Hurons*, who were converted to Chriſtianity by the Jeſuits, though with a great deal of Reluctancy.[1] The Villages of *Silleri*, and of *Saut de la Chaudiere*, are compos'd of three hundred Families of *Abenakis*, who are likewiſe Chriſtians, and among whom the Jeſuits have

[1] The village of Lorette was a mission colony of the Jesuits, founded after the destruction of the Huron mission by the Iroquois (1649). Part of the instructed Hurons sought the fathers at Quebec, and were first established on the Isle of Orleans; later, during the Iroquois war, the remnant was removed to a less-exposed situation, and by 1669 settled at Notre Dame de Foye (now Ste. Foye). A few years later, this colony removed to the village of Lorette (now Ancienne Lorette), and there Lahontan visited them. In 1697, impelled by need of fresh fuel and land, they founded the village of Jeune Lorette, eight miles from Montreal, which became their final home, and where a remnant of the Huron race is still to be found. — Ed.

fetled Miffionaries.[1] I return'd to *Quebec* time enough, and imbarqued under the conduct of a Mafter, that would rather have had a Lading of Goods, than of Soldiers. The North-Eaft Winds wafted us in five or fix days to *Trois Rivieres*, which is the name of a fmall City, feated at the diftance of thirty Leagues from hence. That City derives its name from three Rivers, that fpring from one Channel, and after continuing their divifion for fome fpace re-unite into a joynt Stream, that falls into the River of St. *Laurence*, about half a quarter of a League below the Town. Had we fail'd all Night, the Tides would have carry'd us thither in two days time; but in regard that the River is full of Rocks and Shelves, we durft not venture upon it in the dark; fo, we came to an Anchor every Night, which did not at all difpleafe me; for in the courfe of thirty Leagues, (notwithftanding the darknefs of the Night) it gave me an opportunity of viewing an infinite number of Habitations on each fide of the River, which are not above a Musket-Shot diftant one from another. The Inhabitants that are fetled between *Quebec* and fifteen Leagues higher, diverted me very agreeably with the fifhing of Eels. At low

[1] The mission colony at Sillery was originally founded for the Algonkins, Montagnais, etc.; but its inhabitants were decimated by disease and the ravages of intoxication, so that the converted Abenaki from Maine, who began coming to Canada about 1680, formed the main body of the colony. The mission was maintained here until 1699, when the land which had been ceded in trust for the Indian converts was retroceded to the Jesuit order.

"Le Saut de la Chaudière" was a village on the river of that name, opposite Quebec, where was established about the time Lahontan arrived in Canada, the Abenaki mission of St. François de Sales. In 1700 all the scattered villages were collected in one, which exists till the present time — that of St. François du Lac, in Yamaska County, Quebec. — Ed.

water they ſtretch out Hurdles to the loweſt Water-Mark; and that ſpace of ground being then dry by the retreat of the Water, is cover'd over, and ſhut up by the Hurdles. Between the Hurdles they place at certain diſtances Inſtruments call'd *Ruches*, from the reſemblance they bear to a Bee-hive; beſides Baskets and little Nets belag'd upon a Pole, which they call *Bouteux*, and *Bouts de Quievres*. Then they let all ſtand in this faſhion for three Months in [18] the Spring, and two in the Autumn. Now as often as the Tide comes in, the Eels looking out for ſhallow places, and making towards the Shoar, croud in among the Hurdles, which hinder 'em afterwards to retire with the Ebb-water; upon that they are forc'd to bury themſelves in the abovementioned Ingines, which are ſometimes ſo over-cram'd, that they break. When 'tis low water, the Inhabitants take out theſe Eels, which are certainly the biggeſt, and the longeſt in the World. They ſalt them up in Barrels, where they'll keep a whole year without ſpoiling: And indeed they give an admirable reliſh in all Sauces; nay, there's nothing that the Council of *Quebec* deſires more, than that this Fiſhery ſhould be equally plentiful in all years.

Trois Rivieres is a little paltry Town, ſeated in the Latitude of forty ſix Degrees; 'tis not fortified neither with Stone, nor Pales. The River to which it owes its name, takes its riſe an hundred Leagues to the North-Weſt, from the greateſt ridge of Mountains in the Univerſe. The *Algonkins* who are at preſent an Erratick ſort of Savages, and, like the *Arabs*, have no ſetled Abode; that People, I ſay, ſeldom ſtraggle far from the banks of this River, upon which they have excellent Beaver-hunting. In former times the *Iroquefe* cut off three fourths of that Nation; but they have not dar'd to renew their Incurfions, fince the *French* have Peopled the Countries that lie higher up upon the River of St. *Laurence.* I call'd *Trois Rivieres* a little Town, with reference to the paucity of the Inhabitants; though at the fame time they are very rich, and live in ftately Houfes. The King has made it the Refidence of a Governor, who would die for Hunger, if he did not trade with the Natives for Beavers, when his fmall allowance is out: Befides, a Man that would live there, muft be of the like temper with a Dog, or at leaft he muft take pleafure in fcratching [19] his Skin, for the Flea's are there more numerous than the grains of Sand. I am inform'd, that the Natives of this place make the beft Soldiers in the Country.[1]

Three Leagues higher we enter'd St. *Peter's* Lake, which is fix Leagues long, and had difficulty enough in croffing it; for the frequent Calms oblig'd us to caft Anchor feveral times. It receives three or four Rivers that abound with Fifh; upon the Mouth of which, I defcry'd with my Telefcope very fine Houfes.[2] Towards the Evening we fail'd out of that Lake

---

[1] For the history of Trois Rivières, on the St. Lawrence at the mouth of Maurice River, see Sulte, "La Rivière des Trois Rivières," *Roy. Soc. Proc.*, 1901, pp. 97–116. — ED.

[2] Lake St. Peters was christened Lac d'Angoulême by Cartier; but Champlain crossing it on the day of the saint, changed the name in the latter's honor. It is an enlargement of the St. Lawrence, twenty-five miles long by about nine broad, in the midst of the most fertile region of Lower Canada. It receives several rivers, chief of which are the Du Loup and Maskinonge from the north; the Nicolet, St. Francis, and Yamaska from the south, not including River Richelieu, which enters the St. Lawrence at the upper end of the lake. — ED.

with a fresh Easterly Gale; and though we hoisted up all our Sails, the Current run so strong against us, that 'twas three hours before we could make *Sorel*, which was two small Leagues off.[1] *Sorel* is a Canton of four Leagues in front, in the neighbourhood of which, a certain River conveys the waters of *Champlain* Lake, to the River of St. *Laurence*, after having form'd a Water-fall of two Leagues at *Chambli*.[2] Though we reckon but eight Leagues from *Sorel* to *Monreal*, yet we spent three days in sailing between 'em; by reason partly of slack Winds, and partly of the strength of the Currents. In this course we saw nothing but Islands; and both sides of the River all along from *Quebec* to this place, are so replenish'd with Inhabitants, that one may justly call 'em two continued Villages of sixty Leagues in length.

This place, which goes by the name of *Villemarie*, or *Monreal*, lies in the Latitude of forty five Degrees, and some Minutes; being seated in an Island of the same name, which is about five Leagues broad, and fourteen Leagues long. The Directors of the Seminary of St. *Sulpitius* at *Paris*, are the Proprietors of the Island, and have the nomination of a Bailiff, and several other Magistrates; nay, in former times they had

[1] Fort Sorel was built by an officer of that name (Pierre de Saurel), in 1665. Three years later he married the daughter of a Canadian seigneur, and in 1672 received a grant of the seigniory of Sorel, where he lived until his death in 1682.—ED.

[2] Chambly was named for Jacques de Chambly, captain in the Carignan regiment, whom Tracy sent (1665) to build an advance fort against the Iroquois. He received the surounding land as a seigniory in 1672, but the next year was sent to command in Acadia. Later he removed to Grenada, and Chambly passed to his nephew.—ED.

the priviledge of nominating a Governor.[1] This little Town lies all open without any Fortification [20] either of Stone or Wood: But its ſituation is ſo advantageous, notwithſtanding that it ſtands upon an uneven and ſandy Ground, that it might eaſily be made an impregnable Poſt. The River of St. *Laurence* which runs juſt by the Houſes, on one ſide of this Town, is not Navigable further, by reaſon of its rapidity; for about half a quarter of a League higher, 'tis full of rapid falls, Eddy's, *&c.* Mr. *Perot* the Governor of the Town, who has but a thouſand Crowns a year Sallary; has made ſhift to get fifty thouſand in a few years, by trading with the Savages in Skins and Furs.[2] The Bailiff of the Town gets but little by his place, no more than his Officers: So that the Merchants are the only Perſons that make Money here; for the Savages that frequent the great Lakes of *Canada*, come down hither almoſt every year with a prodigious quantity of

[1] Montreal was a religious colony, founded (1642) by a society of Associates of Montreal, who received the island as a seigniory. In 1663 the number of the Associates being much diminished, the Sulpitians of Paris agreed to take charge of the enterprise, and the seigniory was transferred to them, with the rights here mentioned by Lahontan. The Sulpitians held their seigniorial privileges until the abolition of feudal tenure in 1854; they still retain much land in Montreal and vicinity. — ED.

[2] François Marie Perrot came to Canada with the intendant Talon (1670), whose niece he had married. Upon the request of Talon, the Sulpitians named him governor of Montreal, a grant which was later confirmed by the king. Perrot abused his privileges to enrich himself, and protected the coureurs des bois. Involved in a dispute with Frontenac, the governor arrested Perrot and sent him to France for trial. The ministry, after punishing him by a brief imprisonment in the Bastille, restored him to his governorship, where he remained until 1684. In this year he was appointed governor of Acadia, which position he held for three years. After his recall, he remained in the country as a trader, and in 1690 was captured by the English. The date of his death is unknown. — ED.

Beavers-Skins, to be given in exchange for Arms, Kettles, Axes, Knives, and a thoufand fuch things, upon which the Merchants clear two hundred *per Cent.* Commonly the Governor General comes hither about the time of their coming down, in order to fhare the profit, and receive Prefents from that People. The Pedlers call'd *Coureurs de Bois*, export from hence every year feveral Canows full of Merchandife, which they difpofe of among all the Savage Nations of the Continent, by way of exchange for Beaver-Skins. Seven or eight days ago, I faw twenty five or thirty of thefe Canows return with heavy Cargoes; each Canow was manag'd by two or three Men, and carry'd twenty hundred weight, *i. e.* forty packs of Beaver Skins, which are worth an hundred Crowns a piece. Thefe Canows had been a year and eighteen Months out. You would be amaz'd if you faw how lewd thefe Pedlers are when they return; how they Feaft and Game, and how prodigal they are, not only in their Cloaths, but [21] upon Women. Such of 'em as are married, have the wifdom to retire to their own Houfes; but the Batchelors act juft as our *Eaft-India*-Men, and Pirates are wont to do; for they Lavifh, Eat, Drink, and Play all away as long as the Goods hold out; and when thefe are gone, they e'en fell their Embroidery, their Lace, and their Cloaths. This done, they are forc'd to go upon a new Voyage for Subfiftance.

The Directors of the Seminary of St. *Sulpitius*, take care to fend Miffionaries hither from time to time, who live under the direction of a Superiour, that is very much refpected in the Country. They have Apartments allotted for 'em in a ftately, great, and pleafant Houfe, built of Free-ftone.[1] This Houfe is built after the Model of that of St. *Sulpice* at *Paris;* and the Altar ftands by it felf, juft like that at *Paris.* Their Seignories or Cantons that lye on the South-fide of the Ifland, produce a confiderable Revenue; for the Plantations are good, and the Inhabitants are rich in Corn, Cattle, Fowl, and a thoufand other Commodities, for which they find a Mercat in the City: But the North part of the Ifland lies wafte. Thefe Directors would never fuffer the Jefuits or Recollects to difplay their Banners here; though 'tis conjectur'd, that at the long run they'll be forc'd to confent to it. At the diftance of a League from the Town, I faw at the foot of a Mountain, a Plantation of *Iroquefe* Chriftians, who are inftructed by two Priefts of the Order of *Sulpitius*,[2] and I'm inform'd of a larger

[1] The Seminary of St. Sulpice, whose priests were known as Sulpitians, was founded at Vaugirard in 1640, by Jean Jacques Olier, a young Parisian priest, one of the Associates of Montreal. The next year the Seminary was established at Paris, and by 1657 the first Sulpitian arrived in Canada. At Montreal they were eagerly welcomed, became the curés of the parish, and later seigneurs of the island (see ante, p. 53, note 1). The first superior was Queylus, upon whose retirement (1671) François Casson de Dollier succeeded to the position. The latter came to Canada in 1666 after service in the armies of France. His first office was chaplain in an expedition against the Mohawks; later (1669), he accompanied La Salle on his first voyage of Western exploration. Returning to Montreal the following spring, he served as superior of the Sulpitians until his death (1671–1701). The earliest historian of Montreal, his manuscript was first published in 1871. — ED.

[2] The Sulpitians founded (1677) the Iroquois mission called from its location, La Montagne, where were an Indian village, a school for boys, and another for girls, all aided by a pension from the king. During Frontenac's War (1691) this village was raided and thirty-five prisoners taken. Some years later (1704), the mission was removed to Sault au Récollet, and sixteen years later became the nucleus of the Indian village of Oka on the Lake of Two Mountains, which still exists. See Canadian Indian Department *Report*, 1901, p. 49. — ED.

and more populous Plantation on t'other ſide of the River, at the diſtance of two Leagues from hence, which is took care of by Father *Bruyas* the Jeſuit.[1] I hope to ſet out from hence, as ſoon as Mr. *de la Barre* receives advice from *France;* for he deſigns to leave *Quebec* upon the arrival of the firſt Ship. I reſolve to go to Fort *Frontenac*, upon the Lake that [22] goes by the ſame name. If I may credit thoſe who have been formerly in Action againſt the *Iroqueſe*, I ſhall be able upon my return from this Campaign, to inform you of ſome things that will ſeem as ſtrange to you, as they will be diſagreeable to my ſelf. I am,

SIR,

Yours, &c.

---

[1] The Jesuit mission was known as St. François du Sault, from its location on Sault St. Louis. It was established at La Prairie de la Madeleine in 1669, and in 1676 removed to this place, which is now known as Caughnawaga. Father Jacques Bruyas came to the Canadian mission in 1666, and labored during the rest of his life among the Iroquois. In 1679 he took charge of the mission at Sault St. Louis, where he lived until his death in 1712. He was superior of Canada missions 1693-98, and in 1700-01 was instrumental in adjusting peace with the Iroquois. A linguist of repute, he prepared the first grammar of the Mohawk language. — Ed.

LETTER V.

Dated at *Monreal June* 18. 1684.

In which is contain'd a ſhort account of the Iroqueſe, *with a view of the War and Peace they made with the* French, *and of the means by which it was brought about.*

SIR,

I WROTE to you but four days ago, and did not think to have heard from you ſo ſoon; but this Morning I met with a very agreeable Surpriſal, in receiving a Packet addreſs'd to me by your Brother. You may be ſure I was infinitely well pleas'd, in being given to underſtand what has paſs'd in *Europe* ſince I left it. The knowledge of the Affairs of *Europe* is comfortable to one that's doom'd to another World, ſuch as this is, and I cannot but acknowledge my ſelf infinitely indebted to you, for the exactneſs of your Intelligence. In as much as you require of me an account of the *Iroqueſe*, and would have me to preſent you with a juſt view of their Temper and Government; I would willingly ſatisfie and oblige you in that, or any other point: But in regard [23] that I am oblig'd to ſet out for Fort *Frontenac* the day after to morrow, I have not time to inform my ſelf of things, or to conſult thoſe who have been in the Country before: So that all I can do at preſent, is only to acquaint you with what I have learn'd this Winter, from Perſons that have ſojourn'd twenty years among 'em. As ſoon as I have an opportunity of inlarging my knowledge upon that Head, by a more immediate converſation with themſelves, you may aſſure your ſelf that I'll impart it to you. In the mean time, be pleas'd to accept of what follows.

Theſe *Barbarians* are drawn up in five Cantons, not unlike thoſe of the *Swiſſes*. Tho' theſe Cantons are all of one Nation, and united in one joynt intereſt, yet they go by different names, *viz.* the *Tſonontouans*, the *Goyogoans*, the *Onnotagues*, the *Onoyouts*, and the *Agniès*. Their Language is almoſt the ſame; and the five Villages or Plantations in which they live, lie at the diſtance of thirty Leagues one from another, being all ſeated near the South ſide of the Lake of *Ontario*, or of *Frontenac*. Every year the five Cantons ſend Deputies to aſſiſt at the Union Feaſt, and to ſmoak in the great *Calumet*, or Pipe of the five Nations. Each Village or Canton contains about fourteen thouſand Souls, *i. e.* 1500 that bear Arms, 2000 Superannuated Men, 4000 Women, 2000 Maids, and 4000 Children: Tho' indeed ſome will tell you, that each Village has not above 10000 or 11000 Souls.[1] There has been an Alliance of long ſtanding between theſe Nations and the *Engliſh*, and by trading in Furrs to New-*York*, they are ſupply'd by the *Engliſh*

[1] "Iroquois" was a title bestowed by the French; the tribesmen called themselves "People of the Long House"; to the English, they were known as the "Five Nations." Lahontan gives the five confederates of the league in the French form of their names; the English called them — proceeding in the same order, from west to east — Seneca, Cayuga, Onondaga, Oneida, and Mohawk. Among the Onondaga was the principal council house, where each year the "union feast" was held, and the forthcoming policy deliberated. Lahontan has greatly exaggerated the numbers of these Indians; it is doubtful whether they ever mustered more than 2,500 warriors, implying a population of 10,000 to 12,000. See *Jesuit Relations*, index; Parkman, *Jesuits*, p. lxvi. — ED.

with Arms, Ammunition, and all other Neceſſaries, at a cheaper rate than the *French* can afford 'em at. They have no other conſideration for *England* or *France*, than what depends upon the occaſion they have for the Commodities of theſe two Nations; though after all they [24] give an over-purchaſe; for they pay for them four times more than they are worth. They laugh at the Menaces of our Kings and Governors, for they have no notion of dependence, nay, the very word is to them inſupportable. They look upon themſelves as Sovereigns, accountable to none but God alone, whom they call *The Great Spirit.* They waged War with us almoſt always, from the firſt ſettlement of our Colonies in *Canada*, to the firſt years of the Count of *Frontenac*'s Government. *Meſſieurs de Courſelles*, and *de Traci*, both of 'em Governors-General, made Head againſt the *Agniès* upon the *Champlain* Lake, in Winter as well as in Summer; but they could not boaſt of any great Succeſs.[1] They only burnt their Villages, and carry'd off ſome hundred of their Children, of whom the abovemention'd *Iroqueſe* Chriſtians are ſprung. 'Tis true, they cut off ninety or an hundred Warriours; but in compenſation for

[1] The Iroquois had harassed New France almost from its inception. Alexandre de Prouville, marquis de Tracy, was chosen (1664) lieutenant-general of French colonies in America. An old army officer who had served with efficiency in the West Indies, his arrival (1665) was hailed with joy by the distressed colonists. Shortly after came Daniel de Rémy, sieur de Courcelle, the newly-appointed governor, and detachments of the Carignan regiment. Courcelle's first expedition against the Iroquois, in the winter of 1665-66, was without success. Whereupon Tracy took up the matter, and in the autumn of 1666 led an expedition via Lake Champlain, which burned the Mohawk towns and cowed these savages into an advantageous peace. The following year (1667) Tracy returned to France, to die there three years later. Courcelle remained as governor until 1672, when failing health caused his retirement, he being replaced by Count de Frontenac. — Ed.

that, ſeveral *Canadans*, and ſeveral Soldiers of the Regiment of *Carignan*, being unprovided againſt the unſufferable cold of the Climate, loſt their Limbs, and even their Life it ſelf. Count *Frontenac* who ſucceeded Mr. *Courſelle*,[1] perceiving that the *Barbarians* had the advantage of the *Europeans*, as to the waging of War in that Country; upon this apprehenſion, I ſay, he declin'd ſuch fruitleſs Expeditions, which were very chargeable to the King, and us'd all his efforts to diſpoſe the Savages to a ſincere and laſting Peace. This judicious Governor had three things in view; The firſt was to incourage the greateſt part of the *French* Inhabitants, who would have abdicated the Colony, and return'd to *France*, if the War had continued. His ſecond Topick was, that the concluſion of a Peace would diſpoſe an infinity of People to marry, and to grub up the Trees, upon which the Colony would be better Peopled and inlarg'd. The third Argument that diſſuaded him from carrying [25] on the War, was a deſign of purſuing the diſcovery of the *Lakes*, and of the *Savages* that live upon their banks, in order to ſettle a Commerce with 'em, and at the ſame time to ingage them in our intereſts, by good Alliances, in caſe of a Rupture with the *Iroqueſe*. Upon the conſideration of theſe Reaſons, he ſent ſome *Canadans* by way of a formal Embaſſy to the *Iroqueſe* Villages, in order to acquaint them,

[1] Louis de Baude, count de Frontenac (born in 1620), had from his fifteenth year seen service in French armies, and was also an accomplished courtier. He was made lieutenant-general of New France in 1672, and while the most able of the governors, his imperious disposition and autocratic temper involved him in many disputes. The opposition became so great that he was recalled in 1682. Seven years later, the peril of the colony was such that Frontenac was again summoned to defend it. This he did vigorously, his expedition of 1696 crushing the Iroquois, and saving Canada to the French. He died at Quebec November 28, 1698. — ED.

that the King being inform'd that a groundlefs War was carried on againft them, had fent him from *France* to make peace with 'em. At the fame time the Ambaffadors had orders to ftipulate all the advantages they could obtain with reference to the Commerce. The *Iroquefe* heard this Propofal with a great deal of Satisfaction; for *Charles* II. King of *England*, had order'd his Governor in *New-York* to reprefent to 'em, that if they continu'd to wage War with the *French*, they were ruin'd, and that they would find themfelves crufh'd by the numerous Forces that were ready to fail from *France*. In effect, they promis'd to the Ambaffadors that four hundred of their number fhould meet Count *Frontenac*, attended by an equal number of his Men, at the place where Fort *Frontenac* now ftands. Accordingly, fome Months after, both the one and the other met at the place appointed, and fo a Peace was concluded. Mr. *de la Salle* was very ferviceable to this Governor, in giving him good and feafonable Advices, which I cannot now enter upon, being oblig'd to make fome preparations for my Voyage.[1] When the Campaign is over, you may expect to hear from me. In the mean time, I am,

SIR,

Yours, &c.

---

[1] Lahontan here refers to Frontenac's expedition of 1673, which built Fort Frontenac, and made peace with the Iroquois. La Salle was one of the messengers sent to Onondaga to summon the chiefs to council. See Parkman, *La Salle* (Boston, 1892), chap. vi.

Thomas Dongan, governor of New York (1682–88), was an Irish gentleman who had served in both English and French armies in Europe, and had acted as lieutenant-governor of Tangiers. He attempted to thwart the plans of the French, to control the Iroquois and monopolize the trade with the interior, which conduct brought upon him reprimands from the English king, then subservient to the crown of France.— ED.

LETTER VI.

Dated at *Monreal June* 20. 1684.

Being an ample Defcription of the Canows made of Birch-bark, in which the Canadans *perform all their Voyages; with an account of the manner in which they are made and manag'd.*

SIR,

I THOUGHT to have fet out as this day; but in regard that our Complement of great Canows is not yet brought up, our Voyage is put off for two days. Having fo much leifure time upon my Hands, I have a mind to imploy it in prefenting you with a fhort view of thefe flender Contrivances in which the *Canadans* perform all their Voyages: And this will furnifh you with an *Idæa* of the *Voiture* of this Country. I faw but now above an hundred Canows, fome great and fome little; but confidering that the former are only proper for Martial Expeditions, and long Voyages, I fhall confine my Defcription to that fort. Even the great ones are of different fizes; for they run from ten to twenty eight Foot long. Indeed the leaft of all hold but two Perfons fet upon their Breech, as in a Coffin; and are apt to over-fet, if the Paffengers move to one fide or t'other: But thofe of a larger fize will eafily afford ftowage for fourteen Perfons; tho' they are commonly mann'd only with three Men, when they are imploy'd in tranſporting Proviſions and Merchandize; and even then they'll carry twenty hundred weight. The largeſt ſort are ſafe and [27] ſteddy, when they are made of the Bark of the Birch-tree, which comes off with hot Water in the Winter time. The greateſt Trees afford the beſt Barks for Canows; but oftentimes the Bark of one Tree is not ſufficient. The bottom of the Boat is all of one piece, to which the ſides are ſo artfully ſew'd by the Savages, that the whole Boat appears as one continu'd Bark. They are trimm'd and ſtrengthn'd with wicker Wreaths, and ribs of Cedar-Wood, which are almoſt as light as Cork; the Wreaths are as thick as a Crown-piece; but the Bark has the thickneſs of two Crowns, and the Ribs are as thick as three. On the two ſides of the Boat, there runs from one end to the other two principal Head-bars, in which the ends of the Ribs are inchas'd, and in which the Spars are made faſt, that run a-croſs the Boat and keep it compact. Theſe Boats have twenty Inches in depth, that is, from the upper edge to the Platform of the Ribs; their length extends to twenty eight Foot, and the width at the middle Rib is computed to be four Foot and a half. They are very convenient upon the account of their extream lightneſs, and the drawing of very little Water; but at the ſame time their brittle and tender Fabrick, is an Argument of an equivalent inconveniency; for if they do but touch or grate upon Stone or Sand, the cracks of the Bark fly open, upon which the Water gets in, and ſpoils the Proviſions and Merchandize: Every day there is ſome new chink or ſeam to be gumm'd over. At Night they are always unloaded, and carried on ſhoar where they are made faſt with Pegs, leſt the Wind ſhould blow 'em away: For they are ſo light, that two Men carry 'em upon their ſhoulders with eaſe. This conveniency of lightneſs and eaſie carriage, renders 'em very ſerviceable in the Rivers of *Canada*, which are full of Cataracts, Water-falls, and Currents: For in theſe Rivers we are oblig'd either to tranſport [28] 'em over-land where ſuch obſtructions happen, or elſe to tow 'em along where the Current is not over-rapid, and the ſhoar is acceſſible. Theſe Boats are of no uſe for the Navigation of Lakes; for the Waves would ſwallow 'em up, if they could not reach the ſhoar when a wind ariſes.[1] 'Tis true, the Inhabitants venture in 'em for four or five Leagues, from one Iſland to another; but then 'tis always in calm Weather, and nothing is made uſe of but Oars; for beſides the riſque of being over-ſet, the Goods are in danger of being dammag'd by the Water, eſpecially the Furs which are the moſt valuable part of the Cargoe. When the ſeaſon ſerves, they carry little Sails; but if the Wind be but a little brisk, tho' they run right afore it, 'tis impoſſible to make any uſe of it without running the riſque of Ship-wrack. If their courſe lies directly South, they cannot put up ſail without the wind ſtands at one of the eight points, between North-Weſt and North-Eaſt; and if a wind happens to ſpring any where elſe, (unleſs it comes from the Land which they coaſt along) they

[1] For a brief description of the process of making a birch bark canoe, see McKenney, *Tour of the Lakes* (Baltimore, 1827), pp. 319, 320. Lahontan errs in saying that these craft were unfitted for the navigation of the lakes; he was later to learn of their usefulness on those waters. — ED.

are oblig'd to put in to the ſhoar with all poſſible expedition, and unload the Boat out of hand, till ſuch time as a calm returns.

As for the working of theſe Boats, the Canow-Men ply ſometimes on their Knees, namely, when they run down the ſmall Water-falls; ſometimes ſtanding, when they ſtem a Current by ſetting the Boat along with Poles; and ſometimes ſitting, *viz.* in ſmooth and ſtagnating water. The Oars they make uſe of are made of Maple-wood, and their form is repreſented in the annex'd Cutt. The Blade of the Oar is twenty Inches long, ſix Inches broad, and four Lines thick: The Handle is about three Foot long, and as big as a Pigeons Egg. When they have occaſion to run up againſt rapid Currents, they make uſe of Poles made of Pine-wood; and the ſetting of the Boat along with theſe, [29] is what they call *Piquer de fond.* The Canows have neither Stern nor Prow, for they run to a point at both ends: Neither have they Keels, Nails or Pegs, in the whole Structure. The Steerſman, or he who Conns the Boat, rows without interruption as well as the reſt. The common purchaſe of ſuch a Boat is eighty Crowns; but it do's not laſt above five or ſix years.

This day I have received advice, that Mr. *de la Barre* has rais'd the Militia in the neighbourhood of *Quebec*, and that the Governor of this Iſland has receiv'd orders to have that of the adjacent *Cantons* in readineſs to march. I am,

SIR,

Yours, &c.

LETTER VII.

Dated at *Monreal Novemb.* 2. 1684.

Defcribing the Courfe of the River of St. Laurence, *from* Monreal *to the firft great Lake of* Canada; *with the Water-falls, Cataracts, and Navigation of that River: As alfo Fort* Frontenac, *and the Advantages that accrue from it. Together with a Circumftantial account of the Expedition of Mr.* de la Barre, *the Governor-General, againft the* Iroquefe; *the Speeches he made, the Replies he receiv'd, and the final Accommodation of the difference.*

SIR,

THANK God I have finifh'd this Campaign, and am now return'd in fafety to this place. To prefent you with the Hiftory of our Campaign, be [30] pleas'd to know that in two or three days after the date of my laft, I imbarqu'd on board of a Canow that was work'd by three expert Canow-Men. Every Canow contain'd two Soldiers; and we all row'd up againft the Current of the River till we arriv'd at *Saut de St. Louis*, about three Leagues above this Town, which is a little Water-fall, but fo rapid, that our Watermen were forc'd to ftand in the water up to their Middle, in order to drag the Canows againft the Stream for half a quarter of a League.[1]

[1] Sault St. Louis was the name originally given to Lachine Rapids, just above Montreal, by Champlain (1611), apparently in memory of a lad named Louis who

We reimbarqu'd above this Pafs, and row'd about twelve Leagues up the River, and thro' the Lake of St. *Louis*, till we arriv'd at a place call'd the *Cafcades*, where we were forc'd to turn out and carry our Boats and Baggage over-land, about half a quarter of a League. 'Tis true, we might have tow'd our Boats againft the Stream in this place with fome labour; but there was a Cataract a little above it, which they call *le Cataracte du Trou*. I had taken up a notion that the only difficulty of failing up the River, confifted in the trouble of Land-carriage; but when I came to be a Spectator of the matter, I found that the ftemming of the Currents whether in towing of the Canows, or in fetting them along with Poles, was equally laborious. About five or fix Leagues higher we came to the Water-falls call'd *Sauts des Cedres*, and *du Buiffon*, where we were forc'd to tranfport our Boats five hundred paces over Land. Some Leagues above that, we enter'd the Lake of St. *Francis*, which is faid to be twenty Leagues in Circumference; and having crofs'd it, met with as ftrong Currents as before, particularly at a fall call'd *Long Saut*, where we had recourfe to Land-carriage for half a League. Then

was drowned at this place. The head of navigation upon the St. Lawrence, Cartier ascended to this point on his second voyage (1535), and explored the region in 1541. The name "Lachine" commemorates the derision excited among the enemies of La Salle; upon his embarkation thither for the West (1669), they said he was headed for China (La Chine), an allusion to the then prevalent notion that in the West might be found a transcontinental waterway which should prove a short-cut to China. The term "La Chine" was equivalent to our "China-town." The Lachine Rapids are the most dangerous on the St. Lawrence, and are now avoided by the Lachine canal, eight and a half miles long, on the northern side. In descending, however, specially-constructed passenger steamers "shoot the rapids," a favorite amusement among the people of Montreal. — ED.

we were forc'd to drag up the Boats againſt the rapid Stream; and after a great deal of fatigue came at laſt to a Paſs call'd *la Galete*, from whence we had but twenty Leagues ſailing to Fort *Frontenac.*[1] This [31] Paſs was the laſt difficulty we had to ſurmount; for above it the water was as ſtill as that of a Pool, and then our Watermen ply'd with their Oars in ſtead of Poles.

The *Maringouins*, which we call *Midges*, are unſufferably troubleſom in all the Countries of *Canada*. We were haunted with ſuch clouds of 'em, that we thought to be eat up; and ſmoaking being the only Artifice that could keep 'em off, the Remedy was worſe than the Diſeaſe: In the Night-time the People ſhelter themſelves from 'em in Bowers or Arbours, made after the following manner. They drive into the Ground Stakes or little branches of Trees, at a certain diſtance one from another, ſo as to form a ſemicircular Figure; in which they put a Quilt and Bedcloaths, covering it above with a large Sheet that falls down to the Ground on all ſides, and ſo hinders the Inſects to enter.

We landed at Fort *Frontenac* after twenty days ſailing; and immediately upon our arrival, Mr. *Duta* our Commander in chief, view'd the Fortifications of the place, and three large Barques that lay at Anchor in the Port.[2] We repair'd the

[1] Lahontan here describes in some detail the passage from Montreal to Lake Ontario. For a similar description in reverse order, with enumeration of the rapids, see Journal of Father Bonnecamps (1749), in *Jesuit Relations*, lxix, pp. 195, 197. The Long Sault of the St. Lawrence is now paralleled by the Cornwall canal. — Ed.

[2] Captain Du Tas (Tartre) was in command of the advance guard sent to convey provisions to Fort Frontenac. See New York *Colonial Documents*, ix, p. 234. He

Fortifications in a very little time, and fitted up the three Barques. This Fort was a Square, confifting of large Curtains flanked with four little Baftions; thefe Flanks had but two Battlements, and the Walls were fo low, that one might eafily climb upon 'em without a Ladder. After Mr. *de la Salle* concluded the Peace with the *Iroquefe*, the King beftow'd upon him and his Heirs the property of this place; but he was fo negligent, that inftead of enriching himfelf by the Commerce it might have afforded, he was confiderably out of pocket upon it.[1] To my mind this Fort is fituated very advantageoufly for a Trade with the five *Iroquefe* Nations: For their Villages lye in the Neighbourhood of the *Lake*, upon which they may tranfport their Furs in Canows with more [32] eafe, than they can carry 'em over-land to New-*York*. In time of War I take it to be indefenfible; for the Cataracts and Currents of the River are fuch, that fifty *Iroquefe* may there ftop

stopped but a brief time in the colony, but again brought reinforcements in 1690, when Frontenac sent him to guard the St. Lawrence. He served in the English Channel in 1692; went to Hudson Bay (1695), and the following year was in the campaign in Acadia.— Ed.

[1] Courcelle had recommended the site of Fort Frontenac (Catarakouy) on his expedition of 1671. His successor, acting upon the suggestion, advanced up the St. Lawrence in 1673, and built the stockade on the present site of Kingston, Ontario. Two years later, La Salle, strongly endorsed by Frontenac, obtained from the court at Versailles a grant of the fort and district as a seigniory. Had La Salle been a mere merchant, he would, as Lahontan suggests, have made his fortune therefrom. Using it merely as the base of Western exploration, he became involved in financial difficulties, and upon the departure of his patron Frontenac it was seized by his enemies, headed by La Barre (1683). Upon the order of the king, it was restored the following year to La Salle's lieutenant. At the outbreak of Frontenac's War (1689), Denonville gave orders for the destruction of this fort; but Frontenac restored it in 1695, and the French maintained it until its capture by the British in 1758.— Ed.

five hundred *French*, without any other Arms but Stones. Do but confider, Sir, that for twenty Leagues together the River is fo rapid, that we dare not fet the Canow four paces off the fhoar; Befides, *Canada* being nothing but a Forreft, as I intimated above, 'tis impoffible to travel there without falling every foot into Ambufcades, efpecially upon the banks of this River, which are lin'd with thick Woods, that render 'em inacceffible. None but the Savages can skip from Rock to Rock, and fcour thro' the Thickets, as if 'twere an open Field. If we were capable of fuch Adventures, we might march five or fix hundred Men by Land to guard the Canows that carry the Provifions; but at the fame time 'tis to be confider'd, that before they arriv'd at the Fort, they would confume more Provifions than the Canows can carry; Not to mention that the *Iroquefe* would ftill out-number 'em. As to the particulars relating to the Fort, I fhall take notice of 'em when I come to give a general defcription of New-*France*.

While we continued at Fort *Frontenac*, the *Iroquefe* who live at *Ganeouffe* and *Quentè*, at the diftance of feven or eight Leagues from thence,[1] threw in upon us Harts, Roe-bucks, Turkeys and Fifh; in exchange for Needles, Knives, Powder

[1] In 1668 several Cayugas, asking for a missionary, came to Montreal from a new settlement recently made on Quinté Bay, on the north shore of Lake Ontario. The Sulpitians sent out two of their members, who maintained the mission until 1673, when Frontenac granted the Recollects the chaplaincy of his new fort. Hennepin was stationed here, and administered to the mission for several years. See Hennepin, *New Discovery* (Thwaites's ed., Chicago, 1903), pp. 47, 97. The mission was abandoned during the Iroquois disturbances just preceding the outbreak of Frontenac's War (or about 1687).— Ed.

and Ball. Towards the end of *Auguſt* Mr. *de la Barre* joyn'd us; but he was dangerouſly ill of a Feaver, which rag'd in like manner among moſt of his Militia; ſo that only our three Companies were free from Sickneſs. This Feaver was of the intermitting kind; and the convulſive Motions, Tremblings, and frequency of the Pulſe that attended the cold Fit, were ſo violent, that moſt of our ſick Men dy'd in the ſecond or third Fit. Their Blood was [33] of a blackiſh brown colour, and tainted with a ſort of yellowiſh Serum, not unlike *Pus* or corrupt Matter. Mr. *de la Barre's* Phyſician, who in my opinion knew as little of the true cauſes of Feavers as *Hippocrates* or *Galen*, and a hundred thouſand beſides; this mighty Phyſician, I ſay, pretending to trace the cauſe of the Feaver I now ſpeak of, imputed it to the unfavourable qualities of the Air and the Aliment. His plea was, that the exceſſive heat of the ſeaſon, put the Vapours or Exhalations into an over-rapid Motion; that the Air was ſo over-rarify'd, that we did not ſuck in a ſufficient quantity of it; that the ſmall quantity we did receive was loaded with Inſects and impure Corpuſculum's, which the fatal neceſſity of Reſpiration oblig'd us to ſwallow; and that by this means nature was put into diſorder: He added, that the uſe of Brandy and ſalt Meat ſower'd the Blood, that this ſowerneſs occaſion'd a ſort of Coagulation of the Chyle and Blood, that the Coagulation hindered it to circulate thro' the Heart with a due degree of Celerity; and that thereupon there inſued an extraordinary Fermentation, which is nothing elſe but a Feaver. But after all, to my mind this Gentleman's

Syfteme was too much upon the *Iroquefe* ftrain; for at that rate the Diftemper muft have feiz'd all without diftinction, whereas neither our Soldiers nor the feafon'd *Canadans* were troubled with it; for it raged only among the Militia, who being unacquainted with the way of fetting the Boats with Poles, were forc'd at every turn to get into the water and drag 'em up againft the rapid Stream: Now, the waters of that Country being naturally cold, and the heat being exceffive, the Blood might thereupon freeze by way of *Antiperiftafis*, and fo occafion the Feaver I fpeak of, purfuant to the common Maxim, *Omnis repentina mutatio eft periculofa*, i. e. *All fudden changes are of dangerous Confequence.*

[34] As foon as Mr. *de la Barre* recover'd, he imbarqu'd in order to continue his march; tho' he might have eafily known, that after halting fourteen or fifteen days at that Fort, when the feafon was fo far advanc'd, he could not pretend to compafs the end of his Expedition. We row'd Night and Day the Weather being very calm, and in five or fix days came before the River of *Famine*, where we were forc'd to put in upon the apprehenfion of a Storm.[1] Here we met with a Canow that Mr. *Dulhut* had fent from *Miffilimakinac*, with advice, that purfuant to orders he had ingag'd the *Hurons*,

[1] Rivière la Famine was previously identified with Onondaga (Oswego) River, but later investigations have proven that it was Salmon River, Oswego County, N. Y. See N. Y. *Colonial Documents*, ix, p. 242. The region was not named for lack of supplies in La Barre's army, but from some previous Indian famine. La Barre encamped on the northwest side of the river, opposite the present Port Ontario. See Hawley, *Early Chapters of Cayuga History* (Auburn, 1879).—Ed.

Outaoua's, and ſome other People, to joyn his Army; in which he had above two hundred brave * Foreſt Rangers. Theſe News were very acceptable to Mr. *de la Barre;* but at the ſame time he was very much perplexed; for I'm perſwaded he repented oftner than once, of his entring upon an Expedition that he foreſaw would prove Succeſsleſs; and to aggravate the danger of his Enterpriſe, the *Iroqueſe* had at that time an opportunity to fall upon us. In fine, after a mature conſideration of the Conſequences, and of the Difficulties that ſtood in the way, he ſent back the Canow to Mr. *Dulhut*, with orders to diſmiſs the Foreſt Rangers and Savages immediately, where ever he was, and by all means to avoid the approaching to his Troops. By good luck Mr. *Dulhut* had not yet reach'd *Niagara*, when he receiv'd theſe Orders; with which the Savages that accompany'd him were ſo diſſatisfied, that they threw out all manner of Invectives againſt the *French* Nation.[1]

**See* Coureurs de Bois *in the Table.*

As ſoon as Mr. *de la Barre* had diſpatch'd this Canow, he

[1] Daniel Greysolon DuLuth (duLhut), "king of coureurs des bois," had been an officer in the French army. Coming to Canada before 1674, he set out four years later on an expedition to the Sioux country, and remained in the Northwest for over twelve years, exploring, trading, and securing the Indians in the French interest. He was so powerful that his services were sought by successive governors. He brought an Indian force to the aid of Denonville in 1687; and in 1694 was fighting the Iroquois under Frontenac. Two years later he was commandant at Fort Frontenac, and died in 1710. See McLennan "Gentlemen of the King's Guard," in *Harper's Magazine*, Sept., 1893; and "Death of DuLuth" in *Roy. Soc. Proc.*, 2d series, ix, pp. 39-47. The Huron and Ottawa who composed his party upon the occasion here cited by Lahontan, were from those tribes that had fled from the Iroquois attacks and settled under French protection at Fort Mackinac.— Ed.

ſent Mr. *le Moine* to the Village of the *Onnontagues*, which lay about eighteen Leagues up the River. This Mr. *le Moine* was a Gentleman of *Normandy*, and highly eſteem'd by the *Iroqueſe*, who [35] call'd him *Akoueſſan*, i. e. *the Partridge.*[1] His Orders were, to indeavour by all means to bring along with him ſome of the old ſtanders of that Nation; and accordingly he return'd in a few days, accompany'd with one of their moſt conſiderable Grandees, who had a Train of thirty young Warriours, and was diſtinguiſh'd by the Title of the *Grangula.*[2] As ſoon as he debarqued, Mr. *de la Barre* ſent him a Preſent of Bread and Wine, and of thirty Salmon-Trouts, which they fiſh'd in that place in ſuch plenty, that they brought up a hundred at one caſt of a Net: At the ſame time he gave the Grandee to underſtand, that he congratulated his Arrival, and would be glad to have an Interview with him after he had reſted himſelf for ſome days. You muſt know that he had us'd the precaution of ſending the ſick back to the Colony,

[1] Charles Le Moyne, sieur de Longueuil, was a native of Dieppe, born in 1624. He came to Canada in 1641, and after four years among the Huron with the Jesuits, settled at Montreal. There he acted for many years as interpreter of the colony, and captain of militia. In 1655 he was captured by the Iroquois, who were so impressed by his intrepidity that they adopted him into their tribe, and sent him home unharmed. The value of his services to the colony was so great that he was ennobled by the king (1668). His sons distinguished themselves in the history of the colony; the eldest, first baron of Longueuil, was governor of Canada; Iberville and Bienville were the founders of Louisiana.— Ed.

[2] By this Latinized form Lahontan designates the Iroquois chieftain known by the French as La Grande Gueule (Big Mouth), in allusion to his oratorical ability. His Indian name was Otréouaté, and he belonged to the Onondaga tribe. Although not one of their great chiefs, he was a wily diplomatist, and owed his influence to skill in oratory and powers of dissimulation. For his signature in the totems of his clan, see N. Y. *Colon. Docs.*, ix, p. 386.— Ed.

that the *Iroquese* might not perceive the weaknefs of his Forces; and to favour the Stratagem, Mr. *le Moine* reprefented to the *Grangula*, that the Body of the Army was left behind at Fort *Frontenac*, and that the Troops he faw in our Camp, were the General's Guards. But unhappily one of the *Iroquese* that had a fmattering of the *French* Tongue, having ftroul'd in the Night-time towards our Tents, over-heard what we faid, and fo reveal'd the Secret. Two days after their arrival, the *Grangula* gave notice to Mr. *de la Barre* that he was ready for an Interview; and accordingly an hour being appointed, the whole Company appear'd as the figure reprefents it.

The *Grangula* fat on the Eaft fide, being plac'd at the head of his Men, with his Pipe in his Mouth, and the great *Calumet* of Peace before him. He was very attentive to the following Harangue, pronounc'd by our Interpreters; which you cannot well underftand, without a previous explication of the *Calumet*, and the *Coliers* that it mentions.

[36] The *Calumet of Peace* is made of certain Stones, or of Marble, whether red, black, or white. The Pipe or Stalk is four or five foot long; the body of the *Calumet* is eight Inches long, and the Mouth or Head in which the Tobacco is lodg'd, is three Inches in length; its figure approaches to that of a Hammer. The red *Calumets* are moft efteem'd. The Savages make ufe of 'em for Negotiations and State Affairs, and efpecially in Voyages; for when they have a *Calumet* in their hand, they go where they will in fafety. The *Calumet* is trimm'd with yellow, white, and green Feathers,

and has the ſame effect among the Savages, that the Flag of friendſhip has amongſt us; for to violate the Rights of this venerable Pipe, is among them a flaming Crime, that will draw down miſchief upon their Nations.[1] As for the *Coliers*, they are certain ſwathes of two or three Foot in length, and ſix Inches in breadth; being deck'd with little Beads made of a certain ſort of ſhells that they find upon the Sea ſhoar, between New-*York* and *Virginia*. Theſe Beads are round, and as thick as a little Pea; but they are twice as long as a grain of Corn: Their colour is either blew or white; and they are bor'd thro' juſt like Pearl, being run after the ſame manner upon ſtrings that lye ſideways one to another. Without the intervention of theſe *Coliers*, there's no buſineſs to be negotiated with the Savages; for being altogether unacquainted with writing, they make uſe of them for Contracts and Obligations. Sometimes they keep for an Age the *Coliers* that they have receiv'd from their Neighbours; and in regard that every *Colier* has its peculiar Mark, they learn from the old Perſons, the Circumſtances of the time and place in which they were deliver'd; but after that age is over, they are made uſe of for new Treaties.[2]

---

[1] On the uses of the calumet, see *Jesuit Relations*, index. The red stone is known as "catlinite," from the artist George Catlin, who was the first to explore and describe the quarries at Pipestone, Minnesota. — Ed.

[2] These "collars" (so called by the French; the English entitled them "belts") were made of wampum, of which Lahontan has here described the primitive type in the form of shells. Later they were made of beads. See *Jesuit Relations*, viii, note 70; also Hale, "Indian Wampum Records" in *Popular Science Monthly*, February, 1897. Belts of wampum were always used in the negotiation of Indian treaties; they were sent with envoys as credentials, preserved by a chief as the ensign of his authority, employed in ransom and atonement for crime, and also as ornament and in place of money. The English term was "wampum"; that of the French, "porcelain."—Ed.

[37] *Mr.* de la Barre's *Harangue, was to this purpoſe.*

'The King, my Maſter, being inform'd that the five '*Iroqueſe* Nations have for a long time made infractions 'upon the meaſures of Peace, order'd me to come hither with 'a Guard, and to ſend *Akoueſſan* to the Canton of the *Onno*'*tagues*, in order to an Interview with their principal Leaders, 'in the Neighbourhood of my Camp. This great Monarch 'means, that you and I ſhould ſmoak together in the great '*Calumet* of Peace, with the Proviſo, that you ingage in the 'name of the *Tſonnontouans*, *Goyoguans*, *Onnotagues*, *Onnoyoutes*, 'and *Agnies*, to make reparation to his Subjects, and to be 'guilty of nothing for the future, that may occaſion a fatal 'rupture.

'The *Tſonnontouans*, *Goyogouans*, *Onnotagues*, *Onnoyoutes* and '*Agnies*, have ſtrip'd, rob'd, and abus'd all the Foreſt-Rangers, 'that travel'd in the way of Trade to the Country of the '*Illineſe*, of the *Oumamis*, and of ſeveral other Nations, who 'are my Maſter's Children.[1] Now this uſage being in high 'violation of the Treaties of Peace concluded with my Prede'ceſſor, I am commanded to demand Reparation, and at the

[1] According to Parkman, La Barre had brought this about by giving leave to the Iroquois to plunder La Salle's canoes. The Indians had taken advantage of this permission to seize several canoes and employés of the governor himself. See Parkman, *Frontenac*, pp. 86, 87.

The Illinois Indians, of Algonquian stock, were encountered by the French in the state to which they have given their name. La Salle had founded his colony among them, only to have it raided by the Iroquois. See Hennepin, *New Discovery* (Thwaites's ed.), pp. 337-342. The Miami (Oumamis) were first encountered by white men in Wisconsin. On their migrations see *Wis. Hist. Colls.*, xvi, pp. 41, 99, 127, 285, 361, 398.—Ed.

'ſame time to declare, that in caſe of their refuſal to comply 'with my demands, or of relapſing into the like Robberies, 'War is poſitively proclaim'd.

This Colier *makes my words good.*

'The Warriours of theſe five Nations have introduc'd the '*Engliſh* to the *Lakes*, belonging to the King my Maſter, and 'into the Country of thoſe Nations to whom my Maſter is a 'Father: This they have done with a deſign to ruine the 'Commerce of his Subjects, and to oblige theſe Nations to 'depart from their due Allegiance; notwithſtanding the Re-'monſtrances of the late Governor [38] of New-*York*, who ſaw 'thro the danger that both they and the *Engliſh* expos'd them-'ſelves to. At preſent I am willing to forget thoſe Actions; 'but if ever you be guilty of the like for the future, I have 'expreſs orders to declare War.

This Colier *warrants my Words.*

'The ſame Warriours have made ſeveral barbarous Incur-'ſions upon the Country of the *Illineſe*, and the *Oumamis*. 'They have maſſacred Men, Women, and Children; they 'have took, bound, and carried off an infinite number of the 'Natives of thoſe Countries, who thought themſelves ſecure 'in their Villages in a time of Peace. Theſe People are my 'Maſter's Children, and therefore muſt hereafter ceaſe to be 'your Slaves. I charge you to reſtore 'em to their Liberty, 'and to ſend 'em home without delay; for if the five Nations 'refuſe to comply with this demand, I have expreſs orders to 'declare War.

This Colier *makes my words good.*

'This is all I had to ſay to the *Grangula*, whom I deſire to 'report to the five Nations, this Declaration, that my Maſter 'commanded me to make. He wiſhes they had not oblig'd 'him to ſend a potent Army to the Fort of * *Cat*-'*aracouy*, in order to carry on a War that will 'prove fatal to them: And he will be very much 'troubled, if it ſo falls out, that this Fort which is a work of 'Peace, muſt be imploy'd for a Priſon to your Militia. Theſe 'miſchiefs ought to be prevented by mutual endeavours: The '*French* who are the Brethren and Friends of the five Nations, 'will never diſturb their Repoſe; provided they make the ſatis-'faction I now demand, and prove religious obſervers of their 'Treaties. I wiſh my words [39] may produce the deſir'd 'effect; for if they do not, I am oblig'd to joyn the Governor 'of New-*York*, who has orders from the King his Maſter, to 'aſſiſt me to burn the five Villages, and cut you off.

* *The* French *call it Fort* Frontenac.

This Colier *confirms my word.*

'While Mr. *de la Barre*'s Interpreter pronounc'd this Harangue, the *Grangula* did nothing but look'd upon the end of his Pipe: After the Speech was finiſh'd he roſe, and having took five or ſix turns in the Ring that the *French* and the Savages made, he return'd to his place, and ſtanding upright ſpoke after the following manner to the General, who ſat in his Chair of State.

* *This Title they give to the Governor-General of* Canada.

'* *Onnontio*, I honour you, and all the 'Warriors that accompany me do the ſame: 'Your Interpreter has made an end of his 'Diſcourſe, and now I come to begin mine. 'My Voice glides to your Ear, pray liſten to my words.

'*Onnontio*, in ſetting out from *Quebec*, you muſt needs have 'fancy'd that the ſcorching Beams of the Sun had burnt down 'the Foreſts which render our Country unacceſſible to the '*French;* or elſe that the Inundations of the Lake had ſur-'rounded our Cottages, and confin'd us as Priſoners. This 'certainly was your thought; and it could be nothing elſe but 'the curioſity of ſeeing a burnt or drown'd Country, that 'mov'd you to undertake a Journey hither. But now you 'have an opportunity of being undeceiv'd, for I and my war-'like Retinue come to aſſure you, that the *Tſonontouans*, *Goyogo-'uans*, *Onnontagues*, *Onnoyoutes* and *Agnies*, are not yet deſtroy'd. 'I return you thanks in their name, for bringing into their 'Country the *Calumet* of Peace, that your Predeceſſor receiv'd 'from their hands. At the ſame time I congratulate your [40] 'Happineſs, in having left under Ground '* the bloody Axe, that has been ſo often 'dy'd with the blood of the *French*. I muſt 'tell you, *Onnontio*, I am not aſleep, my Eyes are open; and 'the Sun that vouchſafes the light, gives me a clear view of a 'great Captain at the head of a Troop of Soldiers, who ſpeaks 'as if he were aſleep. He pretends that he do's not approach

* *Burying the Axe ſignifies Peace.*

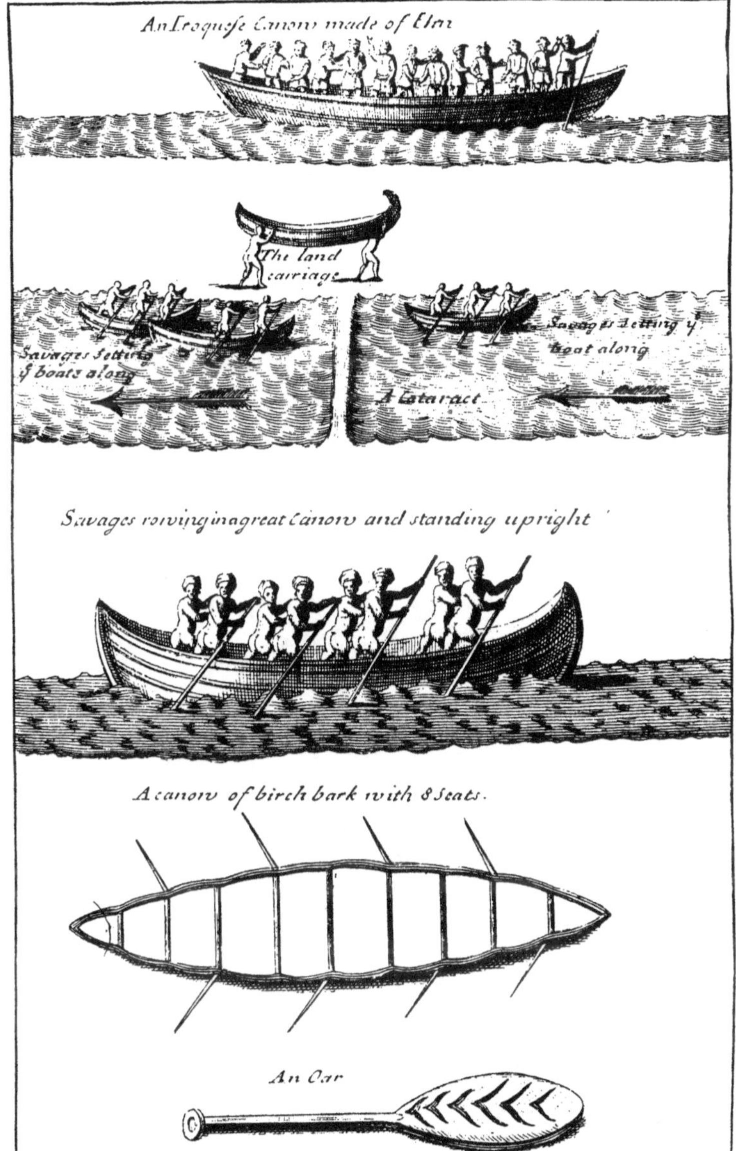
An Iroquese Canow made of Elm
The land carriage
Savages setting ye boats along
Savages setting ye boat along
A Cataract
Savages rowing in a great Canow and standing upright
A canow of birch bark with 8 Seats.
An Oar

'to this Lake with any other view, than to ſmoak with the '*Onnotagues* in the great *Calumet;* but the *Grangula* knows 'better things, he ſees plainly that the *Onnontio* mean'd to 'knock 'em on the Head, if the *French* Arms had not been ſo 'much weaken'd.

'I perceive that the *Onnontio* raves in a Camp of ſick 'People, whoſe lives the great Spirit has ſav'd by viſiting 'them with Infirmities. Do you hear, *Onnontio*, our Women 'had took up their Clubbs; and the Children and the old 'Men, had viſited your Camp with their Bows and Arrows, 'if our Warlike Men had not ſtop'd and diſarm'd 'em, when '*Akoueſſan* your Ambaſſadour appear'd before my Village. 'But I have done, I'll talk no more of that.

'You muſt know, *Onnontio*, we have robb'd no *French-Men*, 'but thoſe who ſupply'd the *Illineſe* and the *Oumamis* (our 'Enemies) with Fuſees, with Powder, and with Ball: Theſe 'indeed we took care of, becauſe ſuch Arms might have coſt 'us our life. Our Conduct in that point is of a piece with 'that of the Jeſuits, who ſtave all the barrels of Brandy that 'are brought to our Cantons, leſt the People getting drunk 'ſhould knock them in the Head. Our Warriours have no 'Beavers to give in exchange for all the Arms they take from 'the *French;* and as for the old ſuperannuated People, they 'do not think of bearing Arms.

[41] *This* Colier *comprehends my word.*

'We have conducted the *Engliſh* to our '*Lakes, in order to traffick with the *Outaouas*, 'and the *Hurons;* juſt as the *Algonkins* con-

* *They pretend to the property of the Lakes.*

'ducted the *French* to our five Cantons, in order to carry on a 'Commerce that the *Englifh* lay claim to as their Right. We 'are born Freemen, and have no dependance either upon the '*Onnontio* or the †*Corlar*.[1] We have a power to 'go where we pleafe, to conduct who we will 'to the places we refort to, and to buy and fell 'where we think fit. If your Allies are your 'Slaves or Children, you may e'en treat 'em as fuch, and rob ''em of the liberty of entertaining any other Nation but your 'own.

† Corlar *is the Title of the Governor of New*-York.

This Colier *contains my word.*

'We fell upon the *Illinefe* and the *Oumamis*, becaufe they 'cut down the trees of Peace that ferv'd for limits or bound-'aries to our Frontiers. They came to hunt Beavers upon 'our Lands; and contrary to the cuftom of all the Savages, 'have carried off whole Stocks, ||both Male and 'Female. They have ingag'd the *Chaouanons* 'in their intereft, and entertain'd 'em in their 'Country.[2] They fupply'd 'em with Fire-Arms, 'after the concerting of ill defigns againft us. 'We have done lefs than the *Englifh* and the

|| *Among the Savages, 'tis a capital Crime to deftroy all the Beavers of a Setlement.*

---

[1] The significance of the word Onontio, by which the Iroquois designated the governor of Canada, was said to be "great" or "beautiful mountain," and to have been a translation of the name of the second governor, Montmagny. Corlaer, the Indian name for the governor of New York, was derived from Van Curler, an early Dutch trader who had much influence among the Mohawk.—ED.

[2] The Shawnee (French Chaouanon) were an Algonquian tribe, concerning whose migrations and relations there has been considerable controversy. La Salle found them in the Ohio country, where in the eighteenth century they were a terror to the Western settlers of the United States. See *Jesuit Relations*, xlvii, p. 316; lxi, p. 249; *Wis. Hist. Colls.*, xvi, pp. 48, 364; xvii, index.—ED.

'*French*, who without any right, have uſurp'd the Grounds 'they are now poſſeſs'd of; and of which they have diſlodg'd 'ſeveral Nations, in order to make way for their building of 'Cities, Villages, and Forts.

[42] *This* Colier *contains my word.*

'I give you to know, *Onnontio*, that my Voice is the Voice 'of the five *Iroqueſe* Cantons. This is their Anſwer, pray 'incline your Ear, and liſten to what they repreſent.

'The *Tſonontouans*, *Goyogouans*, *Onnontagues*, *Onnoyoutes*, and '*Agnies* declare, that they interr'd * the 'Axe at *Cataracouy*, in the preſence of your 'Precedeſſor, in the very center of the Fort; 'and planted the Tree of Peace in the ſame 'place, that it might be carefully preſerv'd; 'that 'twas then ſtipulated, that the Fort ſhould be us'd as a 'place of retreat for Merchants, and not a refuge for Soldiers; 'and that inſtead of Arms and Ammunition, it ſhould be made 'a Receptacle of only Beaver-Skins, and Merchandize Goods. 'Be it known to you, *Onnontio*, that for the future you ought 'to take care, that ſo great a number of Martial-Men as I now 'ſee, being ſhut up in ſo ſmall a Fort, do not ſtifle and choak 'the Tree of Peace. Since it took Root ſo eaſily, it muſt 'needs be of pernicious conſequence to ſtop its growth, and 'hinder it to ſhade both your Country and ours with its 'Leaves. I do aſſure you, in the name of the five Nations, 'that our Warriors ſhall dance the *Calumet* Dance under its

* *Interring the Axe, ſignifies the making of a Peace; and the digging of it up imports a Declaration of War.*

† *This Phrase signifies keeping the Peace.*

'branches; that they shall rest in Tranquility upon their † Matts, and will never 'dig up the Axe to cut down the Tree of 'Peace; till such time as the *Onnontio* and the *Corlar*, do either 'joyntly or separately offer to invade the Country, that the 'great Spirit has dispos'd of in the favour of our Anceſtors.

[43] *This* Colier *contains my word; and the other comprehends the power granted to me by the five Nations.*

Then the *Grangula* addreſs'd himſelf to Mr. *le Moine*, and ſpoke to this purpoſe.

'*Akoueſſan*, take Heart, you are a Man of Senſe; ſpeak and 'explain my meaning; be ſure you forget nothing, but declare 'all that thy Brethren and thy Friends repreſent to thy chief '*Onnontio*, by the voice of the *Grangula*, who pays you all 'Honour and Reſpect, and invites you to accept of this Pre'ſent of Beavers, and to aſſiſt at his Feaſt immediately.

'This other Preſent of Beavers is ſent by the five Nations 'to the *Onnontio*.

As ſoon as the *Grangula* had done, Mr. *le Moine* and the Jeſuits that were preſent, explain'd his anſwer to Mr. *de la Barre*,[1] who thereupon retir'd to his Tent and ſtorm'd and bluſter'd, till ſome body came and repreſented to him, that, *Iroca Progenies neſcit habere modos*, i. e. *The* Iroqueſe *are always upon extreams.* The *Grangula* danc'd after the *Iroqueſe* manner,

[1] Father Jacques Bruyas was interpreter upon this occasion. See *ante*, p. 56, note 1.—Ed.

by way of prelude to his Entertainment; after which he regal'd ſeveral of the *French.* Two days after he and his Martial-Retinue return'd to their own Country, and our Army ſet out for *Monreal.* As ſoon as the General was on board, together with the few healthy Men that remain'd, the Canows were diſpers'd, for the Militia ſtraggled here and there, and every one made the beſt of his way home. Our three Companies indeed kept together, becauſe all of us, both Officers and Soldiers, were carried in flat-bottom'd Boats, made of Deal on purpoſe for our uſe. However, I could have wiſh'd to have run down the falls and Cataracts [44] in the ſame Canow that brought me up, for every body thought we ſhould have been caſt away at theſe Paſſes, which are full of Eddy's and Rocks; and 'twas never heard before, that ſuch Precipices were paſs'd with Deal Boats either upwards or downwards. But we were forc'd to run all hazards, and had certainly been ſwallow'd up in thoſe Mountains of Water, if we had not oblig'd ſeveral Canows to ſhoot the Cataracts at the head of our Boats, in order to ſhew us the way; at the ſame time we had prepar'd our Soldiers for rowing, and ſhieving upon occaſion. Do but conſider, Sir, that the Currents run as faſt as a Cannon Ball; and that one falſe ſtroak of the Oar, would have run us unavoidably upon the Rocks; for we are oblig'd to ſteer a Zig-zag courſe purſuant to the thread of the Stream, which has fifty windings. The Boats which are loaded are ſometimes loſt in thoſe places. But after all, tho' the riſque we run be very great, yet by way of Compenſation, one has the ſatisfaction of running a great way in a little time; for we run from *Galete* to this Town in two days time, notwithſtanding that we croſs'd the two ſtagnating Lakes I took notice of before.

As ſoon as we landed, we receiv'd advice that the *Chevalier de Callieres* was come to ſupply the room of Mr. *Perrot*, the Governor of this place.[1] Mr. *Perrot* has had ſeveral ſcuffles with Mr. *de Frontenac*, and Mr. *de la Barre;* of which you may expect a farther account, when I am better inform'd. All the World blames our General for his bad Succeſs: 'Tis talk'd publickly, that his only deſign was to cover the ſending of ſeveral Canows to traffick with the Savages in thoſe Lakes for Beaver-Skins. The People here are very buſie in wafting over to Court a thouſand Calumnies againſt him; both the Clergy and the Gentlemen of the long Robe, write to his diſadvantage. Tho' after all, the whole charge is [45] falſe; for the poor Man could do no more than he did.[2] Juſt now, I was inform'd that Mr. *Hainaut*, Mr. *Montortier*, and Mr. *Durivau*, three Captains of Ships, are arriv'd at *Quebec*, with a deſign to paſs the Winter there, and to aſſiſt him as Counſellors; and that the

[1] Louis Hector, sieur de Callières-Bonnevue was born in 1646 or 1647, and early adopted the profession of arms. Coming to Canada in 1684 as governor of Montreal, he soon proved himself an important factor in the defense of the colony. He ably seconded the measures of Frontenac, and upon his death (1698) was appointed his successor. He brought Frontenac's war with the Iroquois to a successful issue, and made a peace (1701) with this redoubtable foe. His death occurred in 1703.—Ed.

[2] For La Barre's own account of the expedition, see N. Y. *Colon. Docs.*, ix, pp. 239–243. The account of his detractors, headed by the intendant Meules, follows, pp. 244–248.—Ed.

laſt of theſe three has brought with him an Independent Company, to be commanded by himſelf.[1]

I ſhall have no opportunity of writing again before the next Spring; for the laſt Ships that are to return for *France* this year, are now ready to ſail.

I am, SIR, Yours, &c.

[1] These officers, whose names are given, Desnots, Montortié, and Du Rivau Huet, came out in charge of reinforcements in the autumn of 1684, but were permitted to return the following year. See N. Y. *Colon. Docs.*, ix, p. 250; *Canadian Archives*, supplement, 1899, pp. 269, 270.—Ed.

LETTER VIII.

Dated at *Monreal, June* 28. 1685.

Reprefenting the Fortifications of Monreal, *and the indifcreet Zeal of the Priefts, who are Lords of that Town: With a Defcription of* Chambli, *and of the Commerce of the Savages upon the great Lakes.*

SIR,

I HAVE juft receiv'd yours, by a fmall Veffel of *Bourdeaux* loaded with Wine; which is the firft that came to *Quebec* this Year. I am mightily pleas'd to hear that the King has granted to *Mr. de la Salle* four Ships, to go upon the Difcovery of the Mouth of the *Miffifipi;* and cannot but admire your Curiofity, in defiring to know the Occurrences of this Place, and how I fpent my time in the Winter.

Mr. *de Callieres* was no fooner poffefs'd of his Government, than he order'd all the Inhabitants of this Town, and of the adjacent Country, to cut down and bring in great Stakes, of fifteen Foot in length, [46] to fortifie the Town. During the Winter, thefe Orders were purfued with fo much Application, that all things are now ready for making the Inclofure; in which five or fix hundred Men are to be imploy'd. I fpent part of the Winter in Hunting with the *Algonkins*, in order to a more perfect knowledge of their Language; and the reft I ſpent in this Place, with a great deal of uneaſineſs: for, here we cannot enjoy our ſelves, either at Play, or in viſiting the Ladies, but 'tis preſently carried to the Curate's ears, who takes publick notice of it in the Pulpit. His Zeal goes ſo far, as even to name the Perſons: and ſince he refuſes the Sacrament of the Holy Supper to Ladies of Quality, upon the moſt ſlender Pretences, you may eaſily gueſs at the other ſteps of his Indeſcretion. You cannot imagine to what a pitch theſe Eccleſiaſtical Lords have ſcrew'd their Authority: They excommunicate all the Masks, and wherever they ſpy 'em, they run after 'em to uncover their Faces, and abuſe 'em in a reproachful manner: In fine, they have a more watchful eye over the Conduct of the Girls and married Women, than their Fathers and Husbands have. They cry out againſt thoſe that do not receive the Sacrament once a Month; and at *Eaſter* they oblige all ſorts of Perſons to give in Bills to their Confeſſors. They prohibit and burn all the Books that treat of any other Subject but Devotion. When I think of this Tyranny, I cannot but be inrag'd at the impertinent Zeal of the Curate of this City. This inhumane Fellow came one day to my Lodging, and finding the Romance of the Adventures of *Petronius* upon my Table, he fell upon it with an unimaginable fury, and tore out almoſt all the Leaves. This Book I valued more than my Life, becauſe 'twas not caſtrated; and indeed I was ſo provok'd when I ſaw it all in wrack, that if my Landlord had not held me, I had gone immediately to that turbulent Paſtor's [47] Houſe, and would have pluck'd out the Hairs of his Beard with as little mercy as he did the

Leaves of my Book. Thefe Animals cannot content themfelves with the ftudying of Mens Actions, but they muft likewife dive into their Thoughts. By this Sketch, Sir, you may judge what a pleafant Life we lead here.

The 30th of the laft *March* the Ice melted; and the River being then open, I was fent with a fmall Detachment to *Chambli:* for commonly the Sun refumes its Vigour here much about that time. *Chambli* ftands on the brink of a Bafin, about five or fix Leagues off this Place: That Bafin is two Leagues in Circumference, and receives the Lake of *Champlain* by a Water-fall that is a League and a half in length; out of which there arifes a River that difembogues at *Sorel* into the River of St. *Laurence*, as I intimated above in my fourth Letter. In former times this Place had a great Trade in Beaver-skins, which is now decay'd: for the *Soccokis*, the *Mahingans*, and the *Openangos*, us'd formerly to refort thither in fhoals, to exchange their Furs for other Goods; but at prefent they are retir'd to the *Englifh* Colonies, to avoid the purfuit of the *Iroquefe.*[1] The *Champlain* Lake, which lies above that Water-fall, is eighty Leagues in circumference. At the end of this Lake we met with another, call'd *S. Sacrement*, by which one may go very eafily to *New-York*, there being but

[1] These were tribes who had formerly occupied Acadia and Maine, and had migrated with the Abenaki to the St. Lawrence. The Sokoki (Soccoki) were Abenaki whose habitat was the Saco River, and whose enmity with the Mohawk was of long standing. One of this tribe, Squanto, led the attack on the English settlement at Saco, Sept. 18, 1675. The Openangoes were the Algonquian of New Brunswick, called by the English Quoddy Indians. The Mahican (Mohegan) was a numerous Algonquian tribe, whose first habitat was the valley of the Hudson, later that of the Connecticut. The French usually called them Loups (Wolves). — Ed.

a Land-carriage of two Leagues from thence to the River *Du Fer*, which falls into the *Manathe*.[1] While I was at *Chambli*, I ſaw two Canows loaded with Beaver-skins paſs privately by that way; and 'twas thought they were ſent thither by *Mr. de la Barre*. This ſmuggling way of Trade is expreſly prohibited: for they are oblig'd to carry theſe Skins before the Office of the Company, where they are rated at an Hundred and 60 *per Cent.* leſs than the *Engliſh* buy 'em at in their Colonies.[2] But the little Fort that ſtands at the bottom [48] of the Water-fall, upon the brink of the Baſin of *Chambli*, being only ſingle Palliſadoes, it cannot hinder People to paſs that way; eſpecially conſidering that the Proſpect, of ſo great a profit, renders the Paſſengers the more daring. The Inhabitants of the adjacent Villages are very much expos'd to the Incurſions of the *Iroqueſe* in time of War. Notwithſtanding the weakneſs of the Fort, I continued in that place a Month and a half, and then I return'd hither, where *Mr. de la Barre* arriv'd ſome days after; being accompany'd with Mr. *Hennaut*,

[1] The Indian name for Lake George was Andiatarocté, "where the lake is shut in." The Jesuit missionary Jogues named it (1646) Lac du St. Sacrement. In 1755 Sir William Johnson changed the name in honor of the English king. The River Du Fer is the north branch of the Hudson which falls into the "Manathe," i. e. the river of Manhattan. — ED.

[2] The Compagnie des Indes Occidentales was created May 24, 1664, and given the monopoly of the fur-trade of Canada. Upon the protestation of the colony's merchants, the company relinquished the monopoly in favor of the right to levy a duty of one-fourth of the beaver skins and one-tenth of the moose skins imported from Canada. The company was dissolved in 1674, but the king retained the duties in the same form, and farmed them out for 350,000 livres. The farmer formed a company, sometimes spoken of as the "Company of Domain." This is the one to which Lahontan here refers. The price paid for beaver was regulated by edict. — ED.

Mr. *Montortier*, and Mr. *du Rivau*. Much about the ſame day there arriv'd 25 or 30 Canows, belonging to the *Coureurs de Bois*, being homeward bound from the great Lakes, and laden with Beaver-skins. The Cargo of each Canow amounted to 40 Packs, each of which weighs 50 pound, and will fetch 50 Crowns at the Farmers Office. Theſe Canows were follow'd by 50 more of the *Outaouas* and *Hurons*, who come down every Year to the Colony, in order to make a better Market than they can do in their own Country of *Miſſilimakinac*, which lies on the Banks of the Lake of *Hurons*, at the Mouth of the Lake of the *Illineſe*.[1] Their way of Trading is as follows.

Upon their firſt Arrival, they incamp at the diſtance of five or ſix hundred Paces from the Town. The next day is ſpent in ranging their Canows, unloading their Goods, and pitching their Tents, which are made of Birch Bark. The next day after, they demand Audience of the Governour General; which is granted 'em that ſame day in a publick place. Upon this Occaſion, each Nation makes a Ring for it ſelf; the *Savages* ſit upon the Ground with their Pipes in their Mouths, and the Governour is ſeated in an arm'd Chair; after which, there ſtarts up an Orator or Speaker from one of theſe Nations, who makes an Harangue, importing, 'That his 'Brethren are come to viſit the Governour general, and to 'renew [49] with him their wonted Friendſhip: That their 'chief View is, to promote the Intereſt of the *French*, ſome of

[1] For the early history of Mackinac (Missilimakinac) see Thwaites, "Story of Mackinac," in *How George Rogers Clark Won the Northwest* (Chicago, 1903). Illinois Lake (Lac d' Ilinois) was an early name for Lake Michigan. — Ed.

'whom being unacquainted with the way of Traffick, and 'being too weak for the tranſporting of Goods from the 'Lakes, would be unable to deal in Beaver-skins, if his Breth-'ren did not come in perſon to deal with 'em in their own 'Colonies: That they know very well how acceptable their 'Arrival is to the Inhabitants of *Monreal*, in regard of the 'Advantage they reap by it: That in regard the Beaver-skins 'are much valued in *France*, and the *French* Goods given in 'exchange are of an inconſiderable Value, they mean to give 'the *French* ſufficient proof of their readineſs to furniſh 'em 'with what they deſire ſo earneſtly: That by way of prepara-'tion for another Years Cargo, they are come to take in 'Exchange, Fuſees, Powder, and Ball, in order to hunt great 'numbers of Beavers, or to gall the *Iroqueſe*, in caſe they offer 'to diſturb the *French* Settlements: And, in fine, That in con-'firmation of their Words, they throw a Purcelain *Colier* 'with ſome Beaver-skins to the *Kitchi-Okima* (ſo they call the 'Governour-General) whoſe Protection they lay claim to in 'caſe of any Robbery or Abuſe committed upon 'em in the 'Town.[1]

The Spokeſman having made an end of his Speech, returns to his Place, and takes up his Pipe; and then the Interpreter explains the Subſtance of the Harangue to the Governour, who commonly gives a very civil Anſwer, eſpecially if the Preſent be valuable: in conſideration of which, he likewiſe

[1] See Lahontan's explanation of this term in his Table, post. John Long, an English trader of a century later, gives nearly the same form for the Algonquian word. See Long, *Voyages and Travels* (Thwaites's ed., Cleveland, 1904), p. 242.—ED.

makes them a Prefent of fome trifling things. This done, the Savages rife up, and return to their Hutts to make fuitable Preparations for the enfuing Truck.

The next day the Savages make their Slaves carry the Skins to the Houfes of the Merchants, who bargain with 'em for fuch Cloaths as they want. All the Inhabitants of *Monreal* are allow'd to traffick with [50] 'em in any Commodity but Wine and Brandy; thefe two being excepted upon the account that when the Savages have got what they wanted, and have any Skins left, they drink to excefs, and then kill their Slaves; for when they are in drink, they quarrel and fight; and if they were not held by thofe who are fober, wou'd certainly make Havock one of another.[1] However, you muft obferve, that none of 'em will touch either Gold or Silver. 'Tis a comical fight, to fee 'em running from Shop to Shop, ftark naked, with their Bow and Arrow. The nicer fort of Women are wont to hold their Fans before their eyes, to prevent their being frighted with the view of their ugly Parts. But thefe merry Companions, who know the brisk She-Merchants as well as we, are not wanting in making an Offer, which is fometimes accepted of, when the Prefent is of

[1] The sale of liquor to the Indians had long agitated the colony. Champlain forbade the traffic (1633), except under strict control; but by 1660 it had attained such excesses that Bishop Laval pronounced excommunication against all colonists who sold brandy to savages, and the following year secured a royal edict punishing the crime with death. The excitement in the colony was so great that the edict was revoked, and in Frontenac's first governorship a compromise established, whereby the carrying of liquor into the woods was prohibited, but a moderate sale allowed in the colony. The question never ceased to be agitated by the missionaries, and the evasions of the ordinance by coureurs des bois were a standing grievance. — ED.

good Mettle. If we may credit the common Report, there are more than one or two of the Ladies of this Country, whoſe Conſtancy and Vertue has held out againſt the Attacks of ſeveral Officers, and at the ſame time vouchſaf'd a free acceſs to theſe naſty Lechers. 'Tis preſum'd their Compliance was the Effect of Curioſity, rather than of any nice Reliſh; for, in a word, the Savages are neither brisk, nor conſtant. But whatever is in the matter, the Women are the more excuſable upon this Head, that ſuch Opportunities are very unfrequent.

As ſoon as the Savages have made an end of their Truck, they take leave of the Governour, and ſo return home by the River of *Outaouas*.[1] To conclude, they did a great deal of good both to the Poor and Rich; for you will readily apprehend, that every body turns Merchant upon ſuch occaſions.

I am, *SIR*, *Yours*, &c.

---

[1] The Ottawa River was at first called River of the Algonkins, and Rivière des Prairies. Its present name arose not from its being the habitat of the Ottawa tribe, but because it was the route by which the Ottawa came to Canada from the "upper country" (*pays en haut*). — Ed.

LETTER IX.

Dated at *Boucherville*, Octob. 2. 1685.

Being an Account of the Commerce, and Trade of Monreal: *Of the Arrival of the Marquis of* Denonville *with ſome Troops; and of the recalling of* Mr. de la Barre. *With a curious Deſcription of certain Licenſes for Trading in Beaver-skins in the remote Countries.*

SIR,

I RECEIV'D your ſecond Letter three Weeks ago, but could not ſend a ſpeedier Anſwer, by reaſon that none of our Ships have yet ſet Sail for *France*. Since you want to know the nature of the Trade of *Monreal*, be pleas'd to take the following Account.

Almoſt all the Merchants of that City act only on the behalf of the *Quebec* Merchants, whoſe Factors they are. The Barques which carry thither dry Commodities, as well as Wine and Brandy, are but few in number; but then they make ſeveral Voyages in one Year from the one City to the other. The Inhabitants of the Iſland of *Monreal*, and the adjacent Cantons, repair twice a Year to the City of *Monreal*, where they buy Commodities fifty *per Cent.* dearer than at *Quebec*. The Savages of the neighbouring Countries, whether ſettled or erratick, carry thither the Skins of Beavers, Elks, Caribous, Foxes, and wild Cats; all which, they truck for Fuſees, Powder, Lead, and other Neceſſaries. There every one is allow'd to trade; and indeed 'tis the beſt place for the getting of an Eſtate in a ſhort time. All the Merchants have ſuch a perfect good underſtanding one with another, that they all ſell at the ſame price. [52] But when the Inhabitants of the Country find their Prices exorbitant, they raiſe their Commodities in proportion. The Gentlemen that have a Charge of Children, eſpecially Daughters, are oblig'd to be good Husbands, in order to bear the Expence of the magnificent Cloaths with which they are ſet off; for Pride, Vanity, and Luxury, reign as much in *New France* as in *Old France*. In my opinion, 'twould do well, if the King would order Commodities to be rated at a reaſonable Price, and prohibit the ſelling of Gold or Silver Brocadoes, Fringes, and Ribbands, as well as Points and rich Laces.

The Marquis of *Denonville* is come to ſucceed Mr. *de la Barre* in the quality of Governour-General; for the King has recall'd Mr. *de la Barre*, upon the Accuſations laid againſt him by his Enemies. To be ſure, you who are in *France* know better than I, that Mr. *de Denonville* was *Maitre de Camp* to the Queen's Regiment of Dragoons, which Place he ſold to Mr. *Murcey* when the King beſtow'd this Government upon him; and, that he brought with him ſome Companies of Marines, beſides his Lady and his Children: for it ſeems the danger and inconveniencies that attend ſuch a long and troublefome Voyage, made no Impreffion upon her.[1] This Governour ftay'd at firft fome Weeks at *Quebec*, after which he came to *Monreal*, with 500 or 600 Men of Regular Troops, and fent back the Captains *Hainaut*, *Montortier*, and *du Rivo*, with feveral other Officers. His Army is now in Winter Quarters all round *Monreal.* My Quarters are at a Place call'd *Boucherville*, which lies at the diftance of three Leagues from *Monreal.*[2] I have been here fifteen Days, and in all appearance fhall live more happily than in the Town, abating for the Solitude; for at leaft I fhall have no other oppofition to encounter in the cafe of Balls, Gaming, or Feafting, but the zealous Freaks of a filly Prieft. I am inform'd, that the Governour [53] has given Orders to compleat the Fortifications of *Monreal*,[3] and is now ready to embarque for *Quebec*, where our Governours commonly pafs the Winter. The Savages I fpoke of in my laft, met the *Iroquefe* upon the great River of the *Outaouas*, who inform'd 'em that the *Englifh* were making Preparations to tranfport to their Villages in *Miffilimakinac*, better and cheaper Commodities than thofe they had from the

[1] Jacques Réné de Brisay, marquis de Denonville, had served in the French armies for thirty years. He was a zealous and pious officer, but unequal to the difficulties of the situation in Canada; recalled in 1689, he was given honorable preferment at court. Madame de Denonville was the last French woman of rank to honor Canada with her presence at the government house. — ED.

[2] Boucherville was founded in 1667 by Pierre Boucher, formerly governor of Trois Rivières, and the first Canadian ennobled by the king. The Boucher family was one of the most important in the colony. See Sulte, "Pierre Boucher et son Livre" in *Can. Roy. Soc. Proc.*, series ii, vol. ii, sec. i, pp. 99–168. — ED.

[3] Montreal until this time had scarcely any military protection. In 1685 six hundred men were employed, under a royal engineer, in erecting a palisade over twelve feet in height, with five gates and five posterns. — ED.

French. This piece of News did equally alarm the Gentlemen, the Pedlers call'd *Coureurs de Bois*, and the Merchants; who, at that rate, would be confiderable Lofers: for you muft know, that *Canada* fubfifts only upon the Trade of Skins or Furrs, three fourths of which come from the People that live round the great Lakes: So that if the *Englifh* fhould put fuch a Defign in execution, the whole Country would fuffer by it; efpecially confidering, that 'twould fink certain Licenfes: an Account of which will be proper in this place.

Thefe Licenfes are granted in Writing by the Governours General, to poor Gentlemen and old Officers who have a Charge of Children. They are difpos'd of by the King's Orders; and the Defign of 'em is, to enable fuch Perfons to fend Commodities to thefe Lakes. The Number of the Perfons thus impower'd, ought not to exceed twenty five in one Year: but God knows how many more have private Licenfes. All other Perfons, of what Quality or Condition foever, are prohibited to go or fend to thefe Lakes, without fuch Licenfes, under the pain of Death.[1] Each Licenfe extends to the lading of two great Canows; and whoever procures a whole or a half Licenfe for himfelf, may either make ufe of it himfelf, or fell it to the

[1] The licenses (congés) for trade in the Western country were established in the latter years of Frontenac's first administration, partly, as Lahontan says, as a measure of charity or relief, partly as a means of restricting the coureurs des bois. The abuses were so great that in 1697 the king revoked all licenses and abolished the system. At the close of Queen Anne's War (1702–13), the licenses were again issued, and utilized as a means for provisioning expeditions against the Foxes and the other recalcitrant Indians of the upper country. See *Wis. Hist. Colls.*, xvi, xvii. This policy was maintained throughout the French regime. Henry describes it as still existing in 1765; see his *Travels and Adventures* (Bain's ed., Boston, 1901), pp. 183, 184.—Ed.

higheſt Bidder. Commonly they are bought at ſix hundred Crowns a-piece. Thoſe who purchaſe 'em are at no trouble in finding Pedlars or Foreſt-Rangers to undertake the long Voyages, which fetch the moſt conſiderable [54] Gains, and commonly extend to a Year, and ſometimes more. The Merchants put into the two Canows ſtipulated in the Licenſe, ſix Men with a thouſand Crowns-worth of Goods, which are rated to the Pedlars at fifteen *per Cent.* more than what they are ſold for in ready Money in the Colony. When the Voyage is perform'd, this Sum of a thouſand Crowns commonly brings in ſeven hundred *per Cent.* clear profit, and ſometimes more, ſometimes leſs; for theſe Sparks call'd *Coureurs de Bois* bite the Savages moſt dexterouſly, and the lading of two Canows, computed at a thouſand Crowns, is a Purchaſe for as many Beaver-skins as will load four Canows: Now, four Canows will carry a hundred and ſixty Packs of Skins, that is, forty a-piece; and reckoning each Pack to be worth fifty Crowns, the value of the whole amounts to eight thouſand Crowns. As to the Repartition of this extravagant Profit, 'tis made after the following manner: In the firſt place, the Merchant takes out of the whole bulk ſix hundred Crowns for the Purchaſe of his Licenſe; then a thouſand Crowns for the prime Coſt of the exported Commodities. After this, there remains 6400 Crowns of Surpluſage, out of which the Merchant takes forty *per Cent.* for Bottomree, which amounts to 2560 Crowns; and the Remainder is divided equally among the ſix *Coureurs de Bois*, who get little more than 600 Crowns a-piece: and indeed I muſt ſay 'tis fairly earn'd; for their Fatigue is inconceivable.

In the mean time, you muft remark, that over and above the foregoing profit, the Merchant gets 25 *per Cent.* upon his Beaver-skins by carrying them to the Office of the Farmers General, where the Price of four forts of Beaver-skins is fix'd. If the Merchant fells thefe Skins to any private Man in the Country for ready Money, he is paid in the current Money of the Country, which is of lefs value than the Bills of Exchange that the Director of [55] that Office draws upon *Rochel* or *Paris;* for there they are paid in *French* Livres, which are twenty *Sols*, whereas a *Canada* Livre is but fifteen *Sols.* This Advantage of 25 *per Cent.* is call'd *le Benefice;* but take notice, that 'tis only to be had upon Beaver-skins: for, if you pay to a *Quebec* Merchant 400 *Canada* Livres in Silver, and take from him a Bill of Exchange upon his Correfpondent in *France*, his Correfpondent will pay no more than 300 *French* Livres, which is a juft Equivalent.

This is the laft Intelligence I fhall give you for this Year, which has already brought in a very cold *Autumn.* The *Quebec* Ships muft fet Sail in the middle of *November*, purfuant to the wonted Cuftom. I am,

SIR,

Yours, &c.

LETTER X.

Dated at *Boucherville July* 8. 1686.

Relating the Arrival of Mr. de Champigni, *in the room of Mr.* de Meules, *who is recall'd to* France; *the arrival of the Troops that came along with him, the curiofity of the Rackets, and the way of hunting Elks; with a Defcription of that Animal.*

SIR,

THOUGH I have not heard from you this year, yet I will not flight this opportunity of writing to you. Some Ships from *France* are arriv'd at *Quebec*, and have brought over Mr. *de Champigni Noroua*, [56] with fome Companies of Marines. He comes to fupply the place of Mr. *de Meules*, whom the King recalls upon the unjuft complaints that are made of him. He is charg'd with preferring his private Intereft to the publick Good; but the charge is falfe, and he will eafily clear himfelf. I am apt to believe he may have carry'd on fome underhand Commerce, but in fo doing he injur'd no body; nay, on the contrary he has procur'd Bread for a thoufand poor Creatures, that without his Affiftance would have ftarv'd for Hunger. This new Intendant is defcended of one of the moft Illuftrious Families of the Robe in *France.* He is faid to be a Man of Honour, and Fame entitles his

Lady to a diftinguifhing Merit: I underftand, he and Mr. *Denonville* are bound fpeedily for *Monreal*, where they mean to take a review of the Inhabitants of this Ifland, and of the Neighbouring Cantons.[1] Probably, they take fuch precautions in order to fome new effort againft the *Iroquefe*. Laft Winter we had no new Occurrences in the Colony. I fpent the whole Winter at the hunting of Orignals or Elks along with the Savages, whofe Language I am learning, as I have intimated to you feveral times.[2]

The hunting of Elks is perform'd upon the Snow, with fuch *Rackets* as you fee defign'd in the annex'd Cutt. Thefe *Rackets* are two Foot and a half long, and fourteen Inches broad; their ledges are made of a very hard Wood, about an Inch thick, that faftens the Net juft like a Tennis Racket, from which they differ only in this; that thofe for the Tennis are made of Gut-ftrings, whereas the others are made of little thongs of the skins of Harts or Elks. In the Cut, you may perceive two little fpars of Wood, which run a-crofs to render the Net firmer and ftiffer. The hole that appears by the two Latchets, is the place in which they put the Toes and fore-

---

[1] Jean Bochart de Champigny was one of the most able and faithful of Canadian intendants. He was sent (1686) to replace Jacques de Mueles, who had come out with La Barre (1682), but had proven his bitter enemy, and was also complained of by the new governor Denonville. Champigny lived in concord with the latter, with whose politics he coincided. The harmony with Frontenac was less sincere; but in the last years of the latter, they became good friends. Champigny was recalled to France (1702) to take position as intendant at Havre. — ED.

[2] The "original" or elk of Canada is not to be confounded with the American elk or wapiti (*Cervus Canadensis*), called La Biche by the French; this is the moose of northern North America (*Cervus alches*). See Caton, *Antelope and Deer of North America* (New York, 1877). — ED.

part of the Foot; ſo that 'tis tied faſt by [57] the two Latchets, which run twice round about the Heel, and every ſtep they make upon the Snow, the fore-part of the Foot ſinks into that hole, as often as they raiſe their Heel. By the help of this Contrivance they walk faſter upon the Snow, than one can do with Shoes upon a beaten path: And indeed 'tis ſo neceſſary for them, that 'twould be otherwiſe impoſſible not only to hunt and range the Woods, but even to go to Church, notwithſtanding they are ſo near; for commonly the Snow is three or four Foot deep in that Country during the Winter. Being oblig'd to march thirty or forty Leagues in the Woods in purſuit of the above-mention'd Animals, I found that the fatigue of the Journey equal'd the pleaſure of it.

The *Orignal* is a ſort of Elk, not much different from that we find in *Muſcovy.* 'Tis as big as an *Auvergne* Moyle, and much of the ſame ſhape, abating for its Muzzle, its Tail, and its great flat Horns, which weigh ſometimes 300, and ſometimes 400 weight, if we may credit thoſe who pretend to have weigh'd 'em. This Animal uſually reſorts to planted Countries. Its Hair is long and brown; and the Skin is ſtrong and hard, but not thick. The Fleſh of the *Orignal,* eſpecially that of the Female ſort, eats deliciouſly; and 'tis ſaid, that the far hind Foot of the Female kind, is a Cure for the Falling-Sickneſs; it neither runs nor skips, but its trot will almoſt keep up with the running of a Hart. The Savages aſſure us, that in Summer 'twill trot three Days and three Nights without intermiſſion. This ſort of Animals commonly gather into a body towards the latter end of Autumn; and the Herds are largeſt in the beginning of the Spring, at which time the ſhe ones are in rutting; but after their heat is over, they all diſperſe themſelves. We hunted 'em in the following manner: Firſt of all, we went 40 Leagues to the Northward of the River of St. *Laurence*, [58] where we found a little Lake of three or four Leagues in Circumference, and upon the banks of that Lake, we made Hutts for our ſelves of the barks of Trees, having firſt clear'd the Ground of the Snow that cover'd it. In our Journey thither, we kill'd as many Hares and Woodhens, as we could eat. When we had fitted up our Hutts, the Savages went out upon the diſcovery of the Elks, ſome to the Northward, and ſome to the South, to the diſtance of two or three Leagues from the Hutts. As ſoon as they diſcover'd any freſh foot-ſteps, they detach'd one of their number to give us notice, to the end, that the whole Company might have the pleaſure of ſeeing the chace. We trac'd theſe foot-ſteps ſometimes for one, and ſometimes for two Leagues, and then fell in with five, ten, fifteen or twenty Elks in a body; which preſently betook themſelves to flight, whether a part or in a Body, and ſunk into the Snow up to their Breaſt. Where the Snow was hard and condenſated, or where the froſt following wet Weather had glaz'd it above, we came up with 'em after the chace of a quarter of a League: But when the Snow was ſoft or juſt fallen, we were forc'd to purſue 'em three or four Leagues before we could catch 'em, unleſs the Dogs happen'd to ſtop 'em where the Snow was very deep. When we came up with them, the Savages fired upon 'em with Fuſees. If the Elks be much inrag'd they'll ſometimes turn upon the Savages, who cover themſelves with Boughs in order to keep off their Feet, with which they would cruſh 'em to pieces. As ſoon as they are kill'd, the Savages make new Hutts upon the ſpot, with great Fires in the middle; while the Slaves are imploy'd in fleaing 'em, and ſtretching out the Skins in the open Air. One of the Soldiers that accompany'd me, told me one Day, that to withſtand the violence of the Cold, one ought to have his Blood compos'd of Brandy, [59] his Body of Braſs, and his Eyes of Glaſs: And I muſt ſay, he had ſome ground for what he ſpoke, for we were forc'd to keep a Fire all round us, all the Night long. As long as the Fleſh of theſe Animals laſts, the Savages ſeldom think of ſtirring; but when 'tis all conſum'd, they then look out for a new Diſcovery. Thus they continue to hunt, till the Snow and the Ice are melted. As ſoon as the great thaw commences, 'tis impoſſible for 'em to travel far; ſo that they content themſelves with the killing of Hares and Partridges, which are very numerous in the Woods. When the Rivers are clear of the Ice, they make Canows of the Elk-skins, which they ſow together very eaſily, covering the Seams with a fat ſort of Earth inſtead of pitch. This work is over in four or five days time, after which they return home in the Canows with all their Baggage.

This, Sir, was our Diverſion for three Months in the Woods. We took fifty ſix Elks, and might have kill'd twice as many, if we had hunted for the benefit of the Skins. In the Summer ſeaſon, the Savages have two ways of killing 'em, both of which are equally troubleſom. One conſiſts in hanging a Rope-gin between two Trees, upon a Paſs ſurrounded with Thorns; the other is compafs'd by crauling like Snakes among the Trees and Thickets, and approaching to 'em upon the Leeward fide, fo that they may be fhot with a Fufee. Harts and Caribous are kill'd both in Summer and Winter, after the fame manner with the Elks; excepting that the Caribou's, which are a kind of wild Affes, make an eafie efcape when the Snow is hard, by vertue of their broad Feet; whereas the Elk finks as faft as he rifes.[1] In fine, I am fo well pleas'd with the hunting of this Country, that I have refolv'd to imploy all my leifure time upon the Exercife. The Savages have promifed, that in three Months time [60] I fhall fee other forts of chafes, which will prove lefs fatiguing, and more agreeable. I am,

SIR,

Yours, &c.

---

[1] Caribou is the American woodland reindeer, *Rangifer caribou* or *tarandus*. By the term "hart," Lahontan intends the common deer, *Cervus virginianus*.—Ed.

LETTER XI.

Dated at *Boucherville May* 28. 1687.

Being a curious Deſcription of the Hunting of divers Animals.

SIR,

YOU complain that the laſt year you receiv'd but one of my Letters, dated *July* 8. and with the ſame breath aſſure me, that you writ two to me, neither of which is come to hand. I receiv'd a Letter from you this Day, which is ſo much the more acceptable, that I thought you had been dead, and that I find you continue to give proof of your remembrance of me. I find by your Letter, that you have an agreeable reliſh for the curious Elk-Hunting in this Country, and that a further account of our other hunting Adventures, would meet with a welcome Reception. This Curioſity, indeed, is worthy of ſo great a Hunts-Man as your ſelf; but at preſent I muſt beg your excuſe as to the Beaver-hunting, for I know nothing of it yet but by hear-ſay.

In the beginning of *September*, I ſet out in a Canow upon ſeveral Rivers, Marſhes, and Pools, that diſembogue in the Champlain Lake, being accompany'd with thirty or forty of the Savages that are very expert in Shooting and Hunting, and perfectly [61] well acquainted with the proper places for finding Water-foul, Deer, and other fallow Beaſts. The firſt

Poſt we took up was upon the ſide of a Marſh or Fen of four or five Leagues in Circumference; and after we had fitted up our Hutts, the Savages made Hutts upon the Water in ſeveral places. Theſe Water-Hutts are made of the branches and leaves of Trees, and contain three or four Men: For a Decoy they have the skins of Geeſe, Buſtards, and Ducks, dry'd and ſtuff'd with Hay, the two feet being made faſt with two Nails to a ſmall piece of a light plank, which floats round the Hutt. This place being frequented by wonderful numbers of Geeſe, Ducks, Buſtards, Teals, and an infinity of other Fowl unknown to the *Europeans;* when theſe Fowls ſee the ſtuff'd Skins ſwimming with the Heads erected, as if they were alive, they repair to the ſame place, and ſo give the Savages an opportunity of ſhooting 'em, either flying, or upon the Water; after which the Savages get into their Canows and gather 'em up. They have likewiſe a way of catching 'em with Nets, ſtretch'd upon the ſurface of the Water at the Entries of the Rivers. In a word, we eat nothing but Water-fowl for fifteen Days; after which we reſolv'd to declare War againſt the Turtle-Doves, which are ſo numerous in *Canada*, that the Biſhop has been forc'd to excommunicate 'em oftner than once, upon the account of the Damage they do to the Product of the Earth. With that view, we imbarqued and made towards a Meadow, in the Neighbourhood of which, the Trees were cover'd with that ſort of Fowl, more than with Leaves: For juſt then 'twas the ſeaſon in which they retire from the North Countries, and repair to the Southern Climates; and one would have thought, that all the Turtle-Doves upon Earth had choſe to paſs thro' this place. For the eighteen or twenty days that we ſtay'd there, I firmly believe that a thouſand [62] Men might have fed upon 'em heartily, without putting themſelves to any trouble. You muſt know, that through the middle of this Meadow there runs a Brook, upon which I and two young Savages ſhot ſeveral Snipes, Rayles, and a certain ſort of Fowl call'd *Bateurs de faux*, which is as big as a Quail, and eats very deliciouſly.[1]

In the ſame place we kill'd ſome *Musk-Rats*, or a ſort of Animals which reſemble a Rat in their ſhape, and are as big as a Rabbet. The Skins of theſe Rats are very much valued, as differing but little from thoſe of Beavers. Their Teſticles ſmell ſo ſtrong of Musk, that no Civet or Antilope that *Aſia* affords, can boaſt of ſuch a ſtrong and ſweet ſmell. We spy'd 'em in the Mornings and Evenings, at which time they uſually appear upon the Water with their Noſe to the Windward, and betray themſelves to the Huntſmen, by the curling of the Water. The *Fouteraux*, which are an amphibious ſort of little Pole-Cats, are catch'd after the ſame manner. I was likewiſe entertain'd upon this occaſion, with the killing of certain little Beaſts, call'd *Siffleurs*, or Whiſtlers, with alluſion to their wonted way of whiſtling or whizzing at the Mouth of their Holes in fair Weather. They are as big as Hares, but ſomewhat ſhorter, their Fleſh is good for nothing, but their Skins are recom-

[1] Many early travellers speak of the number of wild pigeons (*Ectopistes migratoria*). See *Jesuit Relations*, index. Batteurs de faux are the North American rail (*Porzana Carolina*) — in French, rale de la Caroline. This identification is made by M. Dionne, curator of Laval University, Quebec. — Ed.

mended by their rarity. The Savages gave me an opportunity of hearing one of thefe Creafures whiftle for an hour together, after which they fhot it.[1] To gratifie the curiofity I had to fee fuch diverfity of Animals, they made a diligent fearch for the Holes or Dens of the *Carcaioux*, and having found fome at the diftance of two or three Leagues from the Fen upon which we were pofted, they conducted me to the place. At the break of day we planted our felves round the Holes, with our Bellies upon the Ground; and left fome Slaves to hold the Dogs a Musket-fhot behind [63] us. As foon as thefe Animals perceiv'd Day-light, they came out of their Holes, which were immediately ftop'd up by the Savages, and upon that the Dogs fetch'd 'em up with eafe. We faw but two of 'em, which made a vigorous defence againft the Dogs, but were ftrangled after a difpute of half an hour. Thefe Animals are not unlike a Badger, only they are bigger, and more mifchievous.[2] Tho' our Dogs shew'd a great deal of Courage in attacking the *Carcaioux*, they betray'd their Cowardice the next day in a rencounter with a Porcupine, which we fpy'd upon a little Tree. To obtain the pleafure of feeing the Porcupine fall, we cut down the Tree; but neither the Dogs nor we durft go near it: The Dogs only bark'd and jump'd round it; for it darted its long and hard hair like fo many Bodkins, three or

---

[1] Muskrats (*Fiber zibethicus*) are widely distributed over the North American continent. The "whistler" is the hoary marmot (*Arctomys pruniosus*). M. Dionne thinks that "foutereaux" must be mink (*Lutreola vison*), which is amphibious, preys on fish, and is a foe to the muskrat. — ED.

[2] Carcajou is the usual Canadian term for the wolverine (*Gulo luscus*), also called at times the "beaver eater."— ED.

four paces off. At laſt we pelted it to death, and put it upon the fire to burn off its Darts; after which we ſcalded it like a Pig, took out the Intrails, and roaſted it: But tho' 'twas very fat, I could not reliſh it ſo well as to comply with the aſſertion of the Natives, who alledge, that it eats as well as a Capon or a Partridge.

After the Turtle-Doves had all paſs'd over the place, in queſt of their Southern retreats, the Savages offer'd to ſend ſome of their number with Canows to conduct me home, before the Rivers and Lakes were frozen over; for themſelves were to tarry out for the Elk-hunting; and they imagin'd that the Cold and Hardſhip attending that Exerciſe, had made me ſick of it the year before. However, we had then a Month good before the commencement of the Froſt, and in that interval of time, they proffer'd to entertain me with more diverting Game than any I had ſeen before. They propos'd to go fifteen or ſixteen Leagues further up the Country, aſſuring me, that they knew of a certain place that had the moſt advantageous ſituation [64] in the World, both for Pleaſure and Profit, and that afforded great plenty of Otters, of the Skins of which they mean'd to make a great Cargoe. Accordingly we pull'd down our Hutts, and having imbarqu'd in our Canows, ſail'd up the River, till we came to a little Lake of two Leagues in Circumference, at the end of which we ſaw another greater Lake, divided from this by an Iſthmus of 150 Paces in length. We pitch'd our Hutts at the diſtance of a League from that Iſthmus; and ſome of the Savages fiſh'd for Trouts, while the reſt were imploy'd in laying Traps for the

Otters upon the brinks of the Lake. Thefe Traps are made of five Stakes plac'd in the form of an oblong Quadrangle, fo as to make a little Chamber, the Door of which is kept up, and fupported by a Stake. To the middle of this Stake they tye a ftring which paffes thro' a little fork, and has a Trout well faften'd to the end of it. Now, when the Otter comes on fhoar, and fees this bait, he puts above half his Body into that fatal Cage, in order to fwallow the Fifh; but he no fooner touches, than the ftring to which 'tis made faft pulls away the Stake that fupports the Door, upon which an heavy and loaded Door falls upon his Reins and quafhes him. During our Pilgrimage in that part of the Country, the Savages took above two hundred and fifty *Canada* Otters; the Skins of which are infinitely prittier than thofe of *Mufcovy* or *Sweden*. The beft of 'em which are not worth two Crowns in this place, are fold in *France* for four or five, and fometimes for ten, if they are black and very rough. As foon as the Savages had fet their Traps, they gave orders to their Slaves to go round the Lake every Morning, in order to take out the amphibious Animals. After that they conducted me to the above-mention'd Ifthmus, where I was furpriz'd to fee a fort of a Park or Fence made of Trees, fell'd one upon another, [65] and interlac'd with Thorns and Branches; with a quadrangular inclofure of Stakes at the end of it, the entry of which was very narrow. They gave me to know, that they ufed to hunt Harts in that place, and promis'd to divert me with the fhew, as foon as the Inclofures were a little mended. In effect, they carry'd me two or three Leagues off, upon ſuch Roads as had nothing on either ſide but Fens and Marſhes; and after they had diſpers'd themſelves, ſome on one hand and ſome on the other, with a Dog for every Man; I ſaw a great many Harts running to and again, in queſt of places of Safety. The Savage that I kept company with, aſſur'd me, that he and I had no occaſion to walk very faſt, becauſe he had took the ſtraighteſt and the neareſt Road. Before us we ſaw above ten Harts, which were forc'd to turn back, rather than throw themſelves into the Marſh, of which they could never get clear. At laſt, after walking a great pace, and running now and then, we arriv'd at the Park, and found the Savages lying flat upon the Ground all round it, in order to ſhut up the entry of the ſtake Incloſure as ſoon as the Harts enter'd. We found thirty five Harts in the place, and, if the Park had been better fenc'd, we might have had above ſixty; for the nimbleſt and lighteſt of 'em, skip'd over before they came to enter the Incloſure. We kill'd a great many of 'em, but ſpar'd the Dams, becauſe they were great with young. I ask'd of the Savages the Tongues and the Marrow of the Harts, which they gave me very readily. The Fleſh was very fat, but not delicious, excepting ſome few bits about the Ribs. But after all, this was not our only Game; for two days after we went a Bear-hunting, and the Savages who ſpend three parts of four of their life in Hunting in the Woods, are very dexterous at that Exerciſe, eſpecially in ſingling out the Trunks of the Trees upon [66] which the Bears Neſtle. I could not but admire their knowledge in that Point, when, as we were walking up and down in a Foreſt, at the diſtance of an hundred Paces one from another, I heard one Savage call to another, *Here's a Bear.* I askt 'em how he knew that there was a Bear upon the Tree which he knock'd with his Axe; and they all reply'd, that 'twas as eaſily diſtinguiſh'd as the print of an Elks foot in the Snow. For five or ſix times they never miſs'd; for after they had knock'd two or three times upon the Trunk of the Tree, the Bear came out of its hole, and was preſently ſhot. The *Canada* Bears are extream black, but not miſchievous, for they never attack one, unleſs they be wounded or fir'd upon. They are ſo fat, eſpecially in the Autumn, that they can ſcarce walk: Thoſe which we kill'd were extream fat, but their fat is good for nothing but to be burnt, whereas their Fleſh, and, above all, their Feet are very nice Victuals. The Savages affirm, that no Fleſh is ſo delicious as that of Bears; and indeed, I think they are in the right of it. While we rang'd up and down in queſt of Bears, we had the pleaſure of ſpying ſome Martins and wild Cats upon the branches of the Trees, which the Savages ſhot in the Head to preſerve their Skin. But the moſt Comical thing I ſaw, was the Stupidity of the Wood-hens, which ſit upon the Trees in whole Flocks, and are kill'd one after another, without ever offering to ſtir. Commonly the Savages ſhoot at 'em with Arrows, for they ſay they are not worth a ſhoot of Powder, which is able to kill an Elk or an Hart. I have ply'd this ſort of Fowling in the Neighbourhood of our Cantons or Habitations in the Winter time, with the help of a Dog who found out the Trees by ſcent, and then bark'd; upon which I approach'd to the Tree, and found the Fowls upon the Branches. When the thaw came, I went two or three Leagues further [67] up the Lake, in Company with ſome *Canadeſe*, on purpoſe to ſee that Fowl flap with its Wings. Believe me, Sir, this ſight is one of the greateſt Curioſities in the World; for their flapping makes a noiſe much like that of a Drum all about, for the ſpace of a Minute or thereabouts; then the noiſe ceaſes for half a quarter of an Hour, after which it begins again. By this noiſe we were directed to the place where the unfortunate Moor-hens ſat, and found 'em upon rotten moſſy Trees. By flapping one Wing againſt the other, they mean to call their Mates; and the humming noiſe that inſues thereupon, may be heard half a quarter of a League off. This they do only in the Months of *April*, *May*, *September*, and *October;* and, which is very remarkable, a Moorhen never flaps in this manner, but upon one Tree. It begins at the break of day, and gives over at nine a Clock in the Morning, till about an hour before Sunſet that it flutters again, and continues ſo to do till Night: I proteſt to you, that I have frequently contented my ſelf with ſeeing and admiring the flapping of their Wings without offering to ſhoot at 'em.

Beſides the pleaſure of ſo many different ſorts of Diverſion, I was likewiſe entertain'd in the Woods with the company of the honeſt old Gentlemen that liv'd in former Ages. Honeſt *Homer*, the amiable *Anacreon*, and my dear *Lucian*, were my inſeparable Companions. *Ariſtotle* too deſir'd paſſionately to go along with us, but my Canow was too little to hold his bulky Equipage of Peripatetick Silogiſms: So that he was e'en fain to trudge back to the Jeſuits, who vouchſaf'd him a very honourable Reception. I had a great deal of reafon to rid my felf of that great Philofopher's Company; for his ridiculous Jargon, and his fenfelefs Terms, would have frighted the Savages out of their wits. Farewell, Sir, I am now arriv'd at once at the end of [68] my Game and my Letter. I have heard no News from *Quebec*, where they continue to make mighty Preparations for fome confiderable Enterprife. Time will difcover a great many things, an Account of which I mean to tranfmit to you by the Ships that are to leave this Harbour in the end of *Autumn*. I conclude with my ufual Compliment,

Yours, &c.

LETTER XII.

Dated at *St. Helens*, over againſt *Monreal*,[1]
June 8. 1687.

The Chevalier de Vaudreuil *arrives in* Canada *with ſome Troops. Both the Regular Troops and the Militia, are poſted at* St. Helens, *in a readineſs to march againſt the* Iroqueſe

SIR,

I HAVE ſuch a budget-full of News, that I know not where to begin. I receiv'd Letters but now from Mr. *Senelay*'s Office; by which I have Advice, that Orders are ſent to Mr. *Denonville* to allow me to go for *France*, upon my private Concerns.[2] No longer ſince than Yeſterday, he told me I ſhould have Leave to go after the Campaign is over. My Relations write, that the procuring of this Leave coſt 'em a great deal of pains; and that the ſooner I come to *Paris*, 'twill be the better for me.

The Governour arriv'd at *Monreal* three or four days ago,

[1] St. Helen Island, in the St. Lawrence opposite Montreal, was named by Champlain in honor of his wife. It was the seigniory of Jacques Le Moyne, sieur de Ste. Hélène, second son of Longueuil, who distinguished himself in the opening of Frontenac's War, and fell at the siege of Quebec (1690). The island, where the troops rendezvoused for Denonville's expedition, is now a public park. — Ed.

[2] Jean Baptiste Colbert, marquis de Seignelay, eldest son of the great Colbert, succeeded his father (1683) as minister of the marine, which office he administered until his death in 1690. The colonies were controlled by this department of the French administration. — Ed.

with all the Militia of the Country, who lie now incamp'd along with our Troops in that Iſland. Mr. *D'Amblemont* has been at *Quebec* this Month, with five or ſix ſecond Rate Ships, having [69] ſail'd from *Rochel* thither in 28 days. He brought over with him ten or twelve Companies of Marines, who are to guard the Colony while we invade the *Iroqueſe* Country.[1] 'Tis ſaid, that laſt Year Mr. *Denonville* ſent ſeveral *Canadeſe*, that were known and eſteem'd by the Savages, our Allies, who live upon the Banks of the Lakes and the adjacent Countries, with Orders to engage 'em to favour our Deſign of extirpating the *Iroqueſe*. In the Winter he made Magazines of Ammunition and Proviſions, and now he has ſent ſeveral Canows, laden with Proviſions, to Fort *Frontenac*, and given Orders for the building of an infinite number of ſuch Boats as I deſcrib'd in my fourth Letter, for the Tranſporting of our twenty Companies of Marines. The Militia who are incamp'd in this Iſland along with our Troops, make fifteen hundred Men, and are join'd by five hundred of the converted Savages that live in the Neighbourhood of *Quebec* and the Iſland of *Monreal*. The Chevalier *Vaudreuil*, who is come from *France* to Command our Troops, is reſolv'd to appear in the Field, notwithſtanding the Fatigue of his Paſſage to *Canada*[2]: and the

---

[1] D'Amblemont commanded the royal ships sent out with reinforcements. There were now about sixteen hundred regular troops in the colony. — Ed.

[2] Philippe de Rigaud, Chevalier de Vaudreuil, came to Canada in 1687 as commander of the king's regiment. Three years later he married a Canadian, and permanently threw in his fortunes with the colony. His services were of sufficient value to secure him a marquisate (1702), when he was appointed governor to succeed Callières, an office held until his death in 1726. His son was the last French governor of Canada. — Ed.

Governour of *Monreal* is of the ſame mind. Mr. *de Champigni*, the Intendant of this Country, went from hence to Fort *Frontenac* two days ago. The day after to morrow, Mr. *de Denonville* means to march at the Head of his little Army, being accompany'd with an ancient *Iroqueſe*, that is very much reſpected by the five Cantons. The Hiſtory and various Adventures of this old Gentleman, are too tedious to bear a Relation in this place. Every body is apprehenſive that this Expedition will prove as ſucceſleſs as that of Mr. *de la Barre:* And if their Apprehenſions are not diſappointed, the King lays out his Money to no purpoſe. For my own part, when I reflect upon the Attempt we made three Years ago, I can't but think it impoſſible for us to ſucceed. Time will diſcover the Conſequences of [70] this Expedition; and perhaps we may come to repent, tho' too late, of our complying with the Advice of ſome Diſturbers of the Publick Peace, who project to enlarge their private Fortunes in a general Commotion. I lay this down for an unconteſted Truth, that we are not able to deſtroy the *Iroqueſe* by our ſelves: beſides, what occaſion have we to trouble 'em, ſince they give us no Provocation? However, let the Event be what it will, I ſhall not fail upon my Return to tranſmit you a Journal of our Actions, unleſs it be, that I embarque for *Rochel*, and deliver it my ſelf: In the mean time, believe me to be,

SIR,

Yours, &c.

LETTER XIII.

Dated at *Niagara*, *Aug*. 2. 1687.

Repreſenting the unfavourable Iſſue of the Campaign made in the Iroqueſe *Country; the Diſcovery of an Ambuſcade; and the iſſuing of Orders for the Author to march with a Detachment to the great Lakes.*

SIR,

IT has been a Maxim in all Ages, That the Events of things are not always anſwerable to Mens Expectations: When Men form to themſelves a promiſing proſpect of compaſſing their Ends, they frequently meet with the mortification of ſeeing themſelves diſappointed. This I ſpeak by way of application to my ſelf; for inſtead of going for *France*, purſuant to the Contents of the Letter I writ to you [71] two Months ago, I am now oblig'd to ſtraggle to one End of the World, as you'll find by the following Journal of our Expedition.

We broke up from *St. Helens* much about the time I ſpoke of in my laſt. Mr. *de Champigni* went before us with a ſtrong Guard, and arriv'd in a Canow at Fort *Frontenac*, eight or ten days before we came up. As ſoon as he arriv'd, he ſent two or three hundred *Canadeſe* to ſurpriſe the Villages of *Kente* and *Ganeouſſe*, which lie at the diſtance of ſeven or eight Leagues from the Fort, and are inhabited by a ſort of *Iroqueſe*, that deſerv'd no other Uſage than what they met with. Our *Canadeſe* had no great difficulty in maſtering them; for they ſurpris'd 'em when they leaſt thought of any Alarm, and brought 'em Priſoners to Fort *Frontenac*, where they were tied to Poſts with Cords round their Necks, Hands, and Feet. We arriv'd at the Fort on the firſt of *July*, after the encountering of ſeveral Difficulties among the Water-falls, Cataracts, and Currents, that I formerly deſcrib'd to you in my Account of Mr. *de la Barre*'s Expedition. We were more perplex'd in this Voyage than the former; for our Boats were ſo heavy, that we could not tranſport 'em over Land as we did the Canows, but were oblig'd to drag 'em up through the impracticable Paſſes with the force of Men and Ropes. Immediately upon our Debarquing, I went ſtraight to the Fort, where I ſaw the miſerable Priſoners in the abovemention'd Poſture. The ſight of this piece of Tyranny fill'd me at once with Compaſſion and Horror; but in the mean time the poor Wretches ſung Night and Day, that being the cuſtomary Practice of the People of *Canada* when they fall into the hands of their Enemies. They complain'd, 'That they were betray'd without any ground; 'that in compenſation for the care they had took ever ſince 'the Peace to furniſh the Garriſon with Fiſh and Veniſon, they 'were bound and [72] tied to Poſts, and whip'd in ſuch a 'manner, that they could neither ſleep, nor guard off the Flies; 'that the only Requital they met with for procuring to the '*French* a Commerce in the Skins of Beavers and other Ani'mals, was, to be doom'd to Slavery, and to ſee their Fathers, 'and the ancient Men of their Country, murder'd before their 'eyes. Are theſe the *French*, ſaid they, that the *Jeſuits* cry'd 'up ſo much for Men of Probity and Honour? Even the 'cruelleſt ſort of Death that Imagination it ſelf can reach, 'would be nothing to us in compariſon with the odious and 'horrible Spectacle of the Blood of our Anceſtors, that is ſhed 'ſo inhumanely before our eyes. Aſſuredly, the five Villages 'will revenge our Quarrel, and entertain an everlaſting and 'juſt Reſentment of the tyrannical Uſage we now meet with.' I made up to one of theſe Wretches that was about five and twenty Years old, and had frequently regal'd me in his Hutt, not far from the Fort, during my ſix Weeks Service in that Place in the Year of Mr. *de la Barre*'s Expedition. This poor Man being Maſter of the *Algonkin* Language, I gave him to know, that I was heartily griev'd to ſee him in that diſmal Poſture; that I would take care to have Victuals and Drink convey'd to him twice a day, and would give him Letters for my Friends at *Monreal*, in order to his being us'd more favourably than his Companions. He reply'd, That he ſaw and was very well acquainted with the Horror that moſt of the *French* were affected with, upon the view of the Cruelty they underwent; and, that he ſcorn'd to be fed, or us'd more civily than his Fellow Priſoners. He gave me an account of the manner in which they were ſurpris'd, and how their Anceſtors were maſſacred; and truly, I do not believe that any one can be touch'd with more cutting and bitter Reflexions than this poor Man was, when he recounted the many Services he had done the *French*, during [73] the whole courſe of his Life: At laſt, after many Sighs and Groans, he bow'd down his Head, and wrap'd himſelf up in Silence. *Quaque poteſt narrat, reſtabant ultima flevit.* But this was not the only thing that affected me, when I beheld the miſery of theſe innocent Creatures: I ſaw ſome young Savages of our ſide burn their Fingers with Fire in their lighted Pipes; which provok'd me to threſh 'em ſoundly: but I was ſeverely reprimanded for my pains, and confin'd to my Tent for five or ſix days, where I only repented that I had not dealt my blows in a double meaſure. Theſe Savages reſented the matter ſo highly, that they ran preſently to their Hutts, and flew to their Fuſees, in order to kill me. Nay, all that could be done was ſcarce ſufficient to appeaſe 'em; for the Diſpute came to that heighth, that they would have left us, if it had not been that our Men aſſur'd 'em I was || drunk, that all the *French* were prohibited to give me either Wine or Brandy, and that I ſhould certainly be impriſon'd as ſoon as the Campaign were over. However, the poor Wretches, the Priſoners, were carried to *Quebec;* from whence they are to be ſent to the *French* Galleys.[1] Much about that time, the Sieur *de la Foreſt*, one of the Mr. *de la Salle*'s Officers, arriv'd at the Fort in a great Canow, being conducted

|| *Among the Savages, drunken Perſons are always excus'd: for, the Bottle attones for all Crimes.*

[1] For the treacherous action of Denonville in seizing these friendly Iroquois, reprisals were made on the colony. See Parkman, *Frontenac*, pp. 167–183. Thirty-six were shipped to France as the first installment for the royal galleys. See *Jes. Rel.*, lxiii, p. 281. The remnant that survived were reprieved and sent back under Frontenac's care (1689). See list in *Collection de Manuscrits relatifs à la Nouvelle France* (Quebec, 1883), i, p. 454. The French edition of Lahontan gives a more extended and vivid narration of his own peril upon this occasion. — Ed.

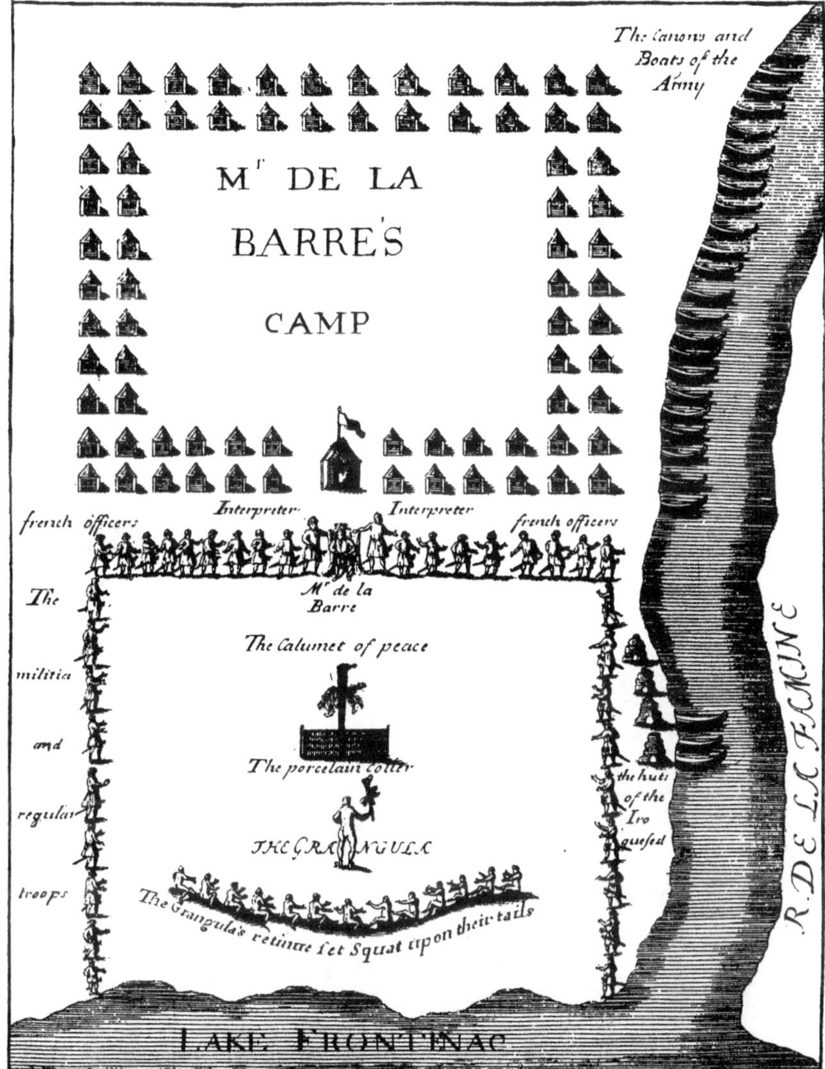

The Canons and Boats of the Army
Mr DE LA BARRE'S CAMP
Interpreter
Interpreter
french officers
french officers
Mr de la Barre
The militia and regular troops
The Calumet of peace
The porcelain coller
the huts of the Iroquese
THE GRANGULA
The Grangula's retinue set Squat upon their tails
LAKE FRONTENAC
R. DE LA FAMINE

thither by eight or ten *Coureurs de Bois.*[1] He gave Mr. *de Denonville* to underſtand, that a Party of the *Illineſe* and the *Oumamis* waited for the *Hurons* and the *Outaouas* at the Lake of *St. Claire*, in order to joyn 'em, and to march with joint Forces to the River of the *Tſonontouans*, that being the place of their general Rendezvous.[2] He added, that in the Lake of the *Hurons* near *Miſſilimakinac*, Mr. *de la Durantais*,[3] aſſiſted by the Savages, our Allies, had taken an *Engliſh* Company conducted by ſome *Iroqueſe*, who had fifty [74] thouſand Crowns-worth of Goods in their Canows, to be diſpos'd of in exchange

[1] François Dauphine, sieur de la Forest, was one of La Salle's trusted lieutenants. Born in 1648, he arrived in the colony with his chief (1675), who left him (1678) in charge of Fort Frontenac. Thence he was summoned (1680–81) to accompany La Salle and carry succor to Illinois. In 1683, his fort was treacherously seized by La Barre, La Forest being offered the command if he would forsake La Salle's interests. He preferred to seek redress in France, where an order was issued restoring all to him, in trust for his absent chief. In 1685, he was relieved of Fort Frontenac, and joined Tonty in Illinois, whence he issued to aid this expedition. In 1690 La Forest and Tonty received a grant of Fort St. Louis, in Illinois; this being revoked in 1702. La Forest then became La Mothe's lieutenant at Detroit, and in 1710 was appointed commandant of this post, which position he held until 1714, dying at Boucherville five years later. — ED

[2] As the sequel shows, the rendezvous was at Irondequoit Bay, Monroe County, N. Y. The "River of the Tsonontouans" was Irondequoit Creek, a highway toward the towns of that nation. — ED.

[3] Olivier Morel de la Durantaye, born at Nantes in 1641, came to Canada with the regiment de Carignan. A brief contemporary biography (*Can. Arch.*, 1899, Supp., p. 26) is as follows: "In 1662, ensign; in 1665, captain; in 1663, commandant over the Ottawa country by order of the Court; in 1689, captain on half-pay in Canada; in 1694, captain *enpied* in that country, where he has settled. A good officer. An honest man; ready for any service; entitled to a company." After retiring from his command at Mackinac (1683–89), he aided in Frontenac's War, and was esteemed the first soldier in the colony. He died in 1717, leaving descendants who still live in Canada. — ED.

with the Nations that dwell upon thefe Lakes: as alfo, That Mr. *Dulhut* had taken another *Englifh* Convoy, being affifted by the *Coureurs de Bois*, and the Savages, who had fhar'd the former Capture; and that he had kept the *Englifh* and *Iroquefe* as Prifoners, as well as their Commander, who was call'd Major *Gregory.*[1] In fine, he reprefented to Mr. *de Denonville*, that 'twas high time for him to fet out from Fort *Frontenac*, if he mean'd to appear at the general Rendezvous, where the Auxiliary Troops fent from the Lakes would arrive very fpeedily. The next day, being the 3d of *July*, the Sieur *de la Foreft* embarqued again for *Niagara*, and fteer'd to the North-fide of the Lake. At the fame time we embarqued, and ftood to the oppofite fide of the Lake, being favour'd by the Calms which in that Month are very common.

By good luck, our whole Body arriv'd almoft at one and the fame time in the River of the *Tfonontouans;* and upon that occafion, the Savages, our Allies, who draw Predictions from the moft trifling Accidents, fhew'd their wonted Superftition in taking this for an infallible Prefage of the utter Deftruction of the *Iroquefe:* tho' after all they prov'd falfe Prophets, as you will find by the fequel of this Letter. The fame Night that we Landed, we hawl'd our Canows and Boats out of the Water, and fet a ftrong Guard upon 'em. This done, we

---

[1] For an account of the capture of the English and Dutch traders commissioned by Dongan, see Parkman, *Frontenac*, pp. 145–147; *N. Y. Colon. Docs.*, ix, pp. 318–322, 363. Colonel Patrick MacGregory emigrated with a colony from Scotland to Maryland, in 1684; later, he removed to New York and engaged in the Indian trade. He was released from imprisonment and sent back to New York in the autumn of 1687, and next year was employed against the Indians in Maine. He was killed during the Leisler rebellion in New York, 1691. — ED.

built a Fort of Stakes or Pales, where we left the Sieur *Dorvillers* with four hundred Men to guard our Shipping and Baggage.[1] The next day, a young *Canadese*, call'd *Fontaine Marion* was unjuftly fhot to death. His cafe ftood thus: Having travell'd frequently all over this Continent, he was perfectly well acquainted with the Country, and with the Savages of *Canada;* and after the doing of feveral good Services to the King, defir'd Leave from the Governour general to continue [75] his Travels, in order to carry on fome little Trade: but his Requeft was never granted. Upon that he refolv'd to remove to *New England*, the two Crowns being then in Peace. The Planters of *New England* gave him a very welcome Reception; for he was an active Fellow, and one that underftood almoft all the Languages of the Savages. Upon this Confideration he was employ'd to conduct the two *Englifh* Convoys I fpoke of but now, and had the Misfortune to be taken along with them. Now, to my mind, the Ufage he met with from us was extream hard; for, we are in Peace with *England:* and befides, that Crown lays Claim to the Property of the Lakes of *Canada.*

The next Day we began our March towards the great Village of the *Tfonontouans*, without any other Provifions than ten Biskets a Man, which every one carry'd for himfelf.[2]

[1] François Chorel, sieur de St. Romain *dit* d' Orvilliers, was born near Lyons in 1639, came to Canada about 1660, and was prominent in military affairs in the colony until his death in 1709. Denonville placed him in charge of Fort Frontenac (1685–87), and he commanded in person one division of his expedition. — ED.

[2] The great village of the Seneca was situated in Ontario County, just south of the present town of Victor. See map in Cayuga County Historical Society *Collections*, iii, and *Jes. Rel.*, li, p. 293. — ED.

We had but feven Leagues to march in a great Wood of tall Trees, upon a fmooth even Ground. The *Coureurs de Bois*, with a Party of the Savages, led the Van, and the reft of the Savages brought up the Rear, our Regular Troops and our Militia being pofted in the middle. The firft Day the Army march'd four Leagues, and the advanc'd Guards made no Difcovery. The fecond Day our advanc'd Parties march'd up to the very Fields of the Village without perceiving any thing, tho' they paft within a Piftol-fhot of five hundred *Tfonontouans*, who lay flat upon the Ground, and fuffer'd 'em to pafs and repafs without moleftation. Upon their Intelligence we march'd up with equal Precipitation and Confufion, being bouy'd up with the Apprehenfion that the *Iroquefe* had fled, and that at leaft their Women, Children, and fuperannuated Perfons would fall into our hands. When we arriv'd at the bottom of the Hill upon which the Ambufcade was plac'd, at the diftance of a quarter of a League from the Village, they began to raife their wonted Cry, which [76] was follow'd by the firing of fome Muskets. Had you but feen, Sir, what Diforder our Troops and Militia were in amidft the thick Trees, you would have joyn'd with me, in thinking that feveral thoufands of *Europeans* are no more than a fufficient number to make head againft five hundred Barbarians. Our Battalions were divided into ftraggling Parties, who fell in to the right and left, without knowing where they went. Inftead of firing upon the *Iroquefe*, we fir'd upon one another. 'Twas to no purpofe to call in the Soldiers of fuch and fuch a Battalion, for we could not fee thirty Paces off: In fine, we were fo diſorder'd, that the Enemy were going to cloſe in upon us with their Clubs in their hands; when the Savages of our ſide having rally'd, repuls'd the Enemy, and purſu'd 'em to their Villages with ſo much fury, that they brought off the Heads of eighty, and wounded a great many. In this Action we loſt ten Savages, and a hundred *French:* We had twenty or two and twenty wounded, in which number was the good Father *Angeleran* the Jeſuit,[1] who receiv'd a Musket-ſhot in thoſe Parts which *Origen* choſe to lop off, in order to qualify himſelf for inſtructing the Fair Sex without the diſturbance of Paſſion, or the danger of Scandal. When the Savages brought in the Heads of their Enemies to Mr. *de Denonville*, they ask'd him why he halted, and did not march up? He made Anſwer, That he could not leave his wounded Men behind, and that he thought it proper to encamp, that the Surgeons might have time to dreſs their Wounds. To obviate this Pretence, the Savages offer'd to make Litters for the tranſporting of 'em to the Village that lay but a little way off. But our General did not approve of their Advice; upon which, notwithſtanding his Remonſtrances, they drew up into a Body, and tho' they conſiſted of ten different Nations, agreed in a joynt Reſolution of purſuing their Enemy, in hopes of taking, at [77] leaſt their Women, their Old-men, and their Children.

[1] Father Jean Enjalran (born in 1639) came to Canada in 1676, and the following year was sent to the Ottawa mission at Mackinac, where he remained until 1688, acting as superior of Ottawa missions for the last seven years. He had been instrumental in persuading the savages to join this expedition. The next year (1688) he went to France, but was again in Canada until 1701, when he returned to his native land for the last time, and died there in 1718. — ED.

Our General being acquainted with their Refolution, gave 'em to know, that he earneftly defir'd they would reft for one day, and not depart from his Camp, and that the next day he would burn their Villages, and ftarve 'em to Death by fpoiling their Crops. But they took this Compliment fo ill, that moft of 'em return'd to their own Country; remonftrating, 'That 'the *French* came out to fetch a Walk, rather than to wage 'War, fince they would not take the Advantage of the beft 'Opportunity in the World: That their Ardour, like a flafh 'of Fire, was extinguifh'd as foon as kindled: That 'twas a 'fruitlefs Adventure, to draw together fo many Warriours, 'from all Parts, to burn fome Hutts of Bark, that the Enemy 'could rebuild in four days: That the *Tfonontouans* did not 'matter the fpoiling of their Corn, for that the other *Iroquefe* 'Nations were able to fupply 'em: And in fine, That fince 'they had joyn'd the *French* twice together to no purpofe, 'they would never truft 'em for the future, in fpite of all the Remonftrances they could make.' Some are of the opinion, that Mr. *de Denonville* ought to have gone farther; and others affirm, that 'twas impoffible for him to do more than he did. For my part, I fhall not venture upon any Decifion of the matter; thofe who fit at the Helm are moft liable to be perplex'd. To purfue the bare matter of Fact; we march'd next day to the great Village, and carry'd our wounded Men upon Litters: but we found nothing there but Afhes; for the *Iroquefe* had burnt the Village themfelves, by way of Precaution. Then we fpent five or fix days in cutting down the *Indian* Corn with our Swords. From thence we march'd to the two little Villages of the *Thegaronhies* and the *Danoncaritaoui*, which lay about two or three Leagues off.[1] Having done the like Exploits there, we return'd to the Lake ſide. In all theſe Villages we [78] found plenty of Horſes, black Cattel, Fowl, and Hogs. All the Country round afforded us a very charming, pleaſant, and even Proſpect. The Foreſts thro which we march'd were repleniſh'd with Oak, Wall-nut, and wild Cheſnut-Trees.

Two days after we imbarqu'd for *Niagara*, which lay thirty Leagues off, and arriv'd there in four days. As ſoon as the Troops had debarqu'd, we imploy'd 'em in making a Fort of Pales with four Baſtions, which was finiſh'd in three days.[2] Here we mean to leave 120 Soldiers under the command of Mr. *des Bergeres*, with Ammunition and Proviſions for eight Months.[3] The Fort ſtands on the South ſide of the Streight of *Herriè* Lake, upon a Hill; at the foot of which, that Lake falls into the Lake of *Frontenac*. Yeſterday the Savages our

---

[1] These villages were in the vicinity of Honeoye Falls, Monroe County, N. Y. See Hawley, "Jesuit Missions among the Senecas," in Cayuga Co. Hist. Soc. *Collections*, iii, pp. 25, 26. — Ed.

[2] It had long been a favorite plan of the leaders of New France to place a fort at Niagara, and thus intercept the fur-trade which passed through the Great Lakes to the Iroquois and English. La Salle built a block house on this site in 1679, which was destroyed by the Senecas; see Hennepin, *New Discovery*. Dongan (1686) complained that Denonville was planning to build "a fort at Ohinagero on this side the lake, within my Master's territoryes without question." *N. Y. Colon. Docs.*, iii, p. 455. Denonville ordered the demolition of this fort, Sept. 15, 1688. A permanent French fort was begun on this site in 1726, being captured by the English (1759), and later surrendered to the Americans (1796). See Severance, *Old Trails on the Niagara Frontier* (Buffalo, 1899). — Ed.

[3] Chevalier de Troyes was left first in command at this fort, where he died in the following year. See *N. Y. Colon. Docs.*, ix, pp. 335, 368, 396. Raymond Blaise des Bergères, sieur de Rigauville, was captain of a company stationed at Niagara; later he was major at Three Rivers. His son commanded at Niagara (1732–36). — Ed.

Allies took leave of Mr. *de Denonville*, and made a Speech after their ufual manner; in which, among other things, they infinuated, That they were pleas'd to fee a Fort fo conveniently plac'd, which might favour their retreat upon any Expedition againft the *Iroquefe;* That they depended upon his promife, of continuing the War till the five Nations fhould be either deftroy'd or difpoffefs'd of their Country; That they earneftly defir'd that part of the Army fhould take the Field out of hand, and continue in it both Winter and Summer, for that they would certainly do the fame on their part; and in fine, That for as much as their Alliance with *France* was chiefly grounded upon the promifes the *French* made of liftening to no Propofals of Peace, till the five Nations fhould be quite extirpated; they therefore hop'd they would be as good as their Word; efpecially confidering that a Ceffation of Arms would fully the honour of the *French*, and infallibly difengage their Allies. Mr. *de Denonville* gave them frefh affurances of his intention to carry on the War, in fpite of all the efforts of the *Iroquefe;* and in a [79] word, protefted that he would profecute this defign fo vigoroufly, that in the end thefe *Barbarians* fhould be either quite cut off, or oblig'd to fhift their Seats.

The General call'd for me that very day, and acquainted me, that in regard I underftood the Language of the Savages, I was to go with a Detachment to cover their Country purfuant to their Requeft. At the fame time he affur'd me, he would inform the Court of the Reafons that mov'd him to detain me in *Canada*, nothwithftanding that he had orders to give me leave to go home. You may eafily guefs, Sir, that I was thunderſtruck with theſe News, when I had fed my ſelf all along with the hopes of returning to *France*, and promoting my Intereſt, which is now ſo much thwarted. However, I was forc'd to be contented; for the greater Power bears the ſway all the World over. Purſuant to my orders, I made all ſuitable preparations for my Voyage, without loſs of time. I took leave of my Friends, who ſingled out the beſt Soldiers for me; and made me Preſents of Cloaths, Tobacco, Books, and an infinity of other things, that they could ſpare without any inconveniency, becauſe they were then upon their return to the Colony, which affords every thing that one can deſire. By good luck, I brought my Aſtrolabe with me from *Monreal*, which will enable me to take the Latitudes of this Lake, and to make ſeveral other uſeful Obſervations; for in all appearance, I ſhall be out two years or ſuch a matter. The Men of my Detachment are brisk proper fellows, and my Canows are both new and large. I am to go along with Mr. *Dulhut*, a *Lions* Gentleman, who is a Perſon of great Merit, and has done his King and his Country very conſiderable Services. Mr. *de Tonti* makes another of our Company[1]; and a Company of Savages is to follow us. Mr. *de Denonville* will ſet out [80]

[1] Henry de Tonty was a Neapolitan, whose father invented the insurance system called from his name, "tontine." Tonty entered the French service at the age of eighteen, and won distinction in the army, where he lost one of his hands. In 1677 he met La Salle, and embarked on his enterprise of discovery, accompanied him to the Illinois, and there took command of Fort St. Louis. After La Salle's death this fort was granted to Tonty and La Forest as a seigniory, and there for ten years or more they held command. Tonty assisted Cadillac in founding Detroit (1701), after which he was ordered to aid Iberville in Louisiana, where he died of yellow fever in 1704. See Legler, "Henry de Tonty," Parkman Club *Papers* (Milwaukee, 1896).—ED.

for the Colony by the North fide of the Lake of *Frontenac*, in two or three days. He defigns to leave at Fort *Frontenac*, a number of Men and Ammunition equal to what he leaves here. I herewith tranfmit fome Letters for my Relations, which I beg you would convey to their Hands. If I meet with any opportunity, I'll fend you a Journal of my Voyage the next year. In the mean time, I am,

SIR,

Yours, &c.

LETTER XIV.

Dated at *Miſſilimakinac May* 26. 1688.

The Author leaves Niagara, *and has an Incounter with the* Iroqueſe *at the end of the Land-Carriage. The after part of his Voyage. A Deſcription of the Country. He arrives at Fort St.* Joſeph *in the Mouth of the Lake of* Hurons. *A Detachment of the* Hurons *arrive at the ſame place. After an Ingagement, they ſet out for* Miſſilimakinac. *A ſtrange Adventure of Mr.* de la Salle's *Brother.* Miſſilimakinac *deſcrib'd.*

SIR,

I AM at a loſs to determine whether 'tis owing to Stupidity, or greatneſs of Mind, that the loſs of my Eſtate, which I infallibly foreſee, do's not at all affect me. Your Letter is but too ſhrewd a confirmation of my Prophecy: However, I cannot but purſue your ſeaſonable advice in writing to Court; [81] in the meantime ſuffer me to ſatisfie my promiſe, in preſenting you with a relation of my Voyages.

I imbarqued at *Niagara Auguſt* 3. on board a Canow mann'd with eight Soldiers of my Detachment; and after running three Leagues againſt the Current of the Streight, came that ſame day to the place where the Navigation ſtops. There I met with the Sieur *Griſolon de la Tourette*, Brother to Mr. *Dulhut*, who had ventur'd to come from *Miſſilimakinac* with a ſingle Canow to joyn the Army.[1] The 4*th* we commenc'd our great Land-Carriage to the Southward, being oblig'd to tranſport our Canows from a League and a half below the great Fall of *Niagara*, to half a League above it. Before we got at any beaten or level Path, we were forc'd to climb up three Mountains, upon which an hundred *Iroqueſe* might have knock'd us all on the head with Stones.[2] While we were imploy'd in this tranſport Service, we were alarm'd twice or thrice; which caution'd us to keep a ſtrict guard, and to tranſport our Baggage with all poſſible Expedition: Nay, after all our precautions we were forc'd to leave one half of our Baggage about half way, upon the diſcovery of a thouſand *Iroqueſe* that march'd towards us. Do you judge, Sir, if we had not ſome reaſon to be alarm'd; and whether we would ſtand to Sacrifice all to the natural principle of Self preſervation; tho' indeed we were in danger of loſing our Lives as well as our Baggage: for we had not imbarqued above the Fall half a quarter of an hour, when the Enemy appear'd upon the Streight ſide. I aſſure you, I 'ſcap'd very narrowly; for about a quarter of an hour before, I and three or four Savages had

[1] Claude Greysolon de la Tourette, younger brother of Duluth, assisted him in all his adventures, and ably seconded his measures. In 1678 he accompanied him to the upper country, and when Duluth built the fort on Lake Nipigon (1683), he named it La Tourette and placed his brother in charge. Their uncle patron bequeathed his possessions to the younger nephew in 1691, and at the time of Duluth's death, La Tourette was living in Lyons, France. The report which he made to Denonville after this encounter with Lahontan, is found in *N. Y. Colon. Docs.*, ix, p. 343. — ED.

[2] For a description of the "three Mountains," which are the three levels of the cliff above Lewiston, see Parkman, *La Salle*, p. 132, note. Hennepin first described the portage path; see *New Discovery*, pp. 103, 104, 324. — ED.

gone five hundred paces out of our Road, to look upon that fearful Cataract; and 'twas as much as I could do, to get at the Canows before they put off. To be taken by ſuch cruel Fellows, [82] was to me no trifling thing.

*Il morir e niente, ma il vivere brugiando & troppo. To die is nothing, but to live in the midſt of Fire * is too much.*

* The Priſoners taken by the *Iroqueſe* are frequently burnt.

As for the Waterfall of *Niagara;* 'tis ſeven or eight hundred foot high, and half a League broad. Towards the middle of it we deſcry an Iſland that leans towards the Precipice, as if it were ready to fall. All the Beaſts that croſs the Water within half a quarter of a League above this unfortunate Iſland, are ſuck'd in by force of the Stream: And the Beaſts and Fiſh that are thus kill'd by the prodigious fall, ſerve for food to fifty *Iroqueſe*, who are ſetled about two Leagues off, and take 'em out of the water with their Canows. Between the ſurface of the water that ſhelves off prodigiouſly, and the foot of the Precipice, three Men may croſs in a breaſt without any other dammage, than a ſprinkling of ſome few drops of water.[1]

To return to the Story of the thouſand *Iroqueſe;* I muſt tell you, that we croſs'd the Streight with all the vigour we were

[1] The first allusion to Niagara Falls is found in the account of Cartier's voyage, in 1535. Champlain heard many relations of the falls from the Indians, but never saw them in person. Hennepin's appears to be the first detailed description by an eye witness; but he characteristically exaggerates the height and noise of the cataract. See *New Discovery*, pp. 54–56, with illustration.

The Seneca village mentioned by Lahontan must have been a temporary camp. The Senecas lived east of Genesee River until after Denonville's expedition, and had no permanent village near Niagara until a number of years later. — ED.

maſters of, and after rowing all Night, arriv'd next Morning at the mouth of the Lake, which appear'd to be indifferent rapid. Then we were ſecure from all danger, for the *Iroqueſe* Canows are ſo dull and large, that they cannot ſail near ſo quick as thoſe made of Birch-bark. The former are made of Elm-bark, which is very heavy, and their form is very aukard; for they are ſo long and broad that thirty Men row in them, two abreaſt, whether ſitting or ſtanding, and the ſides are ſo low, that they dare not venture 'em upon the Lakes, tho' the wind be very ſlack. We coaſted along the North-Coaſt of the Lake of *Erie*, being favour'd by the Calms, which are in a manner conſtant in that ſeaſon, eſpecially in the Southern Countries. Upon the brink of this Lake we frequently ſaw [83] flocks of fifty or ſixty Turkey's, which run incredibly faſt upon the Sands: And the Savages of our Company kill'd great numbers of 'em, which they gave to us in exchange for the Fiſh that we catch'd. The 25*th* we arriv'd at a long point of Land which ſhoots out 14 or 15 Leagues into the Lake; and the heat being exceſſive, we choſe to tranſport our Boats and Baggage two hundred paces over-land, rather than coaſt about for thirty five Leagues.[1] *Septemb.* 6. We enter'd the Streight of the Lake of *Hűron*, where we met with a ſlack Current of half a League in breadth, that continued till we arriv'd in the Lake of St. *Claire*, which is twelve Leagues in Circumference. The 8*th* of the ſame Month we ſteer'd on to the other end, from whence we had but ſix Leagues to run againſt the ſtream,

[1] Long Point, Lake Erie, which Hennepin called "Cape St. Francis." — Ed.

till we arriv'd in the Mouth of the Lake of *Hurons*, where we landed on the 14*th*. You cannot imagine the pleaſant proſpect of this Streight, and of the little Lake; for their banks are cover'd with all ſorts of wild Fruit-Trees. 'Tis true, the want of Agriculture ſinks the agreeableneſs of the Fruit; but their plenty is very ſurpriſing.[1] We ſpy'd no other Animals upon the ſhoar, but Herds of Harts, and Roe-bucks: And when we came to little Iſlands, we ſcour'd 'em, in order to oblige theſe Beaſts to croſs over to the Continent, upon which they offering to ſwim over, were knock'd on the head by our Canow-men that were planted all round the Iſlands. After our arrival at the Fort, of which I was order'd to take poſſeſſion, Mr. *Dulhut* and Mr. *de Tonti* had a mind to reſt themſelves for ſome days, as well as the Savages that accompany'd us. This Fort, which was built by Mr. *Dulhut*, was Garriſon'd upon his own charges by the *Coureurs de Bois*, who had taken care to ſow in it ſome Buſhels of *Turkey*-Wheat, which afforded a plentiful Crop, that prov'd of great uſe to me.[2]

[1] Hennepin says that he named Lake St. Clair, and gives its Iroquois name as "Otsi Keta." All early travellers remark on the beauty of the landscape and the abundance of wild fruit in the vicinity of Detroit. See *Wis. Hist. Colls.*, xvi, pp. 129, 366. — Ed.

[2] It was part of Denonville's plan to bar the English from the upper lakes by erecting a fort at Detroit River. Accordingly in 1686 he sent word to Duluth to proceed thither and erect a stockade. In the autumn of that year, Duluth collected fifty coureurs des bois, and built the post, which he named Fort St. Joseph — not on the site of Detroit, but where St. Clair River flows from Lake Huron, apparently near the present Fort Gratiot, Michigan. See *N. Y. Colon. Docs.*, ix, pp. 300, 302. A contemporary description says: "Our Fort covers a square of one Arpent in extent, without the Bastions, and is very advantageously Situated on an Eminence, separated from the River by a gentle slope of about forty paces, which forms a very pleasant

The Garrison surrendred their Post very [84] chearfully to my Detachment; and then pursued their Commerce with our Savages, for every one had leave to go where he pleas'd. This gave me an opportunity of sending two Canows under a guard of Soldiers, to dispose of a great Roll of Tobacco of 200 weight, that Mr. *Dulhut* had kindly presented me with; for that honest Gentleman inform'd me, that my Soldiers might easily purchase Corn in exchange for Tobacco, sooner than for any other Commodities. I am oblig'd to him as long as I live; but I am much affraid, the Treasurer of the Navy will make him no better compensation for this piece of Service, than for a thousand other disbursements upon the King's account. The Soldiers I sent with the Tobacco, return'd in the latter end of *November*, and brought with 'em the Reverend Father *Avenau* the Jesuit, who found no occasion to trouble himself with preaching up Abstinence from Meat in the time of *Lent*.[1] They brought advice, that a Party of the *Hurons* being prepar'd to march out of their Villages, to attack the *Iroquese* Beaver-hunters, would speedily repair to the Fort to rest themselves. In the mean time I waited with impatience

Glacis [parapet]. Care has been taken to place it at the narrowest part of the River, which is here a gunshot in width." *Wis. Hist. Colls.*, xvi, p. 128. The further history of Fort St. Joseph, which Lahontan was to command, is related by him.

"Turkey wheat" is maize or Indian corn, so called from a vague notion that it was first found in Turkey. — ED.

[1] Father Claude Aveneau came to Canada in 1685, and was assigned next year to the Ottawa mission at Mackinac. One would judge from Lahontan's remark that this missionary acted as chaplain of Fort St. Joseph throughout the winter of 1687–88. He passed the remainder of his life in the West, for many years serving in the Miami mission, and finally dying at Quebec in 1711. — ED.

for the arrival of one *Turcot*,[1] and four more of the *Coureurs de Bois*, who were to come to me in the beginning of *December*, along with ſome other Huntſmen that Mr. *de Denonville* had promis'd to ſend me: But hearing nothing of 'em, and our Commons being at that time very ſhort, I ſhould have been very much pinch'd, if four young *Canadeſe* who were expert Huntſmen, had not tarry'd with me all Winter. The abovemention'd Party of the *Hurons* arriv'd *Decemb.* 2. being headed by one *Saentſouan*, who left me his Canow and his Baggage, to keep till he return'd; for he could not poſſibly continue his Navigation longer, upon the account that the ſurface of the water began then to be cover'd with Ice. Theſe Savages choſe to march [85] over-land to the Fort of *Niagara*, where they expected to receive intelligence before they enter'd the Country of the *Iroqueſe*. They march'd ten days, *i. e.* fifty Leagues, without ſeeing one Soul. But at laſt their Scouts perceiv'd the foot-ſteps of ſome Huntſmen, which they trac'd at a great pace for a whole Night, the Snow being then a foot deep. Towards the break of day they return'd, and gave notice to their Fellow-Adventurers, that they had diſcover'd ſix Hutts, with ten Men lodg'd in each of 'em. Upon this Intelligence the whole party made a halt, in order to paint their faces, to prepare their Arms, and to concert proper Meaſures. The attack was ſo form'd, that two Men made

[1] A habitant by this name was captured by the Iroquois in 1652. As coureur des bois, he was accused of taking refuge among the English to escape his crimes — *N. Y. Colon. Docs.*, ix, p. 133. He appears to have been pardoned and again received in favor by the French authorities. — Ed.

ſoftly up to the two doors of the Hutts with their Clubs in their Hands, to knock down any one that offer'd to come out, while the reſt were imploy'd in firing their pieces. And the Action was crown'd with wonderful Succeſs; for the *Iroqueſe* being ſurpriz'd and ſhut up in their bark Priſons, there was but two out of ſixty four that made their eſcape; and theſe two being naked and deſtitute of Fire-Arms, could not but periſh in the Woods. Three of the *Hurons* indeed were kill'd upon the ſpot, but to attone for that loſs, the Agreſſors carry'd off fourteen Priſoners, and four Women. This done, they march'd back to my Fort with all poſſible Expedition. Among the Captive Slaves, there were three who had made part of the number of the 1000 *Iroqueſe* that thought to have ſurpris'd us the year before, when we were imploy'd in the great Land-Carriage at *Niagara*. They gave us to underſtand, that the Fort of *Niagara* was block'd up by eight hundred *Iroqueſe*, who mean'd to appear before my Poſt without any delay. This troubleſom piece of news gall'd me to the laſt degree, for fear of being reduc'd to extremities; and with that view I was a very nice Husband of what Corn I had [86] left. I was not apprehenſive of being attack'd by 'em, for the Savages never fight fairly, neither do they ever attempt to pull up Paliſſadoes; but I was affraid that they would ſtarve us out by cramping our Huntſmen in their due range. However, the *Hurons* continuing fifteen days in my Fort to refreſh themſelves, I us'd the precaution of ingaging them to aſſiſt my Huntſmen in providing Meat: But as ſoon as they took leave of me in order to return home, our hunting was at an end and the Gates were kept ſhut.

At laſt, finding that my Proviſions were almoſt out, I reſolv'd to go to *Miſſilimakinac*, to buy up Corn from the *Hurons* and the *Outaouans*.[1] Accordingly, having left ſome Soldiers to guard the Fort in my abſence, I imbarqu'd with the reſt of my Detachment on the firſt of *April*, with a gentle South-Eaſt Gale; by the help of which we inſenſibly croſs'd the Bay of *Saguinan*. That little Gulf is ſix hours over, and in the middle of it there are two little Iſlands, which afford a very ſeaſonable ſhelter when a wind ariſes in the croſſing over. Before you have croſs'd this Bay, the Coaſt is all a long full of Rocks and Shelves, one of which that I ſaw was ſix Leagues broad: But above it the Coaſt is clean and low, eſpecially towards the Sand-River, which lies half way between that Bay and a place call'd *l'Anſe du Tonnere*.[2] Now this laſt place is reckon'd thirty Leagues off the Bay. Having paſt that, we had but thirty Leagues more to ſail; which we did without any danger, by the help of an Eaſt-South-Eaſt Gale, that ſwell'd the Waves prodigiouſly. In the Mouth of the *Illineſe* Lake we met the party of the *Hurons* that I mention'd before; and four or five hundred *Outaouas*, who were bound home, after having ſpent the Winter in hunting of Beavers upon the River of *Saguinan*. Both they and we were forc'd to

[1] In the French edition, Lahontan explains that to abandon one's post would be censured in the Old World; in the New, it is regarded as a species of heroism. — Ed.

[2] The description of Saginaw Bay, River Au Sable (Sand River), and Thunder Bay is easily recognized. — Ed.

lye by in that place for three or [87] four days, by reafon of the Ice: After which the Lake was clear'd, and we crofs'd it together. When the *Hurons* came afhoar, they confulted among themfelves how to difpofe of their Slaves: After which they made a Prefent of one of 'em to Mr. *de Juchereau*, who commanded in that place[1]; but the poor wretch was prefently fhot to Death. Another of 'em was prefented to the *Outaouas*, who granted him his Life, for fuch reafons as you would eafily apprehend, if you were better acquainted with the policy and cunning of that fort of Men, whom you now take for Beafts.

I arriv'd in this place on the 18*th* of *April*, and my uneafinefs and trouble took date from the day of my arrival: For I found the *Indian* Corn fo fcarce by reafon of the preceding bad Harvefts, that I defpair'd of finding half fo much as I wanted. But after all, I am hopeful, that two Villages will furnifh me with almoft as much as I have occafion for. Mr. *Cavelier* arriv'd here *May* 6, being accompany'd with his Nephew, Father *Anaftafe* the Recollet, a Pilot, one of the Savages, and fome few *Frenchmen*, which made a fort of a party-colour'd Retinue. Thefe *Frenchmen* were fome of thofe that Mr. *de la Salle* had conducted upon the difcovery of

[1] This was probably Charles Juchereau de St. Denis, eldest son of Nicolas, sieur de Beauport, who the previous year had been employed as a messenger to Mackinac by Denonville. During the absence of La Durantaye (1687–88) he commanded the post. In later years he became councillor of the king, and lieutenant general of Montreal; he assisted Iberville in founding Louisiana, and in 1702 built a post near the mouth of the Ohio. A younger brother, Louis, undertook a remarkable exploration into New Mexico, and lived for many years at Natchitoches. — Ed.

Miffifipi. They give out, that they are fent to *Canada*, in order to go to *France*, with fome Difpatches from Mr. *de la Salle* to the King: But we fufpect that he is dead, becaufe he do's not return along with 'em. I fhall not fpend time in taking notice of their great Journey over-land; which by the account they give cannot be lefs than eight hundred Leagues.[1]

Miffilimakinac, the place I am now in, is certainly a place of great Importance. It lies in the Latitude of forty five Degrees, and thirty Minutes; but as for its Longitude, I have nothing to fay of it, for reafons mention'd in my fecond Letter. 'Tis not above half a League diftant from the *Illinefe* Lake, [88] an account of which, and indeed of all the other Lakes, you may expect elfe-where. Here the *Hurons* and *Outaouas* have, each of 'em, a Village; the one being fever'd from the other by a fingle Paliffadoe: But the *Outaouas* are

[1] These were the survivors of La Salle's last and fatal expedition, which was to have founded a colony at the mouth of the Mississippi. See Parkman, *La Salle*, pp. 356–446; Sulte, "Le Mort de La Salle," in *Can. Roy. Soc. Proc.*, 2d series, iv, pp. 3–32.

Abbe Jean Cavelier, the elder brother of the explorer, was born in Rouen, and became a Sulpitian priest. He had preceded La Salle to Canada, and often vexed him by his censoriousness. Joining this last expedition, he led the few survivors of the party, after the murder of La Salle, back from Texas to Canada; and concealed the death of the explorer from all his friends en route, partly to secure his brother's property. He died in 1717 at the house of his sister in Rouen.

Jean Cavelier, the younger, was a nephew of La Salle, a lad of fourteen when he embarked with his uncle at La Rochelle (1684). Returning to France, he entered the army.

Father Anastase Douay was, according to Hennepin, a native of Hainault. This was his first journey to America, and his published *Memoir* is largely used as a source for the expedition. After his return to Europe he was vicar of the Recollects at Cambray, and in 1699 embarked the second time for Louisiana, with Iberville, to found a mission among the Cenis. — Ed.

beginning to build a Fort upon a Hill, that ftands but 1000 or 1200 paces off. This Precaution they were prompted to by the murder of a certain *Huron*, call'd *Sandaouires*, who was affaffinated in the *Saguinan* River by four young *Outaouas*. In this place the Jefuits have a little Houfe, or Colledge adjoyning to a fort of a Church, and inclos'd with Pales that feparate it from the Village of the *Hurons*. Thefe good Fathers lavifh away all their Divinity and Patience to no purpofe, in converting fuch ignorant Infidels: For all the length they can bring 'em to, is, that oftentimes they'll defire Baptifm for their dying Children, and fome few fuperannuated Perfons confent to receive the Sacrament of Baptifm, when they find themfelves at the point of Death.[1] The *Coureurs de Bois* have but a very fmall fettlement here; though at the fame time 'tis not inconfiderable, as being the Staple of all the Goods that they truck with the South and the Weft Savages; for they cannot avoid paffing this way, when they go to the Seats of the *Illinefe*, and the *Oumamis*, or to the Bay *des Puants*,[2] and to the River of *Miffifipi*. The Skins which they import from

[1] During the French regime Michillimackinac (now Mackinac) was the capital of the Northwest. It had been occupied by traders for many years; but the first Jesuit mission was not begun until Marquette established that of St. Ignace in 1671. A few years later the fort was built and garrisoned. Mackinac Island is 45° 54′ north latitude by 80° 30′ west longitude; but the Mackinac of Lahontan's time lay on the north shore of the strait, as his map plainly indicates. For further details of the history of this place, see Thwaites, "Story of Mackinac," in *How George Rogers Clark Won the Northwest* (Chicago, 1903). — Ed.

[2] Bay des Puants (Stinkards) was the French name for Green Bay, Wisconsin. The origin of the term arose from the significance of the name of the Winnebago (men from the bad-smelling water). For further details, see *Wis. Hist. Colls.*, xvi, p. 3; Thwaites, *Stories of the Badger State* (New York, 1900), p. 30. — Ed.

theſe different places, muſt lye here ſome time before they are tranſported to the Colony. *Miſſilimakinac* is ſituated very advantageouſly; for the *Iroqueſe* dare not venture with their ſorry Canows, to croſs the Streight of the *Illineſe* Lake, which is two Leagues over; beſides that the Lake of the *Hurons* is too rough for ſuch ſlender Boats: And as they cannot come to it by Water, ſo they cannot approach to it by Land, by reaſon of the Marſhes, Fens, and little Rivers, which 'twould be very difficult to croſs; not to mention that the Streight of the *Illineſe* Lake lies ſtill in their way.

[89] You can ſcarce believe, Sir, what vaſt ſholes of white Fiſh are catch'd about the middle of the Channel, between the Continent and the Iſle of *Miſſilimakinac.* The *Outaouas* and the *Hurons* could never ſubſiſt here, without that Fiſhery; for they are oblig'd to travel above twenty Leagues in the Woods, before they can kill any Harts or Elks, and 'twould be an infinite fatigue to carry their Carcaſes ſo far over Land. This ſort of white Fiſh in my opinion, is the only one in all theſe Lakes that can be call'd good; and indeed it goes beyond all other ſorts of River Fiſh. Above all, it has one ſingular property, namely, that all ſorts of Sauces ſpoil it, ſo that 'tis always eat either boil'd or broil'd, without any manner of ſeaſoning.[1] In the Channel I now ſpeak of the Currents are ſo ſtrong, that they ſometimes ſuck in the Nets, though they are two or three Leagues off. In ſome ſeaſons, it ſo falls out that the Currents

[1] There are several species of the whitefish of the lakes. The common one, *Coregonus clupeiformis*, is the largest and the best food. These fish formed an important article of Indian diet. — ED.

run three days Eaſtward, two days to the Weſt, one to the South, and four Northward ; ſometimes more, and ſometimes leſs. The cauſe of this diverſity of Currents could never be fathom'd, for in a calm, they'l run in the ſpace of one day to all the points of the Compaſs, *i. e.* ſometimes one way, ſometimes another, without any limitation of time; ſo that the deciſion of this matter muſt be left to the Diſciples of *Copernicus.* Here the Savages catch Trouts as bigh as one's Thigh, with a ſort of Fiſhing-Hook made in the form of an Awl, and made faſt to a piece of Braſs wire, which is joyn'd to the Line that reaches to the bottom of the Lake.[1] This ſort of Fiſhery is carried on not only with Hooks, but with Nets, and that in Winter, as well as in Summer : For they make holes in the Ice at a certain diſtance one from another, thro' which they conduct the Nets with Poles. The *Outaouas* and the *Hurons* have very pleaſant Fields, in which they ſow *Indian* Corn, Peaſe, [90] and Beans, beſides a ſort of Citruls,[2] and Melons, which differs much from ours, and of which I ſhall take occaſion to ſpeak in another place. Sometimes, theſe Savages ſell their Corn very dear, eſpecially when the Beaver-hunting happens not to take well: Upon which occaſion they make ſufficient repriſals upon us for the extravagant price of our Commodities.

As ſoon as I have bought up ſixty ſacks of Corn, each of

[1] This is the Mackinac trout (*Salvelinus namycush*), which often grows to great size. Its flesh is inferior to that of the whitefish. — Ed.

[2] Citrouille, or summer squash (*Cucurbita polymortha*) was raised extensively by the North American Indians. — Ed.

which may weigh fifty pound, I am to march with my Detachment alone to *St. Mary*'s Fort, in order to ingage the *Sauteurs* or the Inhabitants of *Saut Saint Marie*, to joyn the *Outaouas*[1]; after which we mean to march with joynt Forces to the Country of the *Iroquese*. Besides these, there's a party of a hundred *Hurons* ready to march, under the Command of the great Leader *Adario*, whom the *French* call the *Rat;* but they do not march our way. I shall write to you with the first Opportunity after my return from this Expedition.[2] Perhaps the Jesuits will send your Letters for me along with Mr. *Denonville*'s to Fort St. *Joseph*, where I am to reside. I shall expect their arrival with the utmost impatience. In the mean time I send you a Letter directed to Mr. *de Seignelai*, the purport of which I have here subjoyn'd. 'Twill be a very sensible obligation laid upon me, if you vouchsafe to believe that I always am,

SIR,

Yours, &c.

---

[1] The Saulteurs were a Chippewa tribe, so named by the French from first encountering one of their bands at Sault Ste. Marie; the name was afterwards extended to the entire tribe. Sault Ste. Marie was visited by traders as early as 1616, and the Jesuit mission thereat was established in 1669. In early days it took precedence of Mackinac; but after the discovery of the Mississippi, the latter place increased in importance, as being upon the path thither, and by 1689 the Sault was practically abandoned, except as a station on the trade route to the far Northwest.—ED.

[2] This is Lahontan's first mention of the famous chief, to whom he ascribes his *Dialogues*. Kondiaronk, to give him his Huron name, was a savage of much ability, who played a prominent part in Frontenac's War (1689–97). His skill in diplomacy, and in confederating the tribes, makes of him a precursor of Pontiac and Tecumseh. He was strongly attached to Frontenac, and accepted his counsel. Charlevoix says that he was a Christian convert, and often preached at Mackinac. Dying at Montreal during an important peace conference (1701), he was interred with elaborate rites. See Charlevoix, *Histoire de Nouvelle France* (Shea's trans.), v, pp. 145–148.—ED.

[91] *The Letter directed to Mr.* de Seignelay.

Honoured Sir,

I AM the Son of a Gentleman that ſpent three hundred thouſand Crowns in deepening the Water of the two *Gaves* of *Bearn:* He had the good luck to compaſs his End by conveying a great many Brooks to theſe two Rivers; and the Current of the *Adour* was by that means ſo far ſtrengthen'd as to render the Bar of *Bayonne* paſſable by a fifty Gun Ship, whereas in former times a Frigot of ten Guns durſt not venture over it. 'Twas in conſideration of this great and ſucceſſful Attempt, that his Majeſty granted to my Father and his Heirs for ever, certain Duties and Taxes, amounting to the Sum of three thouſand Livres a Year. This Grant was confirm'd by an Act of the Council of State, dated *January* 9. 1658, Sign'd *Boſſuet*, Collated, *&c.* Another Advantage accruing to the King and the Province from my Father's Services, conſiſts in the bringing down of Maſts and Yards from the *Pyrenean* Mountains, which could never have been effected, if he had not by his Care, and by the disburſing of immenſe Sums, enlarged the quantity of Water in the *Gave* of *Oleron* to a double proportion. Theſe Duties and Taxes which had been juſtly intail'd upon him and his Heirs, ceas'd to be ours when he dy'd; and to inflame the Diſgrace, I loſt his Places, *viz.* that of being a Honorary Judge of the Parliament of *Pau*, and Chief

Juftice in Eyre for the Province of *Bearn;* all which were mine by Inheritance.[1] Thefe Loffes are now follow'd by an unjuft Seizure that fome pretended Creditors have made of the Barony of *la Hontan*, [92] of a piece of Ground that lies contiguous to it, and of a hundred thoufand Livres that lay in the hands of the Chamber of *Bayonne*. Thefe faithlefs Creditors have no other reafon to fue me, but that I am now in the fagg end of the World, and that they are rich, and fupported by the Credit and Protection of the Parliament of *Paris*, where they hope to make good their unjuft Pretenfions in my Abfence. Laft Year I obtain'd Leave to return to *France*, in order to take care of this matter; but now Mr. *de Denonville* has fent me with a Detachment to thefe Lakes; from whence I humbly petition that your Honour would vouchfafe me Leave to come home the next Year, and at the fame time honour me with your Protection. I am, with all poffible refpect,

Your Honours, &c.

---

[1] For a further account of the services of Lahontan's father, Isaac Lom d'Arce, baron de Lahontan and d'Esleich, see Roy, "Le Baron de Lahontan," in *Can. Roy. Soc. Proc.*, 1st series, xii, pp. 67–69, 166–173. — ED.

LETTER XV.

Dated at *Miſſilimakinac Sept.* 18. 1688.

Deſcribing the Fall call'd Saut St. Marie, *where the Author perſwades the Inhabitants to joyn the* Outaouas, *and march againſt the* Iroqueſe. *And containing an Account of the Occurrences of the Voyage between that Place and* Miſſilimakinac.

SIR,

I AM now return'd from the *Iroqueſe* Country, and have quitted the Fort of *St. Joſeph*, againſt my Will. I cannot allow my ſelf to doubt, but that you took care of the Letter directed for Mr. *de Seignelay*, which I tranſmitted to you three Months ago.

[93] I ſet out from hence in my Canow, *June* 2. And after my Arrival at the Water-fall call'd *Saut Sainte Marie*, I perſwaded forty young Warlike Fellows to joyn the Party of the *Outaouas* that I mention'd in my laſt. This *Saut Sainte Marie* is a Cataract, or rather a Water-fall of two Leagues in length, which gives vent to the Waters of the upper Lake, and at the bottom of which, not far from the Jeſuits Houſe, there's a Village of the *Outchipoues*, aliàs *Sauteurs*.[1] This Place is a great Thoroughfare for the *Coureurs de Bois* that trade with the

[1] For an interesting Indian legend of the origin of Sault Ste. Marie, see *Jes. Rel.*, liv, p. 201. — ED.

Northern People, who ufually repair to the brinks of that Lake in the Summer. The continual Fogg that rifes from the upper Lake, and fpreads over the adjacent Country, renders the Ground fo barren, that it bears no Corn. The 13th of the fame Month I fet out from the abovemention'd Village, being accompany'd by the forty young *Sauteurs*, who embark'd in five Canows, each of which held eight Men. The 16th we arriv'd at the Ifle of *Detour*, where my Soldiers and the Party of the *Outaouas* had tarry'd for me two days.[1] The firft day was fpent by the *Outaouas* and the *Sauteurs* in Warlike Feafts, Dancing, and Singing, purfuant to their wonted Cuftom: The next day we all embark'd, and traverfing from Ifle to Ifle, made the Ifland of *Manitoualin* in four days. This Ifland is 25 Leagues long, and feven or eight broad. In former times 'twas poffefs'd by the *Outaouas* of *Talon*, call'd the *Otontagans;* who were diflodg'd by the Progrefs of the *Iroquefe*, that has ruin'd fo many Nations.[2] We coafted upon that Ifle a whole day; and being favour'd by a Calm, crofs'd from Ifle to Ifle

[1] Isle of Detour was the present Drummond Island, which lies east of Detour Strait—the passage to St. Mary's River; the Indian name was "Pontaganipy." In 1815 the island obtained its present title in honor of Sir Gordon Drummond, then lieutenant-governor of Canada. See Cook, *Drummond Island* (Lansing, Mich., 1896).—ED.

[2] Grand Manitoulin Island appears to have been the original home of the Ottawa—first called by the French "cheveux relevez," from their custom of wearing the hair erect. See *Jes. Rel.*, xiv, note 9. After the devastation of the Huron country by the Iroquois (1649–51), many of the vanquished Huron fled to Manitoulin; later, the entire island appears to have been deserted. The *Relation* of 1670–72 speaks of a tribe of Ottawa who had betaken themselves to this island, their former home; probably this was the band led by chief Talon (named for the intendant of Canada), whom Hennepin encountered in this country. See his *New Discovery*, pp. 316, 317. The present Indian population is an admixture of Huron and Ottawa.—ED.

till we made the Eaſt-ſide of the Lake. In this Paſſage we croſs'd between two Iſlands that were ſix Leagues diſtant the one from the other; and upon that occaſion our Watermen, who were not us'd to venture ſo far out in their ſlender Boats, were fain to tugg hard at their Oars.[1] The Savages ſtood out at firſt, and refus'd to [94] venture ſo far from Land, for they would rather have gone fifty Leagues about; but at laſt I over-perſwaded 'em, by repreſenting that I would have been very loth to venture my own Perſon, if I had not been ſufficently provided againſt all danger by an exact knowledge of the Winds and the Storms. The Calm continuing, we made the River of *Theonontatè* on the 25th. The next day there ſprung up a Gale from the Weſt-ſouth-weſt, which kept us back for four or five days; but our ſtop was of no great advantage to us, for it rain'd ſo heavily, that we could not hunt. This Country is the ancient Seat of the *Hurons*, as it appears from the Name they give to their Nations in their own Language, *viz. Theonontateronons*, *i. e.* the Inhabitants of *Theonontate*. But after the *Iroqueſe* had, upon divers occaſions, taken and defeated great numbers of 'em, the reſt quitted the Country to avoid the like Fate.[2] We re-embark'd on the

[1] Scadding (*Canadian Journal*, new series, xiii, p. 313) identifies the two islands as those now known as Fitzwilliam, and the Isle of Caves off Cape Hurd, both across the entrance of Georgian Bay. He identifies the River Theonontaté with the Maitland, in Huron County, Ontario. It was more probably the Nottawausaga, in Simcoe County, where the Tionnontaté had their earliest home. — Ed.

[2] The Tionnontaté, called by the French Tobacco Huron or Petuns, were known to the earliest French explorers. Their ancient seat was in Simcoe County, but all the peninsula between Georgian Bay and lower Lake Huron was known as the "Country of the Ancient Hurons." This is the tribe among whom Marquette had

29th, and on the 1ſt of *July* arriv'd at Fort *St. Joſeph*, where the Soldiers I had left waited for us with great Impatience. Having landed ſome Sacks Corn at the Fort, we ſet out again on the 3d of *July*, and purſued our Courſe with all diligence, in order to an early Appearance in the *Iroqueſe* Country. We ſail'd through the Streight or Neck, and ſtood to the South-ſide, of the Lake *Erie;* and being favour'd by the Weather, arriv'd on the 17th in the River of *Conde*, which I ſhall have occaſion to take notice of in deſcribing the Lakes of *Canada*.[1] Immediately, upon our Landing, the Savages fell to work in cutting down Trees, and making a Redoubt of Stakes, or Pales, for the Security of our Canows and Baggage, and for a ſafe Retreat to our ſelves in caſe of neceſſity.

The 20th they march'd, each Man being provided with a light Covering, a Bow, and ſome Arrows, (or elſe a Fuſee) and a little Bag containing ten pound weight of the Flowr of the *Indian* Corn. [95] They thought it moſt convenient to keep to the Banks of the River, upon which the *Goyogoans* are

his Mackinac mission of St. Ignace; they afterwards settled at Detroit, and were known to the English as Wyandots. On the Iroquois war which expelled them from their ancient home, see Parkman, *Jesuits*, pp. 403-410. On their later history and migrations, see Shea, in *Historical Magazine*, v, pp. 262-265. A remnant still exists on a reservation near Amherstburg, Ont. — Ed.

[1] This name, "River de Conde," appears to be peculiar to Lahontan, from whom Pownall quotes it in his description of 1754 (*N. Y. Colon. Docs.*, vi, p. 896). In our author's later description, and upon his map he exaggerates the size and length of the stream, which from its location must be either Mill Creek, Erie County, Pa., whence the portage ran to the sources of the Allegheny, or Chautauqua Creek, in New York, whence the usual portage to the lake of that name was about six miles. Scadding thinks it was Cattaraugus Creek; but the portage thence to the Allegheny was much longer than Lahontan describes, *post*. — Ed.

wont to fifh for Sturgeon; for that Fifh, which is fix foot in length, comes out of the Lakes in hot Weather, and fwims up the Rivers.[1] They had refolv'd likewife, if they found the Country clear, to march up and furprife the Villages of the *Goyogoans:* but they were foon eas'd of that trouble; for they had not march'd two days when their Scouts defcry'd three hundred *Iroquefe:* and on the other hand the *Iroquefe* fpy'd them to fuch purpofe, that the Scouts efcap'd very narrowly, and had much ado to return to the body of the Party, which immediately betook themfelves to flight. I was mightily furpris'd when I heard the Centinel of our Redoubt cry out, *Aux Armes, our Men are beaten and purfued;* but I was yet more furpriz'd when I faw the Fugitives run at full fpeed, when there was no body behind them. When they came up they were all filent for half an hour, purfuant to their Ufe and Wont; after which their Leader recounted to me the Particulars of the Adventure. I thought at firft that their advanc'd Guards had miftook the number of the Enemies; for I knew that the *Outaouas* had not the Reputation of too much Courage: but the next day a Party of the *Iroquefe* appear'd in fight of our Redoubt, which gave me occafion to believe that they were in the right of it. Nay, this Truth was afterwards confirmed by a certain Slave call'd *Chaouanon*, who made his efcape to the Redoubt, and affur'd me, that the *Iroquefe* were not lefs than four hundred; to which he added, that they expected to be joyn'd by fixty more that had march'd fome

[1] Lahontan here correctly describes the habits of the lake sturgeon (*Acipenser rubicundus*) which spawns in the small streams. — Ed.

A General Map of
NEW FRANCE
Com. call'd CANADA
H. Moll S.
Mouth of ye Great Lake of ye ASSINIPOVALS
Cities and Towns
French & English Villages
Villages of the Savages
Savage Vill. dest. by ye Iroquese
The Forts with a Cross about 'em are abandon'd
The Countries for Beaver hunting, that I know of
Waterfalls and Catar. in ye Rivers
Land Carriages from one place to another.
The prick'd line that runs from St. Laurence Bay points out the course of my Voyage to Missilimakinac
The lines run in this fashion from Missilimakinac by ye East side of ye Lake of Hurons to ye South of Lake Errie and so to Conde River, after which they run back by ye West side of Huron Lake to Missilimakinac: these lines delineate the course we steer'd in our Expedition agst the Iroquese.
This Serpentine line shews ye Course of my Return from Missilimakinac to Monreal, by the way of R. d'France, is the River Crusé, and the Great R. of Outaouas.
This faint line represents ye way that ye Ilinese march thro' a vast tract of ground to make War against ye Iroquese: The same being ye Passage of ye Iroquese in their incursions upon ye other Savages, as far as the River Missisipi
HUDSONS BAY
James Bay
TERRA DE LABRADOR or ESKIMAUX
Bay of St. Laurence
NEW SCOTLAND
Acadia
NEW ENGLAND
NEW YORK
N. York
N. Iersey
PENSILVANIA
ATLANTICK OCEAN
IROQUOIS
LAKE OF HURON
ILINESE LAKE
SUPERIEUR or UPPER LAKE
NEMIPICON LAKE
ERRIE or CONTI LAKE
LAKE FRONTENAC
Missisipi River
St. Laurens River
Long River
Little Fort of St. Germain which hinders ye Assinipovals to come down to Port Nelson
Port Nelson
Fort of Kamanistigoyan
English Fort
Quebec
Trois Rivers
Monreal
Boston
C. Cod
Long I.
Nantucket Isle
Nantucket Sand
C. Sable
C. Breton
Anticoste Isle
Villages of the Missiouris
Osages R.
Otentas R.
F. Crevecoeur
Land Carriage of Ouisconsinc
Ouisconsine R.
Fall of Kakalin
Kikapous
Saut St. Maria
Missilimakinac
Landing Place
Conde R.
Ouabach R.
Andastoguerenons
0 30 60 120 180 240 300
English Miles
0 10 20 40 60 80 100
English and French Leagues

Months before to the Country of the *Oumamis*. He inform'd us farther, That while the Marquis *de Denonville* was concerting meafures for a Peace with the five Nations, an *Englifhman*, of the Name of *Aria*, accompany'd with fome others, endeavour'd to diffwade them from Peace, by Orders [96] from the Governour of *New York*.[1] In the mean time the Savages having prefs'd me to affift at a Council of War, they propos'd to lie by for a fair Wind, and then to embark. They reprefented, that they defign'd to fail to the end of the Lake, where they would infallibly light upon the fixty *Iroquefe* that I mention'd above; but withal, that they could not agree to fet out in a Calm, becaufe that after their quitting the Redoubt, and launching out, a contrary Wind might force 'em afhore, where their Throats might be cut if the Enemy purfu'd 'em. I reply'd, That 'twas then fuch fine Weather, that we had nothing to expect but Calms; that if we tarry'd longer in this Place, our Enemies would thereby gain time to make Canows in order to a Purfuit; that fince the favourablenefs of the Wind was fo uncertain, we ought to embark without lofs of time; that we might fail in the Night, and fculk in the Daytime behind Rocks and Points of Land; and, that by this means the Enemy would be at a lofs to know whether we ftood to the South or to the North fide of the Lake. The Savages made Anfwer, That 'twas true their tarrying might be every way prejudicial; but 'twas equally true, that my Expedient

[1] For the negotiations between Governors Denonville and Dongan, see *N. Y. Colon. Docs.*, iii, pp. 438–564; ix, 388–404. By the "Englishman Aria," Lahontan doubtless intends Arnout Cornelisse Viele, whom Dongan employed as his messenger to the Iroquois. — Ed.

was dangerous: However, they confented to embark along with us, and for that end gumm'd their Canows. We embark'd on the 24th at night, and the Weather being fair, clear, and calm, made a great deal of way that night, and the fucceeding day. The next Evening we came to an Anchor, defigning to fleep for three or four hours, but not to ftir out of the Canows. About Midnight we weigh'd our little wooden Anchors, and one half of the Men row'd while the other was at reft. Thus did we continue to fteer with a great deal of Precaution and Care, rowing all night, and lying by all day.

July 28. when we were lying almoft all afleep in a Creek of a little Ifland, the Watch defcrying fome [97] Canows that made towards us, wak'd fome Savages that had gone a-fhore to fleep the more conveniently. The Noife having alarm'd us all, we prefently made our felves ready to get in head of thefe Canows; but at the fame time, tho' we were but half a League off, we could not diftinguifh who they were, by reafon that the Sun-beams falling perpendicularly, made the Surface of the Water look like a Looking-glafs. Indeed there being but two of 'em, we reckon'd they were mann'd with *Iroquefe*, and that each of 'em contain'd at leaft twenty Men: upon which fufpicion, the Leader of the *Sauteurs* offered to go a-fhore with his Men, and poft himfelf at the Entry of a Wood, from whence he would foftly follow the Canows without being difcover'd, till fuch time as we forc'd 'em a-fhore. At the fame time he propos'd that the *Outaouas* and my Detachment fhould fuffer 'em to be within a Musket-fhot of the Ifland before we dif-cover'd our felves, or offer'd to give 'em chafe, upon the apprehenſion that if we follow'd 'em cloſer, they would be ſo far from getting on ſhore, that they would fight as deſperate, and chooſe rather to be kill'd or drown'd than to be taken. This Propoſal was lik'd, and every thing was manag'd accordingly. As ſoon as our unknown Enemy perceiv'd us, they made the Shore with all imaginable Precipitation; and juſt when they were going to knock their Priſoners on the Head, the *Sauteurs* fell upon 'em, but miſs'd of their aim in taking 'em all alive; for they fought to the laſt gaſp, like Men that knew no Medium betwixt Conqueſt and Death. *Una ſalus victis nullam ſperare ſalutem.* This Engagement happen'd while we landed: however, the *Sauteurs* came off with Honour, for they loſt only four Men, and of twenty *Iroqueſe* they kill'd three, wounded five, and took the reſt Priſoners, ſo that not one of 'em eſcap'd. The *Iroqueſe* had along with them eighteen Slaves of the *Oumamis*, who were all wounded, and ſeven big-belly'd [98] Women, from whom we had Intelligence that the reſt of their Party were then upon their Return by Land upon the Banks of the Lake, having thirty four Priſoners, of both Sexes; and that they could not then be far off. When this Intelligence was laid before us, the *Outaouas* were of the opinion that we ſhould reſt ſatisfied with the Feats we had done, upon the Plea that the above-mention'd four hundred *Iroqueſe* would certainly get before us. On the other hand, the *Sauteurs* maintain'd that they had rather periſh than fail to attempt the Reſcue of theſe Priſoners, and the Defeat of the whole Party; and that if no body would ſecond 'em, they would make the Attempt by themſelves. The Bravery of this Reſolution oblig'd me to encourage and egg on the *Outaouas*. I remonſtrated to 'em, that in regard the *Sauteurs* ingroſs'd the Glory of the former Action, they had more reaſon than we to decline the riſque of a ſecond Engagement: that if we refus'd to back 'em, our Cowardice would cover us with everlaſting Infamy: and, that in order to render the Attack more ſecure, we ought to uſe a ſpeedy Precaution in finding out ſome Point or Elbow of Land where our Canows, our Baggage, and our Priſoners might be lodg'd ſafe. The *Outaouas* had a great deal of Reluctancy to the matter; however, after conſulting among themſelves, they comply'd with the Propoſal, more for Shame, than out of true Courage. Having laid down that joint Reſolution, we made up a little ſort of a Fence in ſeven or eight hours, and then ſent out Scouts on all hands, while the main Body was kept in readineſs to march upon the firſt Alarm.

Auguſt 4. two of our Spies return'd upon full ſpeed, to acquaint us that the *Iroqueſe* were not above three Leagues off, and that they advanc'd towards us; and withal, that upon the Road there was a little Brook, upon which an Ambuſcado might be conveniently laid. This Advice animated our Savages ſo much, [99] that they run immediately to take Poſſeſſion of that Advantageous Poſt: but they knew not how to make the right uſe of it. The *Outaouas* were too haſty in firing; and by ſhooting at too great a diſtance, gave all the Enemies an opportunity of making their Eſcape, abating for ten or twelve whoſe Heads were brought into the little Fort where I ſtay'd. The Slaves indeed were all retaken, and ſo reſcued from the Cruelty of theſe Tygers; which encourag'd us to reſt ſatisfied. When the Expedition was over, we ſtow'd theſe poor Wretches in our Canows, and ſteer'd with all Expedition to the Streight or Neck of the Lake of *Huron*, which we made on the 13th. We enjoy'd a great deal of Pleaſure in ſtemming the Current of that Streight; the Iſlands of which, that I mention'd above, were cover'd with Roe bucks. This opportunity we did not ſlight; nor did we grudge our ſtopping upon theſe Iſlands for eight days; during which time we were buſied in Hunting, and refreſh'd our ſelves with plenty of excellent Fruit that was fully ripe. Here the wounded and retaken Priſoners had an opportunity of reſting, and of drinking the Broth of ſeveral ſorts of Meat; and we had time to broil as much Meat as we could ſtow in our Canows, not to mention the great numbers of Turkeys that we were oblig'd to eat upon the ſpot, for fear that the heat of the Seaſon would ſpoil 'em.

In that ſpace of time the poor wounded Savages were carefully purg'd with ſuch Roots as the *Americans* are well vers'd in; which I mean to explain to you in its proper time and place; and they wanted not good Reſtoratives of Jelly-broth. The 24th we re-embark'd, and arriv'd at Night at Fort *St. Joſeph*, where I found a Party of eighty *Oumamis* commanded by one *Michitonka*, who being lately return'd from *Niagara*, expected my Arrival with the utmoſt impatience. When I landed, I was ſurpris'd to ſee the [100] Fort cramm'd with Savages; but on the other hand, they were equally aſtoniſh'd to find in our Company their Country-men, to whoſe hard Fortune they had been altogether Strangers.

The joyful Meeting fill'd the Air with Acclamations, and Panegyricks rung all about to an extravagant degree. I wiſh, Sir, you had been there to partake of the Pleaſure of ſo fine a Show: had you been preſent, you would have join'd with me in owning that all our *French* Rhetorick cannot reach ſuch pithy and ſignificant Figures, eſpecially upon the ſcore of *Hyperbole*'s, as made up the bulk of the Harangues and Songs that theſe poor People utter'd with Rapture and Tranſport. *Michitonka* acquainted me, that after he went to the Fort of *Niagara*, with a Deſign to make ſome Expedition into the Country of the *Tſonontouans*, he found that the *Scurvey* had made ſuch a terrible havock in that Fort, that it had ſweept off the Commander, and all the Soldiers, bating twelve, who had the good luck to get over it, as well as Mr. *de Bergeres*, who by the advantage of a hale Conſtitution had ſtemm'd the raging Violence of that Diſtemper.[1] He inform'd me farther, That Mr. *Bergeres* having reſolv'd to ſet out with his twelve Men for the Fort of *Frontenac*, had deſir'd of him a Reinforcement of ſome young *Oumamis*, which was granted him; that after Mr. *Bergeres* had embark'd, himſelf march'd over Land to the Country of the *Onnontagues*, where he rejoin'd the Reinforcement he had granted to Mr. *de Bergeres*, and underſtood from them, that during the Winter the *Scurvey* had carried off as many Soldiers at Fort *Frontenac* as at *Niagara;* and, that Mr. *de Denonville* was negotiating a Peace with the *Iroqueſe*.

The Governour of Fort *Frontenac* had requeſted *Michitonka*

[1] For the official report of this disaster, and the abandonment of the fort at Niagara, see *N. Y. Colon. Docs.*, ix, pp. 386–388. — Ed.

to engage in no Enterprife, and to return home with his Men; upon which that Leader being in full March homeward, was attack'd by three hundred [101] *Onnontagues*, whom he durft not engage otherwife than in a running Fight, by which he loft four Men. Being inform'd of all thefe Circumftances, I confulted with the three different Nations that were then pofted in my Fort. After a mature Reflection upon the Intelligence that was laid before 'em, they came to this Refolution; That fince the Marquis *de Denonville* had a mind to clap up a Peace, and the Fort of *Niagara* was abdicated, the Fort I then commanded would be of no ufe; that fince I had neither Provifions nor Ammunition for above two Months, I fhould be oblig'd at the end of thefe two Months to retreat to the Place from whence I now write; that at that time of the Year our Navigation would be uneafie and dangerous; that in regard I lay under an indifpenfible neceffity of making my Retreat, 'twas of no great moment whether I march'd off two Months fooner or later; and, in fine, that fince I had receiv'd no frefh Orders, nor no Succors, 'twas my Bufinefs to go off along with them. This Refolution, which was a fufficient Argument to fway me, afforded matter of joy to the Soldiers, who were afraid of being oblig'd to a more rigorous courfe of Abftinence in that Poft than they had formerly undergone; for the meafures of a critical Abftinence do not fit well upon a Soldiers Stomach. In fine, purfuant to our joint Refolution, we fet fire to the Fort on the 27th, and embarked that fame day, and keeping clofe to the South fhore of the Lake that I took notice of in my laft, arriv'd here on the 10th of *September*.

The *Oumamis* march'd over Land to their own Country, and carry'd with 'em the Wounded, who were then in a condition to march.

Upon my Arrival in this Place, I found here Mr. *de la Durantay*, whom Mr. *Denonville* has invefted with the Commiffion of Commander of the *Coureurs de Bois* that trade upon the Lakes, and in the Southern Countries of *Canada*. The Governour has fent me [102] Orders to return to the Colony if the Seafon and other Circumftances permit; or to tarry here till the Spring if I forefee unfurmountable Difficulties in the Paffage. In the mean time he has fent me Effects to anfwer the Pay of my Detachment, and to fubfift 'em in the Winter. Thefe Orders would be extream acceptable to me, if I could but contrive how to return to the Colony; but that feems to be abfolutely impoffible, and both the *French* and the Savages agree that it is fo. There are in that Paffage fo many Water-falls, Cataracts, and Places where there's a neceffity of tedious Land-carriages, that I dare not run fuch Hazards with my Soldiers, who cannot work the Boats but upon ftagnating Water. Upon that confideration I have thought it more proper to halt here till the next Year; at which time I defign to take the Advantage of the Company of fome *Frenchmen* and Savages, that promife to take into each of their Canows one of my Men. In the mean time, I am upon the point of undertaking another Voyage, for I cannot mew my felf up here all this Winter. I defign to make the beft ufe of my time, and to travel through the Southern Countries that I have fo often heard of, having engag'd four or five good Huntſmen of the *Outaouas* to go along with me.

The Party of the *Hurons* that I mention'd in the beginning of my Letter, return'd hither two Months ago, and brought with 'em an *Iroqueſe* Slave, whom their Leader preſented to Mr. *de Iuchereau*, the late Colonel of the *Coureurs de Bois* and whom that Colonel order'd to be immediately ſhot. The crafty Leader acted upon that occaſion a very cunning and malicious part, the fatal Conſequences of which I eaſily foreſee: He intruſted no body with the Secret but my ſelf; for he is my true Friend, and he knows that I am his. However, I muſt go no farther upon this matter, leſt my Letter ſhould be intercepted. Tho' after all, if the Blow were not already given, [103] or if 'twere poſſible to remedy it, my Friendſhip ſhould not hinder me from acquainting Mr. *de Denonville* with the Intrigue, that he might get clear of it as well as he could. If it pleaſes God to allow me a ſafe Return to *France*, I ſhall tell you the Story by word of mouth.

I underſtand by your laſt, that the King has preferr'd his Almoner, the Abbot of *St. Valiers*, to the Biſhoprick of *Quebec;* and that this Biſhop was conſecrated in St. *Sulpice*'s Church.[1]

[1] The Abbé de St. Vallier had been Bishop Laval's vicar-apostolic since 1685; but at the desire of the latter was consecrated bishop, Jan. 25, 1688. Jean Baptiste de la Croix Chevrière, known as St. Vallier from his benefice, was a native of Grenoble (1653) who had served as chaplain of Louis XIV. He was second bishop of Quebec, retaining the office until his death (1727). During his long term of service, he was frequently absent in France (1694–97); again (1700–04), when he was captured by the English on his return voyage, and kept a prisoner five years. He did not finally reach Quebec until 1713. For his portrait see *Jes. Rel.*, lxiv, frontispiece. — Ed.

This piece of News would be very welcome to me, if I thought he would be leſs rigid than Mr. *de Laval*, his Predeceſſor. But what likelyhood is there that the new Biſhop will be of a tractable temper? If 'tis true that he has refus'd other good Biſhopricks, he muſt be as ſcrupulous as the Monk *Dracontius*, that St. *Athanaſius* cenſures for not accepting of a Preſentation to a Biſhoprick that was offer'd him. In fine, if he is of that ſcrupulous Temper, his critical Strictneſs will ſcarce go down in this Country; for the People are already tyr'd out with his Predeceſſor's Excommunications.

I am,

SIR,

Yours, &c.

[104] LETTER XVI.

Dated at *Miſſilimakinac*, *May* 28. 1689.

Containing an Account of the Author's Departure from, and Return to, Miſſilimakinac. *A Deſcription of the Bay of* Puants, *and its Villages. An ample Deſcription of the* Beavers; *follow'd by the Journal of a remarkable Voyage upon the Long River, and a Map of the adjacent Country.*

SIR,

THANK God, I am now return'd from my Voyage upon the *Long River*, which falls into the River of *Miſſiſipi*. I would willingly have trac'd it up to its Source, if ſeveral Obſtacles had not ſtood in my way. I ſet out from hence the 24th of *Sept.* accompany'd with my own Detachment, and the five Huntſmen I mention'd in my laſt; who indeed did me a great deal of Service. All the Soldiers were provided with new Canows loaded with Proviſions and Ammunition, and ſuch Commodities as are proper for the Savages. The Wind, which ſtood then in the North, wafted me in three days to the Bay of *Pouteouatamis*, that lay forty Leagues off. The mouth of that Bay is in a manner choak'd with Iſles, and the Bay it ſelf is ten Leagues broad, and twenty five Leagues long.[1]

[1] Now Green Bay, Wis., usually called by the French Baye des Puants; see p. 146, note 2, *ante*. Charlevoix says that the Potawatomi formerly inhabited these islands at the mouth of the bay, after being driven by the Iroquois from their seats in lower Michigan. — ED.

The 29th we came to a little deep fort of a River, which difembogues at a place where the Water of the Lake fwells three foot high in twelve hours, and decreafes as much in the fame compafs of time. Our tarrying there three or four days gave me an opportunity of making this Remark.[1] The Villages of the *Sakis*, the *Pouteouatamis*, and fome *Malominis*, are [105] feated on the fide of that River, and the Jefuits have a Houfe or College built upon it.[2] This is a place of great Trade for Skins and *Indian* Corn, which thefe Savages fell to the *Coureurs de Bois*, as they come and go, it being the neareft and moft convenient Paffage to the River of *Miffifipi*. The Soil of this Country is fo fertile, that it produces (in a manner without Agriculture) our *European* Corn, Peafe, Beans, and feveral other Fruits that are not known in *France*. As foon as I landed, the Warriours of thefe three Nations came by turns to my Apartment, to regale me with the *Calumet-Dance*, and with the *Captains-Dance;* the former being a fignification of Peace and Friendfhip, and the latter of Refpect

[1] The Fox River, first called by the French Rivière des Puants, later Rivière des Rénards (Foxes) from the tribe encountered on its banks. The Jesuits entitled it St. Francis River, but the name did not persist. The Jesuits also remarked the tides in the bay. See *Jes. Rel.*, lvi, pp. 137–139; lvii, pp. 301–305; lx. pp. 205–207. —Ed.

[2] The Sauk, Potawatomi, and Menominee tribes were all of Algonquian stock, and had their habitat about the mouth of the Fox, although the latter tribe were more often upon the river of the same name.

The Jesuit mission of St. Francis Xavier was founded on the shores of Green Bay by Father Claude Allouez in 1669; two years later a chapel was built upon the site of the present city of De Pere. In 1899 the citizens of that place, inspired thereto by the Wisconsin Historical Society, erected a monument near the site of this pioneer missionary station. See *Wis. His. Soc. Proc.*, 1899, p. 105. — Ed.

and Efteem.[1] I return'd the Compliment with a Prefent of fome Rolls of *Brafil* Tobacco, which they value mightily, and fome ftrings of *Venice* Beads, with which they embroider their Coats. Next Morning I was invited to a Feaft with one of the three Nations; and after having fent to 'em fome Difhes and Plates, purfuant to the Cuftom of the Country, I went accordingly about Noon. They began with congratulating my Arrival, and after I had return'd them thanks, fell a finging and dancing one after another, in a particular manner, of which you may expect a circumftantial account when I have more leifure. The Singing and Dancing lafted for two hours, being feafon'd with Acclamations of Joy and Jefts, which make up part of their ridiculous Mufick. After that the Slaves came to ferve,[2] and all the Company fat down after the *Eaftern* fafhion, every one being provided with his Mefs, juft as our Monks are in the Monaftery-Halls.

Firft of all four Platters were fet down before me, in the firft of which there were two white Fifh only boil'd in Water; in the fecond the Tongue and Breaft of a Roe-buck boil'd; in the third two Woodhens, the hind Feet or Trotters of a Bear, and [106] the Tail of a Beaver, all roafted; and the fourth contain'd a large quantity of Broth made of feveral forts of

[1] For the calumet dance see Marquette's detailed description in *Jes. Rel.*, lix, pp. 129–137. In its modern form it is described in U. S. Bur. of Ethnol. *Report*, 1881–82, pp. 276–282. — ED.

[2] Slavery among the Indians was due entirely to prisoners taken in war. It was a mild form, slaves being usually treated as members of the family, and having the hope of exchange or ransom by their own tribe. From the Indians it spread to the French in Illinois, and was authorized by edict in 1709. See Lafontaine, "De l'esclavage en Canada," in Montreal Historical Society *Memoires*, 1858. — ED.

Meat. For Drink they gave me a very pleaſant Liquor, which was nothing but a Syrrup of Maple beat up with Water; but of this more elſewhere. The Feaſt laſted two Hours; after which I intreated one of the Grandees to ſing for me; for in all the Ceremonies made uſe of among the Savages, 'tis cuſtomary to imploy another to act for 'em. I made this Grandee a Preſent of ſome pieces of Tobacco, in order to oblige him to act my part till Night. Next day, and the day after, I was oblig'd to go to the Feaſts of the other two Nations, who obſerv'd the ſame Formalities. The moſt curious thing I ſaw in the Villages, was ten or twelve tame Beavers, that went and came like Dogs from the Rivers to the Cottages, without ſtragling out of the Road. I ask'd the Savages if theſe Animals could live out of the Water; and receiv'd this anſwer, that they could live aſhoar as well as Dogs, and that they had kept ſome of 'em above a year, without ſuffering them to go near the Rivers: From whence I conclude, that the *Caſuiſts* are out in not ranging Ducks, Geeſe, and Teals, in the number of Amphibious Animals, as the Naturaliſts are wont to do. I had heard the ſame ſtory from ſeveral *Americans* before; but being apprehenſive that there were different Species of Beavers, I had a mind to be better inform'd: And indeed there is a particular kind of 'em, which the Savages call the *Terreſtrial*, or Land-Beaver; but at the ſame time they tell you, theſe are of a different Species from the Amphibious ſort; for they make Holes or Dens in the Earth, like Rabbets or Foxes, and never go near the Water unleſs it be to drink. They are likewiſe call'd by the Savages, the lazy or idle kind, as being expell'd by the other Beavers from the Kennels in which thefe Animals are lodg'd, to the [107] number of 80. Thefe Kennels I mean to defcribe afterwards; in the mean time I only take occafion to acquaint you, that the idle fort being unwilling to work, are expell'd by the others, juft as Wafps are by Bees; and are fo teas'd by 'em, that they are forc'd to quit the Kennels, which the better and more induftrious Race huddles up to themfelves in the Fens. This fupine Beaver refembles the other fort in its Figure, excepting that the Hair is rub'd off the Back and the Belly, which is occafion'd by their rubbing againft the Earth when they return to, or ftir out from their Holes.[1]

The Writers of Natural Hiftory are very much out, in fancying that the Beavers cut off their own Tefticles, when purfued by the Huntfmen; for that which the Phyficians call *Caftoreum*, is not lodg'd in the Tefticles, but in a certain Bag that Nature feems to have form'd on purpofe for thefe Animals, and this Bag they make ufe of to clear their Teeth, after the biting of fome gummy Shrub. But fuppofing the Tefticles to be the proper Receptacle of the Caftor, we muft ftill conceive that 'tis impoffible for a Beaver to pull out his Tefticles, without rending the Nerves of the Groin, in which they are feated juft by the Sharebone. 'Tis manifeft that *Elian* and feveral other Naturalifts, were fcarce acquainted with Beaver-hunting; for had they known any thing of the matter, they

[1] The beaver is easily domesticated, and becomes as tame as a kitten. Stories of idle beavers are numerous, but apochryphal; they arise from some disorder in the form of a parasite, which occasionally attacks the animal. See Martin, *Castorologia, or the Canadian Beaver* (London and Montreal, 1892), pp. 157, 168, 233.—Ed.

would never have talk'd of the purſuing of theſe Animals, which never go from the ſide of the Pond where their Kennels are built; and which dive under water upon the leaſt noiſe, and return to their Dens when the danger is over. If theſe Creatures were but ſenſible of the reaſon for which War is declar'd againſt 'em, they would flea themſelves alive; for 'tis their Skin only that the Huntſmen want, the value of the Caſtor being nothing in compariſon with that. A great Beaver is twenty ſix Inches long, from [108] the hind-Head, to the root of the Tail. 'Tis about three Foot and eight Inches round, its Head is ſeven Inches long, and ſix broad; its Tail is fourteen Inches long, and ſix broad, and about the middle it has the thickneſs of an Inch and two lines. The figure of the Tail is Oval; the Scale with which 'tis cover'd, and which performs the Office of what the Phyſicians call the *Epidermis* or Scarf-skin, is an irregular Hexagon. The Beaver carries upon its Tail the Clay, the Earth and other Materials of which they make their Banks and Kennels, or Hutts, by a wonderful Inſtinct. Its Ears are ſhort, round and hollow; its Legs are five Inches long, its Feet ſix Inches and eight Lines, and its Paws are three Inches and a half from the Heel to the end of the great Toe. Its Paws are form'd much like a Man's Hand, and they make uſe of 'em in feeding, as Apes do. The five Toes are joyn'd like thoſe of a Duck, with a Membrane of a Slate colour. Its Eyes are of the leſſer ſize, in proportion to the bulk of its Body, and bear the figure of a Rats Eyes. Before its Muzzle there are four Fore-Teeth or Cutters, *viz.*

two in each Jaw, as in a Rabbet, befides which it has fixteen Grinders, that is, eight in the upper, and as many in the lower Mandible. The Cutters are above an Inch long, and ¼ of an Inch broad, being very ftrong and fharp like a Cutlas; for a Beaver affifted by its Affociates, (if I may fo call its fellow Beavers) cuts down Trees as big as a Hogfhead; which I could never have believ'd, if I had not obferv'd with my own Eyes, above twenty Trunks of Trees cut down in that fafhion. A Beaver has two lays of Hair; one is long, and of a fhining black colour, with a grain as big as that of Mans Hair; the other is fine and fmooth, and in Winter fifteen lines long: In a word, the laft is the fineft Down in the World. The Skin of fuch a Beaver as I have now defcrib'd, will be two pound weight, but the [109] price varies according to the goodnefs. In Winter and Autumn the Flefh of a Beaver eats very well, if it be roafted. Thus, Sir, I have prefented you with an exact Defcription of thefe reputed Amphibious Animals which make fuch Structures, that all the Art of Man can fcarce equal. Upon another occafion perhaps I may give you a circumftantial Account of their wonderful Structure, which I decline at prefent, becaufe the Digreffion would be too tedious.[1]

To return to my Voyage. After our arrival in the Bay of *Pouteouatamis*, we bid adieu to the Navigation upon the Lakes of *Canada;* and fetting out *September* 30, arriv'd *October* 2. at the foot of the fall of *Kakalin*, after ftemming fome little Cur-

[1] Lahontan's description of the beaver is not inaccurate, and shows habits of keen observation. For full description see Martin, *op, cit.* — Ed.

rents in the River of *Puants*.[1] The next day we accomplifh'd the fmall Land-carriage, and on the *5th* arriv'd before the Village of *Kikapous*, in the Neighbourhood of which I incamp'd the next day, in order to receive Intelligence. That Village ftands upon the brink of a little Lake, in which the Savages fifh great quantities of Pikes and Gudgeons.[2] I found only thirty or forty Men fit for War in the place, for the reft were gone a Beaver-hunting fome days before. The *7th* I reimbarq'd, and rowing hard made in the Evening the little Lake of *Malominis*, where we kill'd Bucks and Buftards enough for Supper. We went afhoar that Night, and built Hutts for our felves upon a point of Land that fhoots out; by break of day I went in a Canow to the Village, and after an hours Conference with fome of the Savages, prefented 'em with two Rolls of Tobacco, and they by way of Acknowledgment, made me a prefent of two or three Sacks of Oatmeal: For the fides of

[1] The Grand Kakaling, twenty-one miles from the mouth of Fox River, was a series of rapids, the river falling fifty-two feet in the course of a mile. The name signified "the fishing ground for pickerel." The modern town of Kaukauna is on the river bank at this place. See Tanner, "Early Kaukauna" in *Wis. Hist. Soc. Proc.*, 1899, pp. 212–217. The other rapids of Fox River, ascending from the mouth, were those at De Pere, Little Kakalin (now called Little Rapids), the Croche (above Wrightstown), Grand Kakalin (at Kaukauna), Little Chute (still so named), the Cedars (at Kimberly), Grand Chute (at Appleton), and Winnebago Rapids (at Neenah). See *Jes. Rel.*, liv, p. 306.—Ed.

[2] The Kickapoo were an Algonquian tribe closely associated with the Mascoutin. They were first encountered in Wisconsin, but drifted over various portions of Michigan and Illinois, finally crossing the Mississippi (about 1725), and making their homes in Iowa. See *Wis. Hist. Colls.*, xvi, xvii, index. A remnant of this tribe still exists upon reservations in Kansas and Oklahoma. The village mentioned here by Lahontan is not described by his contemporaries. It would seem to have been on Lake Winnebago, between Neenah and Oshkosh.—Ed.

the Lake are cover'd with a ſort of Oats, which grows in tufts with a tall Stalk, and of which the Savages reap plentiful Crops.[1] The *9th* I arriv'd at the foot of *Outagamis* Fort, where I found but [110] few People; however, they gave me a very kind Reception, for after dancing the *Calumet* before the Door of my Hutt, they made me a Preſent of Veniſon and Fiſh. Next day they convey'd me up the River, to the place where their folks were hunting the Beavers. The *11th* we imbarq'd, and landed the *13th* upon the ſhoar of a little Lake, where the Head of that Nation reſided.[2] After we had rear'd up our Hutts, that General gave me a Viſit, and inquir'd which way I intended to move. I made anſwer, that I was ſo far from deſigning to march toward the *Nadoueſſious* his Enemies, that I ſhould not come near 'em by 100 Leagues[3]; and to con-

[1] The "Lake of Malhominis" was probably the present Grand Lake Butte des Morts, where, as now, grew great expanses of wild rice or oats. The French called the Menominee "Folle Avoines," the name for this plant (*Zizania aquatica*) which formed a staple food for Indians in the Northwest. See Jenks, "Wild-rice Gatherers of the Upper Lakes," in U. S. Bur. of Ethnol. *Report*, No. 19. Father Allouez mentioned the wild rice in this lake on his journey of 1670. See *Jes. Rel.*, liv, pp. 217–219, 307. — Ed.

[2] The location of the Outagami or Fox Indian villages has been much discussed. See *Wis. Hist. Colls.*, xvi, p. 39. The most that can be said is, that they were probably in Waupaca County, on Wolf River, or some of its affluents.

The Outagami or Fox (Fr., Rénard) Indians were of Algonquian stock, first encountered in Wisconsin, which was their permanent home until driven by the French across the Mississippi, about the middle of the eighteenth century. Their wars upon the French (1712–47) undermined the empire of the latter in the Northwest. See *Wis. Hist. Colls.*, xvii. In 1730 they amalgamated with the Sauk. Remnants of the Sauk and Fox tribes are still extant in Iowa, Nebraska, and Oklahoma. — Ed.

[3] Nadouessioux, usually abreviated to Sioux, was the name given by the Algonquian tribes to the great Western stock, who called themselves Dakota. The term Nadouessioux meant "snake-like ones," or "enemy." At this time they were hostile

firm the innocence of my Intentions, I pray'd him to ſend ſix Warriours to accompany me to the long River, which I deſign'd to trace up to its Source. He reply'd that he was extream glad to find that I carry'd neither Arms nor Cloaths to the *Nadoueſſious;* that he ſaw I had not the equipage of a *Coureur de Bois*, but that on the contrary, I had ſome diſcovery in my view. At the ſame time he caution'd me not to venture too far up that Noble River, by reaſon of the multitudes of People that I would find there, though they have no ſtomach for War: He mean'd, that ſome numerous Party might ſurpriſe me in the Night-time. In the mean time, inſtead of the ſix Warriours that I deſir'd, he gave me ten, who underſtood the Lingua, and knew the Country of the *Eokoros*, with whom his Nation had maintain'd a Peace of twenty years ſtanding. I ſtay'd two days with this General, during which time he regal'd me nobly, and walk'd about with me to give me the Satisfaction of obſerving the diſpoſure of the Cottages of the Beaver-hunters; a deſcription of which, you may expect in another place; I preſented him with a Fuſee, twelve Flint-ſtones, two pound of Powder, four pound of Ball, and a little Axe, and I gave each of his two Sons a [111] great Coat, and a Roll of *Braſil* Tobacco. Two of the ten Warriours that he gave me, could ſpeak the Language of the *Outaouas*, which I was well pleas'd with; not that I was a ſtranger to their own Language, for between that and the *Algonkin* there is no great difference,

to the Fox, but in their eighteenth-century wars upon the French were their allies. For information concerning the Siouan people, see references in Hennepin, *New Discovery*, p. 225, note.—ED.

but in regard that there were ſeveral words that puzled me. My four *Outaouas* were tranſported with this little Reinforcement, and were then ſo incouraged, that they told me above four times, that we might venture ſafely ſo far as the Plantation of the Sun. I embarqed with this ſmall Guard the 16*th* about Noon, and arriv'd that Night at the Land-carriage of *Ouiſconſinc*, which we finiſh'd in two days, that is, we left the River of *Puants*, and tranſported our Canows and Baggage to the River *Ouiſconſinc*, which is not above three quarters of a League diſtant, or thereabouts.[1] I ſhall ſay nothing of the River we left, but that 'twas Muddy, full of Shelves, and incloſed with a ſteep Coaſt, Marſhes, and frightful Rocks.

The 19*th* we embarqu'd upon the River *Ouiſconſinc*, and being favour'd by a ſlack Current, arriv'd in four days at the place, where it empties it ſelf into the River *Miſſiſipi*, which is about half a League broad in that part. The force of the Current, and the breadth of that River, is much the ſame as that of the *Loire*. It lies North-Eaſt, and South-Weſt; and its ſides are adorn'd with Meadows, lofty Trees and Firs. I obſerv'd but two Iſlands upon it, though there may be more,

---

[1] Lahontan certainly allows too little time for the passage from the Outagami village to the Fox-Wisconsin portage — not less than 100 miles, following the meanderings of the river.

The Fox-Wisconsin portage was a noted place in the early history of Western discovery. Apparently Radisson and Groseilliers were (1655) the first white men to traverse it. Marquette describes it in 1672. A contemporary writer (1682) says it was "through an oak grove and a flooded meadow."—*Wis. Hist. Colls.*, xvi, p. 106. The portage was about a mile in length; later, the French built a corduroy road through the swamp, and established a rude wagon carriage for their batteaux. —*Wis. Hist. Colls.*, x, pp. 221, 222. A government ship canal now spans the distance. — ED.

which the darknefs of the Night hid from us as we came down.[1] The 23*d* we landed upon an Ifland in the River *Miffifipi*, over againft the River I fpoke of but now, and were in hopes to find fome wild Goats there, but had the ill fortune to find none. The day after we croft to t'other fide of the River, founding it every where, as we had done the day before, and found nine foot water in the fhalloweft place. The [112] 2*d* of *November* we made the Mouth of the *Long River*, having firft ftem'd feveral rapid Currents of that River, though 'twas then at loweft Ebb. In this little paffage we kill'd feveral wild Beeves which we broil'd, and catch'd feveral large Dabs. On

[1] The distance from the portage to the mouth of the Wisconsin is 145 miles. Its stage of water was in Lahontan's time doubtless much higher than now, although early canoeists speak of being embarrassed by its numerous shifting sand-bars. Until the depletion of the great pine forests in north-central Wisconsin, it was an important lumbering stream. From the time of the erection of Wisconsin Territory (1836) until about 1890 there was much popular agitation in favor of dredging both the Fox and Wisconsin, in order to connect Lake Michigan with Mississippi River — in other words, adapting what was, in the French regime, the most popular fur-trade route between the great lakes and the great river, to the requirements of modern steam navigation. Large sums of money have been spent by the federal government in surveys on the sprawling and sand-bar-ridden Wisconsin, and in a lockage system on the lower Fox; but it has at last come to be recognized by most engineers that the route is impracticable without an unwarranted expenditure of public funds. The Fox as far up as Lake Winnebago has a strong current, and its rapids are the basis of the present federal-built water powers; the upper Fox is sluggish, shallow, and frequently fringed with wild-rice swamps. There is to-day occasional navigation by flat-bottomed steamers as far as Berlin, but only small launches can proceed to the portage. On the Wisconsin, which in spring and autumn overflows to the width of a mile or more, steam craft are seldom seen; the passage of a small launch, perhaps once or twice a season, arousing general curiosity. Lahontan's description, although brief, is not inexact, and appears to be that of one who had seen the alternating cliffs and meadows which border the Wisconsin, one of the most beautiful of Western streams. See chapters on the Fox-Wisconsin waterway in Thwaites, *Down Historic Waterways* (Chicago, new ed., 1903). — Ed.

the 3*d* we enter'd the Mouth of the *Long River*, which looks like a Lake full of Bull-rufhes; we found in the middle of it a narrow Channel, upon which we fteer'd till Night, and then lay by to fleep in our Canows. In the Morning I enquir'd of my ten *Outagamis*, if we had far to fail before we were clear of the Rufhes, and receiv'd this anfwer, that they had never been in the Mouth of that River before, though at the fame time they affur'd me, that about twenty Leagues higher, the Banks of it were clad with Woods and Meadows. But after all we did not fail fo far, for about ten a Clock next Morning the River came pretty narrow, and the Shoar was cover'd with lofty Trees; and after continuing our courfe the reft of that day, we had a profpect of Meadows now and then. That fame Night we landed at a point of Land, with a defign to drefs our broil'd Meat, for at that time we had none frefh. The next day we ftop'd at the firft Ifland we faw, in which we found neither Man nor Beaft; and the Evening drawing near, I was unwilling to venture far into it, fo we e'en contented our felves with the catching of fome forry Fifh. The 6*th* a gentle Gale fprung up, which wafted us to another Ifland about 12 Leagues higher, where we landed. Our paffage to this place was very quick, notwithftanding the great calm that always prevails upon this River, which I take to be the leaft rapid River in the World. But the quicknefs of the paffage was not the only furprifal, for I was amaz'd that I faw no Harts, nor Bucks, nor Turkeys, having met with 'em all along in the other parts of my Difcovery. The 7*th* the fame Wind drove us [113] to a third Ifland, that lay ten or twelve Leagues off the former, which we quitted in the Morning. In this third Ifland our Savages kill'd thirty or forty Pheafants, which I was not ill pleas'd with.

The 8*th* the Wind proving unferviceable to us, by reafon that 'twas intercepted by Hills cover'd with Firs, we ply'd our Oars; and about two in the Afternoon, defcry'd on the left Hand large Meadows, and fome Hutts at the diftance of a quarter of a League from the River. Upon this Difcovery, our Savages and ten of the Soldiers jump'd upon the fhoar, and directed their courfe to the Houfes, where they found fifty or fixty Huntfmen prepar'd to receive 'em, with their Bows and Arrows. As foon as the Huntfmen heard the voice of the *Outagamis*, they threw down their Arms, and prefented the Company with fome Deer that they had juft kill'd, which they likewife help'd to carry to my Canows. The Benefactors were fome of the *Eokoros*, who had left their Villages, and come thither to hunt. I prefented 'em, more out of Policy, than Acknowledgment, with Tobacco, Knives and Needles, which they could not but admire. Upon this, they repair'd with expedition to their Villages, and gave their Affociates to underftand, what a good fort of People they had met with; which had fo much influence, that the next day towards the Evening, there appear'd upon the River fide above two thoufand Savages, who fell a dancing as foon as they defcry'd us. Thereupon, our *Outagamis* went afhoar, and after a fhort Conference, fome of the principal Savages imbarqu'd on board of our Canows, and fo we all fteer'd to the chief Village, which we did not reach till Midnight. I order'd our Hutts to be made up on a point of Land near a little River, at the diftance of a quarter of a League from the Village. Though the Savages prefs'd me extreamly to lodge in one of their Villages, yet none [114] went with 'em but the *Outagamis*, and the four *Outaouas*, who at the fame time caution'd the Savages not to approach to our Camp in the Night-time. Next day I allow'd my Soldiers to refrefh and reft themfelves; and went my felf to vifit the Grandees of this Nation to whom I gave Prefents of Knives, Ciffars, Needles, and Tobacco. They gave me to underftand, that they were infinitely well pleas'd with our arrival in their Country, for that they had heard the Savages of other Nations fpeak very honourably of the *French*. I took leave of 'em on the 12*th*, and fet out with a Convoy of five or fix hundred Savages, who march'd upon the fhoar, keeping pace with our Canows. We pafs'd by another Village that lay to the right Hand, and ftop'd at a third Village that was five Leagues diftant from the firft, but did not difimbarque: For all that I defign'd, was to make a Prefent to the leading Men of the Village, from whom I receiv'd more *Indian* Corn, and broil'd or dry'd Meat, than I had occafion for. In fine, I pafs'd from Village to Village without ftopping, unlefs it were to incamp all Night, or to prefent the Savages with fome Trinkets; and fo fteer'd on to the laft Village, with a defign to get fome Intelligence. As foon as we arriv'd at the end of this Village, the Great Governour, who indeed was a venerable old Gentleman, fent out Hunters to bring us good Cheer. He inform'd me, that fixty Leagues higher I fhould meet with the Nation of the *Effanapes*, who wag'd War with him; that if it had not been for their being at War, he would have given me a Convoy to their Country; that, however he mean'd to give up to me ſix Slaves of that Country, which I might carry home, and make uſe of as I ſaw occaſion; and that in ſailing up the River, I had nothing to fear, but the being ſurpriz'd in the Night-time. In fine, after he had inſtructed me in ſeveral very uſeful Circumſtances, I immediately [115] made every thing ready for my Departure.

The Commanders of this People acquainted me, that they had twelve Villages peopled by 20000 Warriours; that their number was much greater before the War, which they wag'd at one time with the *Nadoneſſis*, the *Panimoha*, and the *Eſſanapes.* The People are very civil, and ſo far from a wild Savage temper, that they have an Air of Humanity and Sweetneſs. Their Hutts are long, and round at the top, not unlike thoſe of our Savages; but they are made of Reeds and Bulruſhes, interlac'd and cemented with a ſort of fat Earth. Both the Men and the Women go naked all over, excepting their Privities. The Women are not ſo handſom, as thoſe who live upon the Lakes of *Canada.* There ſeems to be ſomething of Government and Subordination among this People; and they have their Houſes fortified with the branches of Trees, and Faſcines ſtrengthen'd with fat Earth.

The 21*ſt* we imbarqu'd at the break of day, and landed that Night in an Iſland cover'd with Stones and Gravel, having paſs'd by another at which I would not put in, becauſe I would not ſlight the opportunity of the Wind, which then ſtood very fair. Next day the Wind ſtanding equally fair, we ſet out and continued our courſe all that Day, and the following Night; for the ſix *Eſſanapes* inform'd us, that the River was clean, and free from Rocks and Beds of Sand. The 23 we landed early in the Morning on the right ſide of the River, in order to careen one of our Boats that ſprung a Leak. While that was a doing, we dreſt ſome Veniſon that had been preſented me by the Commander of the laſt Village of the *Eokoros;* and the adjacent Country being repleniſh'd with Woods, the Savages of our Company went a ſhooting in the Foreſts; but they ſaw nothing but ſmall Fowls, that they did not think fit to ſhoot at. As ſoon as we reimbarqu'd, the Wind fell all of a ſudden, and ſo [116] we were forc'd to ply the Oars; but moſt of the Crew having ſlept but little the Night before, they row'd but very faintly, which oblig'd me to put in at a great Iſland two Leagues higher; the ſix *Eſſanapes* Slaves having inform'd me, that this Iſland afforded great plenty of Hares, which I found to be true. Theſe Animals had a lucky Inſtinct in taking ſhelter in this Iſland, for there the Woods are ſo thick, that we were forc'd to ſet fire to ſeveral places, before we could diſlodge 'em.

Having made an end of our Game, my Soldiers fed heartily, and thereupon fell ſo ſound aſleep, that I could ſcarce get 'em wak'd upon a falſe Alarm, occaſion'd by a Herd of Wolves that made a noiſe among the Thickets upon the Continent. We reimbarqued next day at ten a Clock in the Morning, and did not run above twelve Leagues in two days, by reaſon that the Savages of our Company would needs walk along the River ſide with their Guns, to ſhoot Geeſe and Ducks; in which they had very good Succefs. After that we incampt juft by the Mouth of a little River on the right Hand, and the *Eſſanapes* Slaves gave me notice, that the firft of their Villages was not above fixteen or eighteen Leagues off. Upon this Information, I fent, by the advice of the Savages of our Company, two of the Slaves to give notice of our arrival. The 26*th* we row'd briskly, in hopes to reach the firft Village that day; but being retarded by the huge quantities of floating Wood, that we met in feveral places, we were forc'd to continue all Night in our Canows. The 27*th* about ten or eleven a Clock we approach'd to the Village, and after putting up the great *Calumet* of Peace upon the Prow of our Canows, lay upon our Oars.

Upon our firft appearance, three or four hundred *Eſſanapes* came running to the fhoar, and, after dancing juft over againft us, invited us afhoar. As foon [117] as we came near the fhoar, they began to jump into our Canows; but I gave 'em to know by the four *Eſſanapes* Slaves, that I defir'd they fhould retire, which they did immediately. Then I landed, being accompany'd with the Savages of our Company, namely, the *Outagamis*, and the *Outaouas*, and with twenty Soldiers. At the fame time I gave orders to my Sergeants, to land and poft Centries. As we ftood upon the fhoar, all the *Eſſanapes* proftrated themfelves three or four times before us, with their Hands upon their Foreheads; after which we were convoy'd to the Village with fuch Acclamations of Joy, as perfectly ftun'd us. Upon our arrival at the Gate, our Conductors ftop'd us, till the Governour, a Man of fifty years of Age, march'd out with five or fix hundred Men arm'd with Bows and Arrows. The *Outagamis* of my Company perceiving this, charg'd 'em with Infolence in receiving Strangers with their Arms about 'em, and call'd out in the *Eokoros* Language, that they ought to lay down their Arms. But the *Eſſanapes* Slaves that I had fent in the day before, came up to me, and gave me to underftand, that 'twas their cuftom to ftand to their Arms on fuch occafions, and that there was no danger in the cafe. However, the obftinate *Outagamis* oblig'd us to retire immediately to our Canows: Upon which the Leading Officer, and the whole Battalion, flung their Bows and Arrows afide all on a fudden. Then I return'd, and our whole Company enter'd the Village with their Fufees in their Hands, which the Savages admir'd mightily. The Leader of the Savages conducted us to a great Hutt, which look'd as if no body had liv'd in it before. When I and my twenty Soldiers had enter'd the place, they ftop'd the *Outagamis*, affirming, that they did not deferve the priviledge of entring within the Cottage of Peace, fince they had endeavour'd to create a difference, and occafion [118] a War between us and the *Eſſanapes.* In the mean time I order'd my Men to open the Door, and to call out to the *Outagamis*, that they fhould offer no manner of Injury: But the *Outagamis* in ftead of coming in, prefs'd me to return with all expedition to the Canows, which accordingly I did, without lofs of time, and carry'd with me the four *Eſſanapes* Slaves, in order to leave 'em at the firft Village we came to. We had no fooner imbarqued, than the two other Slaves came to acquaint me that the Governor would ftop me in his River; but the

Outagamis made anſwer, that he could not do that, without throwing a Mountain into it. In fine, we did not ſtand to diſpute the matter; and tho' 'twas then late, we row'd ſtraight to the next Village, which lay about three Leagues off. During the time of this paſſage, I us'd the precaution of taking from my ſix Slaves an exact information of the Conſtitution of their Country, and particularly of the principal Village. They having aſſur'd me, that the Capital Canton was ſeated upon a ſort of a Lake, I took up a Reſolution of not ſtopping at the other Villages, where I ſhould only loſe time, and laviſh my Tobacco, and ſteering directly to the *Metropolitan* in order to complain to their Generaliſſimo.

We arriv'd at the Capital Canton on the 3*d* of *November*,[1] and there met with a very honourable Reception. The *Outagamis* of our Company complain'd of the affront they had receiv'd; but the Head General being already inform'd of the matter, made anſwer, that they ought to have carry'd off the Governour or Leading Officer, and brought him along with them. In paſſing from the firſt Village to this we run fifty Leagues, and were follow'd by a Proceſſion of People, that were much more ſociable than the Governour that offer'd us that Affront. After our Men had fitted up our Hutts at [119] the diſtance of a Cannon ſhot from the Village; we went in a joynt body with the *Outagamis* and the *Outaouas*, to the *Cacick* of that Nation; and in the mean time the *Eſſanapes* Slaves were brought before him by ten of my Soldiers.

[1] According to Lahontan's own chronology this should be December, not November. — ED.

I was actually in the prefence of this petty King, when thefe Slaves fpent half an hour in proftrating themfelves feveral times before him. I made him a Prefent of Tobacco, Knives, Needles, Ciffars, two Firelocks with Flints, fome Hooks, and a very pretty Cutlas. He was better fatisfied with thefe trifling things, which he had never feen before, than I could have been with a plentiful Fortune. He teftified his Acknowledgment of the Gift, by a Counter-prefent that was more folid, though not much more valuable, as confifting of Peafe, Beans, Harts, Roe-bucks, Geefe and Ducks, of which he fent great plenty to our Camp: And indeed, we were extreamly well fatisfied with fuch a feafonable Prefent. He gave me to know, That, fince I defign'd to vifit the *Gnacfitares*, he would give me a Convoy of two or three hundred Men: That the *Gnacfitares* were a very honeft fort of People; and that both they and his People were link'd by a common intereft in guarding off the *Mozeemlek*, which were a turbulent and warlike Nation. He added, that the Nation laft mention'd were very numerous; that they never took the Field without twenty thoufand Men at leaft: That to repref the Incurfions and Infults of that dangerous Enemy, the *Gnacfitares* and his Nation had maintain'd a Confederacy for fix and twenty years; and that his Allies (the *Gnacfitares*) were forc'd to take up their Habitation in Iflands, where the Enemy cannot reach 'em. I was glad to accept of his Convoy, and return'd him many thanks. I ask'd four Pirogues of him, which he granted very frankly, allowing me to pick and choofe that number out of fifty. Having thus concerted my Meafures, I [120] was refolv'd to loſe no time; and with that view order'd my Carpenters to plane the Pirogues; by which they were thinner and lighter by one half. The poor innocent People of this Country, could not conceive how we work'd with an Axe; every ſtroke we gave they cry'd out, as if they had ſeen ſome new Prodigy; nay, the firing of Piſtols could not divert 'em from that Amazement, though they were equally ſtrangers both to the Piſtol and the Axe. As ſoon as my Pirogues were got ready, I left my Canows with the Governour or Prince, and beg'd of him that they might remain untouch'd by any body; in which point he was very faithful to me.

I cannot but acquaint you in this place, that the higher I went up the River, I met with more diſcretion from the Savages. But in the mean time I muſt not take leave of the laſt Village, without giving ſome account of it. 'Tis bigger than all the reſt, and is the Reſidence of the Great Commander or Generaliſſimo, whoſe Apartment is built by it ſelf towards the ſide of the Lake, and ſurrounded with fifty other Apartments, in which all his Relations are lodg'd. When he walks, his way is ſtrow'd with the leaves of Trees: But commonly he is carry'd by ſix Slaves. His Royal Robes are of the ſame Magnificence with thoſe of the Commander of the *Okoros:* For he is naked all over, excepting his lower parts, which are cover'd with a large Scarf made of the barks of Trees. The large extent of this Village might juſtly intitle it to the name of a City. The Houſes are built almoſt like Ovens, but they are large and high; and moſt of 'em are of Reeds cemented with fat Earth. The day before I left this place, as I was walking about, I ſaw

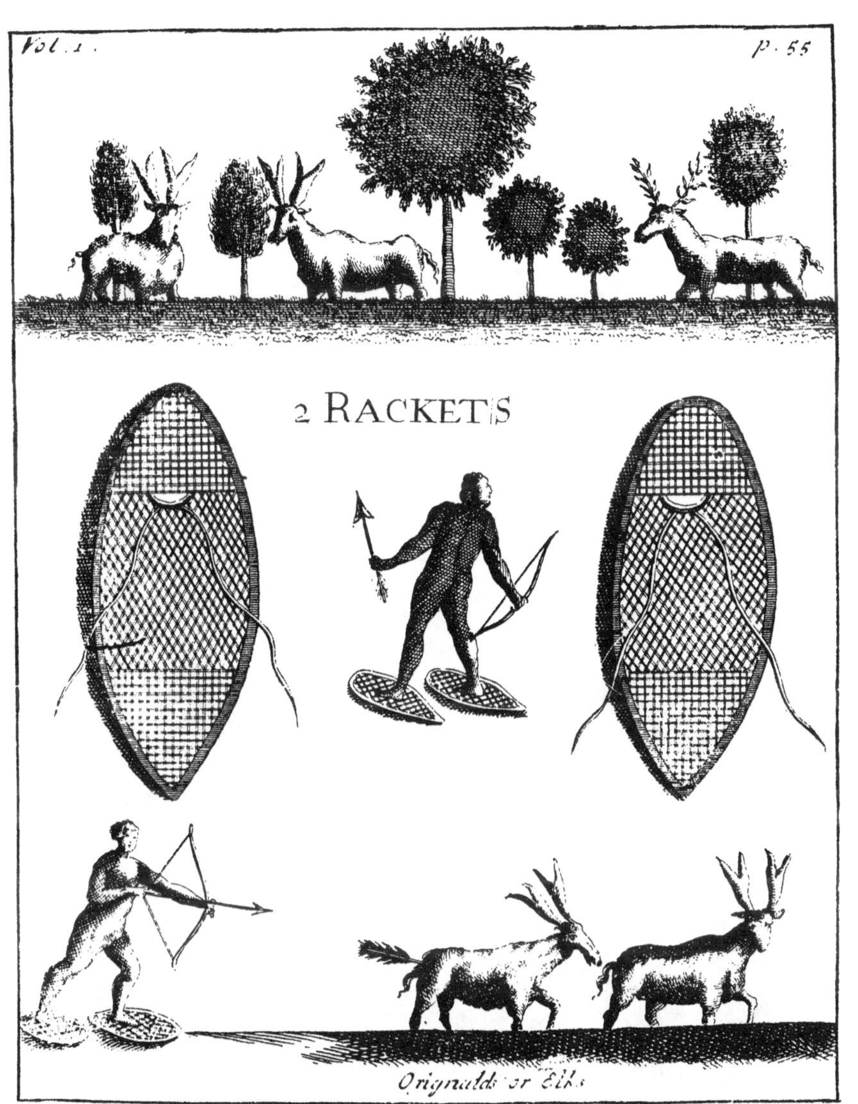
Vol. 1.
p. 55
2 RACKETS
Orignalds or Elks

thirty or forty Women running at full ſpeed; and being ſurpris'd with the ſpectacle, ſpoke to the *Outagamis* to order my four Slaves to ſee what the matter was; for theſe Slaves were my only Interpreters in [121] this unknown Country. Accordingly they brought me word, that 'twas ſome new married Women, who were running to receive the Soul of an old Fellow that lay a dying. From thence I concluded, that the People were *Pythagoreans;* and upon that Apprehenſion, ask'd 'em how they came to eat Animals, into which their Souls might be transfus'd: But they made anſwer, that the Tranſmigration of Souls is always confin'd to the reſpective Species, ſo that the Soul of a Man cannot enter into a Fowl, as that of a Fowl cannot be lodg'd in a quadruped, and ſo on. The *Okoros*, of both Sexes, are fully as handſom and as clever, as this People.

December the 4*th*, I took leave of this Village, having ten Soldiers on board of my Pirogue, beſides the ten *Oumamis*,[1] the four *Outaouas*, and the four *Eſſanapes* Slaves, that I have mention'd ſo often. Here ended the Credit and Authority of the *Calumet* of Peace, for the *Gnacſitares* are not acquainted with that Symbol of Concord. The firſt day we had enough to do to run ſix or ſeven Leagues, by reaſon of the Bulruſhes with which the Lake is incumber'd. The two following days we ſail'd twenty Leagues. The 4*th* day a Weſt-North-Weſt wind ſurpris'd us with ſuch a boiſterous violence, that we were forc'd to put aſhoar, and lay two days upon a ſandy Ground,

[1] This must be a misprint for Outagamis, as no previous mention has been made of Oumanis (Miamis) accompanying him. — Ed.

where we were in danger of ftarving for Hunger and Cold; for the Country was fo barren, that we could not find a chip of Wood wherewith to warm our felves, or to drefs our Victuals; and as far as our Eye could reach, there was nothing to be feen but Fens cover'd with Reeds and Clay, and naked Fields. Having indur'd this Hardfhip we fet out again, and row'd to a little Ifland, upon which we incamp'd, but found nothing there but green Fields; however, to make fome amends we fifh'd up great numbers of little Trouts, upon which we fed very heartily. At laft, after [122] failing fix days more, we arriv'd at the Point or Lands-end of that Ifland which you fee mark'd in my Map with a Flower-de-luce. 'Twas then the 19th day of *December*, and we had not yet felt all the rigorous Hardfhips of the Cold. As foon as I had landed and fitted up my Tents or Hutts, I detach'd my *Effanapes* Slaves to the firft of the three Villages that lay before us; for I had avoided ftopping at fome Villages in an Ifland upon which we coafted in the Night-time. The Slaves return'd in a great Alarm, occafion'd by the unfavourable Anfwer they receiv'd from the *Gnacfitares*, who took us for *Spaniards*, and were angry with them for conducting us to their Country. I fhall not be minute in every Particular that happen'd, for fear of tyring your Patience. 'Tis fufficient to acquaint you, that upon the Report of my Slaves I immediately embark'd, and pofted my felf in another Ifland that lay in the middle between the great Ifland and the Continent; but I did not fuffer the *Effanapes* to be in my Camp. In the mean time the *Gnacfitares* fent expeditious Couriers to the People that live eighty

Leagues to the Southward of them, to defire they would fend fome of their number to examine us; for that People were fuppos'd to be well acquainted with the *Spaniards* of *New Mexico.* The length of the Journey did not difcourage 'em, for they came as chearfully as if it had been upon a National Concern: and after taking a view of our Cloaths, our Swords, our Fufees, our Air, Complexion, and manner of Speech, were forc'd to own that we were not true *Spaniards?* Thefe Confiderations, join'd to the Account I gave 'em of the Reafons upon which I undertook the Voyage, of the War we were ingag'd in againft *Spain*, and of the Country to the Eaftward that we poffefs'd; thefe, I fay, had fo much influence, as to undeceive 'em. Then they invited me to encamp in their Ifland, and brought me a fort of [123] Grain not unlike our Lentils, that grows plentifully in that Country. I thank'd 'em for their Invitation, and told 'em that I would not be oblig'd to diftruft them, nor give them any occafion to diftruft me. However, I crofs'd with my Savages and ten Soldiers well arm'd; and after breaking the Ice in certain places (for it had freez'd hard for ten or twelve days) I landed within two Leagues of one of their Villages, to which I walk'd up by Land. 'Tis needlefs to mention the Particulars of the Ceremony with which I was receiv'd, it being the fame with what I defcrib'd upon other occafions; I fhall only take occafion to acquaint you, that my Prefents made a wonderful Impreffion upon the Minds of thefe People, whom I fhall call a rafcally Rabble, tho' at the fame time they are the politeft Nation I have yet feen in this Country. Their Governour bears the

Figure of a King more than any of the other Commanders of the Savages. He has an abſolute Dominion over all the Villages which are deſcrib'd in my Map. In this and the other Iſlands I ſaw large Parks, or Incloſures, ſtock'd with wild Beeves for the uſe of the People. I had an Interview for two hours together with the Governour, or the *Cacick;* and almoſt our whole Conference related to the *Spaniards* of *New Mexico,* who, as he aſſured me, were not diſtant from his Country above eighty *Tazous*, each of which is three Leagues. I muſt own indeed, I was as curious upon this Head as he was; and I wanted an Account of the *Spaniards* from him, as much as he did from me: In fine, we reciprocally inform'd one another of a great many Particulars relating to that Head. He requeſted me to accept of a great Houſe that was prepar'd for me; and his firſt piece of Civility conſiſted in calling in a great many Girls, and preſſing me and my Retinue to ſerve our ſelves. Had this Temptation been thrown in our way at a more ſeaſonable time, it had prov'd irreſiſtible; but 'twas not an agreeable Meſs [124] for Paſſengers that were infeebled by Labour and Want. *Sine Cerere & Baccho friget Venus.* After he made us ſuch a civil Proffer, the Savages, upon my inſtance, repreſented to him, that my Detachment expected me at a certain hour, and that if I ſtay'd longer, they would be in pain for me. This Adventure happen'd on the 7th of *January*.

Two days after, the *Cacick* came to ſee me, and brought with him four hundred of his own Subjects, and four *Mozeemlek* Savages, whom I took for *Spaniards.* My Miſtake was occaſion'd by the great difference between theſe two *American* Nations; for, the *Mozeemlek* Savages were cloath'd, they had a thick buſhy Beard, and their Hair hung down under their Ears; their Complexion was ſwarthy, their Addreſs was civil and ſubmiſſive, their Meen grave, and their Carriage engaging. Upon theſe Conſiderations I could not imagine that they were Savages, tho' after all I found my ſelf miſtaken. Theſe four Slaves gave me a Deſcription of their Country, which the *Gnacſitares* repreſented by way of a Map upon a Deer's Skin; as you ſee it drawn in this Map. Their Villages ſtand upon a River that ſprings out of a ridge of Mountains, from which the Long River likewiſe derives its Source, there being a great many Brooks there which by a joint Confluence form the River. When the *Gnacſitares* have a mind to hunt wild Beeves, they ſet out in Pirogues, which they make uſe of till they come to the Croſs mark'd thus (+) in the Map, at the Confluence of two little Rivers. The Hunting of the wild Bulls, with which all the Valleys are cover'd in Summer, is ſometimes the occaſion of a cruel War: For the other Croſs (+) which you ſee in the Map is one of the Boundaries or Limits of *Mozeemlek;* and if either of theſe two Nations advances but a little beyond their Limits, it gives Riſe to a bloody Engagement. The Mountains I ſpoke of but now, are ſix Leagues broad, and ſo high [125] that one muſt caſt an infinity of Windings and Turnings before he can croſs 'em. Bears and wild Beaſts are their only Inhabitants.

The *Mozeemleck* Nation is numerous and puiſſant. The four Slaves of that Country inform'd me, that at the diſtance of 150 Leagues from the Place where I then was, their principal River empties it ſelf into a Salt Lake of three hundred Leagues in Circumference, the mouth of which is about two Leagues broad: That the lower part of that River is adorn'd with ſix noble Cities, ſurrounded with Stone cemented with fat Earth: That the Houſes of theſe Cities have no Roofs, but are open above like a Platform, as you ſee 'em drawn in the Map: That beſides the abovemention'd Cities, there were above an hundred Towns, great and ſmall, round that ſort of Sea, upon which they navigate with ſuch Boats as you ſee drawn in the Map: That the People of that Country made Stuffs, Copper Axes, and ſeveral other Manufactures, which the *Outagamis* and my other Interpreters could not give me to underſtand, as being altogether unacquainted with ſuch things: That their Government was Deſpotick, and lodg'd in the hands of one great Head, to whom the reſt paid a trembling Submiſſion: That the People upon that Lake call themſelves *Tahuglauk*, and are as numerous as the Leaves of Trees, (ſuch is the Expreſſion that the Savages uſe for an Hyperbole:) That the *Mozeemlek* People ſupply the Cities or Towns of the *Tahuglauk* with great numbers of little Calves, which they take upon the abovemention'd Mountains: and, That the *Tahuglauk* make uſe of theſe Calves for ſeveral ends; for, they not only eat their Fleſh, but bring 'em up to Labour, and make Cloaths, Boots, *&c.* of their Skins. They added, That 'twas their Misfortune to be took Priſoners by the *Gnacſitares* in the War which had laſted for eighteen Years; but, that they hoped a Peace would be ſpeedily concluded,

[126] upon which the Prifoners would be exchang'd, purfuant to the ufual Cuftom. They glory'd in the poffeffion of a greater meafure of Reafon than the *Gnacfitares* could pretend to, to whom they allow no more than the Figure of a Man; for they look upon 'em as Beafts otherwife. To my mind, their Notion upon this Head is not fo very extravagant; for I obferv'd fo much Honour and Politenefs in the Converfation of thefe four Slaves, that I thought I had to do with *Europeans:* But, after all, I muft confefs, that the *Gnacfitares* are the moft tractable Nation I met with among all the Savages. One of the four *Mozeemlek* Slaves had a reddifh fort of a Copper Medal hanging upon his Neck, the Figure of which is reprefented in the Map. I had it melted by Mr. *de Tonti*'s Gun-fmith, who underftood fomething of Mettals; but it became thereupon heavier, and deeper colour'd, and withal fomewhat tractable. I defir'd the Slaves to give me a circumftantial Account of thefe Medals; and accordingly they gave me to underftand, that they are made by the *Tahuglauk*, who are excellent Artizans, and put a great value upon fuch Medals. I could pump nothing farther out of 'em, with relation to the Country, Commerce and Cuftoms of that remote Nation. All they could fay was, that the great River of that Nation runs all along Weftward, and that the falt Lake into which it falls is three hundred Leagues in Circumference, and thirty in breadth, its Mouth ftretching a great way to the Southward. I would fain have fatisfied my Curiofity in being an eye-witnefs of the Manners and Cuftoms of the *Tahuglauk;* but that being impracticable, I was forc'd to be inftructed at

ſecond hand by theſe *Mozeemlek* Slaves; who aſſur'd me, upon the Faith of a Savage, that the *Tabuglauk* wear their Beards two Fingers breadth long; that their Garments reach down to their Knees; that they cover their Heads with a ſharp-pointed Cap; that they [127] always wear a long Stick or Cane in their hands, which is tipp'd, not unlike what we uſe in *Europe;* that they wear a ſort of Boots upon their Legs which reach up to the Knee; that their Women never ſhew themſelves, which perhaps proceeds from the ſame Principle that prevails in *Italy* and *Spain;* and, in fine, that this People are always at War with the puiſſant Nations that are ſeated in the Neighbourhood of the Lake; but withal, that they never diſquiet the ſtrowling Nations that fall in their way, by reaſon of their Weakneſs: An admirable Leſſon for ſome Princes in the World, who are ſo much intent upon the making uſe of the ſtrongeſt hand.

This was all I could gather upon that Subject. My Curioſity prompted me to deſire a more particular Account; but unluckily I wanted a good Interpreter: and having to do with ſeveral Perſons that did not well underſtand themſelves, I could make nothing of their incoherent Fuſtian. I preſented the poor miſerable Slaves with ſomething in proportion to the Cuſtom of that Country, and endeavour'd to perſwade 'em to go with me to *Canada*, by making 'em ſuch Offers as in their eſteem would appear like Mountains of Gold: but the love they had for their Country ſtifled all Perſwaſion; ſo true it is, that Nature reduc'd to its juſt Limits cares but little for Riches.

In the mean time it began to thaw, and the Wind chop'd about to the South-weſt; upon which I gave notice to the great *Cacique* of the *Gnacſitares*, that I had a mind to return to *Canada*. Upon that occaſion I repeated my Preſents; in compenſation of which, my Pirogues were ſtow'd with Beef as full as they could hold. This done, I embark'd, and croſs'd over from the little Iſland to the Continent, where I fix'd a great long Pole, with the Arms of *France* done upon a Plate of Lead. I ſet out the 26th of *January*, and arriv'd ſafe on the 5th of *February* in the Country [128] of the *Eſſanapes*. We had much more pleaſure in ſailing down the River, than we had in going up; for we had the agreeable diverſion of ſeeing ſeveral Huntſmen ſhooting the Water-Fowl, that are plentiful upon that River. You muſt know, that the Stream of the Long River is all along very ſlack and eaſie, abating for about three Leagues between the fourteenth and fifteenth Village; for there indeed its Current may be call'd rapid. The Channel is ſo ſtraight, that it ſcarce winds at all from the Head to the Lake. 'Tis true 'tis not very pleaſant; for moſt of its Banks have a diſmal Proſpect, and the Water it ſelf has an ugly Taſte: but then its Uſefulneſs attones for ſuch Inconveniencies; for, 'tis navigable with the greateſt eaſe, and will bear Barques of fifty Tun, till you come to that place which is mark'd with a Flower-de-luce in the Map, and where I put up the Poſt that my Soldiers chriſten'd *la Hontau's Limit*. *March* 2. I arriv'd in the *Miſſiſipi*, which was then much deeper and more rapid than before, by reaſon of the Rains and Land-floods. To ſave the Labour of Rowing, we then left our Boats to the Current, and arriv'd on the 10th in the Iſland of *Rencontres*, which took its Name from the Defeat of 400 *Iroqueſe*, accompliſh'd there by 300 *Nadoueſſis*. The Story of the Encounter is briefly this: A Party of 400 *Iroqueſe* having a mind to ſurpriſe a certain People in the Neighbourhood of the *Otentas* (of whom more anon) march'd to the Country of the *Illineſe*, where they built Canows, and were furniſh'd with Proviſions. After that they embark'd upon the River *Miſſiſipi*, and were diſcover'd by another little Fleet that was ſailing down the other ſide of the ſame River. The *Iroqueſe* croſs'd over immediately to that Iſland, which is ſince call'd *Aux Rencontres*. The *Nadoueſſis*, *i. e.* the other little Fleet, being ſuſpicious of ſome ill Deſign, without knowing what People they were, (for they had no knowledge of the [129] *Iroqueſe* but by Hear-ſay; upon this ſuſpicion, I ſay, they tugg'd hard to come up with 'em. The two Armies poſted themſelves upon the point of the Iſland, where the two Croſſes are put down in the Map; and as ſoon as the *Nadoueſſis* came in ſight, the *Iroqueſe* cry'd out in the *Illineſe* Language, *Who are ye?* To which the *Nadoueſſis* anſwer'd, *Some body:* And putting the like Queſtion to the *Iroqueſe*, receiv'd the ſame Anſwer. Then the *Iroqueſe* put this Queſtion to 'em, *Where are you a going?* To hunt Beeves, reply'd the *Nadoueſſis*. *But pray*, ſays the *Nadoueſſis*, *what's your buſineſs? To hunt Men*, reply'd the *Iroqueſe*. *'Tis well*, ſays the *Nadoueſſis*, *we are men*, *and ſo you need go no farther*. Upon this Challenge the two Parties diſembark'd, and the Leader of the *Nadoueſſis* cut his Canows to pieces; and after reprefenting to his Warriours that they behov'd either to Conquer or Die, march'd up to the *Iroquefe;* who receiv'd 'em at firft Onfet with a Cloud of Arrows: But the *Nadoueffis* having ftood their firft Difcharge, which kill'd 'em eighty Men, fell in upon 'em with their Clubs in their hands, before the others could charge again; and fo routed 'em entirely. This Engagement lafted for two hours, and was fo hot, that two hundred and fixty *Iroquefe* fell upon the fpot, and the reft were all taken Prifoners. Some of the *Iroquefe* indeed attempted to make their Efcape after the Action was over; but the victorious General fent ten or twelve of his Men to purfue 'em in one of the Canows that he had taken: and accordingly they were all overtaken and drown'd. The *Nadoueffis* having obtain'd this Victory, cut off the Nofes and Ears of two of the clivereft Prifoners; and fupplying 'em with Fufees, Powder, and Ball, gave 'em the liberty of returning to their own Country, in order to give their Country-men to underftand, that they ought not to employ Women to hunt after Men any longer.[1]

[130] The 12th we arriv'd at the Village of the *Otentas*, where we took in a plentiful Provifion of *Turkey* Corn, of which thefe People have great ftore. They inform'd us, that their River was pretty rapid, and took its Rife from the neighbouring Mountains; and that the upper part of it was adorn'd with feveral Villages inhabited by the People call'd *Panimaha*,

[1] This tale appears to have been an invention of Lahontan; none of his contemporaries describes any such encounter between the Sioux and the Iroquois. — Ed.

Paneaſſa, and *Panetonka*.[1] But conſidering that I was ſtraitned for time, and that I ſaw no probability of learning what I wanted to know with reference to the *Spaniards*, I took leave of 'em the next day, which was the 13th, and in four days time, by the help of the Current and our Oars, made the River of the *Miſſouris*.[2] This done, we run up againſt the Stream of that River, which was at leaſt as rapid as the *Miſſiſipi* was at that time; and arriv'd on the 18th at the firſt Village of the *Miſſouris*, where I only ſtop'd to make the People ſome Preſents that procur'd me a hundred Turkeys, with which that People are wonderfully well ſtock'd.[3] After that, we row'd hard againſt the Stream, and landed next night near the ſecond Village. As ſoon as I arriv'd, I detach'd a Sergeant with ten Soldiers to convoy the *Outagamis* to the Village, while the reſt of my Crew were buſied in fitting up our

[1] River Otentas is an early name for the Des Moines, so called from the tribe encountered near its mouth. Marquette's map shows the Otontantas, whom Shea, *Early Voyages on the Mississippi* (Albany, 1861), identifies with the Oto, evidently the same as the Authoutantas of LeClercq and Hennepin. The Oto were a Siouan tribe who by the beginning of the nineteenth century had migrated west of the Missouri, and were settled on Platte River with the remnant of the Missouri tribe. The Panimaha, Paneassa, and Panitonka were divisions of the Pawnees, of Caddoan stock. The Panimaha were later called Pawnee Loups. By the close of the eighteenth century they were all west of the Missouri. — ED.

[2] Missouri River was first seen at its mouth by Jolliet and Marquette, who called it Pekitanoui, meaning Muddy Stream. Marquette surmised that its upper waters might mingle with a stream flowing into the Vermillion Sea (*Pacific Ocean*).— ED.

[3] The Missouri were a Siouan tribe first encountered near the mouth of their great river. It would be fruitless to attempt to locate the villages described by Lahontan; but later, the Missouri dwelt for many years near the mouth of Grand River. From this site they were driven late in the eighteenth century, and amalgamated with the Kansa and Oto. On the movements of all these tribes see Dorsey, "Migrations of Siouan Tribes," in *Amer. Naturalist*, xx, pp. 211-218. — ED.

Hutts and unloading our Canows. It happen'd unluckily that neither the Soldiers nor the *Outagamis* could make the Savages underſtand 'em; and the latter were juſt ready to fall upon 'em, when an old Fellow cry'd out, that the Strangers were not without more company, for that he had diſcover'd our Huts and Canows. Upon this, the Soldiers and the *Outagamis* retir'd in a great Conſternation, and advis'd me to keep a ſtrong Guard all night. About two a clock in the Morning two Men approach'd to our little Camp, and call'd in *Illineſe*, that they wanted an Interview; upon which the *Outagamis*, being extreamly well ſatisfied that there was ſome body among 'em who could underſtand what they ſaid, reply'd [131] in *Illineſe*, that they ſhould be very welcome as ſoon as the Sun appear'd in the Horizon. Neverthleſs, the *Outagamis* reſented the former Affront ſo much, that they importun'd me all night long to ſet fire to the Village, and put all the ſcoundrel Inhabitants to the Sword. I made anſwer to 'em, that 'twas our buſineſs to be wiſer than they, and to bend our Thoughts, not upon a fruitleſs Revenge, but upon the Diſcovery that we were then in queſt of. At the break of Day the two Adventurers of the Night came up to us, and after putting Interrogatories to us for the ſpace of two hours, invited us to come up to their Village. The *Outagamis* reply'd, that the Head or Governour of their Nation ought to have ſaluted us ſooner: and this oblig'd 'em to go back to give him notice. After that we ſaw no body for three hours: but at laſt, when our Impatience was juſt beginning to boil, we perceiv'd the Governour, who accoſted us in a trembling Poſture. He was accompany'd with ſome of his own Men, who were loaded with broil'd or dry'd Meat, Sacks of *Turkey* or *Indian* Corn, dry'd Raiſins, and ſome ſpeckled or particolour'd Buck-skins. In conſideration of this Preſent, I made 'em another of leſs conſequence. Then I brought on a Conference between the *Outagamis* of my Company and the two Night Meſſengers, in order to make ſome diſcovery of the Nature of the Country; but they ſtill ſtop'd our Mouths with this Anſwer, that they knew nothing of the Matter, but that the other Nations that liv'd higher up were able to inform us. Had I been of the ſame mind with the *Outagamis*, we had done noble Exploits in this Place: but I conſider'd that 'twas my buſineſs to purchaſe the Knowledge of ſeveral things, which I could not obtain by burning the Village. To be ſhort, we re-embark'd that ſame day, about two a clock in the Afternoon, and row'd about four Leagues up the River, where we made the River of [132] the *Oſages*, and encamp'd by its Mouth.[1] That Night we had ſeveral falſe Alarms from the wild Beeves, upon which we made ſufficient Repriſals afterwards; for the next day we kill'd many of 'em notwithſtanding that it rain'd ſo heavily that we could ſcarce ſtir out of our Hutts. Towards the Evening, when the Rain was over, and while we were tranſporting two or three of theſe Beeves to our little Camp, we ſpy'd an Army of the Savages upon a full March towards us.

[1] The Missouri was in early nomenclature frequently called "River of the Ozages"; but Lahontan seems here to refer to that now known as Osage River. The Osage Indians were of Siouan origin, closely akin to the Missouri and Kansa. Nearly 2,000 still live (1902) upon their reservation in Oklahoma. — Ed.

Upon that, my Men began to entrench themſelves, and to unload their Pieces with Worms, in order to charge 'em afreſh; but one of the Pieces happening to go off, the whole Body of the Enemy diſappear'd, ſome ſtraggling one way, and ſome another: for theſe People were upon the ſame foot with the Nations that live upon the Long River, foraſmuch as neither of them had ever ſeen or handled Fire-Arms. However, this Adventure mov'd the *Outagamis* ſo much, that to ſatisfie them, I was oblig'd to re-embark that very night, and return the ſame way that I came. Towards Midnight we came before a Village, and kept a profound Silence till Day-break, at which time we row'd up to their Fort; and upon our entring there, and diſcharging our Pieces in the Air, the Women, Children, and ſuperannuated Men, were put into ſuch a Conſternation, that they run from place to place calling out for Mercy. You muſt know, all their Warriours were abroad, and 'twas a Body of them that offer'd to attack us the day before. The *Outagamis* perceiving the Conſternation of the Women and Children, call'd out, that they behov'd to depart the Village, and that the Women ſhould have time to take up their Children. Upon that the whole Crew turn'd out, and we ſet fire to the Village on all ſides. This done, we purſu'd our Courſe down that rapid River, and enter'd the River *Miſſiſipi* on the 25th, early in the Morning: the 26th, about three a clock in the [133] Afternoon, we deſcry'd three or four hundred Savages employ'd in the Hunting of Beeves, which ſwarmed in all the Meads to the Weſtward. As ſoon as the Hunters ſpy'd us, they made a ſign that we ſhould make towards 'em. Being ignorant who, or how numerous they were, we made a halt at firft; but at laft we put in about a Musket-fhot above 'em, calling out to 'em that they fhould not approach to us in a Body. Upon that, four of their number came up to us with a fmiling Countenance, and gave us to know, in the *Ilinefe* Language, that they were *Akanfas.* We could not but credit their Report, for they had Knives and Sciffars hanging upon their Necks, and little Axes about 'em, which the *Ilinefe* prefent 'em with when they meet. In fine, being affur'd that they were of that Nation, which Mr. *de la Salle* and feveral other *French-men* were intimately acquainted with, we landed at the fame place; and they entertain'd us firft with Dancing and Singing, and then with all forts of Meat.[1] The next day they fhew'd us a Crocodile that they had knock'd in the head two days before, by a Stratagem that you'll find defcrib'd in another place: After that they gave us the diverfion of a Hunting Match; for 'tis cuftomary with them, when they mean to divert themfelves, to catch the Beeves by the different Methods laid down in this Cut. I put fome Queftions to 'em relating to the *Spaniards*, but they could not refolve 'em. All that I learn'd from 'em was, that the *Miffouris* and the *Ofages* are numerous and mifchievous

[1] The Akansas (Arkansas) was the name by which the French designated the great Siouan tribe of Quapaw. Dorsey (see p. 200, note 3, *ante*) thinks it was an Illinois term for all that stock who lived on the banks of the Ohio, whence the Quapaw moved southward (before 1540) to the region of the river now known as Arkansas. In the beginning of the nineteenth century numerous bands of Arkansas lived along the river of that name. About three hundred yet survive in Oklahoma. For La Salle's adventures among the Arkansas, see Membre's account in Shea, *Discovery and Exploration of Mississippi Valley* (New York, 1853), pp. 169–172. — Ed.

Nations, equally void both of Courage and Honefty; that their Countries were water'd with very great Rivers; and, in a word, were too good for them.

After we had fpent two days with them, we purfued our Voyage to the River *Ouabach*, taking care to watch the Crocodiles very narrowly, of which they had told us incredible Stories. The next day we enter'd the Mouth of that River, and founded it, [134] to try the truth of what the Savages reported of its depth. In effect, we found there three Fathom and a half Water; but the Savages of our Company alledg'd, that 'twas more fwell'd than ufually.[1] They all agreed, that 'twas Navigable an hundred Leagues up, and I wifh'd heartily, that my time had allow'd me to run up to its Source; but that being unfeafonable, I fail'd up againft the Stream, till we came to the River of the *Illinefe*, which we made on the *9th* of *April* with fome difficulty, for the Wind was againft us the firft two days, and the Currents was very rapid.[2]

All I can fay of the River *Miffifipi*, now that I am to take leave of it, is, that its narroweft part is half a League over, and the fhalloweft is a Fathom and a half deep; and that

[1] The Ohio River was usually designated as the Wabash (Ouabache) below the mouth of the present river of that name. Marquette gave it the title Ouabouskiguo, which the French soon corrupted into Ouabache. The upper reaches of the Ohio were early known by the name it now bears. — Ed.

[2] Jolliet and Marquette named the Illinois River St. Louis. Several names were later given it; Seignelay (by Hennepin), Rivière Divine, etc. For an explanation of these titles see Parkman, *La Salle*, p. 154 note. This river, about three hundred and fifty miles in length, is entirely in the state of the same name. Its easy navigation made it of much value as a connecting link between the great lakes and the Mississippi. — Ed.

according to the information of the Savages, its ſtream is pretty gentle for ſeven or eight Months of the year. As for Shelves or Banks of Sand, I met with none in it. 'Tis full of Iſles which look like Groves, by reaſon of the great plenty of Trees, and in the verdant ſeaſon of the year afford a very agreeable proſpect. Its Banks are Woods, Meadows and Hills. I cannot be poſitive, whether it winds much in other places; but as far as I could ſee, its courſe is very different from that of our Rivers in *France;* for I muſt tell you by the way, that all the Rivers of *America* run pretty ſtraight.

The River of the *Illineſe* is intitled to Riches, by vertue of the benign Climate, and of the great quantities of Deer, Roe-Bucks, and Turkeys that feed upon its brinks: Not to mention ſeveral other Beaſts and Fowls, a deſcription of which would require an intire Volume. If you ſaw but my Journal, you would be ſick of the tedious particulars of our daily Adventures both in Hunting and Fiſhing divers ſpecies of Animals, and in Rencounters with the Savages. In ſhort, the laſt thing I ſhall mention of this [135] River, is, that the Banks are repleniſh'd with an infinity of Fruit-Trees, which we ſaw in a diſmal condition, as being ſtrip'd of their verdure; and that among theſe Fruit-Trees, there are many Vines, which bear moſt beautiful Cluſters of very large Grapes. I ate ſome of theſe Grapes dry'd in the Sun, which had a moſt delicious Taſte. The Beavers are as unfrequent in this, as in the long River, where I ſaw nothing but Otters, of which the People make Furs for the Winter.

I ſet out from the *Illineſe* River on the 10*th* of *April*, and by the help of a Weſt-South-Weſt Wind, arriv'd in ſix days at the Fort of *Crevecoeur*, where I met with Mr. *de Tonti*, who receiv'd me with all imaginable Civility, and is juſtly reſpected and honour'd by the *Iroqueſe.*[1] I ſtay'd three days in this Fort, where there were thirty *Coureurs de Bois* that traded with the *Illineſe.* The 20*th* I arriv'd at the Village of the *Illineſe;* and to leſſen the drudgery of a great Land-carriage of twelve great Leagues, ingag'd four hundred Men to tranſport our Baggage, which they did in the ſpace of four days, being incourag'd by a Bribe of a great Roll of *Braſil* Tobacco, an hundred pound weight of Powder, two hundred weight of Ball, and ſome Arms, which I gave to the moſt conſiderable Men of their number. The 24*th* I arriv'd at *Chekakou*, where my *Outagamis* took leave of me in order to return to their own Country, being very well ſatisfied with a Preſent I made 'em of ſome Fuſees, and ſome Piſtols.[2] The 25*th* I reimbarqued, and by rowing hard in a Calm, made the River of the *Oumamis* on the 28*th*. There I met four hundred Warriours, upon the

[1] If Lahontan had really been at Tonty's fort on the Illinois, he would have known better than to call it Fort Crêvecœur. The latter was the fort built near the site of Peoria, Ill., on La Salle's first journey to Illinois, and destroyed by mutineering soldiers two months later (Jan.–March, 1680). Tonty was at this time in command at Fort St. Louis, built (1682) on "La Rocher" farther up the river near the present Utica. For its later history see p. 133, note 1, *ante*. Lahontan probably intended to say that Tonty was respected and honored by the Illinois, not the Iroquois, against whom he waged frequent wars. — ED.

[2] The portage at Chicago was first made known to the French by the voyage of Jolliet and Marquette, who returned to Mackinac by this route (1672). They reported it as very convenient for settlement (*Jes. Rel.*, lviii, pp. 105, 107); but La Salle wrote less favorably of the site, and that a canal would be very expensive. The connection between Chicago River and the Illinois is now secured by the Chicago drainage canal, between that city and Joliet, Ill. — ED.

very ſame place where Mr. *de la Salle* had formerly built a Fort.[1] Theſe Warriours were then imploy'd in burning three *Iroqueſe*, who, as they ſaid, deſerv'd the Puniſhment; and invited us to ſhare in the pleaſure of the Show; for the Savages take it very ill if one [136] refuſes the diverſion of ſuch real Tragedies. The Tragical ſpectacle made me ſhrink, for the poor wretches were put to inconceiveable Torture; and upon that I reſolv'd to reimbarque with all expedition; alledging for an Apology, that my Men had great ſtore of Brandy with 'em, and would certainly make themſelves drunk, in ſolemniſing their Victory, upon which they would be apt to commit diſorders, that I could not poſſibly prevent. Accordingly I went immediately on board, and after coaſting along the Lake, croſs'd the Bay *de l'Ours*, and landed at *Miſſilimakinac* the 22*d*.[2]

I am inform'd by the Sieur *de S. Pierre de Repantigni*, who travel'd from *Quebec* hither upon the Ice, that Mr. *de Denonville* has took up a reſolution of making a Peace with the *Iroqueſe*, in

[1] The River of the Miamis was that now known as St. Joseph, which flows into Lake Michigan in Berrien County, Mich. La Salle built a fort at this place in November, 1679, which was destroyed the next spring by the deserters from Fort Crêvecœur. In the autumn of the same year it was rebuilt by La Salle's lieutenant La Forest, and there the great explorer spent the ensuing winter. The Jesuits founded a mission to the Miamis about sixty miles up the river, near the present Niles, Mich. The mission and the fort afterwards built were known as St. Joseph. — Ed.

[2] The Bay de l'Ours qui Dort (Bay of Sleeping Bears) was that now called Grand Traverse Bay, Mich. This name appears upon nearly all French maps until the English conquest (1760). The first English maps designate it as Grand Bay; later, it acquired its present appellation. The French name was doubtless given because of a fancied resemblance in the rocky headlands to sleeping bears. — Ed.

which he means to comprehend the other Nations that are his Allies; and with that view had given notice to his Allies, that they ſhould not infeſt the *Iroqueſe*.[1] He acquaints me further, that Mr. *de Denonville* has ſent orders to the Governour of this place, to perſwade the *Rat*, (one of the Commanders of the *Hurons*) to go down to the Colony, with a deſign, to have him hang'd; and that the Savage General being aware of the deſign, has made a publick Declaration, that he will go thither on purpoſe to defie him. Accordingly he deſigns to ſet out to Morrow with a great body of *Outaouas*, and ſome *Coureurs de Bois*, under the command of Mr. *Dulhut*. As for the Soldiers of my Detachment, I have diſpers'd 'em in ſeveral Canows among the Savages, and the *Coureurs de Bois;* but having ſome buſineſs to adjuſt in this place, I am oblig'd to tarry my ſelf ſeven or eight days longer.

This, Sir, is the true account of my little Voyage. I have related nothing but the Eſſential Circumſtances; chooſing to overlook the reſt, which are ſo trifling, as to be unworthy of your Curioſity. [137] As for the *Illineſe* Lake, 'tis three hundred Leagues in Circumference, as you may ſee by the Scale of Leagues upon the Map. 'Tis ſeated in an admirable Cli-

[1] Jean Paul le Gardeur, sieur de St. Pierre de Repentigny, was grandson of a Norman gentleman of good family, who early settled in Canada; and, on his mother's side, of Jean Nicolet, first explorer of Wisconsin. He had seen service in the Northwest, probably under Du Luth. He was in 1689 sent by Denonville with orders for the destruction of Fort Frontenac, and distinguished himself as an officer in both King William's (1689–97) and Queen Anne's (1702–13) wars. In 1718 he built the French post at Chequamegon Bay, on Lake Superior. His son Jacques, second sieur de St. Pierre, was the officer whom Washington encountered upon the Allegheny (1753). — Ed.

mate; its Banks are cloath'd with fine and tall Trees, and have but few Meads. The River of the *Oumamis* is not worth your regard. The Bay *de l'Ours qui dort*, is of an indifferent large extent, and receives the River upon which the *Outaouas* are wont to hunt Beavers every third year. In ſhort, it has neither Shelves, Rocks, nor Banks of Sand. The Land which bounds it on the South ſide, is repleniſh'd with Roe-bucks, Deer, and Turkeys. Farewel, Good Sir: And aſſure your ſelf, that 'twill always be a ſenſible pleaſure to me, to amuſe you with an account of the greateſt Curioſities I meet with.

But now, Sir, I hope you will not take it ill, that the Relation I here give you, is only an Abridgment of my Voyage: For, in earneſt, to be minute upon every particular Curioſity, would require more time and leiſure than I can ſpare. I have here ſent you a view of the ſubſtantial part; and ſhall afterwards hope for an opportunity of recounting to you by word of Mouth, an infinity of Adventures, Rencounters, and Obſervations, which may call up the reflecting faculty of thinking Men. My own Thought is too Superficial to philoſophiſe upon the Origin, the Belief, the Manners and Cuſtoms of ſo many Savages; or to make any advances with reference to the extent of this Continent to the Weſtward. I have contented my ſelf with offering ſome thoughts upon the cauſes of the bad ſucceſs of the Diſcoveries, that ſeveral experienc'd Men have attempted in *America*, both by Sea and Land: And I flatter my ſelf, that my thoughts upon that head are juſt. The freſh Inſtances of Mr. *de la Salle*, and ſeveral other unlucky Diſcoverers, may afford a ſufficient and ſeaſonable caution to

[138] thoſe, who for the future ſhall undertake to diſcover all the unknown Countries of this New World. 'Tis not every one that's qualify'd for ſuch an Enterpriſe, *non licet omnibus adire Corinthum.* 'Twere an eaſie matter to trace the utmoſt limits of the Country that lies to the Weſt of *Canada*, provided it be gone about in a proper Method. In the firſt place, inſtead of Canows, I would have ſuch Adventurers to make uſe of certain Sloops of a peculiar Structure, which might draw but little Water, and be portable, as being made of light Wood; and withall carry thirteen Men, with 35 or 40 hundred weight of Stowage, and be able to bear the ſhock of the Waves in the great Lakes. Courage, Health, and Vigilance, are not ſufficient of themſelves to qualifie a Man for ſuch Adventures; he ought to be poſſeſs'd of other Talents, which are rarely met with in one and the ſame Perſon. The Conduct of the three hundred Men that accompany'd me upon this Diſcovery, gave me a great deal of trouble. It requires a large ſtock of Induſtry and Patience, to keep ſuch a Company up to their Duty. Sedition, Mutinies, Quarrels, and an infinity of diſorders frequently take place among thoſe, who being in remote and ſolitary Places, think they have a right of uſing force againſt their Superiours. One muſt diſſemble, and even ſhut his Eyes upon occaſion, leaſt the growing Evil ſhould be inflam'd: The gentleſt Methods are the ſureſt, for him that commands in Chief; and if any Mutiny or Seditious Plot is in view, 'tis the buſineſs of the inferior Officers to ſtifle it, by perſwading the Mutineers, that the diſcovery of ſuch things to the Commanding Officer, would create a great deal

of uneafinefs. So, the chief Officer muft ftill make as if he were ignorant of what paffes, unlefs it be, that the flame breaks out in his Prefence; then indeed he lies under an indifpenfible Obligation, of inflicting fpeedy [139] and private punifhment, without his prudence directs him to put off the Execution, upon an apprehenfion of fome pernicious confequences that may infue thereupon. In fuch Voyages he muft overlook a thoufand things, which upon other occafions he has all reafon to punifh. He muft counterfeit a downright ignorance of their Intrigues with the She-Savages, of their Quarrels among themfelves, of their negligence in not mounting the Guard, and not obferving the other points of Duty; in a word, he muft pretend to know nothing of an Infinity of fuch Diforders, as have no direct tendency to a Revolt. He ought to ufe the precaution of fingling out a Spy in his little Army, and reward him handfomly for a dexterous Intelligence as to all that happens; to the end that he may remedy the growing diforders either directly or indirectly. This Spie may by good management, and due fecrecy find out the Ringleader of a Club or Cabal; and when the Commanding Officer has receiv'd fuch fatisfaction upon the matter, that there's no room left to doubt of the Criminal's Demerit; 'twill then be very convenient to make away with him, and that with fuch management, that no body fhould know what became of him.

Farther: He ought to give 'em Tobacco and Brandy now and then, to ask their advice upon fome occafions, to fatigue 'em as little as poffible, to call 'em up to dance and make merry, and at the ſame time to exhort 'em to live in a good underſtanding with one another. The beſt Topick he can make uſe of for inforcing their Duty, is Religion, and the Honour of their Country, and this he ought to deſcant upon himſelf: For though I have a great deal of Faith in the power of the Clergy; yet I know that ſort of Men do's more harm than good, in Voyages of this nature; and for that reaſon I'd chooſe to be without their Company. The Perſon [140] who undertakes to go upon a Diſcovery, ought to be very nice and cautious in the choice of his Men; for every one is not fit for his buſineſs. His Men ought to be between 30 and 40 years of Age, of a dry Conſtitution, of a peaceable Temper, of an active and bold Spirit, and inur'd to the fatigues of Voyages. The whole Retinue muſt conſiſt of three hundred Men; and of that number there muſt be ſome Ship-Carpenters, Gun-ſmiths, and Sawyers with all their Tools; beſides Huntſmen, and Fiſhermen with their Tackling. You muſt likewiſe have Surgeons among 'em, but their Cheſt ought to contain nothing but Razours, Lancets, External Medicines for Wounds, Or-vietan and Senna. All the Men of the Detachment, ought to be provided with Buff-Coats and Boots to turn the Arrows; for, as I intimated above, the Savages of the unknown Countries are ſtrangers to Fire-Arms. They muſt be arm'd with a double barrel'd Gun, a double barrel'd Piſtol, and a good long Sword. The Commanding Officer muſt take care to provide a ſufficient quantity of the Skins of Deer, Elks, and Beeves, in order to be ſew'd together, and hung round his Camps upon certain Stakes fix'd at convenient diſtances from one another. I had as many as would go round a ſquare of thirty Foot every way; for each Skin being five Foot deep, and almoſt four Foot broad, I made two pieces of eight Skins a piece, which were rais'd and extended in a Minute. Beſides theſe, he ought to carry with him ſome Pot-Guns of eight Foot in length, and ſix in breadth; with two Hand-Mills for grinding the *Indian* Corn, Nails of all ſizes, Pickaxes, Spades, Hatchets, Hooks, Soap, and Cotton to make Candles of. Above all, he muſt not forget to take in good ſtore of Powder, Brandy, *Braſil* Tobacco, and ſuch things as he muſt preſent to the Savages whoſe Country he diſcovers. Add to this Cargo, an Aſtrolabe, a Semicircle, ſeveral [141] Sea-Compaſſes, ſome Simple, and ſome of Variation, a Load-ſtone, two large Watches of three Inches Diameter; Pencils, Colours, and Paper, for making Journals and Maps, for the deſigning of Land-Creatures, Fowl, Fiſh, Trees, Plants, Grain, and in a word, whatever ſeems worthy of his Curioſity. I would likewiſe adviſe him to carry with him ſome Trumpeters and Fidlers, both for animating his Retinue, and raiſing the admiration of the Savages. With this Equipage, Sir, a Man of Senſe, Conduct, and Action, I mean, a Man that's Vigilant, Prudent, Cautious, and above all, Patient and Moderate, and qualify'd for contriving Expedients upon all occaſions; a Man, I ſay, thus qualify'd, and thus fitted out, may boldly go to all the Countries that lye to the Weſt of *Canada*, without any apprehenſion of danger. As for my own part, I ſeriouſly declare, that if I were poſſeſs'd of all theſe qualities, I ſhould eſteem it my happineſs to be imploy'd upon ſuch an Enterpriſe, both for the Glory of his Majeſty, and my own Satisfaction: For the continu'd diverſity of Objects, did ſo charm me in my Voyages, that I had ſcarce time to reflect upon the fatigue and trouble that I underwent. I am,

SIR,

Yours, &c.

[142] LETTER XVII.

Dated at *Quebec September* 28. 1689.

The Author ſets out from Miſſilimakinac *to the Colony, and deſcribes the Country, Rivers, and Paſſes that he ſaw by the way. The* Iroqueſe *make a fatal incurſion into the Iſland of* Monreal: *Fort* Frontenac *is abandon'd. Count* Frontenac *is ſent to* Canada, *and the Marquis of* Denonville *is recall'd.*

SIR,

I WRIT to you from *Miſſilimakinac* on the 28*th* of *May*. I left that place *June* the 8*th*, and ſet out for *Monreal*, accompany'd with twelve *Outaouas*, who were divided into two Canows, and row'd very hard. The 23*d*, I overtook the *Coureurs de Bois* in the River *Creuſe*, who had got the ſtart of me for ſome days.[1] Mr. *Dulhut* us'd his utmoſt efforts to diſſwade me from going further with ſo weak a Retinue. He would have had me to go down along with him; and remonſtrated to me, that if my twelve Conducters perceiv'd either in the Land-carriage or upon the Rivers, any thing that might call up an apprehenſion of falling into the hands of the *Iroqueſe*, they would deſert me and the Canows, and fly to the

[1] The Rivière Creuse — called by the English Deep River — is not a separate stream, but the long, deep, still part of the Ottawa River, extending for many miles above the Allumettes Rapids and Islands. Lahontan apparently gives that name to all of the Upper Ottawa or to the Mattawan. — ED.

Woods to avoid the Enemy. I rejected his Advice, though I had like to have repented of my refolution not long after; for according to his Prediction, my Canow-Men threaten'd to run away to the Forrefts, at the Fall call'd *Long Saut*[1]: And indeed if they had done it, I had follow'd 'em, upon the reflection, that of two Evils a Man ought [143] to choofe the leaft; but this Storm blew over. In the great River of the *Outaouas*, not far from the River of *Lievre*,[2] I met Mr. *de St. Helene* at the Head of a Party of the *Coureurs de Bois*, who was bound for *Hudfon*'s Bay, in order to retake fome Forts that the *Englifh* had feiz'd upon.[3] He acquainted me with the Prince of *Orange's* Expedition for *England;* and gave me to underftand, that upon his arrival King *James* retir'd to *France*, and that the Prince was proclaim'd King, which feem'd to prefage a bloody and fharp War in *Europe*. I affure you, Sir, this piece of News furpriz'd me extreamly; and notwithftanding that I

---

[1] This was the Long Sault of the Ottawa, not that of the St. Lawrence, for which see p. 68, note 1, *ante*. The former, about three miles in length, is on the Ottawa above the Lake of Two Mountains, and is now avoided by the Grenville Canal. It was at the lower end of these rapids that occurred the heroic defense of Canada by Dollard and his companions (1661). See Parkman, *Old Régime in Canada*, chap. 3. — ED.

[2] Rivière au Lièvre descends from the north and enters the Ottawa about three miles above the upper end of the Long Sault. — ED.

[3] For Jacques le Moyne, Sieur de St. Hélène, see p. 118, note 1, *ante*. He was carrying supplies and despatches to his brother Iberville, who was in command of the forts which the French had captured (1686) in Hudson Bay. Two English ships had been sent to recover these; during St. Hélène's absence, Iberville succeeded in capturing both of these vessels, with their officers and crews. Iberville had sent messengers to the governor of Canada, who left Fort Albany (Fr., St. Anne) Jan. 5, 1689, and came overland on snowshoes. See Charlevoix, *History of New France* (Shea's trans.), iv, pp. 37-40. — ED.

had it from the Mouth of a Man, whofe word I rely very much upon, yet I had all the difficulty in the World to make my felf believe, that a Revolution of fuch Importance could be accomplifh'd in fo fhort a time, without the effufion of Blood; efpecially confidering what a ftrict Alliance there was between our Court, and the Court of *England*, and how much 'twas the intereft of both thefe Monarchs to give mutual affiftance to one another. *July* the 9*th* I arriv'd at *Monreal*, after venturing down feveral fearful Cataracts in the River of the *Outaouas*, and induring the hardfhips of fifteen or twenty Land-carriages, fome of which are above a League in length.

The Navigation is prety fure from *Miffilimakinac* to the River *des François;* for in coafting along the Lake of *Hurons*, we meet with an infinity of Iflands, which ferve for a fhelter.[1] But in going up that River, there's fome difficulty, for it has five Cataracts which oblige us to turn out and carry all overland for thirty, fifty, and a hundred Paces. Having pafs'd that River, we enter'd the Lake of the *Nepicerinis*, from whence we are forc'd to tranfport our Canows and Baggage two Leagues over-land, to another River which has fix or feven Water-falls that we commonly fhoot.[2] From that River we

[1] The distance from Mackinac to the mouth of French River, in Georgian Bay, is nearly 200 miles, taking as direct a course as possible among the islands of the North Channel. French River (River des Français) was so called because it was the accustomed waterway of the French voyageurs, who on account of the hostility of the Iroquois, found the difficult route via the Ottawa, Lake Nipissing, and French River more practicable than the Great Lakes. — Ed.

[2] French River is fifty-five miles long, and filled with rapids and falls. Lake Nipissing was named from the tribe of Algonquian Indians first encountered on its banks, some of whose descendants still live on a reservation on the north bank of the

have another [144] Land-carriage to the River *Creuſe*, which falls with rapid Currents into the great River of the *Outaouas*, near a place call'd *Mataouan*.[1] We continue our courſe upon this great River, till we come to the point of the Iſland of *Monreal*, where 'tis loſt in the great River of St. *Laurence*. Theſe two Rivers joyn one another with very gentle Streams, and quitting their fearful Channels form the little Lake of St. *Louis*. I thought to have loſt my Life at the fall, call'd the fall of St. *Louis*, about three Leagues from *Monreal*, for our Canow having overſet in the Eddy, I was carry'd by the Current to the foot of that Cataract, from whence the Chevalier *de Vaudreuil* drag'd me out by a great chance.[2] The Canows and the Skins belonging to the ſix Savages were loſt; and one of the Savages was drown'd. This is the only time I was in danger, through the whole courſe of my Voyages. As ſoon as I landed here, I repair'd with diligence to a Tavern to refreſh my ſelf, and to make up the loſſes I had ſuſtain'd by a neceſſary Abſtinence. The next day I waited upon Mr. *de Denonville*,

lake. From the eastern end of this lake, the route lay for a mile and a half along Rivière de Vase (Muddy River), whence the Portage au Vase, of about four miles, led over the watershed to Trout Lake, the source of River Mattawan. This river flows east into the Ottawa, is about thirty-four miles long, and has in it fourteen rapids, some of which are very difficult. For details of this route, see Alexander Henry, *Travels and Adventures* (Bain ed.), pp. 28–37; Mackenzie, *Voyages through the Continent of North America* (London, 1801), pp. xxix-xxxvii. — ED.

[1] Mattawan is now a town at the junction of River Mattawan with the Ottawa; it is three hundred miles from Montreal. Champlain utilized this route in his voyage to the Hurons (1615). — ED.

[2] For Lake St. Louis and the fall of the same name, see p. 66, note 1, *ante*. Lachine Rapids were frequently dangerous to the returning voyageur, who had escaped all the perils of the upper country. Jolliet here lost his papers on his return from the famous exploration of 1673. — ED.

and Mr. *de Champigni*, to whom I gave an account of my Voyages, and withal, gave in the News that a great company of the *Coureurs de Bois* and Savages would arrive very ſpeedily; which they did accordingly after fifteen days. The *Rat* I mention'd above came down hither, and return'd home notwithſtanding the threats that were levell'd againſt him. By this Adventure, he ſhew'd that he laugh'd at their Intrigues. But now that I have mention'd his name, I cannot forbear mentioning a malicious Stratagem that this cunning Savage made uſe of laſt year, to prevent the concluſion of a Peace between Mr. *de Denonville* and the *Iroqueſe.*

This Savage is the general and chief Counſellour of the *Hurons;* he is a Man of forty years of Age, and brave in his way. When he found himſelf [145] preſs'd and importun'd by Mr. *de Denonville*, to enter into the Alliance concluded in the year 1687, that I took notice of before; he at laſt comply'd with his deſire, with this reſerve, that the War ſhould not be put to an end till the *Iroqueſe* were totally routed. This clauſe the Governour promis'd to make good, and gave him aſſurances to that purpoſe on the 3*d* of *September*, in the ſame year, which happen'd about two days before I ſet out from *Niagara*, upon my Voyage to the great Lakes. This Savage-General relying upon Mr. *de Denonville*'s promiſe, march'd from *Miſſilimakinac* at the Head of an hundred Warriours as I inſinuated in my 14*th* Letter, in order to invade the *Iroqueſe* Country, and atchieve ſome glorious feats among 'em. In the mean time, to carry on his deſign the more cautiouſly, he thought it proper to paſs by the way of Fort *Frontenac*, where

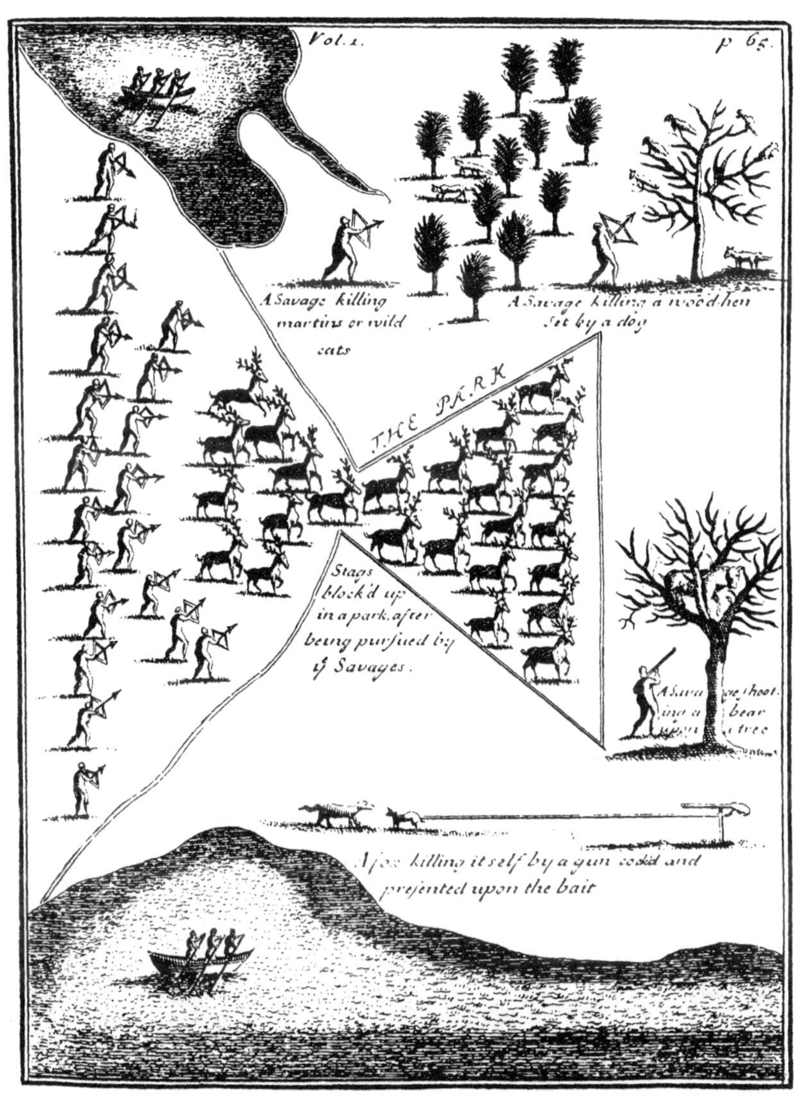
Vol. 1.
p 65.
A Savage killing martins or wild cats
A Savage killing a wood-hen set by a dog
THE PARK
Stags block'd up in a park, after being pursued by 15 Savages.
A Sava ge shoot ing a bear a tree
A fox killing it self by a gun cock'd and presented upon the bait

he might receive ſome intelligence. Upon his arrival at this Fort, the Governour told him that Mr. *de Denonville* was negotiating a Peace with the five *Iroqueſe* Nations, whoſe Embaſſadors and Hoſtages he expected in a ſhort time, in order to conclude and ratifie the Peace, he having orders to conduct 'em to *Monreal:* And that upon that Conſideration, 'twas moſt proper for him and his Warriours to return home, and to paſs no further. The Savage General was mightily ſurpris'd with this unexpected piece of News; eſpecially conſidering that by the means of that Peace, he and his Nation would be given up as a Sacrifice for the Wellfare of the French. When the Governor had made an end of his Remonſtrance, the *Rat* acknowledg'd, that what he offer'd was very reaſonable, but withal, that inſtead of following his Advice, he would go and tarry for the *Iroqueſe* Embaſſadours and Hoſtages at the Cataracts, by which they were oblig'd to paſs. He had not tarry'd there above five or ſix days, before the unhappy Deputies [146] arriv'd with a Train of forty young Men, who were all either kill'd or taken as they diſembarqued. The Priſoners were no ſooner fetter'd, than this crafty General of the *Hurons* repreſented to 'em, that the *French* Governour had ſent him notice to take up that Poſt, in order to lie in wait for a Party of fifty Warriours, that were to paſs that way at a certain ſet time. The *Iroqueſe* being much ſurpris'd with the apprehenſion of the perfidiouſneſs that he charg'd upon Mr. *de Denonville*, acquainted the *Rat* with the deſign upon which they came. Upon that the *Rat* counterfeited a ſort of Rage and Fury; and to play his Cards the better, flew out in invectives againſt Mr. *de Denonville*, declaring, that ſome time or other he would be reveng'd upon that Governour, for making him the Inſtrument of the moſt barbarous Treachery that ever was acted. Then he fix'd his Eyes upon all the Priſoners, among whom was the chief Embaſſadour call'd *Theganeſorens*,[1] and ſpoke to this purpoſe; *Go my Brethren, though I am at War with you, yet I releaſe you, and allow you to go home. 'Tis the Governour of the* French *that put me upon this black Action, which I ſhall never be able to digeſt, unleſs your five Nations revenge themſelves, and make their juſt Repriſals.* This was ſufficient to convince the *Iroqueſe* of the ſincerity of his words; and they aſſur'd him upon the ſpot, that if he had a mind to make a ſeparate Peace, the five Nations would agree to it: However, the *Rat* having loſt one Man in this Adventure, kept an *Iroqueſe* Slave to ſupply the place of the Man he had loſt: And after furniſhing the Priſoners with Guns, Powder, and Ball, in order to their return homeward, march'd to *Miſſilimakinac*, where he preſented the *French* Governour with the Slave that he brought off. The poor wretch was no ſooner deliver'd, than he was condemn'd to be ſhot; for at that time the *French* Garriſon did not know that [147] Mr. *de Denonville* deſign'd to clap up a Peace with the *Iroqueſe*. The condemn'd Priſoner gave an

[1] Teganissoren (Dekanissore) was a famous Onondaga chief who for many years took a prominent part in the councils of the Iroquois, and in the French and English wars. Being much attached to Frontenac, during his rule he was regarded by the English as a French spy. Later, he became attached to the English; but in 1711 notified Vaudreuil of an intended British attack. For his negotiations with the two powers, see *N. Y. Colon. Docs.*, index. — Ed.

account of his Adventure, and that of the Ambaſſadours; but the *French* thought that the fear of Death made the fellow talk idly, and were confirm'd in that thought, by hearing the *Rat* and his Men ſay that he was Light-headed: Inſomuch, that the poor Fellow was put to death, notwithſtanding all the reaſons he could offer. The ſame day that he was ſhot, the *Rat* call'd an old *Iroqueſe* Slave that had ſerv'd him a long while, and told him he had reſolv'd to allow him the liberty of returning to his own Country, and ſpending the reſt of his days among his Friends and Country-men. At the ſame time he gave him to know, that ſince he had been an Eye-witneſs of the barbarous uſage that his Countrymen had met with from the *French*, notwithſtanding what he offer'd in his own defence, it behov'd him to acquaint his Countrymen with the blackneſs of that Action. The manumitted Slave obey'd his orders ſo punctually, that ſoon after the *Iroqueſe* made an Incurſion, at a time when the Governour did not dream of any ſuch thing, for he had us'd the Precaution of giving the *Iroqueſe* to underſtand, that he diſallow'd of the *Rat's* Treachery; inſomuch, that he had a mind to have him hang'd; and upon this proſpect, expected hourly ten or twelve Deputies to conclude the Peace he ſo much deſir'd.[1]

In effect the Deputies did come, but neither their Number nor their Deſign was ſuitable to what the Governour had

[1] Parkman, after careful comparison with other original documents bearing on this story of the Rat's treachery, accepts the account of Lahontan as substantially correct. He thinks the weight of evidence, however, would place the site of the ambuscade at La Famine, rather than the Cascades of the St. Lawrence. See *Frontenac*, p. 176, note. — ED.

promifed to himfelf. Twelve hundred Warriours landed at the Lands-end of the Ifland of *Monreal*, and burnt and fack'd all the Plantations in that Quarter: They maffacred Men, Women, and Children; and Madam *de Denonville*, who was then at *Monreal* with her Husband, did not think her felf fafe in that place. A general Confternation was fpread all about; for the *Barbarians* were not above [148] three Leagues from *Monreal*. They burnt all the adjacent Settlements, and block'd up two Forts.[1] Mr. *de Denonville* fent out a Detachment of a hundred Soldiers and fifty Savages to oppofe 'em, being unwilling to fpare a greater number out of the City: but all the Men of the Detachment were either taken or cut in pieces, excepting twelve Savages, one Soldier, and Mr. *de Longueil* who commanded the Party, and was carried off by the twelve Savages after his Thigh was broke: The other Officers, namely, the *Sieurs de la Raberre*, *Denis*, *la Plante*, and *Villedenè*, were all taken Prifoners.[2] In a word, the *Barbarians* laid almoft the

[1] Lahontan must have been in Montreal at the time of this massacre at Lachine, which occurred August 5, 1689, and was the most appalling in the history of New France. There are several other reports of eye-witnesses, which correspond in the main to this account. The two forts were block-houses known as Forts Rolland and Rémy. For a detailed account, with full list of the victims, see Girouard, *Lake St. Louis*, pp. 117–139. — ED.

[2] Charles Le Moyne, first baron de Longueuil, later governor of New France (1725–26), was eldest son of Charles, seigneur de Longueuil, for whom see p. 74, note 1, *ante*. Longueuil distinguished himself in the Iroquois wars, was for many years governor of Montreal, and one of the most distinguished Canadians. He died in 1729.

Of the other officers, all were finally rescued from the Iroquois, except Lieutenant de la Rabeyre, who was burned at the stake. La Plante did not return to the colony until 1692. After his release, Etienne de Villedonné led troops against the Mohawk (1692–93), and distinguished himself in Acadia (1705). He died in 1726. — ED.

whole Iſland waſte, and loſt only three Men, who having drank to exceſs of the Wine they found in the Plantations, were decoy'd into a Fort by a *Canadeſe* Cow-keeper, that had been their Slave for ſome Years. As ſoon as the three unfortunate *Iroqueſe* arriv'd in the Fort, they were thrown into a Cellar to ſleep themſelves ſober; and, queſtionleſs, as ſoon as they wak'd they repented of their exceſſive drinking. When they wak'd, they fell immediately a ſinging; and when the Garriſon offer'd to fetter 'em, and carry 'em to *Monreal*, they flew to ſome Clubs that lay in the Cellar, and made ſuch a vigorous and brave defence, that the Garriſon was forc'd to ſhoot 'em upon the ſpot. The Cow-keeper being brought before Mr. *de Denonville*, he told him, That the Breach made by the *Rat*'s Contrivance was irreparable; that the five *Iroqueſe* Nations reſented that Adventure with ſo much warmth, that 'twas impoſſible to diſpoſe 'em to a Peace in a ſhort time; that they were ſo far from being angry with that *Huron* for what he did, that they were willing to enter into a Treaty with him, owning that he and his Party had done nothing but what became a brave Man and a good Ally. Doubtleſs this fatal Incurſion was a great Surpriſal to Mr. *de Denonville*, and afforded him a copious Field for Reflection. 'Twas already impoſſible [149] to continue the Poſſeſſion of Fort *Frontenac*, where they began to want Proviſions, and which could not be relieved without expoſing a great many Men to the danger of the Paſſes or Cataracts, which I have mention'd ſo often. There was a downright neceſſity of calling out the Garriſon, and blowing up the Fort; but the difficulty lay in finding a Man to carry Orders for that effect to the Governour, for no body durst undertake it, till the Sieur *Peter d'Arpentigni* offer'd to go all alone through the Forests; and accordingly he went, and did his Business successfully. The Orders were extream welcome to Mr. *de Valrenes*, the Governour of the Fort for the time; who, upon the receiving of 'em, run a Mine under the four Bastions, which, with the Powder he put in, was reckon'd sufficient to blow it up.[1] This done, he embark'd, and came down the River through the Cataracts to *Monreal*, where he found Mr. *de Denonville*, and accompany'd him hither. That Officer did not only abdicate the Fort of *Frontenac*, but set fire to three great Barques that they us'd to ply with upon the Lake, both to awe the *Iroquese* in time of War, and to convey Commodities to 'em in time of Peace. Mr. *de Denonville* acted a prudent part in relinquishing both this Fort and that of *Niagara;* for, in earnest these two Posts are indefensible, by reason of the inaccessible Cataracts, upon which an Ambuscado of ten *Iroquese* may repulse a thousand *Frenchmen* by the throwing of Stones. But after all I must own, that the Welfare and Preservation of our Colonies had an absolute dependance upon these two Forts, which seem'd to insure the utter Destruction of the *Iroquese;* for they could not stir out

[1] Philippe Clément Duvault, sieur de Valrennes, was already a veteran officer when he arrived in Canada in 1685. In that year, he led one division of La Barre's forces, and performed prodigies of valor in the relief of La Prairie de la Madeleine (1691), for which he received high praise from Frontenac. See *N. Y. Colon. Docs.*, ix, pp. 522, 523.—Ed.

of their Villages to Hunt, or to Fiſh, without running the riſque of having their Throats cut by the Savages in Alliance with us, who being then aſſur'd of a ſafe Retreat, would have made continual Incurſions into the Country of thoſe *Barbarians:* [150] And by this means the *Iroqueſe* being unprovided with Beaver-skins to be given in exchange for Guns, Powder, Ball, and Nets, would be ſtarv'd to death, or at leaſt be oblig'd to depart their Country.

In the end of *September* Mr. *de Bonaventure*, Captain and Owner of a Merchant Ship, arriv'd in this Port, and brought the News of Mr. *de Frontenac*'s Reinſtallment in the place of Governour-General of *Canada*,[1] and of the Re-calling of Mr. *de Denonville*, whom the Duke *de Beauvilliers* has recommended to the King, for the place of Sub-Governour to the Princes his Grandſons.[2] Some People are uneaſie at the re-calling of this Governour; and 'tis ſaid, that the Reverend Fathers the Jeſuits, fall under the number of the Malecontents: For if we may credit the reports of the Country, they contributed in a great meaſure, to the re-calling of Mr. *de Frontenac* ſeven or eight years agoe, by acting in concert

[1] Claude Denis, sieur de Bonaventure, belonged to one of the oldest Canadian families, and afterwards rose to the rank of admiral in the navy. In 1691 he co-operated in driving the English from Acadia, and was aid to Iberville in the latter's expeditions. — ED.

[2] Paul, Duke de Beauvilliers, was one of the noted figures of the court of Louis XIV, and famous for his probity and piety. For many years he had served as first gentleman of the bedchamber and chief of the council of finance, and in 1670 was chosen governor of the royal princes. He died in 1714, on which occasion St. Simon drew the remarkable portrait of him which appears in his *Memoirs*. — ED.

with the Intendant of *Chesneau*, and the ſupreme Council, and drawing up Accuſations againſt him which had the deſired effect; though now the King ſhews that he is undeceiv'd, by reinſtating that Gentleman once more in this Government.[1] In the mean time the Stateſmen of the Country that are moſt guilty, know not how to dreſs this kettle of Fiſh; for they make no queſtion but the New Governour will retain a juſt reſentment of what's paſt. But the Gentlemen, Merchants, and other Inhabitants, are making preparations for ſolemniſing his Arrival, which they expect with as much impatience, as the *Jews* do the *Meſſias*. The very Savages that live in the skirts of the Colony, ſhew an uncommon Joy upon the hopes of his return: And indeed, we need not think it ſtrange, for that Governour drew Eſteem and Veneration, not only from the *French*, but from all the Nations of this vaſt Continent, who look'd upon him as their Guardian Angel. Mr. *de Denonville* begins to pack up his Baggage, and that in effect, [151] is all I can ſay of him. 'Tis none of my buſineſs to meddle with an infinity of Affairs, that relate to the Gentleman's private Intereſt. As to the queſtion, whether he has manag'd well or ill, during the courſe of his Government, or whether he was lov'd or hated, I know nothing of the matter.

[1] Jacques Duchesneau, sieur de la Doussinière, was chosen (1675) successor of Talon in the Canadian intendancy. Almost from the first he maligned Count Frontenac, and supported the Jesuit party in opposition. The king, losing patience at their complaints, recalled both Frontenac and Duchesneau May 10, 1682. In the crisis of affairs in New France, Frontenac was sent back (1689) as the one man capable of meeting the difficulties. — ED.

I am at a loſs to know whether he kept a good or a ſorry Table, for indeed I was never at it. Adieu.

I make account to ſet out for *Rochel*, when the Veſſel that brings our new Governour, returns for *France*. I am,

SIR,

Yours, &c.

LETTER XVIII.

Dated at *Quebec November* 15. 1689.

Giving an Account of Mr. de Frontenac*'s Arrival, his Reception, his Voyage to* Monreal, *and the repairing of Fort* Frontenac.

SIR,

THE Intelligence you give me of the adjudging of the Lands of *Labontan*, would have drove me to deſpair; if you had not aſſur'd me at the ſame time, that I might recover it after a Century of years, (if I had the misfortune to live ſo long) upon the condition of reimburſing to the Poſſeſſour, the Sum that he pay'd for it, and of proving that I was actually in the Kings Service in the remote parts of the World, when that Eſtate was ſold. To ſpeak to the purpoſe, Mr. *de Frontenac* has [152] countermanded the leave I had to go for *France*, and has offer'd me a free acceſs to his Pocket and his Table. All the Arguments I offer'd, have no Influence upon him, and ſo I am bound to obey.

This new Governour arriv'd at *Quebec* the 15*th* of *October*. He came on ſhoar at eight a Clock at Night, and was receiv'd by the Supreme Council, and all the Inhabitants in Arms, with Flambeau's both in the City, and upon the Harbour, with a triple Diſcharge of the great and ſmall Guns, and Illuminations in all the Windows of the City. That ſame

Night he was complimented by all the Companies of the Town, and above all, by the Jesuits, who upon that occasion made a very pathetick Speech, though the Heart had less hand in it, than the Mouth. The next day he was visited by all the Ladies, whose inward joy appear'd in their Countenances, as much as in their Words. Several Persons made Fire-works, while the Governour and his Retinue sung *Te Deum* in the great Church. These solemn Demonstrations of Joy, increas'd from day to day, till the new Governour set out for *Monreal;* and the Conduct of the People upon this Head, afforded signal proofs of the satisfaction they had in his return, and of their resting assur'd, that his wise Conduct, and noble Spirit, would preserve the Repose and Tranquility that he always kept up, during his first ten years Government. All the World ador'd him, and styl'd him *Redemptor Patriæ;* to which Title he had a just claim, for all the Inhabitants of these Colonies agree, that when he came first to *Canada*, he found all things in Confusion and Distress. At that time the *Iroquese* had burnt all the Plantations, and cut the Throats of some thousands of the *French;* the Farmer was knock'd on the Head in his Field; the Traveller was murder'd upon the Road, and the Merchant ruin'd for want of Commerce: All the Planters were pinch'd with Famine, [153] the War render'd the Country desolate; and in a word, New-*France* had infallibly perish'd, if this Governour had not made that Peace with the *Barbarians*, that I spoke of in my fifth Letter. The bringing of that Peace to bear, was an action of greater Importance, than you can well imagine; for these *Barbarians* grounded all their Wars upon a perſonal Enmity, whereas the *European* Ruptures depend more upon Intereſt than upon pure Revenge.

Mr. *de St. Valiers* the Biſhop of *Quebec*, arriv'd likewiſe on the 15*th* at the ſame Port. He had imbarqu'd in the preceding Spring, on board of a Bark that he had hir'd to tranſport him to *Acadia*, to *Newfound-land*, and to the other Countries of his Dioceſe. Mr. *de Frontenac* our Governour, ſet out for *Monreal* in a Canow, four or five days after his Arrival; and I had the honour to accompany him. All Indeavours were us'd to diſſwade him from undertaking that Voyage, when the ſeaſon was ſo cold, and ſo far advanc'd: For, as I inform'd you before, the Ice is thicker and ſtronger here in *Octob.* than 'tis at *Paris* in *January;* which, is very ſtrange. Notwithſtanding all the Remonſtrances drawn from the Hardſhips and Inconveniences of the Voyage, he ſlighted the Fatigues of the Water, and threw himſelf into a Canow in the ſixty eighth year of his Age. Nay, he took the abdication of Fort *Frontenac* ſo much to Heart, that he had gone ſtraight thither, if the Nobility, the Prieſts, and the Inhabitants of *Monreal*, had not intreated him with joynt Supplications, not to expoſe his Perſon to the danger of the Falls and Cataracts that lie in that Paſſage. In the mean time ſome Gentlemen of *Canada*, follow'd by a hundred *Coureurs de Bois*, under the command of Mr. *Mantet*, ventur'd upon the Voyage, with intent to learn the State of the Fort. I acquainted you in my laſt Letter, that Mr. *de Valrenes* had blown up the Walls of the Fort, when [154] he made his Retreat; but by good luck, the damage was not ſo great as 'twas took to be; for the Party commanded by Mr. *Mantet*, have already rear'd up the ruinous Wall to the height of ſome Fathoms, and will continue to work upon the repair of the Fort all this Winter.[1] This News Mr. *de Frontenac* receiv'd laſt Night, which was the ſixth after his return to this City.

I had forgot to tell you that he brought with him out of *France*, ſome of thoſe *Iroqueſe* that Mr. *de Denonville* had ſent to the Galleys, as I intimated in my thirteenth Letter; the reſt having periſh'd in their Chains. Of all theſe unfortunate *Barbarians* that he has brought back, the moſt conſiderable is one that goes by the name of *Oreouahè*. He was not us'd as a Galley Slave, in regard that he was the Leader of the *Goyoguans*, and the Governour has lodg'd him in the Caſtle, in conſideration of the eſteem he ſhews both for Mr. *de Frontenac*, and for the *French* Nation. Some flatter themſelves with the hopes, that ſome Accommodation with the five *Iroqueſe* Nations may be effected by his Mediation; and for that end propoſals of Peace are now in agitation: But I have three good reaſons for predicting, that ſuch a Deſign will prove abortive.[2] I have already laid theſe Reaſons before Mr.

[1] Nicholas d'Ailleboust, sieur de Mantet (Mantz, Manteht), belonged to a prominent Canadian family, being grandson of one of the founders of Montreal. Like other promising young men he took to wood-ranging; becoming an associate of DuLuth, he acquired much influence with the Indians of the Northwest. Frontenac employed him upon raiding parties, and he was first to enter Schenectady (1690). His latter years were spent in trading in the upper country, where he is last mentioned in 1709. — ED.

[2] Oureahé (Ourehaoué) was a Cayuga war chief, who had been sent to France through Denonville's treachery. Frontenac had won his good will on the return

de Frontenac, who gave me to know, that after the departure of the Ships, he would difcourfe me upon that Head. I fhall not offer at the particulars of his Interview, with Monfieur and Madam *de Denonville;* till fuch time as you and I have an opportunity of talking under the Rofe. Some Officers accompany Mr. *Denonville* and his Lady to *France*, in hopes of being prefer'd. In all probability the Ships will fet fail to Morrow, for we have now a fair and gentle Wefterly Gale; befides, that the feafon for quitting this Port, is almoft fpent. I am,

SIR, *Yours*, &c.

---

voyage, and employed him in negotiations with the Iroquois. On the ill-success of these first efforts see Parkman, *Frontenac*, pp., 194-207. The chief, however, continued to serve the French, and was rewarded with the pay of a captain until his death in the early eighteenth century. — ED.

[155] LETTER XIX.

Dated at *Monreal October* 2. 1690.

Relating the Attempts upon New-England *and New*-York; *a fatal Embaſſy ſent by the* French *to the* Iroqueſe; *and an ill-concerted Interpriſe of the* Engliſh *and the* Iroqueſe, *in marching by Land to Attack the* French *Colony.*

SIR,

ABOUT fifteen days ſince a Ship of *Rochel* laden with Wine and Brandy, arriv'd in this Harbour; and the Captain took care to convey a Letter from you to my Hands. As to your deſire of having a circumſtantial Account of the Trade of *Canada*, I cannot ſatisfie it at preſent, for I am not as yet ſo thoroughly acquainted with all its Branches. But I aſſure you, that ſome time or other I ſhall ſend you ſuch Memoirs, as will give you ſatisfaction upon that Head. In the mean time, I hope you'll be contented with an account of what paſs'd in this Country ſince the date of my laſt.

As ſoon as Mr. *Denonville* ſet out from *Quebec*, upon his return to *France*, Mr. *de Frontenac* took poſſeſſion of the Fort, which is the common Reſidence of our Governour-General; and order'd one of our beſt Architects to make preparations for rebuilding it as ſoon as he could.

In the beginning of this year, Mr. *d'Iberville* attempted to pillage a ſmall Village in New-*York*, call'd by the *Iroqueſe Corlar;* which name they likewiſe give to all the Governours of that *Engliſh* Colony. [156] This Gentleman, who is a *Canadeſe*, was attended by five hundred *Coureurs de Bois*, and the like number of Savages; and the whole Party made the Expedition over Snow and Ice, notwithſtanding they had three hundred Leagues to march backward and forward, and that the Roads were very rugged and troubleſome. Mr. *d'Iberville* met with wonderful Succeſs, for after he had pillag'd, burnt, and ſack'd that little Village, with the adjacent Cantons, he fell in with a Party of an hundred *Iroqueſe*, and defeated 'em intirely.[1] Much about the ſame time Mr. *de Portneuf*, another *Canada* Gentleman, march'd out at the Head of three hundred Men, one half Savages, and the other half *Coureurs de Bois*, with intent to poſſeſs himself of a Fort belonging to the *Engliſh*, call'd *Kenebeki*, which ſtands upon the Sea-Coaſt of *New-England*, towards the Frontiers of *Acadia*. The Garriſon of this Fort made a brave defence: But there being great quantities of Granado's and other Fire-works thrown in upon 'em,

[1] St. Hélène and Mantet were the leaders of this expedition, which numbered only about two hundred men, not a thousand. Iberville was one of the officers. See *N. Y. Colon. Docs.*, ix, pp. 466–469. The Iroquois party who pursued the victors were not routed, but defeated the rear of the French forces.

Pierre Le Moyne, sieur d'Iberville, was one of the most remarkable of early Canadians, and has been called "The Cid of Canada." Born in 1661, the third son of Charles le Moyne, sieur de Longueuil (see p. 74, note 1, *ante*), he early joined the French navy. His first exploits were in Hudson Bay, where he captured the English forts and vessels. In 1692 he served against the English in Acadia and Newfoundland. After the Peace of Ryswick (1697) he turned his attention to the Mississippi, and led the expedition which founded Louisiana (1699). He attacked the English fleet in the West Indies (1706), dying in July of the same year at Havana. — Ed.

while the Savages (contrary to their Cuſtom) ſcal'd the Paliſſadoes on all hands, the Governour was oblig'd to ſurrender upon Diſcretion. 'Tis ſaid, that in this Action the *Coureurs de Bois* did their duty very bravely, but the Enterpriſe had prov'd ſucceſsleſs without the aſſiſtance of the Savages.[1]

As ſoon as the Rivers were navigable, Mr. *de Frontenac* offer'd to ſend me with Propoſals of Peace to the *Iroqueſe*. But I made anſwer, that ſince his Pocket and his Table had been free to me during the Winter, I could not imagine that he had a mind to be rid of me ſo ſoon. Being oblig'd by this reply to unfold my meaning, I remonſtrated to him, That, the King of *England* having loſt his Crown, and War being proclaim'd, the Governours of New-*England* and New-*York*, would infallibly uſe their utmoſt Efforts to excite theſe Bandito's to redouble their Incurſions; that for that end they would furniſh [157] 'em with Ammunition *gratis*, and even joyn 'em in order to attack our Towns; and above all, that the Intrigue of the *Rat* had ſo provok'd 'em, that in my opinion, 'twas impoſſible to appeaſe 'em. Upon theſe Conſiderations, I humbly beſeech'd him to have ſome other Perſon in his view, in caſe he

[1] The French version of this attack upon Fort Loyal, on the present site of Portland, Maine, is found in *N. Y. Colon. Docs.*, ix, pp. 472, 473. Lahontan has, as usual, exaggerated the number of the attacking party. For the narrative of the British captain, Sylvanus Davis, see *Mass. Hist. Colls.*, 3d series, i, pp. 101–112.

Jacques Robineau, sieur de Portneuf, belonged to the early Canadian noblesse, and was employed as an officer in the Indian and English wars. In 1687 he acted as lieutenant under Denonville. After this attack on Fort Loyal, he served in Acadia, where his brother Villebon was governor, and for several years led raiding parties against the Maine settlements. He died at Quebec in 1715. The flag captured at Fort Loyal hung for many years in the basilica at Quebec. — Ed.

perfifted in his defign of making a Trial of that Nature.[1] The Chevalier *Do* was fingled out for this fatal Embaffy, being attended by one *Colin*, as Interpreter of the *Iroquefe* Language, and two young *Canadans.* They fet out in a Canow, and when they came in fight of the Village of the *Onnontagues*, were receiv'd with the honourable Salvo of feveral good blows, and conducted with the fame Ceremony to the Village. Such a Retinue could not but be difagreeable to the Gentleman that came to make offers of a Peace. The ancient Men being quickly affembled, thought it moft proper to fend 'em back with a favourable Anfwer, and in the mean time to ingage fome of the *Agnies* and *Onnoyotes*, to lye in wait for 'em at the Cataracts of the River, and there kill two, fending the third back to *Quebec*, and carrying the fourth to their Village, where there would be found fome *Englifh* that would fhoot 'em, that is, that would give 'em the fame ufage as the *Rat* did to their Ambaffadours: So true it is, that that Action fticks in their ftomachs. This Project had actually been put in execution, if it had not been for fome of the Planters of New-*York*, who were then among the *Barbarians*, having come thither on purpofe to animate 'em againft us. Thefe Planters knew fo well how to influence the *Barbarians* that were already bent upon Revenge; that a Company of young *Barbarians* burnt 'em all alive, excepting the Chevalier *Do*, whom they tied Hand and Foot, and fent him bound to *Bofton*, with a defign to pump out of him, a view of the condition of our

[1] The French version indicates that Lahontan had been ill, and used his weakness as a plea to be excused from this hazardous embassy. — Ed.

Colonies and Forces.[1] This piece of News [158] we receiv'd two Months after, by ſome Slaves that made their eſcape from the *Iroqueſe;* and Mr. *de Frontenac*, when ſurpris'd with ſuch diſmal News, declar'd, that out of twenty Captains that offer'd to execute that Commiſſion, and would have taken the Imployment for an Honour, I was the only one that had been capable of foreſeeing its bad Succeſs.

June the 24*th*, I imbarqu'd for this place in a ſluggiſh Brigantine, that the Captain of the Governour's Guards had caus'd to be built the foregoing Winter. This venerable Veſſel had the honour to lodge the Intendant and his Lady; and all of us being in no haſte, ſpent ten or twelve days by the way, and feaſted like Kings every Night. Mr. *de Frontenac* mark'd out a Fort in his paſſage to the City of *Trois Rivieres*, which I ſpoke of before. Fifteen days after our arrival in this place, a certain Savage whoſe name was *Plake*, came and gave us notice, that he had diſcover'd a Body of a thouſand *Engliſh*, and five hundred *Iroqueſe* that march'd up to attack us.[2] Upon this Intelligence, all our Troops croſs'd over to

---

[1] This account of the embassy of Chevalier Pierre d'Aux (Do), sieur de Jolliet, is substantially correct. He was a prisoner both in Boston and New York until August, 1692, when having escaped he made his way to Canada in time to furnish Count Frontenac with useful information relative to the English plans. The governor thereupon sent him to France to give an account of the situation of Boston and New York, "and how easily they may be taken." He returned to New France the following year, and then disappears from history. — ED.

[2] La Plaque, nephew of the Great Mohawk (called by the Dutch, Kryn), chief of the praying Indians of Sault St. Louis mission, was useful to the French during Frontenac's War (1689–97). After having given notice of this intended invasion, he set out the following year (1691) to capture prisoners and secure information, which undertaking proved so successful that he was sent to France to report. After

the Meadow of *Madelaine*, oppofite to this City, and there incamp'd, in conjunction with three or four hundred Savages that were our Allies, in order to give the Enemy a warm Reception.[1] Our Camp was no fooner form'd, than Mr. *de Frontenac* detach'd two or three fmall Parties of the Savages to obferve the Enemy. Thefe Parties came foon back, after having furpris'd fome ftragling *Iroquefe* at hunting on the Confines of *Champlaine* Lake: The Prifoners inform'd us, that the *Englifh* being unable to encounter the fatigues of the march, and unprovided with a fufficient ftock of Provifions, both they and the *Iroquefe* were return'd to their own Country.[2] This account being confirm'd by other Savages, our Troops decamp'd, and march'd back to this place, from whence I was detach'd [159] fome days after to command a Party that was to cover the Reapers of Fort *Roland*, which lies in this Ifland.[3] When the Harveft was over I return'd to

his return he continued to serve the French, on two occasions (1692, 1693) leading war parties nearly to the gates of Albany. — Ed.

[1] La Prairie de la Madeleine is six miles above Montreal, on the opposite side of the river. This was supposed to be the point at which the expedition would emerge, coming by way of Lake Champlain and Richelieu River. A small division did attack this point after Frontenac's return to Quebec, carrying off several prisoners. — Ed.

[2] This was part of the expedition fitted out by the British colonies for the capture of Canada. The troops of New York and Connecticut rendezvoused at Wood Creek, on Lake Champlain, under command of General Winthrop of Connecticut; but illness, lack of provisions, and the lukewarm attitude of their Iroquois allies, made it necessary to abandon the attack. See Winthrop's "Journal," in *N. Y. Colon. Docs.*, iv, pp. 193–197. — Ed.

[3] Fort Rolland was built (1670) on the site of the present Lachine, to protect the trading houses of François le Noir, *dit* Rolland, who carried on a large traffic with the Western Indians. During Frontenac's War, it was regularly garrisoned by detachments of soldiers. For full details, see Girouard, *Lake St. Louis*, pp. 70–75. — Ed.

this place, along with the *Hurons* and the *Outaouas*, who had come down from their own Country, in purſuit of their uſual Trade in Skins, an account of which you had in my eight Letter. Theſe Traders continued here fifteen days, and then march'd home.[1]

This, Sir, is a Summary of all our Occurrences of Moment ſince the laſt year. About fifteen days hence, I think to ſet out for *Quebec*, in Mr. *de Frontenac's* Brigantin. I conclude with my uſual Complement,

SIR,

Yours, &c.

[1] The descent of the Northwest Indians for trade this year (1690) was an encouraging circumstance for New France. See *N. Y. Colon. Docs.*, ix, pp. 478–490; Parkman, *Frontenac*, pp. 252–255. — Ed.

LETTER XX.

Dated at *Rochel January* 12. 1691.

Being a Relation of a ſecond and very important Expedition of the Engliſh *by Sea; in which is contain'd a Letter written by the* Engliſh *Admiral to the Count of* Frontenac, *with this Governour's Verbal Answer. As alſo an account of the Authour's departure for* France.

SIR,

I AM arriv'd at laſt at *Rochel*, from whence I now tranſmit you a Relation of all that paſs'd in *Canada*, ſince the date of my laſt Letter. In the ſpace of a few days after that date, Mr. *de Frontenac* receiv'd advice that a ſtrong Fleet of *Engliſh* [160] Ships, amounting to thirty four Sail, was ſeen near *Tadouſſac.*[1] Immediately he got on board of his Brigantine, and order'd all the Troops to imbarque in Canows and Boots, and to row Night and Day to prevent the Enemy; all which was happily put in execution. At the ſame time he gave orders to Mr. *de Callieres*, to bring down as many of the Inhabitants as poſſibly he could. We row'd with ſuch expedition, and diligence, that we arriv'd the 3*d* day at *Quebec.* As

[1] The first report of the approach of the English Fleet reached Frontenac through an Abenaki Indian, who had travelled overland with the tidings. The governor gave this news scant credence until fishing vessels announced the progress of the fleet as far up as Tadoussac. For a brief but succinct account, see *Jes. Rel.*, lxiv, pp. 41–53. — ED.

ſoon as Mr. *de Frontenac* debarqued, he view'd the weakeſt Poſts, and order'd 'em to be fortified without loſs of time: He rais'd Batteries in ſeveral places, and though in that capital City we had but twelve great Guns, and but little Ammunition, yet he ſeem'd to be reſolutely bent upon an obſtinate Reſiſtance to the efforts of the Enemy's Fleet, which in the mean time ſtood catching of Flies, at the diſtance of two Leagues from *Quebec*. We took the advantage of their ſlow approaches, and work'd inceſſantly to put our ſelves in a poſture of defence. Our Troops, our Militia, and our confederate Savages, came up to us on all hands. 'Tis certain, that if the *Engliſh* Admiral had made his Deſcent before our arrival at *Quebec*, or even two days after, he had carry'd the place without ſtriking a blow; for at that time there was not two hundred *French* in the City, which lay open, and expos'd on all hands.[1] But inſtead of doing that, he caſt Anchor towards the point of the Iſland of *Orleans*, and loſt three days in conſulting with the Captains of the Ships, before they came to a Reſolution. He took the Sieur *Joliet* with his Lady and his Mother-in-Laws in a Bark in the River of St. *Laurence*.[2] Three Merchant-men from *France*, and one laden with Beaver-

[1] All authorities apparently agree with Lahontan's judgment, that the capital fault of the English commander was his waste of time. — Ed.

[2] Lahontan is the only contemporary authority who includes Jolliet himself in the list of prisoners. Probably it was only his wife and mother-in-law, who were captured on their way to their seigniory of Anticosti, with M. de Grandville. Louis Jolliet, the famous explorer, was born in Quebec in 1645. Losing his father at an early age, he was reared by the Jesuits. In 1667 he visited France, and the following year organized his first trading and exploring expedition to the Great Lakes, whither he again went, 1670–71. His success brought him a commission to discover the

Skins from *Hudſon* Bay, enter'd the River of *Saguenay*, by the way of *Tadouſſac*, where they ſculk'd, and after hauling their Guns aſhoar, rais'd very good Batteries. [161] To be ſhort, the Officers of the Enemy's Fleet came to a Reſolution after the loſs of three or four days in uſeleſs Conſultations, during which time we were joyn'd on all hands by great numbers of Inhabitants and Soldiers. Purſuant to the reſolution of the Councils of War, the *Engliſh* Admiral, namely, Sir *William Phips*, ſent out his Sloop with a *French* Flag upon its Prow, which made up to the City with ſound of Trumpet.[1] Upon

---

Mississippi, which he accomplished in company with the Jesuit missionary Marquette (1673). Upon his return in July, 1674, Jolliet lost all of his papers by having his canoe swamped in the descent of Lachine Rapids. The following year he married Claire Françoise Bissot, who brought him property on the Gulf of St. Lawrence, where in 1679, he acquired Isles Mingan, and Anticosti a year later. In the former year, he visited Hudson Bay, via the Saguenay and Lake St. John, and was cordially received by the English. Labrador was explored by him in 1694, his death occurring six years later. For the latest research concerning Jolliet, see Gagnon, "Louis Jolliet," in *La Revue Canadienne*, 1900–1902.

Jolliet's mother-in-law was Marie Couillard, who after the death (1675) of Bissot, her first husband, married Jacques de Lalande. She was a woman of much force and ability, and according to other authorities suggested to Phips the exchange of prisoners, and to effect it went in person to Frontenac. She was a sister-in-law of Jean Nicolet, the explorer, and one of her sons was Sieur de Vincennes, an officer of note in the Western country. — ED.

[1] Sir William Phips was born in Pemaquid (Bristol), Maine, in 1651. He was the son of a poor colonist, and tended sheep until he was eighteen years of age, then learned the trade of a ship carpenter. Going to Boston, he there married a wealthy widow, who taught him to read and write. On a visit to England, he secured a commission to search for wrecked Spanish treasure-ships in the West Indies. After one unsuccessful attempt (1684), he raised in 1687 silver and plate amounting to £300,000. For this service knighthood was conferred upon him, and he returned to Massachusetts to lead an expedition which captured Port Royal (May, 1690). After the failure of the Quebec investment, Phips was somewhat discredited, but in 1692 he was appointed governor of Massachusetts, which office he held until his death in London, in 1695. — ED.

this, Mr. *de Frontenac* ſent out another with a *French* Officer to meet it, who found an *Engliſh* Major in the Sloop, who gave him to underſtand, that he had the charge of a Letter from his General, to the Governour of *Canada*, and hop'd he might be allow'd to deliver it himſelf. Upon that the *French* Officer took him into his Sloop, and having blindfolded him, conducted him to the Governour's Chamber; where his Face being uncover'd, he deliver'd him a Letter, the ſubſtance of which was this.

'I Sir *William Phips*, General of the Forces of *New-* '*England*, by Sea and Land, to Count *Frontenac*, Governour 'General of *Quebec*, by Orders from, and in the name of '*William* III and *Mary* King and Queen of *England;* am come 'to make my ſelf Maſter of this Country. But in regard that 'I have nothing ſo much in view, as the preventing of the 'effuſion of Blood, I require you to ſurrender at diſcretion, 'your Cities, Caſtles, Forts, Towns, as well as your Perſons; 'aſſuring you at the ſame time, that you ſhall meet with all 'manner of good Uſage, Civility and Humanity. If you do 'not accept of this Propoſal without any Reſtriction, I will 'indeavour, by the aſſiſtance of Heaven, on which I rely, and 'the force of my Arms, to make a Conqueſt of 'em. I expect 'a poſitive anſwer in writing in the ſpace of an Hour, and in 'the mean time give you notice, that after [162] the com- 'mencement of Hoſtilities, I ſhall not entertain any thoughts 'of Accommodation.

Sign'd, *William Phips.*

After the Interpreter had tranflated the Letter to Mr. *de Frontenac*, who was then furrounded with Officers; he order'd the Captain of his Guards to make a Gibbet before the Fort, in order to hang the poor Major, who in all appearance underftood *French;* for upon the pronouncing of this fatal Sentence, he was like to fwoon away. And indeed I muft fay, the Major had fome reafon to be affected, for he had certainly been hang'd, if the Bifhop and the Intendant, who to his good luck were then prefent, had not interceded on his behalf. Mr. *de Frontenac* pretended, that they were a Fleet of Pyrates, or of Perfons without Commiffion, for that the King of *England* was then in *France*. But at laft the Governour being appeas'd, order'd the Major to repair forthwith on board of his Admiral, againft whom he could defend himfelf the better, for not being attack'd. At the fame time he declar'd, that he knew no other King of *Great Britain*, than *James* II, that his rebellious Subjects were Pyrates, and that he dreaded neither their Force nor their Threats. This faid, he threw Admiral *Phips*'s Letter in the Major's face, and then turn'd his Back upon him. Upon that the poor Ambaffadour took frefh courage, and looking upon his Watch, took the liberty to ask Mr. *de Frontenac*, if he could not have his Anfwer in Writing before the hour elaps'd. But the Governour made anfwer with all the haughtinefs and difdain imaginable, that his Admiral deferv'd no other anfwer, than what flew from the Mouth of Cannons and Muskets. Thefe words were no fooner pronounc'd than the Major was forc'd to take his

Letter again, and being blind-folded, was reconducted to his Sloop, in which he row'd towards the Fleet with all expedition.

[163] The next day about two in the Afternoon, fixty Sloops were fent afhoar with ten or twelve hundred Men, who ftood upon the Sand in very good order. After that the Sloops went back to the Ships, and brought afhoar the like Compliment of Men, which was afterwards joyn'd by a third Complement of the fame number. As foon as thefe Troops were landed, they began to march towards the City with Drums beating, and Colours flying. This Defcent was made over againft the Ifle of *Orleans*, about a League and a half below *Quebec;* but 'twas not fo expeditious, but that our Confederate Savages, with two hundred *Coureurs de Bois*, and fifty Officers, had time to poft themfelves in a Copfe of thick Brambles, which lay half a League off the place of Landing. It being impoffible for fo fmall a Party to come to an open Battle with a numerous Enemy, they were forc'd to fight after the manner of the Savages, that is, to lay Ambufcadoes from place to place in the Copfe, which was a quarter of a League broad. This way of waging War prov'd wonderfully fuccefsful to us, for our Men being pofted in the middle of the Copfe, we fuffer'd the *Englifh* to enter, and then fir'd upon 'em, lying flat upon the ground till they fir'd their pieces; after which we fprung up, and drawing into knots here and there, repeated our fire with fuch fuccefs, that the *Englifh* Militia perceiving our Savages fell into confufion and diforder, and their Battalions were broke; infomuch, that

they betook themſelves to flight, crying out, *Indians*, *Indians*, and gave our Savages the opportunity of making a bloody ſlaughter among 'em, for we found three hundred Men left upon the ſpot, without any other loſs on our ſide, than that of ten *Coureurs de Bois*, four Officers, and two Savages.

The next day the *Engliſh* landed four pieces of braſs Cannon mounted like Field-pieces, and fought [164] very bravely, though they were very ill diſciplin'd. 'Tis certain there was no want of Courage on their ſide, and their want of Succeſs muſt be imputed to their unacqaintedneſs with Military Diſcipline, to their being infeebled by the fatigues of the Sea, and to the ill conduct of Sir *William Phips*, who upon this Enterpriſe could not have done more than he did, if he had been ingag'd by us to ſtand ſtill with his hands in his Pockets. This day paſs'd over more peaceably than the next: For then the *Engliſh* made a freſh attempt to force their paſſage through the Copſe, by the help of their Artillery; but they loſt three or four hundred more in the attempt, and were forc'd to retire with all diligence to the Landing-place: On our ſide we loſt Mr. *de St. Helene*, who dy'd of a wound in his Leg, and about forty *French-men* and Savages. This Victory animated us ſo much, that we purſued the *Engliſh* to their Camp, and lay all Night flat upon the ground juſt by it, with a deſign to attack it by the break of day: But they ſav'd us the labour, for they imbarqued about Midnight with ſuch confuſion, that we kill'd fifty more of 'em, rather by chance, than by dexterity, while they were getting into their Boats. When day came, we tranſported to *Quebec* their Tents and their Cannon, which they had left behind 'em; the Savages being in the mean time imploy'd in ftripping the dead in the Wood.

The fame day that the Defcent was made, Sir *William Phips* weigh'd and came to an Anchor with four great Ships, at the diftance of a Musket-fhot from the lower City, where we had only one Battery of fix or eight Pounders. There he Cannonadoed for twenty four hours fo handfomly, that the fire of the great Guns equal'd that of the fmall Arms. The dammage they did to the roofs of the Houfes, amounted to five or fix Piftoles; for as I inform'd you in my firft Letter, the Walls of the Houfes are fo hard, that a Ball cannot pierce 'em.

[165] When Sir *William Phips* had made an end of thefe glorious Exploits, he fent to demand of Mr. *de Frontenac* fome *Englifh* Prifoners in exchange for the Sieur *Joliet*, with his Wife and his Mother, and fome Seamen; which was forthwith put in execution. This done, the Fleet weigh'd Anchor and fteer'd homeward.[1] As foon as the three Merchantmen that lay fculking in the River of *Saguenay*, faw the Fleet running below *Tadouffac* with full Sail before a Wefterly Gale, they put their Guns aboard, and purfuing their Voyage with great fatisfaction, arriv'd at *Quebec* on the 12*th* of *November*. They had fcarce put their Cargoe on fhoar, when the bitter cold cover'd the River with Ice, which dammag'd their Ships fo much, that

---

[1] There exist many contemporaneous accounts of Phips's expedition. Myrand, *Sir William Phips devant Quebec* (Quebec, 1893), has collected nineteen from archives, with all the details of participants. He accuses Lahontan of exaggerating the numbers of English taking part and wounded in the land battles, *op. cit.*, pp. 267–276. For the rest, however, Lahontan's account is substantially correct. — Ed.

they were forc'd to run 'em aſhoar. This troubleſom Froſt was as uneaſie to me, as to Mr. *de Frontenac;* for I then ſaw that I was oblig'd to paſs another Winter in *Canada*, and Mr. *de Frontenac* was at a loſs, to contrive a way of ſending the King advice of this Enterpriſe. But by good luck, there came all of a ſudden a downfal of Rain, which was follow'd by a Thaw, and was equally acceptable to us both. Immediately the Governour order'd an unrigg'd Frigat to be rigg'd and fitted out; which was done accordingly with ſuch diſpatch, that the Ballaſt, Sails, Ropes, and Maſts, were all in order almoſt as ſoon as the Orders were given out. When the Frigat was ready to ſail, the Governour told me, that the making of *France* as ſoon as ever I could, would be a piece of important Service; and that I ought rather to periſh, than to ſuffer my ſelf to be taken by the Enemy, or to put in at any Port whatſoever by the way. At the ſame time he gave me a particular Letter to Mr. *de Seignelay*, the purport of which was much to my advantage.

I put to Sea the 20*th* of *November*, the like of which was never ſeen in that place before. At the Iſle of *Coudres* we 'ſcap'd luckily, for there the [166] North-Eaſt Wind blew ſo hard upon us, that after we had drop'd Anchor, we thought to have been ſplit in pieces in the Night-time. The reſt of our paſſage was good enough, for we encounter'd but one Storm till we arriv'd at this place. Indeed we met with contrary Winds, about 150 Leagues off the coaſt of *France*, which oblig'd us to traverſe, and lye by for a long time, and 'twas for this reaſon that our paſſage was ſo long.

I hear you are now in *Provence*, and that Mr. *de Seignelai* is gone upon a Voyage to the other World, which is of a quite different nature from that I have juſt perform'd. In earneſt, Sir, his Death is the laſt misfortune to the Navy of *France*, to the Colonies of the two *America's*, and to me in particular, ſince Mr. *de Frontenac's* Recommendatory Letter is thereby render'd uſeleſs to me. I am,

SIR, *Yours*, &c.

LETTER XXI.

Dated at *Rochel July* 26. 1691.

Containing a Deſcription of the Courts or Offices of the Miniſters of State, and a view of ſome Services that are ill rewarded at Court.

SIR,

THE Letter you writ to me two Months agoe came to my Hands at *Paris;* but I could not give you an anſwer there, becauſe I had not then done my buſineſs. Now that I am return'd to *Rochel*, I have leiſure time enough to inform you of all that befell me ſince my return to *France*. As ſoon as I arriv'd at *Verſailles*, I waited upon Mr. *de Pontchartrain*, [167] who ſucceeded Mr. *de Seignelai.* I repreſented to him, that Mr. *de Frontenac* had given me a Letter to his Predeceſſour, in which he took notice of the Services I had done. I remonſtrated to him, that my Eſtate being ſeiz'd upon, and there being ſeveral Law-ſuits to be adjuſted, where my preſence was neceſſary, I hop'd his Majeſty would give me leave to quit his Service. He made anſwer, that he had been inform'd of the ſtate of my Affairs, and that I was allow'd to purſue the management of 'em, till the departure of the laſt Ships that are bound this year for *Quebec*, to which place he mean'd I ſhould return. Having receiv'd this anſwer, I went from *Verſailles* to

Paris, where my Relations drew me into a conſultation of ſeveral Counſellors, who declar'd that my Affairs were ſo perplex'd, that in their opinion, I could not have 'em adjuſted in ſo ſhort a time. In the mean time, the Crowns I was forc'd to lug out for this Conſultation, turn'd my Stomach againſt the going to Law with Perſons that had ſo much intereſt in the Parliament of *Paris;* inſomuch, that I was almoſt in the mind of loſing my Right, rather than to enter upon the Law-ſuit. However, I did not fail to put in for a proviſion upon my confiſcated Eſtate, by vertue of my being actually in the Service. But the ſolliciting of that, coſt me ſo much trouble and charges, that though my powerful Adverſaries had not been able to prevent the obtaining of my requeſt, yet the Sum adjudg'd thereupon, would not be ſufficient to anſwer the charges I was at. *Meſſieurs de Bragelone*[1] are very honourable Gentlemen, as you know very well. 'Tis true, they love Piſtoles better than their Relations, and upon that Principle contented themſelves in doing me the honour of their good Advice, for their Generoſity do's not go much further; and if I had no other refuge than theirs, I ſhould be but in a ſorry condition. The Abbot of *Ecouttes*,[2] who is more liberal, [168] tho' not ſo rich as they, made me a Preſent of a hundred *Louis d'ors*, which I applied to the payment of the Fees, for being receiv'd into the Order of St. *Lazarus*. The Ceremony

[1] Lahontan belonged to the Gascon family of Bragelonne, one member of which had been of the Company of One Hundred Associates, that founded the colony of New France. — ED.

[2] The Abbé de Couttes, who was an uncle of Lahontan, being a brother of his mother, was an ecclesiastic well known at the court of Louis XIV. — ED.

of that Inſtallment was perform'd in Mr. *de Louvois* his Chamber, and did not laſt ſo long as the telling of the Money.[1] I was in hopes that this generous Abbot would have beſtow'd upon me ſome ſimple Benefice that he might have thrown in my way, without injuring himſelf: But it ſeems, a ſcruple of Conſcience ſtood my Enemy. Upon the whole, Sir, I was e'en forc'd at laſt to go to *Verſailles* to ſollicit for a Place, which is the moſt cutting and vexatious Office in the World. Do but conſider, Sir, that in thoſe Royal Apartments Crowns fly, and no body knows where they go. One muſt patiently attend five or ſix hours a day in Mr. *de Pontchartrain's* Apartments, only to ſhew himſelf every time that that Miniſter goes out or comes in.

He no ſooner appears, than every one crowds in to preſent Memorials clogg'd with fifty Reaſons, which commonly fly off as light as the Wind. As ſoon as he receives theſe Petitions, he gives 'em to ſome Secretary or other that follows him; and this Secretary carries 'em to Meſſieurs *de la Touche*, *de Begon*, and *de Saluberri;* whoſe Footmen receive Piſtoles from moſt of the Officers, who without that Expedient, would be in danger of catching cold at the Door of the Office of theſe Deputies. 'Tis from that expedient alone, that their good or bad deſtiny muſt flow. Pray undeceive your ſelf, as to your

[1] St. Lazare was one of the military orders founded in the eleventh century, during the Crusades. It was rich and powerful, and had large property in Paris. In the seventeenth century it was amalgamated with the order of Mont Carmel, and Lahontan is sometimes known as chevalier of Notre Dame du Mont Carmel.

François Michel le Tellier, marquis de Louvois, was the great war minister of the reign of Louis XIV. Among other honors, he received in 1673 the office of vicar general of the orders of St. Lazare and Mont Carmel. — Ed.

p. 75.

An Iroquese Village
The Road
where 1500 Iroquese lay in Ambush
The Hill
Coureurs de bois
Mr. Denonville
Regular troops
Militia
The Road
Confederate savages

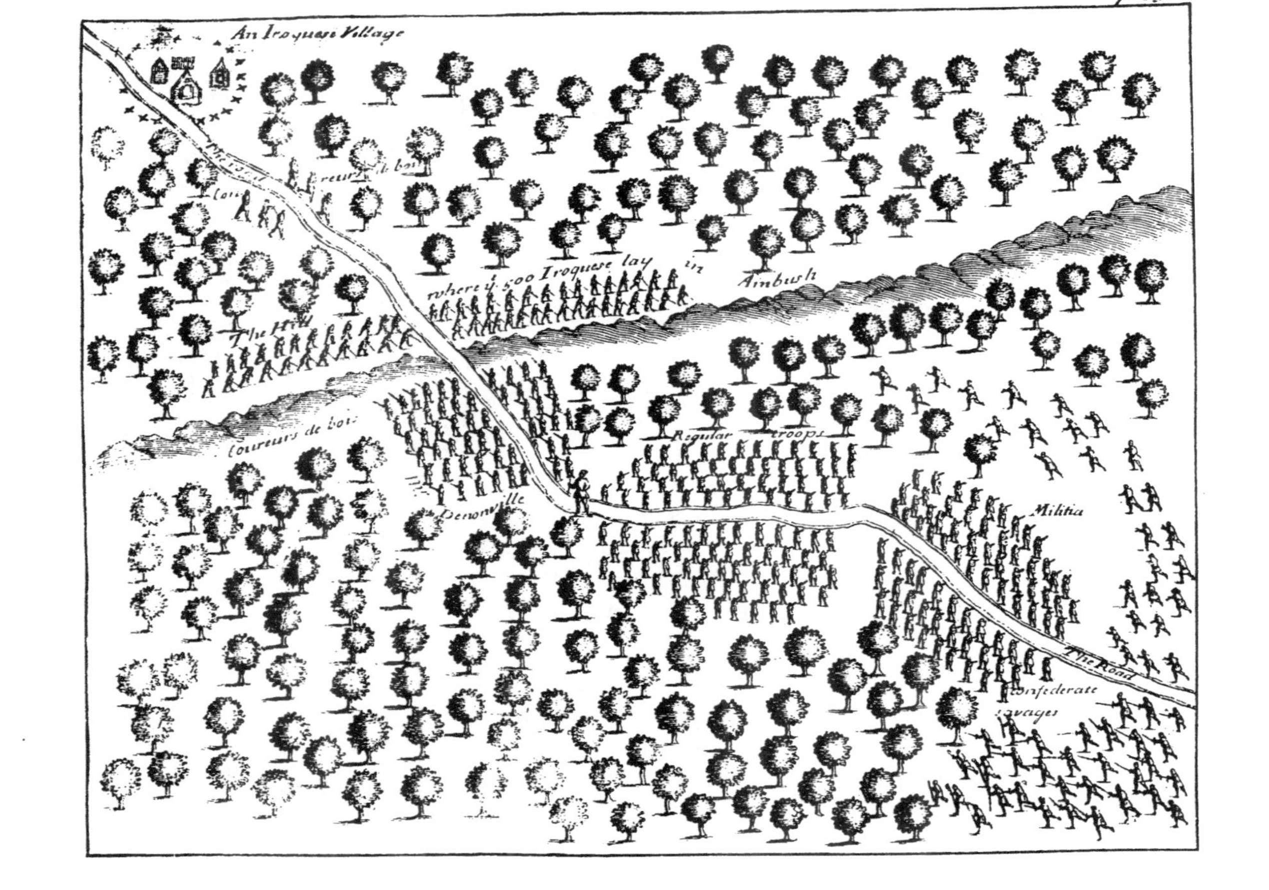

notion of the protection of great Lords: The time is gone in which the Miniſters granted whatever they ask'd for their Baſtards, their Footmen, and their Vaſſals. There is but two or three Princes or Dukes, who being great Favourites, will meddle in protecting thoſe that have no immediate dependance upon 'em: And if theſe do it, 'tis very [169] ſeldom; for you know that the Gentry of *France* is in no great Circumſtances, and theſe great Lords have oftentimes poor Friends of their own, for whom they are oblig'd· to ask places, in order to their Subſiſtence. As the World goes now, the Miniſters are upon ſuch a foot, that they'll refuſe any thing to Perſons of the higheſt Dignity about Court, by replying, the King will have it ſo, or the King will have it otherwiſe. And as for the Topick of Merit; that's ſuch a frightful Monſter, that it can have no Reception in the Miniſters Offices, nay, moſt of the Miniſters are ſtruck with horrour when they think of it. 'Tis the Miniſters, in effect, that diſpoſe of all places, though it appears as if 'twere the King. They do what they pleaſe, without being accountable to him, for he puts all upon the affection and zeal they ought to have for his Service. They carry Extracts to him, in which the merit of the Officers they mean to prefer, is either ſuppos'd or extoll'd. But the Memorials of thoſe they do not like, are far from appearing.

I'm ſorry I ſhould be oblig'd to lay this truth before you; however, I mention no particular Miniſter, for they are not all of that kidney. I know ſome of 'em that would ſcorn to do the leaſt injuſtice to any Man whatſoever; and would not ſuffer their Suiſſes, or their Lackeys, or even their Deputies or Clerks, to intrigue for the preferment of ſuch and ſuch Perſons by the means of Piſtoles. Theſe dexterous Intriguers, do by indirect means make more Officers, than you have hairs on your Head; and 'tis for that reaſon they are ſaluted a League off, and dignify'd as ſeriouſly with the Title of *Monſieur*, as their Maſters are with that of *Monſeigneur* or *Grandeur*. Theſe laſt Titles have been acquir'd by our Miniſters and Secretaries of State, with as much glory, as by our Biſhops. We muſt not think it ſtrange therefore, that even our General Officers [170] have the words *Monſeigneur* and *Grandeur* ſo frequently in their Mouths, provided it be accompany'd with that of your *Excellency*. I ſwear, Sir, I could find matter for a Book of three hundred Pages in Folio, if I had a mind to be particular upon the intrigues of the Officers and Miniſters of State; upon the means by which the Sollicitors compaſs their ends, the notorious Knavery of a certain ſort of People, and the patience with which the Officers muſt be fortified; upon the contempt that thoſe meet with, who have no other Recommendation than Merit, and in a word, upon all the inſtances of Injuſtice, that are practis'd without the King's knowledge.

Let it be as it will, I muſt acquaint you that after a fruitleſs Sollicitation for what I thought I had ſome Title to, in conſideration of my Services, I receiv'd this Anſwer, that the King would order Mr. *de Frontenac* to provide for me as handſomly as he could, when an occaſion offer'd: So that I was forc'd to reſt ſatisfi'd with my Anſwer, and reſolve to continue a

Captain for ever; for I know very well that the Governour of *Canada* can not prefer me to a higher Poſt.[1]

Having left *Verſailles*, I came hither with all expedition, and then went to receive the commands of the Intendant of *Rochefort*. He acquainted me that the Ship call'd *Honorè* was fitting up, and that I might ſail as ſoon as 'twas ready. He recommended to me the Chevalier *de Meaupou*, Madam *Ponchartrain's* Nephew, who is to go along with me.[2] This Gentleman having the curioſity to ſee *Canada*, is come hither from *Paris*, with a handſom Retinue. 'Tis in vain to ſet forth to him the tediousneſs of the Paſſage, the inconveniencies of the Sea, and the diſagreeableneſs of the Country; for all theſe Arguments ſerve only to inflame his Curioſity. The Count *d'Aunay* is to convoy us to the Latitude of Cape *Finiſterre*, at which place [171] he is to take leave of us, and return to *Rochefort*. We only ſtay for a fair Wind to put to Sea. I am,

SIR,

Yours, &c.

[1] The king, in addition to the bestowal of a military order, had already promoted Lahontan to a captaincy. See *Collecion de Manuscrits de la Nouvelle France*, ii, p. 62. The governor of New France had no higher appointment in his power. Roy suggests that most young officers of that time would, at the age of twenty-five, have been content with such honors. — Ed.

[2] Probably the Sieur de Maupeau, who was later president of inquests in the Parliament of Paris and whose son was chancellor, 1763–68. — Ed.

LETTER XXII.

Dated at *Quebec Nov.* 10. 1691.

Which contains an Account of the Authors departure from Rochel *to* Quebec, *of his Voyage to the Mouth of the River St.* Laurence, *of a Ren-counter he had with an* Englifh *Ship which he fought; of the ftranding of his Ship; of his failing through the River St.* Laurence; *of the News he receiv'd, that a Party of the* Englifh *and* Iroquefe *had defeated a Body of the* French *Troops.*

SIR,

TWO days after I wrote to you, we fet fail from the Harbour of *Rochel*, upon our great Voyage to *Canada*. On the 5*th* of *Auguft* we perceiv'd a great Ship, which the Count of *Aunay* gave chafe to, who having a better Sailer, came up with her in three hours time, whereupon fhe on a fudden put up *Genoefe* Colours. Some Guns were fir'd upon the Prow, to oblige her to ftrike; but the Captain was fo obftinate, that Mr. *d'Aunay* was forc'd to give her a Broadfide, which kill'd four or five of the Seamen, whereupon the reft were oblig'd to put out their Long-boat, and carry to his Ship their Paffports and Bills of Lading. On the 10*th*, after [172] they had taken the Latitude, the Pilots thinking that they were even with Cape *Finifter*, Mr. *d'Aunay* fent out his Long-boat, to acquaint me that he was then upon his return home, upon which I wrote him a Letter of thanks. Father *Bechefer* a Jeſuit, who had been many years Superior of the College of *Quebec*, whither he was now going in the ſame Capacity, was forc'd to throw himſelf into this Long-boat, in order to his return into *France*, having found himſelf continually indiſpos'd, from the firſt day we put to Sea.[1] On the 23*d* of *Auguſt* we had a great Storm of Wind from the North-Weſt, which laſted about twenty four hours, being then a hundred Leagues off the Bank of *Newfound-Land. This Bank takes its Name from the Iſland of* Newfound-Land, *a Map of which is here annex'd.*

When the Storm was over, there ſucceeded a Wind from the North-Eaſt, which drove us in ten or twelve hours, to the Mouth of the River of *St. Laurence.* On the 6*th* of *September* we diſcover'd a Ship ſailing from the Coaſt of *Gaſpè*, which bore down upon us with a full ſail. We thought at firſt that they were *French* coming from *Quebec*, but their way of working the Ship diſcover'd to us within an hour after, that they were Enemies. After we knew them, we prepar'd to fight them, and they being about a League to the Windward of us, came quickly down upon us with full Sail, within Musket-ſhot. Preſently they put up *Engliſh* Colours, and gave us a Broadſide; and we put up our own Colours, and paid them home in their own Coyn. The Fight laſted two hours, and both

[1] Thierry Beschefer, Jesuit missionary, came to Canada in 1665, and was for several years stationed among the Iroquois. He had been superior of the Canadian missions since 1680, and in 1688 was prefect of the College of Quebec. After this mention by Lahontan, he disappears from Canadian history, but is thought to have died at Rheims in 1711. — Ed.

ſides fir'd continually one upon another, but the Sea being tempeſtuous, we were oblig'd to ſhear off as Night came on, without ſuffering any other loſs, than the wounding of two Seamen, and the receiving of twenty eight or thirty ſhot in our Maſts, Sails, and Rigging. Two days after we met Mr. *Duta*, Captain of the *Hazardous*, who was homeward bound for [173] *France*, being a Convoy to ten or twelve Merchant Ships. He gave me ſome Refreſhments, and told me ſome news of *Canada*, which were very acceptable. We purſu'd our courſe in ſpight of the South-Eaſt Wind, which oblig'd us to tack about ſeveral ways, till we came to *Portneuf*, near to *Tadouſſac*.[1] In this place we were ſtranded by the fault of the Coaſting-Pilot, who being obſtinate for caſting Anchor near the Land, was like to have been the cauſe of a Shipwrack. At Midnight the Ship was ſo daſh'd againſt the Sand, that I thought ſhe was ſplit in pieces, but the Tide ebbing by degrees, ſhe was left lying upon the Coaſt, without any apparent Damage. I preſently caus'd a Kedger to be dropt in the deep Water belag'd with ſeveral Ropes call'd *Grelins Epiſſes (ſee the Explication Table,)*[2] and the next Morning the Tide returning ſet the Ship afloat, and then we haul'd it in with the Capeſtan. On the 13*th* we caſt anchor near the *Red*

[1] The seigniory of Portneuf lay a league and a half along the St. Lawrence River northeast of Tadoussac, in the present County of Chicoutimi, where is now Portneuf River. The fief was founded in 1636, in favor of the family of Le Neuf de la Poterie; in 1671 it passed by marriage to the Robineau family, who remained barons de Portneuf until the conquest (1760). — ED.

[2] In the French edition of 1728, this term is explained as follows: Grelins episses, cables made fast end to end, interlaced and joined, one to the end of the other by means of iron bolts which are called "cornets d'episse" (spiked horns). — ED.

Ifland, and the next day being the 14*th*, we pafs'd that Channel without danger, by the favour of a frefh Gale from the North-Eaft.

On the 15*th* we caft Anchor at the *Ifle of Hares*[1]: On the 16*th* we pafs'd the *Ifle of Coudres:* On the 17*th* we weather'd the Cape of *Tourmente*, and the next day we anchor'd in this Port. From the Mouth of the River to this place, we had the fineft Sunfhine days that ever were feen: During which time, I had both leifure and opportunity to view the Coafts on the right Hand and the left, while we tack'd about and about as the wind ferv'd. When I faw a great many Rivers on the South fide, I ask'd the Pilots why the Ships us'd to fteer their courfe on the North fide, where there is no Anchorage to be found, but at *Papinachefe*, the feven *Ifles*, and *Portneuf*.[2] They anfwer'd me, that the ordinary Breezes of the rough North-Weft Wind, which blows upon this River for three quarters of a year, were [174] the true caufe why they durft not go far from the North fide; and that no body could enfure a Ship that fhould fteer on the South fide, except it were in the Months of *June*, *July*, and *Auguft*. If it were not for that, I believe it would be more pleafant, more eafie, and lefs dangerous to fail on the South, than on the North fide,

---

[1] Hare Island (Isle au Lièvres) lies in the River St. Lawrence west of Tadoussac. It was so named by Cartier (1545), because many hares were there captured on his voyage of discovery. — Ed.

[2] Seven Islands is a group lying near the northerly shore of the St. Lawrence, protecting a harbor now known as Seven Islands Bay. Papinachois is a small bay at the entrance of a river of that name, in Saguenay County, Quebec. It was named from a tribe of Montagnais Indians, and is said to signify, "I like to laugh a little." — Ed.

becaufe one might caft Anchor every Night at the entrance of thofe Rivers which difcharge themfelves all along that Coaft, and would not be oblig'd to be veering about continually Night and Day, as he is forc'd to do, when he fteers his courfe on the North fide. This, Sir, is all I had to fay at prefent about our failing in this River, which I fhall have occafion to mention to you again. After our Ship caft Anchor before *Quebec*, I landed with the Chevalier *Meaupou*, whom I conducted to the Houfe of Mr. *Frontenac*, who offer'd to him as well as to me, the ufe of his Table and Houfe. I am inform'd that 300 *Englifh*, and 200 *Iroquefe*, approach'd about two Months agoe to the Ifle of *Monreal;* That the Governour of that Ifle tranfported 15 Companies from the other fide of the River, to watch their motions; That a Detachment of the Enemy having furpriz'd our Out-Guards, attack'd the whole Body of them, and our Camp at the fame time with fo much Vigour and Courage, that they kill'd upon the fpot more than three hundred Soldiers, befides two Captains, fix Lieutenants, and five Enfigns; and that after this fatal Expedition, Mr. *Valrenes*, a Captain of the Marines, fet out for *Monreal*, with a Detachment of *French* and Savages, to go to Fort *Chambli*, (for fear the *Iroquefe* fhould attack that Poft) who having met in their paffage a party of *Englifh* and *Iroquefe*, attack'd them vigouroufly, and defeated them.[1]

[1] This account refers to the raiding party sent out from Albany under Peter Schuyler in August, 1691. Schuyler's report is in *N. Y. Colon. Docs.*, iii, pp. 800–805; that of the French ibid, ix, pp. 520–524. Parkman gives a good resumé in *Frontenac*, pp. 289–294. Lahontan has greatly exaggerated the numbers of the slain — in all, about a hundred French were killed and wounded. — Ed.

All thefe different Adventures give me ground to conjecture, that it will be much more difficult [175] than 'tis imagin'd, to make a good Peace with the five Nations of the *Iroquefe*. Mr. *Frontenac* has given the neceffary Orders to all the neighbouring Habitations, that they fhould tranfport a great quantity of Stakes and Lime in the Winter time to the Neighbourhood of this City. Farewel Sir, the laft Ships which are to depart hence for *France*, will fail in three or four days. I am,

SIR, *Yours*, &c.

LETTER XXIII.

Dated at *Nants Octob.* 25. 1692.

Containing an Account of the taking of ſome Engliſh *Veſſels, of defeating a Party of the* Iroqueſe, *of an* Iroqueſe *burnt alive at* Quebec; *of another Party of theſe Barbarians, who having ſurpriz'd ſome* Coureurs de Bois, *were afterwards ſurpriz'd themſelves. Of the Project of an Enterprize propos'd by Mr.* Frontenac *to the Author. Of the Authors departure in a Frigat for* France, *and his ſtopping at* Placentia, *which was attack'd by an* Engliſh *Fleet that came to take that Poſt from us. How the* Engliſh *fail'd in their Deſign, and the Author purſu'd his Voyage.*

SIR,

THIS Letter comes from *Britany*, and not from *Canada*, from whence I parted ſuddenly to return into *France*, about two Months after I receiv'd your Letter, which I could not then anſwer for want of an opportunity. You tell me, that you are ſatisfi'd with the Deſcription I have ſent you of [176] the River St. *Laurence*, and that you would be very glad to have as exact an account of the whole Country of *Canada*. I can ſcarce ſatisfie your deſire at preſent, becauſe I have not yet had time to ſort all my Memoirs, and therefore you muſt not take it amiſs, that I pray you to ſuſpend your curioſity for ſome time. In the mean time, here follows the Relation of ſome things that happen'd in *Canada*, which may be acceptable to you.

Immediately after the Ships parted from *Quebec* the laſt year, Mr. *Frontenac* order'd a Plan to be drawn of a Wall to encompaſs the City, and having tranſported thither all the Materials neceſſary for building ſome Redoubts of Stone, he took care to fortifie it during the Summer.[1] Some days agoe a Gentleman of *New-England* call'd *Nelſon*, was brought priſoner to *Quebec*, who was taken in the River of *Kenebeki*, upon the Coaſt of *Acadia*, together with three Ships belonging to him, and becauſe he was a very gallant Man, Mr. *Frontenac* gave him a Lodging at his own Houſe, and treated him with all manner of Civility.[2] About the beginning of this year,

[1] The plans for fortifying Quebec were made by Levasseur and Beaucourt, two young engineers from France. The walls, which were the first permanent fortifications of Quebec, were about three-quarters of a mile in extent, stretching from Cape Diamond to St. Charles River. — ED

[2] John Nelson, a prominent Boston merchant, was great-nephew of Sir Thomas Temple from whom he had inherited rights to Nova Scotia grants. During the Andros revolution (1689), he headed the party that secured surrender of the fort in Boston harbor, and used all his influence against the tyrannical government. Being an Episcopalian and "of gay and free temper," he was accorded no place in the provisional government, but opposed Phips and his plans. In 1691, he was captured in St. John's River on his way to Port Royal. Frontenac treated him with marked courtesy, as a reward for his kindness to French prisoners in Boston. Having found means to send information to Boston of an expected attack on Pemaquid, Nelson was deported to France, where he was kept in solitary confinement for two years. Removed to the Bastille, he made propositions for an adjustment between the crowns, and was sent to England on parole (1696). Refusing to break his parole, though the king forbade his return to Paris, he went back and remained prisoner until the peace of Ryswick (1697). Upon his release, he had trouble with the English authorities because of his disobedience, but, after an absence of ten years, was finally allowed to return to Boston. In 1707, he supported the king's party in the colony. — ED.

this Governour gave the command of a Party confifting of 150 Soldiers, to Chevalier *Beaucour*, with whom fifty of the Savages that were our Friends were joyn'd, in order to march on the Ice towards Fort *Frontenac*. About thirty or forty Leagues from *Monreal*, they met a Company of fixty *Iroquefe*, who were difcover'd by the Foot-fteps of fome of their Hunters, that had ftragled out of their Cottages, and the next day they were all furpriz'd, and either had their Throats cut, or were made Prifoners. The Sieur *de la Plante* who liv'd in Slavery with thefe Wretches, had the good fortune to be prefent in their Company when they were defeated, and he had certainly been kill'd with his Mafters, if he had not cry'd out with all his Might, *Spare me, I am a Frenchman:* He was one of [177] the four Officers, who had the misfortune to be taken in that fatal Incurfion, which thefe Tygers made into *Monreal*, as I told you in my 17*th* Letter.[1] The Chevalier *Beaucour* return'd again to the Colony with his Party, and brought along with him twelve Prifoners of the *Iroquefe*, who were immediately conducted to *Quebec:* After they arriv'd, Mr. *Frontenac* did very judicioufly condemn two of the wickedeft of the Company, to be burnt alive with a flow Fire. This Sentence extreamly terrified the Governour's Lady, and the Jesuits; the Lady us'd all manner of fupplication to procure a moderation of the terrible Sentence, but the Judge was

[1] Josué Dubois de Berthelot, sieur de Beaucourt, a young engineer, was the second officer on this expedition, and took command when his superior became disabled. Later, he served the colony in many capacities, planning the Quebec fortifications of 1712; acting as army officer in Newfoundland in 1705; and as governor of Three Rivers in 1730. — ED.

inexorable, and the Jefuits employ'd all their Eloquence in vain upon this occafion. The Governour anfwered them, "That it was abfolutely neceffary to make fome terrible ex- "amples of Severity to frighten the *Iroquefe;* That fince thefe "Barbarians burnt almoft all the *French*, who had the mis- "fortune to fall into their Hands, they muft be treated after "the fame manner, becaufe the Indulgence which had hitherto "been fhown them, feem'd to authorize them to invade our "Plantations, and fo much the rather to do it, becaufe they "run no other hazard, than that of being taken, and well kept "at their Mafter's Houfes; but when they fhould underftand "that the *French* caus'd them to be burnt, they would have "a care for the future, how they advanc'd with fo much "boldnefs to the very Gates of our Cities; and in fine, That "the Sentence of Death being paft, thefe two wretches muft "prepare to take a Journey into the other World. This obftinacy appear'd furprizing in Mr. *Frontenac*, who but a little before had favour'd the efcape of three or four Perfons liable to the Sentence of Death, upon the importunate prayer of Madam the Governefs; but though fhe redoubled her earneft Supplications, fhe could not alter his firm Refolution as [178] to thefe two Wretches.[1] The Jefuits were thereupon fent to Baptize them, and oblige them to acknowledge the Trinity, and the Incarnation, and to reprefent to them the

[1] The lady who plead for the Iroquois must have been the intendant's wife, Madame de Champigny, as the Countess de Frontenac never came to New France. The Jesuits later reported that the terrible example made of this Iroquois prisoner had a good effect, in causing that nation to cease or mitigate the tortures of the captured French. — ED.

Joys of Paradiſe, and the Torments of Hell, within the ſpace of eight or ten hours. You will readily confeſs, Sir, that this was a very bold way of treating theſe great Myſteries, and that to endeavour to make the *Iroqueſe* underſtand them ſo quickly, was to expoſe them to their Laughter. Whether they took theſe Truths for Songs, I do not know; but this I can aſſure you, that from the Minute they were acquainted with this fatal News, they ſent back theſe good Fathers without ever hearing them; and then they began to ſing the ſong of Death, according to the cuſtom of the Savages. Some charitable Perſon having thrown a Knife to them in Priſon, he who had the leaſt Courage of the two, thruſt it into his Breaſt, and died of the Wound immediately. Some young *Hurons* of *Lorette*, aged between fourteen and fifteen years, came to ſeize the other, and carry him away to the *Diamant Cape*, where notice was given to prepare a great pile of Wood. He ran to death with a greater unconcernedneſs, than *Socrates* would have done, if he had been in his caſe. During the time of Execution he ſung continually; "That "he was a Warriour, brave and undaunted; that the moſt "cruel kind of Death could not ſhock his Courage, that "no Torments could extort from him any Cries, that his "Companion was a Coward for having kill'd himſelf through "the fear of Torment; and laſtly, that if he was burnt, he "had this Comfort, that he had treated many *French* and "*Hurons* after the ſame manner. All that he ſaid was very true, and chiefly as to his own courage and firmneſs of Soul;

for I can truly ſwear to you, that he neither ſhed Tears, nor was ever perceiv'd to Sigh; but on the contrary, during all the time that he ſuffer'd [179] the moſt horrible Torments that could be invented, and which laſted about the ſpace of three hours, he never ceas'd one Minute from ſinging. The ſoles of his Feet were roaſted before two great Stones red hot, for more than a quarter of an hour; the tops of his Fingers were ſcorch'd in a Stove of lighted Pipes; during which Torture he did not draw back his Hand. After this the ſeveral joynts of his Body were cut off, one after another: The Nerves of his Limbs and Arms were diſtorted with a little Iron Wand, after ſuch a manner, as cannot poſſibly be expreſs'd. In fine, after many other Tortures, the hair of his Head was taken off after ſuch a manner, that there remain'd nothing but the Skull, upon which theſe young Executioners were going to throw ſome burning Sand, when a certain Slave of the *Hurons* of *Lorette*, by the order of Madam the Governeſs, knock'd him on the head with a Club, which put an end to his Martyrdom. As to my ſelf, I vow and ſwear, that the Prologue of this Tragedy, created in me ſo great a Horror, that I had not the curioſity to ſee the end of it, nor to hear this poor Wretch ſing to the laſt moment of his Life. I have ſeen ſo many burnt againſt my Will, amongſt thoſe People where I ſojourn'd, during the courſe of my Voyages, that I cannot think of it without trouble. 'Tis a ſad Spectacle, at which every one is obliged to be preſent, when he happens to Sojourn among theſe Savage Nations, who inflict this cruel kind of Death upon their Prisoners of War; for as I have told you in one of my Letters, all the Savages practise this barbarous Cruelty. Nothing is more grating to a civil Man, than that he is oblig'd to be a Witness of the Torments which this kind of Martyrs suffer; for if any one should pretend to shun this Sight, or express any Compassion for them, he would be esteem'd by them a Man of no Courage.

[180] After the Navigation was open and free, the Sieur St. *Michel* a *Canadan*, set out from *Monreal* for the Beaver Lakes, at the Head of a Party of the *Coreurs de Bois*, with several Canows laden with such Goods as are proper for the Savages. In their passage from *Long-Saut*, to the River of the *Outaouas*, they met sixty *Iroquese*, who surpriz'd them, and cut all their Throats except four, that had the good fortune to escape, and carry the news to *Monreal*.[1] As soon as this fatal accident was known, the Chevalier *Vaudreuil*, put himself in a Canow with a Detachment, and pursu'd this party of *Iroquese*, being follow'd by a hundred *Canadans*, and some confederate Savages. I know not by what chance he had the good fortune to overtake them, but so it was, he surpriz'd them, and attack'd them with Vigour, upon which they fought desperately, but at last they were defeated. This Victory cost us the lives of many of our Savages, and of three or four of our Officers.

[1] St. Michel, the leader, was carried captive to Onondaga, whence he escaped in 1693, just as he was to be burned at the stake. Nearly naked, without food or weapons, he made his way in twenty-four days to Quebec, where he gave warning of an approaching Iroquois raid. — Ed.

The *Iroquefe* that were taken, were carried to the City of *Monreal*, near which place they were regal'd with a Salvo of Baftinadoes.[1]

About the beginning of the Month of *July*, Mr. *Frontenac* having receiv'd fome News from the Commander of the Lakes,[2] fpoke to me of a certain Project, which I had formerly fhown him to be of great Importance: But becaufe he did not fufficiently confider all the advantages that might be reap'd from it, and on the contrary, apprehended a great many difficulties would attend the putting it in execution, he had altogether neglected this Affair, of which I fhall give you the following account.

I obferv'd to you in my 17*th* Letter, the great Importance and Advantage of the Forts of *Frontenac* and *Niagara*, and that in the conjuncture of Circumftances wherein Mr. *Denonville* then found them, it was impoffible to preferve them. You have alfo [181] remarqu'd the advantages which the Savages have over the *Europeans*, by their way of fighting in the Forrefts of this vaft Continent. Since we cannot deftroy the *Iroquefe* with our own fingle Forces, we are neceffarily oblig'd to have recourfe to the Savages that are our Allies: And 'tis certain, as they themfelves forefee, that if thefe *Bar-*

[1] For an account of Vaudreuil's pursuing party, see *N. Y. Colon. Docs.*, ix, pp. 531, 536.—ED.

[2] This was Louis de la Porte, sieur de Louvigny, who was commandant at Mackinac 1690–94. He was an able officer, who saw much service in the colony; was major of Quebec in 1703; led several expeditions to the upper country, notably that of 1716 to Wisconsin; and was drowned in a shipwreck (1725). For fuller details see *Wis. Hist. Colls.*, v, pp. 67–77, 108–110; xvi, index.—ED.

barians could compafs the Deftruction of our Colonies, they would be fubdued by them fooner or later, as it has happen'd to many other Nations, fo they know it to be their Intereft to joyn with us to deftroy thefe *Banditi*'s. Now fince they are well affected to this defign, we muft endeavour to faciliate to them the means of putting it in execution, for you may eafily believe that thefe People, as favage as they are, are not fo void of Senfe, as to travel two or three hundred Leagues from their own Country, to fight againft their Enemies, without being fure of a place of retreat, where they may repofe themfelves, and find Provifions. There is no queftion therefore, but we fhould build Forts upon the Lands of the *Iroquefe*, and maintain them in fpite of their Teeth. This, Sir, is what I propos'd above a year agoe to Mr. *Frontenac*, and it is what he would have me ftill to undertake. I project therefore, to build and maintain three Forts upon the courfe of the Lakes, with fome Veffels that fhall go with Oars, which I will build according to my Fancy; but they being light, and of great carriage, may be manag'd either with Oars or a Sail, and will alfo be able to bear the fhocks of the Waves. I demand fifty Seamen of the *French Bifcay*, for they are known to be the moft dexterous and able Mariners that are in the World. I muft alfo have two hundred Soldiers, chofen out of the Troops of *Canada*. I will build three little Caftles in feveral places, one at the mouth of the Lake *Errie*, which you fee in my Map of *Canada*, under the name of Fort *Suppofè*, befides two [182] others. The fecond I will build in the fame place where it was when I maintain'd it, in the years 1687, and 1688, whereof

I have wrote to you in my 14*th* and 15*th* Letter: and the third at the Mouth of the Bay of *Toronto*, upon the ſame Lake.[1] Ninety Men will be ſufficient to Garriſon theſe three Redoubts, and perhaps a ſmaller number; for the *Iroqueſe* who never ſaw a Canon, but in a Picture, and to whom an ounce of Powder is more precious than a Lewis-D'or, can never be perſwaded to attack any kind of Fortification. I deſire of the King for putting this Project in execution, 15000 Crowns a year, for the Maintenance, Entertainment, Subſiſtance, and pay of theſe 250 Men. It will be very eaſie for me to tranſport with the abovemention'd Veſſels 400 Savages, into the Country of the *Iroqueſe*, whenever I have a mind. I can carry Proviſions for 2000, and tranſport as many Sacks of *Indian* Corn, as are neceſſary for maintaining theſe Forts both in Winter and Summer. 'Tis eaſie to have plenty of Hunting and Shooting in all the Iſles, and to contrive ways for croſſing the Lakes; and it will be ſo much the more eaſie to purſue the *Iroqueſe* in their Canows, and ſink them, that my Veſſels are light, and my Men fight under a Cover. In fine, if you ſaw the Memorial which I am to preſent to Mr. *Pontchartrain*, you would find that this Enterprize is the fineſt and moſt uſeful that can be invented, to diſtreſs the *Iroqueſe* in time of War, and confine them within bounds in time of Peace. Mr.

[1] Toronto Lake was the early name of Lake Simcoe. Lahontan appears to apply it to the entire Georgian Bay, whence the Toronto portage led through the peninsula to Lake Ontario. His intended fort was to control this passage to Canada, as that on Lake Erie commanded the route by the Great Lakes. A contemporary document appears to be concerned with that part of Lahontan's project that related to the post at Detroit. See Roy, *Lahontan*, pp. 94, 95.—ED.

Frontenac has joyn'd to it a private Letter to Mr. *Pontchartrain*, wherein he obſerves to him, that if this Project were well put in execution, theſe terrible Enemies would be oblig'd in two years time, to abandon their Country. After this he adds, that he judges me ſufficiently qualified to go upon ſuch an Interpriſe; and believes I will make my point good. Perhaps he might have light on others that know the Country and Cuſtoms of the Savages better than [183] I do: But by an accident which do's not tend much to my advantage, I have purchas'd the Eſteem and Friendſhip of theſe Savages, which in my opinion was the only reaſon that mov'd Mr. *de Frontenac* to ſingle out me for this Service.

July the 27*th* the Governour having given me his Packet for the Court, and the St. *Ann* Frigat being rigg'd and fitted out according to his Orders, I imbarqu'd in the Port of *Quebec*, and after five days ſailing, we met in the River of St. *Laurence*, over againſt *Monts notre dame*, twelve Merchantmen bound from *France* for *Quebec*, under the Convoy of Mr. *d'Iberville*, Captain of the *Poli.*[1] *Auguſt* the 8*th*, we got clear of the Bay of St. *Laurence*, by the help of a Weſterly Gale, and that in ſuch fair and clear Weather, that we deſcry'd the Iſlands of Cape *Breton* and *Newfound-Land*, as diſtinctly, as if we had been within a Musket-ſhot of 'em. The nine or ten following days were ſo far of a different ſtamp, that we could ſcarce ſee from

[1] Iberville was to continue to the coast of Acadia and attack Fort Pemaquid. The plan proved abortive, because the English authorities were notified by the prisoner Nelson. The "Poli" was wrecked the following year off the coast of Newfoundland. — Ed.

the Prow to the Poop of the Ship, for all of a ſudden there fell the thickeſt and darkeſt Fog that ever I ſaw. At the end of theſe days the Horiſon clearing up, we ſtood in for *New-found-Land*, deſcrying Cape St. *Mary;* and by making all the ſail we could, arriv'd that very day in the Port of *Placentia*.[1]

In that Port I found fifty Fiſhermen, moſt of which were of *French Biſcay*, and thought to have ſet out for *France* along with them in a few days: But they were longer in getting ready than I thought for, and when we were juſt ready to break ground, we were inform'd by ſome Fiſhermen, that five large *Engliſh* Ships were come to an Anchor near Cape St. *Mary*. This Intelligence prov'd very true, for on the 15*th* of *September* they caſt Anchor in ſight of *Placentia*. The 16*th* they weigh'd, and came to an Anchor in the Road, out of the reach of our Guns. Upon this the Governour was not a little perplex'd, for he had but fifty Soldiers in his Fort, and a very [184] ſmall moiety of Ammunition. Beſides, the Fort was commanded by a Mountain, from whence he might be gall'd with Stones flung out of Slings; and 'twas to be fear'd, the *Engliſh* would poſſeſs themſelves of that high Ground. I march'd with ſixty of the Seamen belonging to the Fiſhermen, to prevent their Landing, in caſe they attempted to make a

[1] Placentia, the French post upon Newfoundland, possessed an excellent harbor. Together with a portion of the southern shore of the island, it had been sold (1662) by Charles II to Louis XIV, who immediately erected a fortification at this point. Before King William's War, the defences had fallen into ruin, and the place become the resort of privateers who sallied forth to attack English fishing and trading vessels. Since 1690 the French had been occupied in restoring the stronghold, and rebuilding the fort, named St. Louis. — Ed.

Defcent at a certain place call'd *la Fontaine;* and I compafs'd my end without firing a Gun. In effect, fix or feven hundred *Englifh* put in to the Land in twenty Sloops, with a defign to have landed at that place; upon which my vigorous *Cantabrians* being full of fire and forwardnefs, appear'd too foon upon the fhoar, in fpite of my Teeth, and by that means oblig'd the *Englifh* to take another courfe, and row with all their might to the back of a little Cape, where they threw in a Barrel of Pitch and Tar that burnt two arpents of Thickets. The 18*th* about Noon, perceiving that a little Sloop put off from the Admiral with a white Flag on its Prow, and made towards the Fort, I run in thither immediately. The Governour had took care to fend out one of his own Sloops with the fame Flag, to meet the other, and was furpris'd when fhe return'd with two *Englifh* Officers on board. Thefe Officers gave the Governour to underftand, that the Admiral defir'd he would fend an Officer on board of him, which was done accordingly; for Mr. *de Cofte-belle*[1] and I, went on board of the Admiral, who receiv'd us with all Refpect and Civility, and regal'd us with Sweet-meats, and feveral forts of Wines, with which we drank the Healths of the Admirals of *France*, and *England*. He fhew'd us his whole Ship, to the very Carriages of the Guns,

[1] Sieur Pastour de Costabelle was sent to Placentia in 1687 in command of a detachment of troops. Upon the retirement of the governor, he assumed control until superseded by De Brouillon (1690), under whom he became second in command, and with whom he was a confederate in enriching himself from the profit of the public service. In 1701 Costabelle succeeded De Brouillon as governor of Placentia — an office he held for about twelve years, when he was sent to take charge of Isle Royal (Cape Breton). — Ed.

and then gave the Sieur *de Coſtebelle* to know, that 'twould be a great trouble to him to be oblig'd to take *Placentia* by the force of Arms, in regard that he foreſaw, ſuch an Enterpriſe would prove fatal to the Governour, to the Garriſon, and all the [185] Inhabitants, upon the account that he would find a great deal of difficulty in preventing the Pillaging and other Diſorders; That in order to avoid this Misfortune, 'twould be a prudential part in the Governour to come to a Compoſition. Our Officer being fully acquainted with the Governour's Mind, made anſwer in his name, that he was reſolv'd upon a vigorous defence, and would rather ſpring the place in the Air, than ſurrender it to the Enemies of the King his Maſter. After a mutual exchange of Compliments, we took leave of him, and being ready to get into our Sloop, he told us with embraces, that he was infinitely ſorry he could not ſalute us with his Guns, in the room of which he order'd five or ſix Huzza's, with a *Long live the King*. When we went into the Boat, we return'd him the ſame number of ſhouts, to which he return'd a ſeventh that finiſh'd the Ceremony. Upon our return to the Fort, Mr. *de Coſtebelle* gave the Governour an account of the force of the Admiral's Ship. The St. *Albans* (ſo the Ship was call'd) carried ſixty ſix Guns mounted, and ſix hundred Men Complement, but the other Ships appear'd to be of leſs force.

The next day, which was the 19*th*, they advanc'd within Canon-ſhot of the Fort, where they lay bye, while a Sloop row'd up to the Batteries. The Governour ſent out another

Sloop to know what the matter was, and was anſwer'd, that if he had a mind for a Parley in the time of the Ingagement, he ſhould put up a red Flag for a Signal. I was then poſted at *la Fontaine*, to oppoſe a Deſcent; for that was the only place that could be ſerviceable to the *Engliſh*, in order to maſter *Placentia*. The *Engliſh* ought to have conſider'd, that their Cannon would do no ſervice againſt an impenetrable Rampart, and that they would loſe their labour in ſhooting againſt Flints and Earth. But it ſeems, they were oblig'd by expreſs Orders from the Prince of *Orange*, to do [186] it, and at the ſame time to expoſe themſelves to the danger of being ſunk, which had certainly been effected, if we had had Powder and Ball enough for the Canonading laſted almoſt five hours.

The 20*th* a *French* Pilot who was Priſoner on board of the Admiral, made his eſcape by throwing himſelf into the Sea in the Night-time. He landed at the place where I lay in Ambuſcade; and after he had given me an account of what paſs'd in the Fleet, I ſent him to the Governour's Houſe. He inform'd me, that they had deſign'd a Deſcent with ſeven or eight hundred Men, but alter'd their Reſolution, upon the apprehenſion, that there were fourteen or fifteen hundred Seamen ready to oppoſe them; that they were of the opinion, that my ſixty *Biſcayans* who diſcover'd themſelves upon the ſhoar at *la Fontaine*, in ſpite of all I could do, had no other view but to draw 'em into an Ambuſcade, by tempting 'em to come up. The 21*ſt* they ſet ſail with a North-Eaſt Gale, after having burnt all the Houſes at *Pointe Verte*, where the Governour had ſent a Detachment by way of Precaution that ſame very day; but the ways were ſo impracticable, that the Detachment could not get there in time to oppoſe the Enemy. This one may juſtly ſay, that if it had not been for the Captains of the *Biſcay* Ships that were then at *Placentia*, that place had undoubtedly fallen into the hands of the *Engliſh*: And this I can convince you of, when you and I meet. In this bloody Expedition, the *Engliſh* loſt ſix Men; and on our ſide the Sieur *Boat*, Lieutenant of a *Nantes* Veſſel, had his Arm ſhot off. In fine, the *Engliſh* did all that Men could do, ſo that nothing can be ſaid againſt their Conduct.[1]

October the *6th*, I took ſhipping in purſuit of my Voyage to *France*, being accompany'd with ſeveral other Veſſels. The Weſterly Winds were ſo favourable to us in our paſſage, that we came to an Anchor [187] on the 23*d* at St. *Nazere*, which lies but eight or nine Leagues for this place.[2] I am to ſet out immediately for *Verſailles;* in the mean time, I am,

SIR,

Yours, &c.

---

[1] The English ships were commanded by Commodore Williams, whose management of the attack was later criticized. Comparison with the documentary reports of this expedition, proves that Lahontan was accurate in this account. Charlevoix drew from it largely in his *History*, iv, pp. 222–226. The governor represented to the court the services of Lahontan on this occasion. See Roy, *Lahontan*, p. 97. — Ed.

[2] St. Nazaire is a harbor at the mouth of the Loire River. — Ed.

LETTER XXIV.

Dated at *Nantes May* 10. 1693.

Containing an Account of Mr. Frontenac's *Project, which was rejected at Court, and the reason why it was rejected. The King gives the Author the Lieutenancy of the* Isle of New-found Land, *&c. together with a free Independent Company.*

SIR,

I AM now once more at *Nantes*, from whence I wrote to you in *October last.* I am now return'd from Court, where I presented to Mr. *Pontchartrain* Mr. *Frontenac*'s Letters, and the Memorial I mention'd in my last. I was answer'd, that it would not be proper to execute the Project I propos'd because the forty Seamen which were necessary for my purpose, could not now be allow'd me, and besides the King had given Orders to Mr. *Frontenac*, to make Peace with the *Iroquese* upon any terms whatsoever. This Inconveniency also was found to attend the Project, that after the Forts which I intended to build upon the Lakes were intirely finish'd, the Savages that are our Friends and Confederates, would rather seek after Glory, by making [188] War upon the *Iroquese*, than take pleasure in Hunting the Beavers, which would be a considerable damage to the Colonies of *Canada*, that subsist only as one may say, by the trade of Skins, as I shall shew you more particularly in a proper place. The *Englifh* will by no means take it ill, that we do not build thefe Forts, for befides that, they are too much concern'd for the prefervation of the *Iroquefe*, they will always be ready to furnifh with Merchandize the Savage Nations, that are our Allies, as they have done hitherto. I muft own my felf mightily oblig'd to the *Englifh*, who attack'd us at *Placentia* the laft year; they declar'd publickly, though without any juft ground, after they arriv'd in *England*, that they would infallibly have taken that place, if I had not oppos'd their Defcent. I have already inform'd you, that I did not at all hinder them from Landing at the place where I was pofted with fixty *Bifcayan* Seamen: So that they attribute to me a glorious Action, in which I had no fhare, and by that means have done me fo much Honour, that his Majefty hath beftow'd upon me the Lieutenancy of the Ifle of *Newfound-Land* and *Acadia*, which I never deferv'd upon that fcore. Thus you fee, Sir, that many times fuch Perfons are preferr'd, who have no other Patrons in the World, but pure Chance. However, I fhould have been better pleas'd, if I could have put the abovemention'd Project in execution, for a folitary Life is moft grateful to me, and the manners of the Savages are perfectly agreeable to my Palate. The corruption of our Age is fo great, that it feems the *Europeans* have made a Law, to tear one another in pieces by cruel Ufage and Reproaches, and therefore you muft not think it ftrange, if I have a kindnefs for the poor *Americans*, who have done me fo many favours. I am to fet out the next day after to Morrow, from this [189] place, in order to embark at St. *Nazere*. The

Meſſieurs d'Angui, two *Nantes* Merchants, have taken upon them to maintain the Garriſon of *Placentia*, upon condition of certain Grants made by the Court, who furniſhes them with a Ship, wherein I am to have my Paſſage. Pray ſend me your News by ſome Ships of S. *John de Luz*, which are to ſail from this place within two Months, in order to truck with the Inhabitants of *Placentia*.

I cannot conclude this Letter, without giving you ſome account of a Diſpute I had very lately at my Inn, with a *Portugueze* Phyſician, who had made many Voyages to *Angola*, *Brezil*, and *Goa*. He maintain'd, that the People of the Continent of *America*, *Aſia*, and *Africa*, were deſcended from three different Fathers, which he thus attempted to prove. The *Americans* differ from the *Aſiatics*, for they have neither Hair nor Beard; the features of their Face, their colour and their cuſtoms are different; beſides that, they know neither *meum* nor *tuum*, but have all things in common, without making any property of Goods, which is quite contrary to the *Aſiatic* way of living. He added, that *America* was ſo far diſtant from the other parts of the World, that no body can imagine, how a Voyage ſhould be made into this New Continent, before the uſe of the Compaſs was found out; That the *Africans* being black and flat Nos'd, had ſuch monſtrous thick Lips, ſuch a flat Face, ſuch ſoft woolly Hair on their Head, and were in their Conſtitution, Manners, and Temper, ſo different from the *Americans*, that he thought it impoſſible, that theſe two ſorts of People ſhould derive their Original from *Adam*, whom this Phyſician would have to reſemble a *Turk* or a *Perſian* in his

Air and Figure. I anſwer'd him preſently, that ſuppoſing the Scripture did not give convincing evidence, that all Men in general are deſcended from one firſt Father, yet his reaſoning would not be ſufficient [190] to prove the contrary, ſince the difference that is found between the People of *America* and *Africa*, proceeds from no other cauſe but the different qualities of the Air and Climat in theſe two Continents: That this appears plainly to be true, becauſe a *Negro* Man and Woman, or a Savage Man and Woman, being tranſplanted into *Europe*, will produce ſuch Children there, who in four or five Generations, will infallibly be as white, as the moſt ancient *Europeans*. The Phyſician deny'd this matter of Fact, and maintain'd, that the Children deſcended from this *Negro* Man or Woman, would be born there as black as they are in *Guinea;* but that afterwards the Rays of the Sun being more oblique and leſs ſcorching than in *Africa*, theſe Infants would not have that black ſhining Luſtre, which is ſo eaſily diſtinguiſhed upon the Skin of ſuch *Negroes* as are brought up in their own Country. To confirm his *Hypotheſis*, he aſſur'd me, that he had ſeen many *Negroes* at *Lisbon*, as black as in *Africa*, tho' their Great Grandfather's Grandfather had been tranſplanted into *Portugal* many years agoe. He added alſo, that thoſe who were deſcended from the *Portugueze*, that dwelt at *Angola*, Cape *Vert*, *&c.* about a hundred years agoe, are ſo little tawn'd, that 'tis impoſſible to diſtinguiſh them from the Natives of *Portugal:* He further confirm'd his way of reaſoning, from an unconteſtable matter of fact, for, ſays he, if the Rays of the Sun were the cauſe of the blackneſs of the *Negroes*, from hence it would follow, that the *Brazilians* being ſituate in the ſame degree from the Equator with the *Africans*, ſhould be as black as they are; but ſo they are not, for 'tis certain their Skin appears to be as clear as that of the *Portugueſe*. But this was not all, he maintain'd farther, that theſe who are deſcended from the firſt Savages of *Brazil*, that were tranſported into *Portugal*, above an Age agoe, have as little Hair and [191] Beard as their Anceſtors, and on the contrary, thoſe who are deſcended from the firſt *Portugueze*, who peopl'd the Colonies of *Brazil*, are as hairy, and have as great Beards, as if they had been born in *Portugal*. But after all, continued he, though all that I have ſaid is abſolutely true, yet there are ſome People, who raſhly maintain, that the Children of the *Africans* and *Americans*, will by degrees degenerate in *Europe*. This may happen to thoſe whoſe Mothers receive the imbraces of *Europeans*, which is the reaſon why we ſee ſo many *Mullatto*'s in the Iſles of *America*, in *Spain*, and in *Portugal*: Whereas if theſe Women had been as cloſely kept up in *Europe*, as the *Portugueze* Women are in *Africa* and *America*, the Children of the *Braſilians* would no more degenerate than thoſe of the *Portugueze*. Such Sir, was the reaſoning of this Doctor, who hits the matter pretty juſtly towards the end of his Diſcourſe; but his Principle is moſt falſe, and moſt abſurd, for no Man can doubt, unleſs he be void of Faith, good Senſe and Judgment, but that *Adam* was the only Father of all Mankind. 'Tis certain, that the Savages of *Canada*, and all the other People of *America*, have not naturally either Hair or Beard; that the features of their Face, and their colour ap-

The Dwelling Houses of the TAHUGLAUK, *wich are 80 paces in length according to the Draught that yͤ Mozeemlek slaves gave me upon yͤ Barks of Trees.*

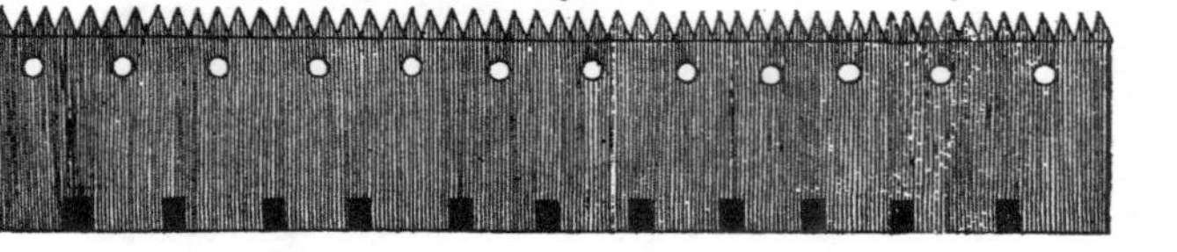

The Vessels us'd by the TAHUGLAUK *in wich 200 men may row; provided they are such as som of yͤ Mozeemlek people drew to me upon yͤ Barks of Trees.*

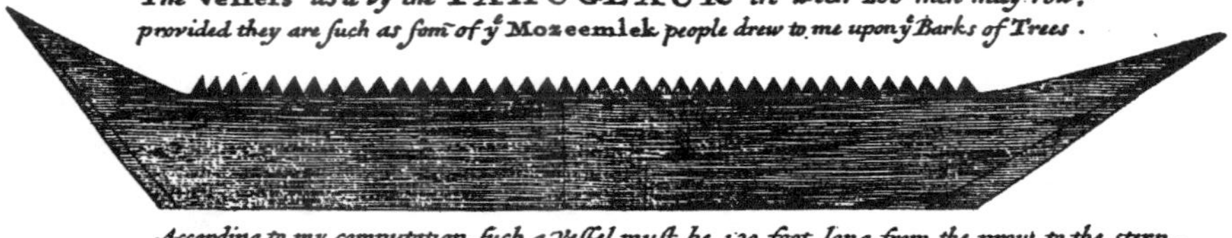

According to my computation such a Vessel must be 130 foot long from the prow to the stern.

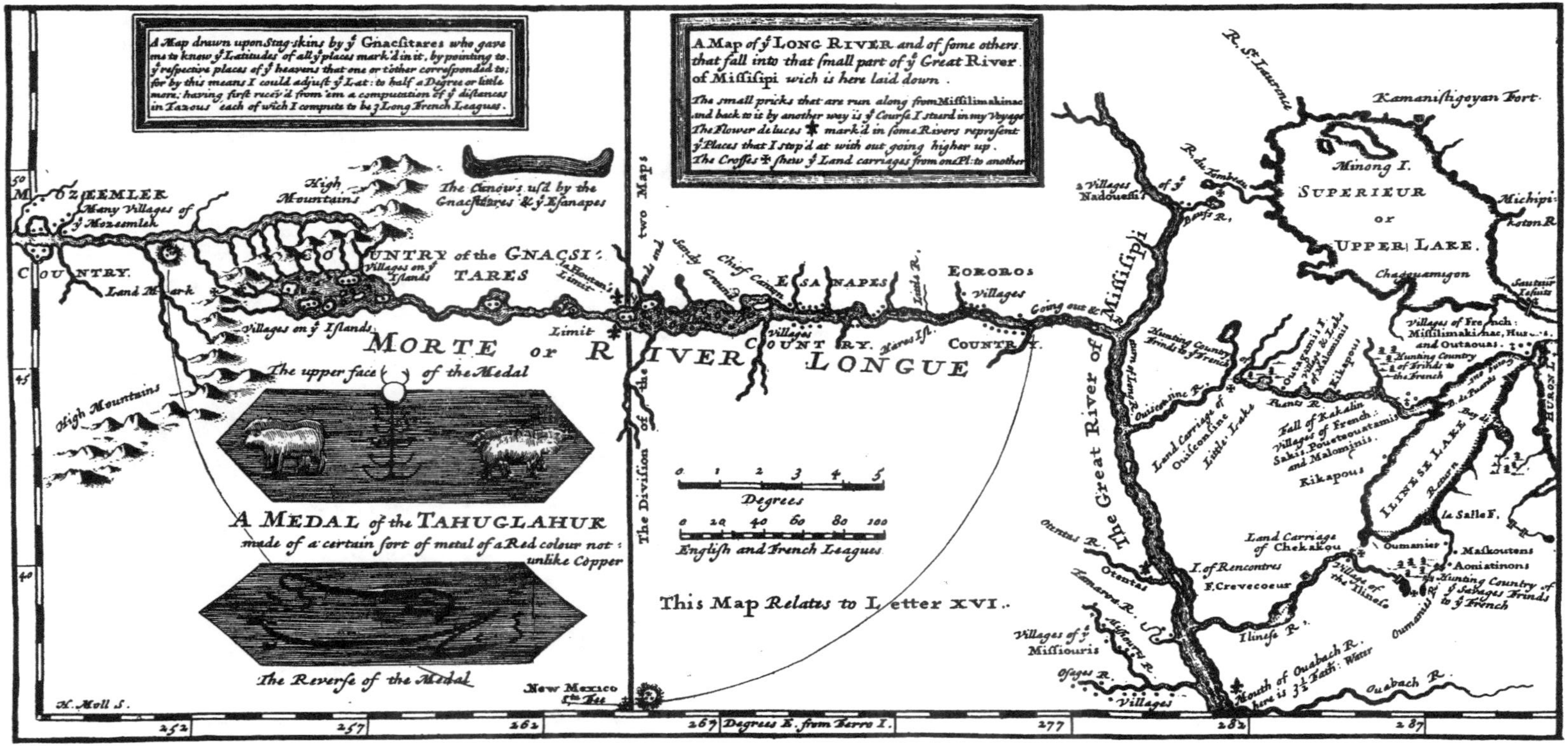

A Map drawn upon Stag-skins by yͤ Gnacsitares who gave me to know yͤ Latitudes of all yͤ places mark'd in it, by pointing to yͤ respective places of yͤ heavens that one or tother corresponded to; for by this means I could adjust yͤ Lat: to half a Degree or little more; having first receiv'd from 'em a computation of yͤ distances in Tazous each of wich I compute to be 3 Long French Leagues.

A Map of yͤ LONG RIVER and of some others that fall into that small part of yͤ Great River of Missisipi wich is here laid down.

The small pricks that are run along from Missilimakinac and back to it by another way is yͤ Course I steerd in my Voyage. The Flower de luces ⚜ mark'd in some Rivers represent yͤ Places that I stop'd at with out going higher up. The Crosses ✠ shew yͤ Land carriages from one Pl: to another.

MOZEEMLEK COUNTRY

Many Villages of yͤ Mozeemlek

Land Mark

High Mountains

The Canows us'd by the Gnacsitares & yͤ Esanapes

COUNTRY of the GNACSITARES

Villages on yͤ Islands

MORTE or RIVER LONGUE

The upper face of the Medal

A MEDAL of the TAHUGLAHUK *made of a certain sort of metal of a Red colour not unlike Copper*

The Reverse of the Medal

The Division of the two Maps

ESANAPES COUNTRY

EOROROS COUNTRY

Chief Canton

Sandy Ground

Villages

Little R.

Hares Isl.

Going out of R.

Degrees 0 1 2 3 4 5

English and French Leagues 0 20 40 60 80 100

This Map Relates to Letter XVI.

The Great River of Missisipi

R. St. Laurence

Kamanistigoyan Fort

Minong I.

SUPERIEUR or UPPER LAKE

Chagouamigon

Michipicoton R.

Sauteur Jesuits

R. du Tombeau

Boeufs R.

3 Villages of yͤ Nadouessis

Villages of French: Missilimakinac, Hurons and Outaouas.

Hunting Country of Friends to the French

Outagamis & Village of Malominis

Kikapous

Puants R.

Fall of Kakalin

Villages of French: Sakis, Pouteouatamis and Malominis

Hunting Country of Friends to yͤ French

Ouisconsinc R.

Land Carriage of Ouisconsinc

Little Lake

ILINESE LAKE

HURON L.

la Salle F.

Oumanies

Maskoutens

Aoniatinons

Hunting Country of yͤ Savages Friends to yͤ French

Land Carriage of Chekakou

Village of the Ilinese

I. of Rencontres

F. Crevecoeur

Ilinese R.

Otentas R.

Otentas

Zamarous R.

Missouris R.

Villages of yͤ Missiouris

Osages R.

Villages

Mouth of Ouabach R. here is 3½ Fath: Water

Ouabach R.

New Mexico 5th Bee

H. Moll S.

252 257 262 267 Degrees E. from Ferro I. 277 282 287

50 45 40

proaching to an Olive, ſhow a vaſt difference between them and the *Europeans.* What is the cauſe of theſe things I know not, and yet I cannot believe them to be the effect of their Air and Food. For at that rate, thoſe who are deſcended from the *French*, that firſt ſetled in *Canada* near a hundred years agoe, and for the moſt part run up and down in the Woods, and live like the Savages, ſhould have neither Beard nor Hair, but degenerate alſo by degrees into Savages, which yet never happens. After this Phyſician had alledg'd all theſe Reaſons, he digreſs'd from this Subject, and having a mind to diſcover his extravagant Opinions, ask'd me what I [192] thought of the Salvation of ſo many *Americans*, to whom in all probability the Goſpel was never preach'd. You may very well believe, that I made no ſcruple to condemn them by wholeſale to Eternal Fire, which he took very ill. 'How can you, ſaid he, 'condemn theſe poor People with ſo much aſſurance: 'Tis 'probable that their firſt Father, having never ſinn'd as our '*Adam* did, had a good Soul, and an upright Heart, ſince his 'Poſterity do exactly obſerve the Law of natural Equity, 'which is expreſs'd in *Latine* in theſe well known words, *Alteri* '*ne feceris quod tibi fieri non vis;* and allow no property of 'Goods, nor any Diſtinction or Subordination among them, 'but live as Brethren, without Diſputes, without Suits, with-'out Laws, and without Malice. But ſuppoſing, added he, 'that they were originally deſcended from *Adam*, we ought 'not to believe, that they are damn'd for their ignorance of 'the Chriſtian Doctrine, for who can tell but God may impute 'to them the Merits of Chriſt's Blood, by ways ſecret and 'incomprehenſible to us; and beſides, (ſuppoſing that Man 'has a Free Will) his Divine Majeſty without doubt will have 'a greater regard to his moral Actions, than to his Worſhip 'and Belief. The want of Knowledge, continued he, is an 'Unhappineſs, but not a Crime, and who can tell but God has 'a mind to be honour'd by infinite ways of paying him Hom-'age and Reſpect, as by Sacrifices, Dances, Songs, and the 'other Ceremonies of the *Americans?* He had ſcarce made an end of his Diſcourſe, when I fell foul upon him with all my might, as to the preceding Points; but after I had given him to underſtand, that if among the *multi vocati, i. e.* thoſe who profeſs the true Religion, who are but a handful of Men, there are found but *Pauci electi*, all the *Americans* muſt be in a very deplorable condition: He anſwer'd me impudently, that I was very raſh [193] to determine who ſhould be in the number of the Reprobate at the laſt Judgment, and to condemn them without giving any Quarter; for, ſays he, this is to inſult the Wiſdom of God, and to make him deal as capriciouſly by his Creatures, as St. *Paul*'s Potter did by his two Veſſels. Nevertheleſs, when he ſaw that I treated him like an impious, unbelieving Wretch, he to be even with me, reply'd in theſe fooliſh words, *Fidem ego hic quæ adhibetur Myſteriis ſacris interpello, ſed fidem illam quæ bonæ mentis ſoror eſt, quæq; rectam rationem amat.* From hence you may judge, Sir, whether this fine Phyſician was able to remove Mountains. I am,

SIR,

Yours, &c.

LETTER XXV.

Dated at *Viana* in *Portugal January* 31. 1694.

The Author's departure from France *for* Placentia. *A Fleet of* 30 Englifh *Ships came to feize upon that place; but is difappointed, and fheers off. The Reafons why the* Englifh *have bad fuccefs in all their Enterprifes beyond Sea. The Author's Adventure with the Governour of Placentia. His departure for* Portugal. *An Engagement with a Flufhing Privateer.*

SIR,

I DO not at all doubt but you will be fenfibly affected with my fad and fatal Mifadventure, which I am now to give you an account of. And firft [194] you muft know, that after we had waited for a fair Wind fifteen or twenty days at St. *Nazere*, we fet fail on the 12*th* of *May* laft. Our Paffage was neither long nor fhort, for we arriv'd at the Harbour of *Placentia* the 20*th* of *June*, having taken an *Englifh* Ship laden with Tobacco, on the edges of the Bank of *Newfound Land*. After I landed, I went to falute Mr. *Brouillon*, Governor of *Placentia*, and declar'd to him how glad I was to obey the Orders of fo wife a Commander.[1] He anfwer'd, that he was much furpriz'd

[1] Jacques François de Brouillon belonged to a good family from Guienne, France, and had served as an infantry officer since 1670. Twenty years later he was honored with the appointment of governor of Placentia, where he arrived early in the spring of 1690. He was an officer of merit, but inclined to peculation, and both merchants

to find, that I had ſollicited to be employ'd there, without acquainting him with it the preceding year; and that he now plainly perceiv'd, that the Project about the Lakes of *Canada*, (which I had mention'd to him) was a mere ſham pretence. I endeavour'd in vain to perſwade him to the contrary; for it was not poſſible for me to undeceive him.[1] Neverthelеſs, I landed my Goods, and hir'd a private Houſe, till ſuch time as I could build one for my ſelf, which I carried on with ſo much diligence, that it was finiſh'd in *September*, by the aſſiſtance of the Ship-Carpenters, who were lent me *gratis*, by all the *Biſcay* Captains. The Sieur *Beray* of St. *John de Luz*,[2] arriv'd at *Placentia* on the 18*th* of *July*, with one of his Ships, and brought me a Letter, wherein you acquaint me, that in regard to your Nephew deſires to viſit *Canada* the next year, you would be very glad to have a Dictionary of the Language of the Savages, together with the Memoirs which I promis'd you.

On the 16*th* of *September* we perceiv'd an *Engliſh* Fleet of twenty four Sail, which caſt Anchor in the Road much about the time that it was diſcover'd. It was commanded by Sir *Francis Wheeler*, who had gone to *Martinico* with a deſign

---

and habitants made frequent complaints under his administration. He remained in Placentia until 1701, when he was transferred to Acadia, serving there as governor until his death in 1705. Indications are not lacking from official sources that Lahontan's accusations against De Brouillon had some justification. See Roy, *Lahontan*, pp. 176–179. — ED.

[1] Roy shows from the letters of De Brouillon himself, that the arrival of Lahontan in the capacity of lieutenant of the king, not only deprived the governor of certain sources of profit, but also of hopes for placing his brother in that position. — ED.

[2] St. Jean de Luz is a small port at the southwestern extremity of France on the Bay of Biscay. It had considerable commerce with Placentia and its fisheries. — ED.

to ſeize that Iſle, and in his return from thence had ſail'd to *New England*, to take in ſome Forces and Ammunition there, in order to make himſelf Maſter [195] of *Placentia*; but when he diſcover'd a Redoubt of Stone lately built upon the top of the Mountain, which I mention'd to you in my laſt Letter but one, he thought it more adviſable to return quietly into *Europe*, than to make a fruitleſs Attempt. We had planted four Canon upon this high Redoubt, which ſo gaul'd the Ships of his Fleet, that they were forc'd to weigh Anchor, and hoiſt Sail ſooner than they intended.[1] The fault of the *Engliſh* upon this occaſion, was, that they did not enter the Harbour the ſame day that they appear'd before the place. I have obſerv'd it many times, that Attempts do commonly miſcarry, by delaying them for a little while; and of this I could give you at leaſt fifteen or ſixteen Inſtances within the compaſs of my own Knowledge. But now I return to the Quarrel the Governour had with me.

Fancying that I had ſollicited my Employments without taking notice of him, he treated me with all manner of Reproaches and Outrages, from the time of my Landing, to that of my Departure, and was not ſatisfy'd with appropriat-

[1] Sir Francis Wheler, born in 1656, entered the navy when twenty-two years of age, and by 1680 was captain of a man of war. The following year he captured two Algerine corsairs, and was knighted by James II in the last year of his reign. After the Revolution (1688) Wheler was made rear-admiral and sent with a squadron to the West Indies. There he made an unsuccessful attack on Martinique (April, 1692), and arrived in Boston June 10, where he requested Phips to coöperate in a second attack upon Quebec. Finding that impracticable, he sailed for Placentia, with the results Lahontan details. The following year (1694) his flag ship foundered off the coast of Gibralter, and the admiral, with all on board, was lost. — Ed.

ing to himſelf the Profits and Advantages of the free Company that was given me, but likewiſe ſtop'd without any ſcruple, the pay of the Soldiers that were employ'd in the Cod-fiſhing by the Inhabitants, and made the reſt work without Wages. I ſhall take no notice of his publick Extortion; for tho' he has formally counteracted the ten Articles contain'd in the Orders of *Lewis* the 10*th*, yet he had ſo many Friends in all the Courts, that he could not be found guilty: There's ſome pleaſure in making Preſents in his way, for by them he has made 50000 Crowns *per fas & nefas*, in the ſpace of three or four years. I ſhould never have done, if I offer'd to give you a particular account of all the trouble and vexation he gave me. I ſhall only mention three Inſtances which crown'd all the reſt.

[196] On the 20*th* of *November*, *i. e.* a Month after our Fiſhermen ſet ſail, while I was entertaining at Supper ſome of the Inhabitants, he came Mask'd into my Houſe, with his Servants, and broke the glaſs Windows, Bottles, and Drinking-Glaſſes, and threw down the Tables, Chairs, Cheſts of Drawers, and every thing that came to hand. Before I had time to get into my Chamber, and take my Piſtols, this inſolent Mob diſappear'd very ſeaſonably; for I would have loaded my Piſtols and purſu'd them, if my Gueſts had not hindred me. Next Morning his Servants fell upon mine, who expected nothing leſs than to be threſh'd to death with Clubs. This ſecond inſult having provok'd my Patience to the laſt degree, I was meditating ſome Revenge upon theſe Aſſaſſins, when the Recollets came and remonſtrated to me, that I muſt diſſem-

ble my Refentment, to prevent any Innovation in the King's Affairs. Then I refolv'd to fhut my felf up, and apply my felf to Study, to divert the vexatious Thoughts, of not being able to pull off my Mask. The third trick which he play'd me, at the end of three days, was this; he fent to arreft two Soldiers, whom I had imploy'd to cut down fome Grafs in the Meadows, about half a League from the Garrifon: They were feiz'd while they were Mowing, bound and carried away Prifoners, under the pretence of being Deferters, becaufe they had lain two Nights out of the Garrifon, without his leave; and, which would have prov'd yet more fatal to thefe innocent Men, he had certainly caus'd 'em to be knock'd on the Head, on purpofe to vex me, if the Recollets, and his own Miffse, had not earneftly interceded on their behalf.

After this Accident, the Recollets advifed me to go and fee him, and to entreat him to put an end to all his Perfecutions, affuring him at the fame time, that I was entirely his Servant and Friend. *Durus eft hic fermo.* Whatever reluctancy I had to yield to an advice fo [197] contrary to nature, which, I muft confefs, ftruggled furioufly within me, yet I offer'd fo much violence to my felf, that I fubmitted to it. I was at his Houfe, went into his Chamber, and being with him all alone, I fpoke to him for a quarter of an hour in the moft fubmiffive Terms, that any Slave could ufe. I am afham'd to make this Confeffion to you, for I blufh to my felf every time I think of fo mean a fubmiffion. However, inftead of his liftening to my Reafons, and treating friendly with me, he fell into a moft furious Paffion, and loaded me with a torrent of moft bitter

Reproaches. In this cafe, Sir, I preferr'd the Service of the King, before the Punctilio's of Honour, for I did nothing but retir'd to my own Houfe, being well fatisfy'd that I was not affaffinated by his Domefticks: But the diforder which this Affair produc'd, would require a long Difcourfe. It will be more to the purpofe, to come to matter of Fact; I do affure you, that he would have laid me up, if the Inhabitants had appear'd to be in his Intereft. He pretended that he had been infulted, and confequently that he was in the right in revenging himfelf, whatever it coft him. But the tragical end of a Governour, whofe Throat was cut in this Country about thirty or forty years agoe, furnifh'd him with abundant matter of Reflexion. He judg'd it therefore his fafeft way to diffemble his Anger, being perfwaded, that if I fhould have run him through with my Sword, the Soldiers and Inhabitants would have favour'd my efcape to the *Englifh*, in the neighbourhood of *Placentia*. In the mean time the Recollets, who had a mind to compofe thefe growing Differences, found no great trouble in reconciling us, for they Remonftrated to him, of what confequence it would be for us to live in a good Correfpondence, and to avoid the troubles that would enfue upon our quarrels. This propofal of an Accomodation, was in appearance [198] moft agreeable to him, and fo much the rather, becaufe he was glad to diffemble his Refentments by the external figns of Friendfhip. So we faw and embrac'd one another with mutual Proteftations of forgetting all that had pafs'd between us.

After this Reconciliation, I had reafon to believe, that

his Heart would not give the lye to his Mouth, becaufe I thought he was not fo imprudent as to inform the Court of fome Trifles, wherein he would appear to have proftituted his Honour; but I was deceiv'd, for he took the pains to add afterwards to the Verbal Procefs he had given in before our Accommodation, fome falfhoods which he ought to have conceal'd. 'Tis needlefs to acquaint you, how by chance his Papers fell into my Hands; that Indifcretion might prove a difadvantage to fome Perfons, whom Heaven blefs. I fhall only tell you, that after the Recollets had feen and read the Allegations contain'd in his Papers, they made no fcruple to advife me to take care of my felf, and ingeneoufly declar'd to me, that they never intended to meddle any more in that Affair, becaufe they perceiv'd that they had innocently contributed to do me a prejudice, by reftoring peace between him and me.[1] This wholfom advice made me perceive the danger to which I fhould be expos'd, if I continued any longer at *Placentia*, infomuch, that the fear I had of being fent to the *Baftile*, after the arrival of the Ships from *France*, made me refolve to abandon all hopes of making my fortune here, and to throw up my Places. After the Inhabitants were acquainted with this News, all of 'em except three or four, came running to my Houfe, to affure me they were ready to fign my Verbal

[1] For copies of De Brouillon's accusations against his lieutenant, taken from the French archives, see Roy, *Lahontan*, pp. 100, 101. It is amusing reading, as one recognizes the unpopularity of the governor with the inhabitants, and the mocking spirit of Lahontan who composed satiric songs concerning his superior, and sang them in the taverns of Placentia. — ED.

Procefs, in cafe I would change my Refolution: But inftead of accepting their offer, I gave them to underftand, having thank'd them firft for their Good-will, that [199] they would bring Mifchief upon themfelves, and be look'd upon at Court as Seditious Perfons, and Difturbers of the publick Peace; fince by a deteftable principle of Politicks, an inferior Perfon is always judg'd to be in the wrong, whatever reafon he may have on his fide. Indeed I would gladly have avoided this fatal neceffity of throwing up my Places, which feem'd infenfibly to lead me to fome great Fortune; but at laft the confinement in the *Baftile*, made fuch a deep impreffion upon my Mind, after I had ferioufly reflected upon the troublefom Circumftances of my Affairs, that I made no fcruple to embark in a little Veffel, which was the only one, and the laft that was to go to *France*. The Propofal I made to the Captain of prefenting him with a 1000 Crowns, was fo well receiv'd, that he engag'd to land me upon the Coaft of *Portugal* for that Sum, upon condition that I fhould keep the Secret. The beft of the matter was, that my Enemy had ufed the precaution of writing to the Governors of *Belle* Ifle, of the Ifle of *Re*, and of *Rochelle*, to feize me as foon as I fhould land.[1] He reckon'd, and not without reafon indeed, that this Veffel would put into one of thefe three Ports: But three hundred Piftoles, dexteroufly convey'd to the hands of fome People that are not much

[1] Three well-known harbors on the west coast of France. Belle Isle lies off from Britanny opposite the bay of Quiberon; Isle de Ré is over against the harbor of La Rochelle in the Bay of Biscay. — ED.

accuſtom'd to finger Gold, have a wonderful effect; for that very Sum, which indeed I was loth to part with, ſav'd me my Liberty, and perhaps my Life.

Purſuant to this Reſolution, I imbarqu'd the 14*th* of the laſt Month, notwithſtanding the riſque that one runs by ſailing in the Winter time, through ſuch a Sea as lies between *Newfound-Land* and *France.* 'Tis needleſs to inform you, that I left at *Placentia* a great deal of Houſhold Furniture, which I could neither ſell nor carry off. 'Twill be more edifying for you to hear the Journal of our Voyage. We incounter'd three terrible Storms in our Paſſage, [200] without any damage; and in the laſt of theſe, which laſted three days, the Wind at North-Weſt, we run a hundred and fifty Leagues without any Sail. This laſt Storm was ſo violent, that the Seamen imbrac'd, and bid an eternal adieu to one another; for every Minute they expected to be ſunk without relief. As this Storm alarm'd us, ſo the contrary Winds from the Eaſt and North-Eaſt, that ſprung upon us a hundred Leagues to the Weſtward of Cape *Finiſterre*, occaſion'd an equal dread; for we were oblig'd to traverſe the Sea for three or four and twenty days, after which we deſcry'd the Cape by vertue of our frequent tackings, and by a ſtrange accident, were attack'd by a *Fluſhing* Privateer, which could not board us, becauſe the Sea roll'd ſo high, but contented her ſelf with firing upon us, and that with ſo little effect, that we did not loſe one Man. Our Maſts and Rigging indeed was ſo dammag'd, that after we were parted from the Privateer, by the help of the Night and a great Fog, we could ſcarce make uſe of our Sails. However, we refitted with all poſſible diligence, and the Captain of the Ship having then a fair pretence to luft out of the direct courſe ſtood to the South-Eaſt in the Night-time. This feign'd courſe did not ſecure us from the Privateer, which might happen to ſteer the ſame courſe; ſo that in the Night-time we put our ſelves in a readineſs to renew the fight in the Day-time. In effect, he did not purſue us, as we apprehended: But about Noon we eſcap'd yet more narrowly, for we were purſu'd by a *Sallyman*[1] in ſight of the Coaſt for four hours, and were within a hairs breadth of being taken, before we got under the Canon of the Fort of this City. Had we been catch'd, the Governour of *Placentia* would have had ſome ground for the joyful Exclamation, *Incidit in Scillam*, &c. But thank God we were only frighted.

[201] As ſoon as we came to an Anchor, I paid down my 1000 Crowns to the Captain, who has reaſon to look upon this Action, as one of the beſt he ever did in his Life-time. The Long-boat was no ſooner in the Water, than I went aſhoar with all my Baggage; and as ſoon as I came into this City, I procur'd Ammunition and Proviſions for the Ship with that Expedition, that the Captain weigh'd Anchor the very next day, and ſo continu'd his courſe to *France*.

As for the Memoirs of the Country of *Canada*, which you have ſo often deſir'd, I have addreſs'd 'em to the *Rochel* Merchant, who convey'd your Letters to me all the while I was in

[1] A Salleeman was a Moorish pirate ship, so called from the port of Sallee on the coast of Morocco. — Ed.

Canada. To theſe I have tack'd a ſmall Catalogue of the moſt neceſſary words of the *Algonkin* Language; which, as I have often told you, is the fineſt and the moſt univerſal Language in that Continent. If your Nephew continues his deſign of undertaking a Voyage to that Country, I would adviſe him to learn theſe words in the time of his Paſſage, that ſo he may be able to ſtay five or ſix Months with the *Algonkins*, and underſtand what they ſay. I have likewiſe ſent you an explication of the Sea-Terms, made uſe of in my Letters. The making of this little Table, was a diverſion to me in my Voyage; for in peruſing my Letters, I drew out ſome remarks which I deſign to impart to you, if I find that the inſuing Memoirs give you ſatisfaction.

You will readily gueſs, that from the year 1683, to this very day, I have renounc'd all manner of ties to my Country. The curious Adventures that I have related to you in Writing ſince that time, will undoubtedly afford an agreeable diverſion to your Friends; provided they are not of the number of thoſe unſufferable Devotees, who would rather be crucifi'd, than ſee an Eccleſiaſtick expos'd. Pray be ſo kind as to write to me to *Lisbon*, and inform [202] me of what you hear, in reference to my concern. You have ſuch good Correſpondents at *Paris*, that you cannot miſs of knowing how things go. I doubt not but my Adverſary feeds himſelf with the hopes, that his uſual Preſents would procure the apprehending of me in *France*, where he thinks I would be the fool to land: But now to be ſure he'll fret his Heart out, for that he cannot gall me to his Wiſhes. However, 'tis as much his intereſt to ſollicit my Death, (purſuant to his unjuſt Charge againſt me) as 'tis my Glory to procure him a long Life. Upon this foot, Sir, the longer he lives, the more revenge I ſhall have; and conſequently I ſhall have an opportunity of an eaſie ſolace for the loſs of my Places, and the Diſgrace I have met with from the King. I am,

SIR,

Yours, &c.

[203] # MEMOIRS

OF

North-*America;*

Containing a Geographical Deſcription of that vaſt Continent; the Cuſtoms and Commerce, of the Inhabitants, &c.

SIR,

IN my former Letters, I preſented you with a view of the *Engliſh* and *French* Colonies, the Commerce of *Canada*, the Navigation upon the Rivers and Lakes of that Country, the courſe of ſailing from *Europe* to *North-America*, the ſeveral Attempts made by the *Engliſh* to maſter the *French* Colonies, the Incurſions of the *French* upon New-*England*, and upon the *Iroqueſe* Country: In a word, Sir, I have reveal'd a great many things, that for reaſons of State or Politicks, have been hitherto conceal'd; inſomuch, that if you were capable of making me a Sacrifice to your Reſentment, 'tis now in your power to ruine me at Court, by producing my Letters.

All that I writ in the foregoing Letters, and the whole ſubſtance of the Memoirs I now ſend you, is truth as plain as the Sun-ſhine. I flatter no Man, and I ſpare no body. I ſcorn to be partial; I beſtow due praiſe upon thoſe who are in no capacity to ſerve [204] me, and I cenſure the Conduct of others, that are capable of doing me an injury by indirect Methods. I am not influenc'd by that principle of Intereſt and Party-making, that is the rule of ſome folks words. I ſacrifice all to the love of Truth, and write with no other view, than to give you a juſt Repreſentation of things as they are. 'Tis beneath me to mince or alter the matter of fact, contain'd either in the Letters I ſent you ſome ten or twelve years agoe, or in theſe Memoirs. In the courſe of my Voyages and Travels, I took care to keep particular Journals of every thing; but a minute relation of all Particulars, would be irkſom to you, beſides, that the trouble of taking a copy of the Journals, before I have an opportunity of ſhewing you the Original, would require more time than I can well ſpare. In theſe Memoirs you'll find as much as will ſerve to form a perfect *Idea* of the vaſt Continent of North-*America*. In the courſe of our Correſpondence from the year 1683, to this time, I ſent you five and twenty Letters, of all which I have kept a double very carefully. My only view in writing of theſe Letters, was to inform you of the moſt eſſential things; for I was unwilling to perplex and confound your Thoughts, with an infinity of uncommon things, that have happen'd in that Country. If you'll conſult my Maps, as you read the abovemention'd Letters, you'll find a juſt Repreſentation of all the places I have ſpoke of. Theſe Maps are very particular, and I dare aſſure you, they are the correcteſt yet extant. My Voyage upon the Long River, gave me an opportunity of making that little Map, which I ſent you from *Miſſilimakinac* in

1699 [1689], with my ſixteenth Letter. 'Tis true, it gives only a bare Deſcription of that River, and the River of the *Miſſouris:* But it requir'd more time than I could ſpare, to make it more compleat, by a knowledge of the adjacent Countries, which have [205] hitherto been unknown to all the World, as well as that great River, and which I would never have viſited, if I had not been fully inſtructed in every thing that related to it, and convoy'd by a good Guard. I have plac'd the Map of *Canada* at the front of theſe Memoirs, and deſire that favour of you, that you would not ſhew it to any body under my Name. To the latter part I have ſubjoyn'd an Explication of the *Marine*, and other difficult Terms, made uſe of in my Letters, as well as in theſe Memoirs; which you'll pleaſe to conſult, when you meet with a word that you do not underſtand.

A ſhort Deſcription of Canada.

You'll think, Sir, that I advance a Paradox, when I acquaint you that New-*France*, commonly call'd *Canada*, comprehends a greater extent of Ground, than the half of *Europe:* But pray mind what proof I have for that Aſſertion. You know that *Europe* extends South and North, from the 35 to the 72 degree of Latitude, or if you will, from *Cadiz* to the North Cape on the confines of *Lapland;* and that it's Longitude reaches from the 9*th* to the 94*th* Degree, that is, from the River *Oby*, to the Weſt Cape in *Yſlandia*. But at the ſame time, if we take the greateſt breadth of *Europe*, from Eaſt to Weſt, from the imaginary Canal, (for Inſtance) between the *Tanais* and the *Volga*, to *Dinglebay* in *Ireland*, it makes but 66 Degrees of Longitude, which contain more Leagues than the Degrees allotted to it towards the Polar Circle, though theſe are more numerous, by reaſon that the degrees of Longitude are unequal: And ſince we are wont to meaſure Provinces, Iſlands, and Kingdoms by the ſpace of Ground, I am of the Opinion, that we ought to make uſe of the ſame Standard, with reſpect to the four parts of the World. The Geographers who parcel [206] out the Earth in their Cloſets, according to their fancy; theſe Gentlemen, I ſay, might have been aware of this advance, if they had been more careful. But, to come to *Canada;*

All the World knows, that *Canada* reaches from the 39*th* to the 65*th* Deg. of Latitude, that is, from the South ſide of the Lake *Erriè*, to the North ſide of *Hudſon*'s Bay; and from the 284*th*, to the 336*th* Degree of Longitude, *viz.* from the River *Miſſiſipi*, to Cape *Raſe* in the Iſland of New-*Foundland.*[1] I affirm therefore, that *Europe* has but 11 Degrees of Latitude, and 33 of Longitude, more than *Canada*, in which I comprehend the Iſland of New-*Foundland*, *Acadia*, and all the other Countries that lye to the Northward of the River of St. *Laurence*, which is the pretended great boundary that ſevers the *French* Colonies from the *Engliſh.* Were I to reckon in all the Countries that lye to the North-Weſt of *Canada*, I ſhould

[1] The claim for Canadian limits as far south as 39° of latitude would extend them nearly to the Ohio River. Longitude was reckoned at this time from west to east entirely around the globe, the prime meridian in most common use being that of the Canary Islands, supposed to be the "Fortunate Isles" of Ptolemy. The longitude of the Mississippi, therefore, at its eastern projection would be about 284°; that of Cape Race was usually estimated at about 330°. — ED.

find it larger than *Europe:* But I confine my ſelf to what is diſcover'd, known and own'd; I mean, to the Countries in which the *French* trade with the Natives for Beavers, and in which they have Forts, Magazines, Miſſionaries, and ſmall Settlements.

'Tis above a Century and a half ſince *Canada* was diſcover'd. *John Veraſan* was the firſt Diſcoverer, though he got nothing by it, for the Savages eat him up.[1] *James Cartier* was the next that went thither, but after ſailing with his Ship above *Quebec*, he return'd to *France* with a ſorry opinion of the Country.[2] At laſt better Sailors were imploy'd in the Diſcovery, and trac'd the River of St. *Laurence* more narrowly: And about the beginning of the laſt Century, a Colony was ſent thither from *Rouan*, which ſetled there after a great deal of oppoſition from the Natives.[3] At this day the Colony is ſo

---

[1] Giovanni da Verrazzano was a Florentine navigator, who, sailing under the French flag, explored the coast of North America (1524) from Carolina to Newfoundland. The authenticity of his narrative has been doubted, and for a long time there was a critical controversy concerning his *Relation;* but its genuineness is now generally accepted by historians. See *Old South Leaflets*, No. 17, and authorities therein cited; also Harrisse, *Discovery of North America* (London and Paris, 1892), pp. 218–228. One of his earliest biographers relates his death upon a later voyage at the hands of the Indians. — ED.

[2] For an account of Cartier's explorations, and the recent investigations concerning them, see Pope, *Jacques Cartier* (Ottawa, 1889); Dionne, *Jacques Cartier* (Quebec, 1889). A version of his *Voyages* was published by Stevens (Montreal, 1890). Cartier made three (possibly four) voyages to North America (1534–42), discovered and explored the St. Lawrence as far as Lachine rapids, and made full reports of his adventures. His accounts are far from being as discouraging as Lahontan represents. — ED.

[3] Lahontan here refers to the first permanent settlement of New France, made by Champlain upon the site of Quebec (1608). The colony was fostered by a company of Rouen merchants — see Biggar, *Early Trading Companies of New France* (Toronto, 1901). The opposition of the aborigines is exaggerated by our author. — ED.

populous, that 'tis computed to contain 180000 Souls.[1] I have already given you ſome account of that Country in [207] my Letters, and therefore ſhall now only point to the moſt noted places, and take notice of what may gratifie your curioſity beyond what you have yet heard.

We are at a loſs to find the Head of the River of St. *Laurence*, for tho' we have traced it ſeven or eight hundred Leagues up, yet we could never reach its ſource; the remoteſt place that the *Coureurs de Bois* go to, being the Lake *Lenemipigon*, which diſimbogues into the *Upper Lake*, as the *Upper Lake* do's into the Lake of *Hurons*, the Lake of *Hurons* into that of *Errié* alias *Conti*, and that of *Errié*, into the Lake of *Frontenac*,[2] which forms this laſt great River, that runs for twenty Leagues with a pretty gentle Stream, and ſweeps thro' thirty more with a very rapid Current, till it reaches the City of *Monreal;* from whence it continues its courſe with ſome moderation to the City of *Quebec;* and after that ſpreads out, and inlarges it ſelf by degrees to its Mouth, which lies a hundred Leagues further. If we may credit the North-Country Savages, this River takes its riſe from the great Lake of the *Aſſinipouals*, which they give out to be larger than any of the Lakes I mention'd but now, being ſituated at the

---

[1] This should be 18,000. Ferland, *Cours d'Histoire du Canada* (Quebec, 1865), ii, p. 390, gives the exact population in 1713 as 18,440, taken from the archives of the diocese of Quebec. — ED.

[2] Lake Lenemipigon was the present Nipigon, north of Lake Superior (Upper Lake). For the first exploration of this region see p. 136, note 1, *ante;* also Thwaites, *Early Western Travels* (Cleveland, 1904), ii, p. 87, note 45. Lake Ontario was frequently called "Frontenac" by the French. — ED.

diſtance of fifty or ſixty Leagues from the Lake of *Lenemipigon*.[1] The River of St. *Laurence* is 20 or 22 Leagues broad at its Mouth, in the middle of which there's an Iſland call'd *Anticoſti*, which is twenty Leagues long. This Iſland belongs to the Sieur *Joliet* a *Canadan*, who has built a little fortify'd Magazine upon it, to guard his Goods and his Family from the Incurſions of the *Eskimaux*, of whom more anon. He deals with the other Savage Nations, namely, the *Montagnois*, and the *Papipanachois* in Arms and Ammunition, by way of exchange for the Skins of Sea-Wolves or Sea-Calves, and ſome other Furs.[2]

Over againſt this Iſland, to the Southward of it, we find the Iſle call'd *L'Iſle Percèe*, which is a great Rock with a paſſage bor'd through it, in which [208] the Sloops can only paſs.[3] In time of Peace the *Biſcayans* of *France*, and the *Normans*, us'd to fiſh for Cod at this place: For here that Fiſh are very plentiful, and at the ſame time larger, and more proper for drying than thoſe of *New-Foundland*. But there are two great Inconveniencies that attend the fiſhing

[1] The Assinipouals were the present Assiniboin Indians, a large Siouan tribe of the Northwest region. The lake here referred to was Winnipeg. — ED.

[2] For Jolliet and the seignoiry of Anticosti, see pp. 243, 244, note 2, *ante*. The Indians mentioned are noticed on p. 261, note 2. — ED.

[3] Isle Percé (now called Percé Rock) is a remarkable cliff of primitive rock separated from the mainland of Gaspé by the action of the waves and ice, which have also worn through it a great arch from which the islet takes its name. The village of Percé, near by, is one of the oldest and most interesting fishing stations on the continent. For an excellent and well-illustrated description, see Clarke, "Percé: a brief sketch of its geology," in *Report* of New York State Paleontologist, 1903. — ED.

upon this Iſland; one is, that the Ships ride in great danger, unleſs they have good Anchors and ſtrong Cables; another Inconvenience is, that this place affords neither Gravel nor Flint-ſtones to ſtretch out the Fiſh upon before the Sun, and that the Fiſhermen are forc'd to make uſe of a ſort of Hurdles.

There are other Fiſhing-places beſides this, which lie ſome Leagues higher up upon the ſame ſide of the River. Such is that call'd *Gaſpè*, where the Ships Crew ſometimes trade in Skins with the *Gaſpeſians*, to the prejudice of the Proprietors of this River. The other places for Cod-fiſh lie toward *Monts notre dame*, in the little Bays or Rivers that empty themſelves into the River of St. *Laurence*.[1]

On the other ſide of the River, there lies the wide extended Country of *Labrador*, or of the *Eskimaux*, who are ſuch a wild barbarous People, that no means whatſoever, have hitherto been able to civiliſe 'em. One would think that good old *Homer* had this People in his view, when he ſpeaks of the Cyclopes; for the Character of the one, ſuits the other admirably well, as it appears from theſe four Verſes, in the ninth

[1] Gaspé is an Indian term signifying "that which is separated," and originally applied only to Cape Forillon, a lonely detached rock at the extremity of the peninsula. It is now extended to the entire broad peninsula between the St. Lawrence and the Bay of Chaleurs, the coast of which is dotted with French-Canadian fishing villages. Monts Notre Dame was the early name for the Chicchack (Shickshock) range, which traverses the peninsula and forms the watershed. The interior of Gaspé is still a forested wilderness, and the home of big game. At several points wealthy Americans have of recent years bought large tracts for game preserves; on the other hand, the lumber industry, also largely capitalized by Americans, is rapidly making inroads into the forest. — Ed.

Book of his *Odyſſea*, which are ſo pretty, that I cannot forbear inſerting them in this place.

Τοῖσιν δ' ὔτ' ἀγοραὶ βυληφόροι ὔτε θέμιδες.
Ἀλλ' οἵγ' ὑψηλῶν ὀρέων ναίοισι κάρηνα
Ἔν σπέεσι γλαφυροῖσι· θεμιστεύει δὲ ἕκαστος
Παίδων ἠδ' ἀλόχων· ὐδ' ἀλλήλων ἀλέγοισι.

[209] That is; this People do not perplex themſelves with voluminous Laws, and vexatious Suits; they delight only in the tops of Mountains, and deep Caves, and every one confines his care to the management of his own Family, without troubling his Head about his Neighbour. The *Danes* were the firſt diſcoverers of this Country, which is full of Ports, Havens, and Bays, that the *Quebec* Barques reſort to in the Summer, in order to truck with the Savages for the Skins of Sea-Calves.[1] The Commerce I ſpeak of, is carried on after this manner. As ſoon as the *Quebec* Barques come to an Anchor, theſe Devils come on board of them in their little Canows made of the Skins of Sea-Calves, in the form of a Weavers Shuttle, with a hole in the middle of it, reſembling that of a Purſe, in which they ſtow themſelves with Ropes, ſitting ſquat upon their Brech. Being ſet in this faſhion they row with little Slices, ſometimes to the Right, and ſometimes to the Left, without bending their Body for fear of Over-

[1] It is not probable that Lahontan here refers to the early discovery of this country by the Norsemen. Gomara, in *Histoire Generalle des Indes Occidentalis et Terres neuves*, translated into French and published in 1569, declares that the Bretons and Danes made the first voyages to Baccaleos — a term used for both the Newfoundland and Labrador coasts. Lahontan is probably following this authority, or a similar one, for his historical remarks; the description of the trading is evidently the report of an eye witness. — ED.

ſetting. As ſoon as they are near the Barque, they hold up their Skins upon the end of the Oar, and at the ſame time make a demand of ſo many Knives, Powder, Ball, Fuſees, Axes, Kettles, *&c.* In fine, every one ſhews what he has, and mentions what he expects in exchange: And ſo when the Bargain is concluded, they deliver and receive their Goods upon the end of a Stick. As theſe pitiful Fellows uſe the precaution of not going on board of our Boats, ſo we take care not to ſuffer too great a number of Canows to ſurround us; for they have carry'd off oftner than once, ſome of our ſmall Veſſels, at a time when the Seamen were buſied in hauling in the Skins, and delivering out the other Goods. Here, we are oblig'd to be very vigilant in the Night-time, for they know how to make great Sloops, that will hold thirty or forty Men, and run as faſt as the Wind: And 'tis for this [210] reaſon that the *Malouins*, who fiſh for Cod at *Petit Nord*, and the *Spaniards* who follow the ſame Fiſhery at *Portochoua*,[1] are oblig'd to fit out long Barques to ſcour the Coaſt and purſue 'em; for almoſt every year they ſurpriſe ſome of the Crew on ſhoar, and cut their Throats, and ſometimes they carry off the Veſſel. We are aſſur'd, that their number of Warriours, or Men that bear Arms, amounts to thirty thouſand; but they are ſuch cowardly fellows, that five hundred *Cliſtino's* from *Hudſons*

[1] French fishers from St. Malo and other Breton towns were among the earliest explorers of the Newfoundland coast. They termed all of the great upper peninsula of the island, from White Bay northward, Petit Nord, and it was their favorite fishing ground. The Spanish Basque fishermen frequented the northwest coast, and their port was Portachua, now called Old Port au Choix. — Ed.

Bay, ufed to defeat five or fix thoufand of them.[1] They are poffefs'd of a very large Country, extending from over againft the Ifles of *Mingan* to *Hudfons* Streight. They crofs over to the Ifland of *Newfound-Land* every day, at the Streight of *Belle* Ifle, which is not above feven Leagues over; but they never came fo far as *Placentia*, for fear of meeting with other Savages there.

Hudfon's Bay adjoyns to this *Terra* of *Labrador*, and extends from the 52*d* Degree and thirty Minutes to the 63 of Latitude. The Original of its name was this. Captain *Henry Hudfon*, an *Englifh* Man by Birth, obtain'd a Ship from the *Dutch*, in order to trace a paffage to *China* through an imaginary Streight to the Northward of North-*America*. He had firft form'd a defign of going by the way of *Nova Zembla;* but upon feeing the Memoirs of a *Danifh* Pilot, who was a friend of his, he drop'd that thought. This Pilot, namely, *Frederick Anfchild*, had fet out from *Norway* or *Yflandia*, fome years before, with a defign to find out a Paffage to *Japan* by *Davis*'s Streight, which is the Chimerical Streight I fpoke of.[2]

[1] The Cristinaux (Killistinoe, Clistino) Indians are a large branch of the Algonquian family, that roam the Hudson Bay country and far to the west. They are now known as the Cree, their present number being reckoned at twelve thousand. For further details of this tribe see Henry, *Travels and Adventures* (Bain, ed., Boston, 1901), p. 246. — ED.

[2] The standard authority for the voyages of Hudson is Asher, *Henry Hudson the Navigator* (London, 1860), printed for the Hakluyt Society, vol. xxvii. The editor in his introduction says that the story of the Danish pilot Anschild (Anskoeld) is a myth, growing out of the expedition of a Pole, Johannes Kolnus, whose voyage (1476) was cited by the geographers of the sixteenth century in distorted terms. See also Read, *Historical Inquiry concerning Henry Hudson* (Albany, 1866); De Costa, *Sailing Directions of Henry Hudson* (Albany, 1869). — ED.

The firft Land he defcry'd was *Savage* Bay, feated on the North fide of the *Terra* of *Labrador;* then fweeping along the Coaft, he enter'd a Streight, which about twenty or thirty years afterwards, was chriften'd *Hudfon*'s Streight. After that, fteering to the Weftward, he came upon fome [211] Coaft that run North and South; upon which he ftood to the North, flattering himfelf with the hopes of finding an open paffage to crofs the Sea of *Jeffo;* but after failing to the Latitude of the Polar Circle, and running the rifque of perifhing in the Ice, I do not know how often, without meeting with any paffage or open Sea, he took up a refolution of turning back; but the Seafon was then fo far advanc'd, and the Ice fo cover'd up the furface of the Water, that he was forc'd to put in to *Hudfon*'s *Bay*, and winter there in a Harbour, where feveral Savages furnifh'd his Crew with Provifions and excellent Skins. As foon as the Sea was open, he return'd to *Denmark.* Now, Captain *Hudfon* being afterwards acquainted with this *Dane*, undertook upon his Journals to attempt a paffage to *Japan* through the Streight of *Davis;* but the Enterprife fail'd, as well as that of one *Button*, and fome others.[1] However, *Hudfon* put in to the Bay that now goes

[1] From 1576 to 1632 there were sixteen English voyages of exploration for a Northwest Passage. That of John Davis, whose name is commemorated in Davis Strait, occurred in 1585. The same navigator made two later voyages to Arctic regions, and was finally murdered by Japanese pirates in the East Indies (1606). See Markham, "Voyages and Works of John Davis, Navigator" (London, 1880), *Publications* of Hakluyt Society, No. 59. Sir Thomas Button followed on the track of Henry Hudson, and explored the great bay bearing the latter's name (1612–13); he was knighted for his services. See Christy, *Voyages of Captain Luke Foxe and Captain Thomas James* (London, 1894), Hakluyt Society, No. 88. — Ed.

by his name, where he receiv'd a great quantity of Skins from the Savages; after that, he difcover'd *New Holland*, which is now call'd *New-York*,[1] and fome other Countries retaining to *New-England:* upon the whole, 'tis not fair to call this Streight and this Bay, by the name of *Hudfon;* in regard that the abovemention'd *Dane*, *Frederick Anfchild*, was the firft difcoverer of them; he being the firft *European* that defcry'd the Countries of North-*America*, and chalk'd out the way to the others. Upon this *Hudfon's* Journals, the *Englifh* made feveral attempts to fettle a Commerce with the *Americans.* The great quantity of Beaver-Skins and other Furs that he purchas'd of the Savages while he Winter'd in the Bay, put the notion into the heads of fome *Englifh* Merchants, who thereupon form'd a Company for the carrying on of this New Commerce. With this view, they fitted out fome Ships under the command of Captain *Nelfon*, who loft fome of 'em in the Ice not far from the [212] Streight, having efcap'd narrowly himfelf. However, he enter'd the Bay, and plac'd himfelf at the Mouth of a great River, which rifes towards the Lake of the *Afimpouals*, and falls into the Bay at a place where he built a Redoubt, and mounted fome Cannon upon it.[2] In the fpace

---

[1] Hudson did not discover the great bay of that name until his fourth voyage (1610–11), whence he never returned. His exploration of New Holland (preferably New Netherlands) occurred upon his third voyage (1609). — Ed.

[2] This voyage of Nelson is hypothetical, apparently invented to account for the name Nelson River. The wintering place at its mouth was named Port Nelson by Button, in honor of his sailing master, who died and was buried there; thence the name extended to the river. In the confusion of Lahontan's account, it is uncertain whether he refers to the organization of the Hudson's Bay Company (1670), or to the

of three or four years after, the *Engliſh* made ſome other little Forts near that River, which prov'd a conſiderable baulk to the Commerce of the *French*, who found that the Savages who us'd to deal with 'em in Furs on the North ſide of the upper Lake, were not then to be ſeen.

It came to paſs in proceſs of time, but how I cannot tell, that one *Ratiſſon*, and one *Grozelier*, met in that great Lake ſome *Cliſtino*'s, who promis'd to conduct 'em to the bottom of the Bay, where the *Engliſh* had not yet penetrated. In effect, the *Cliſtino*'s were as good as their word; for they ſhew'd 'em the place they ſpoke of, beſides ſeveral other Rivers upon which there was a fair proſpect of making ſuch Settlements, as would carry on a great trade in Skins with ſeveral Savage Nations.[1] Theſe two *Frenchmen* return'd to the Upper Lake, the ſame way that they went, and from thence made the beſt of their way to *Quebec*, where they offer'd to the chief Merchants of the place, to carry Ships to *Hudſon*'s Bay; but their

---

incorporation of "The Company of the Merchants of London, Discoverers of the North-West Passage," which latter received its charter in 1612 (Hakluyt Society, No. 89, pp. 642-664). — Ed.

[1] Pierre Esprit Radisson and Médard Chouart des Groseilliers were among the most interesting and daring adventurers of the early years of New France. It is not beyond probability that Lahontan had known them either in Canada or at the English court. Their alleged overland visit to Hudson Bay, on what is known as their "fourth voyage," is open to doubt. For the evidence see Campbell, "Radisson and Groseillers," in Parkman Club *Papers* (Milwaukee, 1896); Wis. Hist. Soc. *Proceedings*, 1895, pp. 88-116; Bryce, *The Remarkable History of Hudson's Bay Company* (Toronto, 1900), pp. 4-7. The latter author (pp. 39-46) has unearthed some new evidence concerning Radisson's later life and death in England (1710). *Radisson's Voyages* (Boston, 1885) are published by the Prince Society, No. 16; see also *Wis. Hist. Colls.*, xi, pp. 64-96; Dionne, "Chouart et Radisson," in Can. Roy. Soc. *Proceedings*, 1893, 1894. — Ed.

Project was rejected. In fine, having met with this repulse, they went to *France*, in hopes of a more favourable hearing at Court: But after the presenting of Memorial upon Memorial, and spending a great deal of Money, they were treated as whimsical Fellows. Upon that occasion the King of *England*'s Ambassadour did not lose the opportunity of perswading them to go to *London*, where they met with such a favourable Reception, that they got several Ships, which they carry'd to the Bay, not without difficulty, and built several Forts in different places, [213] that did great service in promoting the Commerce.[1] Then the Court of *France* repented, though too late, that they did not give ear to their Memorials: and finding no other remedy, resolv'd to dislodge the *English* at any rate. In effect, they attack'd 'em vigorously by Sea and Land, and dispossess'd 'em of all their Forts, excepting Fort *Nelson*, where they could not expect such an easie Conquest.[2] Some years after, the *English* resolv'd to use their utmost efforts to retake these Posts; and their resolution was crown'd with Success, for they dislodg'd the *French* in their turn, and at this day the

[1] The first permanent trading fort (or factory) in Hudson Bay was that erected by Groseilliers upon Rupert River in the autumn of 1668, and christened Fort Charles in honor of the king. The success of this trading venture led to the chartering (1670) of the Hudson's Bay Company. — ED.

[2] Radisson organized an expedition in the French interest in 1682, set out for the bay, captured a ship and the English governor, and built Fort Bourbon not far from Fort Nelson. Upon his return (1684), when France was on the point of dispatching another squadron under his guidance, he deserted to the English, returned to Fort Bourbon, and retook it and its furs in the interest of the Company. The authorities of New France resolved on retribution, and an overland expedition (1685–87), headed by De Troyes and d'Iberville captured all the forts except that upon Nelson River. See p. 217, note 3, *ante*. — ED.

French are making preparations to repay 'em in their own Coin.[1]

That Country is ſo cold for ſeven or eight Months of the year, that the Sea freezes ten Foot deep, the Trees and the very Stones ſplit, the Snow is ten or twelve Foot deep upon the Ground, for above ſix Months of the year, and during that ſeaſon, no body can ſtir out of Doors, without running the riſque of having their Noſe, Ears and Feet mortified by the Cold. The paſſage from *Europe* to that Country is ſo difficult and dangerous, by reaſon of the Ice and the Currents, that one muſt be reduc'd to the laſt degree of miſery, or be blind to a fooliſh heighth, that undertakes ſuch a wretched Voyage.

'Tis now time to paſs from *Hudſon*'s Bay, to the *Superior* or *Upper Lake.* 'Tis eaſier to make this Voyage upon Paper, than to go actually through it; for you muſt ſail almoſt a hundred Leagues up the River of *Machakandibi*, which is ſo rapid and full of Cataracts, that a light Canow work'd by ſix Watermen, ſhall not ſail 'em under thirty or thirty five days. At the head of this River we meet with a little Lake of the ſame name, from whence we are oblig'd to a Land-carriage of ſeven Leagues, to get at the River of *Michipikoton*, which we run down in ten or twelve days, though at the ſame [214] time we

[1] After the first Canadian punitive expedition (see preceding note), each nation made frequent armed attempts to dislodge the other from the lucrative trading posts of Hudson Bay. See the brief summary in Bryce, *Hudson's Bay Company*, pp. 47–55. Lahontan probably refers to the preparations being made for d'Iberville's brilliant expedition of 1697. The French were not finally expelled from the forts on the lower, or James, Bay until after the treaty of Utrecht (1713). — ED.

have ſeveral Land-carriages upon it: For going down this River we paſs ſeveral Cataracts, where we are oblig'd either to carry our Canows by Land, or to drag 'em back again.[1] Thus we arrive at the *Upper Lake*, which is reckon'd to be five hundred Leagues in Circumference, including the windings of the Creeks, and little Gulfs. This little freſh-water Sea is calm enough from the beginning of *May*, to the end of *September*. The South ſide is the ſafeſt for the Canows, by reaſon of the many Bays, and little Rivers, where one may put in in caſe of a Storm. There is no ſetled Savage Nation upon the brinks of the Lake, that I know of. 'Tis true indeed, that in Summer ſeveral Northern Nations come to Hunt and Fiſh in theſe parts, and bring with 'em the Beaver-Skins they have got in the Winter, in order to truck with the *Coureurs de Bois*, who do not fail to meet 'em there every year. The places where the Interview happens, are *Bagouaſch*, *Lemipiſaki*, and *Chagouamigon*.[2] 'Tis ſome years ſince Mr. *Dulhut* built

[1] Probably Lahontan had conversed at Mackinac with natives or coureurs des bois who described the journey from Hudson Bay to Lake Superior. The "River of Machakandibi" is likely the present Moose River, whence the portage to the Michipiciton is not long. — ED.

[2] It is probable that Lahontan had his information concerning Lake Superior from Duluth (see p. 73, note 1, *ante*), who roamed this region for a dozen years. Bagouasch is a river on the north side of the lake, east of Nipigon, where, according to an inscription upon a map of 1756, Duluth had had a fort. Neill, *Minn. Hist. Colls.*, v, p. 417, identifies (but without giving reasons) Lemipisaki with Nipigon; but there is a greater probability that it was Nemitsakouat, at Bois Brulé River, which empties into Lake Superior to the west of Chequamegon Bay; Duluth had a rendezvous with the Indians, on the Bois Brulé. See *Wis. Hist. Colls.*, xvi, p. 108. Chequamegon was a well-known post on the present bay of that name, where a fort was first built by Radisson and Groseilliers. See Thwaites, "Story of Chequamegon," in *How George Rogers Clark Won the Northwest*, etc. (Chicago, 1903). — ED.

a Fort of Pales or Stakes upon this Lake, where he had large Magazines of all ſorts of Goods. That Fort was call'd *Camaniſtigoyan*, and did conſiderable Diſſervice to the *Engliſh* Settlements in *Hudſon*'s *Bay;* by reaſon that it ſav'd ſeveral Nations the trouble of transporting their Skins to that Bay.[1] Upon that Lake we find Copper Mines, the Mettal of which is ſo fine and plentiful, that there is not a ſeventh part loſs from the Oar.[2] It has ſome pretty large Iſlands, which are repleniſh'd with Elks and wild Aſſes; but there's ſcarce any that goes to hunt upon 'em, by reaſon of the danger of croſſing over. In fine, this Lake abounds with Sturgeons, Trouts, and white Fiſh. The Climate is unſufferably cold for ſix Months of the year, and the Snow joyn'd to the Froſt, commonly freezes the Water of the Lake for ten or twelve Leagues over.

[215] From the *Superiour* or *Upper Lake*, I ſteer to that of *Hurons*, to which I allot four hundred Leagues in Circumference. Now to make this Lake, you muſt ſail down by the fall call'd *Saut St. Mary*, which I deſcrib'd in my fifteenth Letter. This Lake is ſituated in a fine Climate, as you'll perceive from

---

[1] Kamanistiquia (Camanistigoyan) was the site of Duluth's first western fort, erected in 1678. It was later abandoned until 1717, when the Canadian authorities sent Sieur de la Noué to restore it. This post was maintained throughout the French regime, and was the site of the famous Fort William, the North West Company's headquarters well into the nineteenth century. It was at the mouth of Three Rivers, and commanded the Grand Portage route to the interior, along what is now the boundary between Minnesota and Ontario. The locations on Lahontan's map are obviously incorrect. — ED.

[2] For early copper mines on the shores of Lake Superior, consult *Wis. Hist. Colls.*, xvi, xvii. — ED.

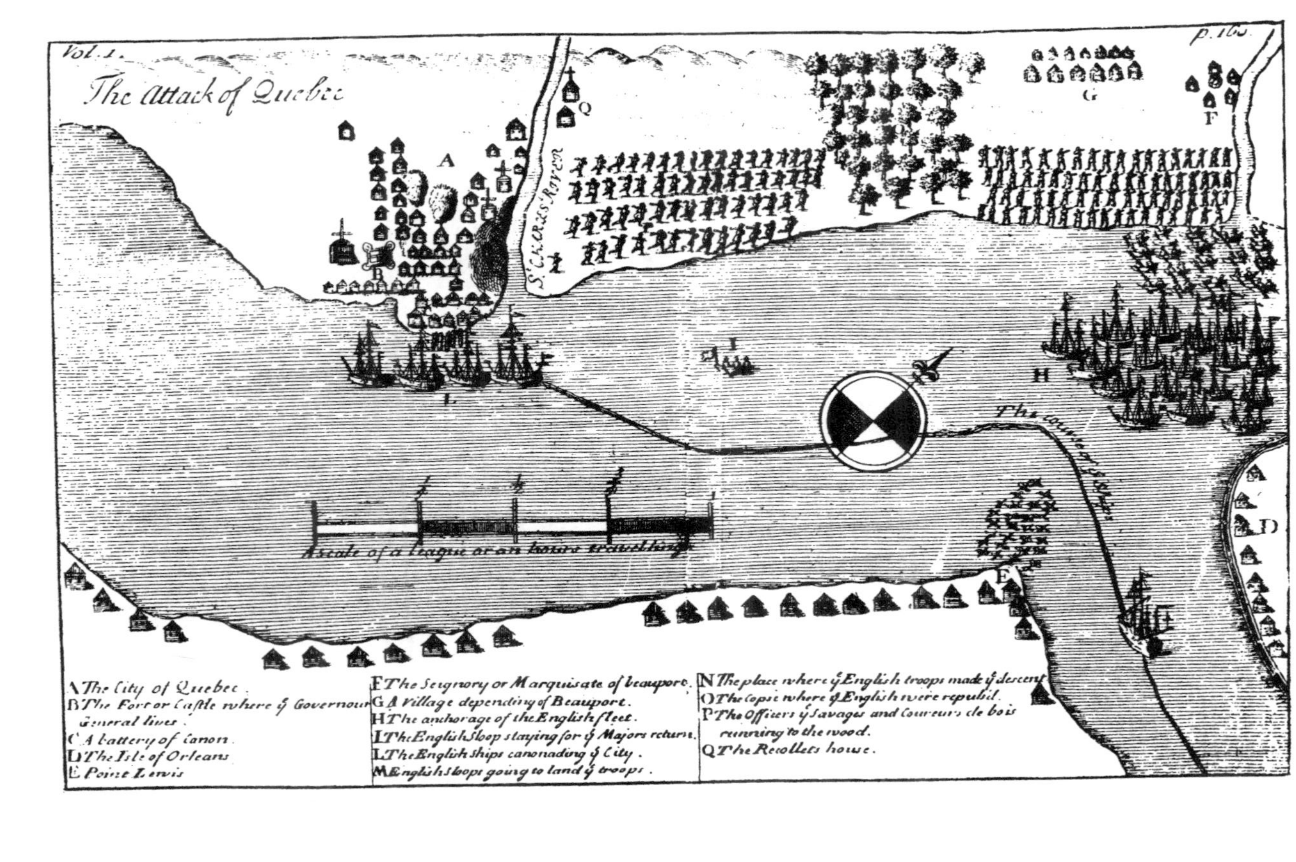
Vol. I.
The Attack of Quebec
S.t Charles River
The course of y.e Ships
A scale of a league or an houre travelling
A The City of Quebec.
B The Fort or Castle where y.e Governour General lives.
C A battery of canon.
D The Isle of Orleans
E Pointe Lewis
F The Seignory or Marquisate of beaupore.
G A Village depending of Beaupore.
H The anchorage of the English fleet.
I The English Sloop staying for y.e Majors return.
L The English ships canonading y.e City.
M English sloops going to land y.e troops.
N The place where y.e English troops made y.e descent.
O The copse where y.e English were repulsd.
P The Officers y.e Savages and Coureurs de bois running to the wood.
Q The Recollets house.

the Map. The North ſide of it is beſt for the Navigation of Canows, by reaſon of the frequency of Iſles which afford ſhelter in bad Weather. The South ſide is pleaſanter, and more convenient for the Hunting of Deer, which are there very plentiful. The figure of this Lake comes near to an equilateral Triangle. Of all its Iſles, that call'd *Manitoualin*, is the moſt conſiderable, being above twenty Leagues long, and ten broad. In former times, the *Outaouas* of the Nations of *Talon* and *Sable* dwelt in it; but the dread they were under upon the account of the *Iroqueſe*, oblig'd both them and their Neighbours to retire to *Miſſilimakinac.* That part of the Continent that faces this Iſland, is inhabited by the *Nockès* and the *Miſſitagues*, in two different Villages, which are twenty Leagues diſtant, the one from the other.[1] Towards the Eaſt end of this Iſland, we fall in with the River *des Francois*, which I took notice of in my ſixteenth Letter. 'Tis as broad as the *Seine* is at *Paris*, and runs not above forty Leagues in length from its ſource in the Lake *Nepicerini*, to its Mouth. To the North-Weſt of this River, there lies the Bay of *Toranto*, which is twenty, or five and twenty Leagues long, and fifteen broad at its Mouth. This Bay receives a River that ſprings from a little Lake of the ſame name, and forms ſeveral Cataracts that

[1] For Manitoulin Island and its inhabitants, see p. 153, note 2, *ante*. The Nocké (Noquets) were an Algonquian tribe that early merged with others of the same family —see *Wis. Hist. Colls.*, xvi, pp. 117, 360; they left their name upon two bays in Upper Michigan. The Mississagua occupied the north shore of Lake Huron, and later built villages in the peninsula between Lakes Erie and Ontario. In 1901 they numbered about eight hundred, settled upon reservations in Ontario.—ED.

are equally impracticable both upon the afcent and defcent.[1] Upon the fide of this River you'll fee a Man's Head mark'd in my Map, which fignifies a large Village of the *Hurons*, that was deftroy'd by the *Iroquefe*. You may go from the fource of this River to the [216] Lake *Frontenac*, by making a Land-carriage to the River of *Tanaouate*, that falls into that Lake.[2] Upon the South fide of the Bay of *Toronto*, you fee the Fort call'd *Fort Suppofè*, which I mention'd in my 23*d* Letter, and about thirty Leagues to the Southward of that, you find the Country of *Theonontate*, which being formerly inhabited by the *Hurons*, was entirely depopulated by the *Iroquefe*.[3]

From thence I pafs directly to my Fort, without amufing you with the different Landskips I met with in the fpace of thirty Leagues. That Fort I have fpoke fo often of already, that without ftopping there, I fhall run directly to the Bay of *Sakinac*, reckoning it needlefs at the fame time, to take any notice of the many Shelves and Rocks that lye hid under the Water for two Leagues off the Coaft. This Bay is fixteen or feventeen Leagues long, and fix broad at its Mouth: In the middle of which we meet with two little Iflands, that are very ferviceable to the Paffengers; for if it were not for the con-

[1] Concerning the Bay of Toronto, see p. 273, note 1, *ante*. The text should read southwest, instead of northwest. — Ed.

[2] Lake Toronto is the modern Simcoe, whence the entire region was often called Toronto; see Scadding, *Toronto of Old* (Toronto, 1893). The "River of Tanouate," which appears upon a map of 1746, is to be identified with the chain of lakes ending in Trent River, falling into Quinté Bay. Lahontan's reference may be to the present Humber River, as the Toronto portage was used upon both or either of these routes. — Ed.

[3] See p. 154, note 2, *ante*. — Ed.

veniency of putting in there, they would be oblig'd for the moſt part, rather to march quite round the Bay, than to run the hazard of croſſing directly over in a Canow.[1] The River of *Sakinac* falls into the bottom of the Bay. This River runs ſixty Leagues in length, with a gentle Current, having only three little Cataracts that one may ſhoot without danger. 'Tis as broad as the *Seine* is at *Seve* Bridge. Once in two years the *Outaouas* and the *Hurons*, are wont to hunt great quantities of Beavers upon the confines of the River of *Sakinac*. Between the River I now ſpeak of, and *Miſſilimakinac*, we meet with no place that is worth our regard. As for *Miſſilimakinac* it ſelf, I have already imparted to you all that I can ſay of that Poſt, which is of ſo great importance to our Commerce, and at the ſame time ſent you a draught of it. I ſhall therefore purſue my courſe to the Lake *Errie*, remembring that I [217] deſcrib'd the *Ilineſe* Lake in my ſixteenth Letter.

The Lake *Erriè* is juſtly dignified with the illuſtrious name of *Conti;* for aſſuredly 'tis the fineſt Lake upon Earth. You may judge of the goodneſs of the Climate, from the Latitudes of the Countries that ſurround it. Its Circumference extends to two hundred and thirty Leagues; but it affords every where ſuch a charming Proſpect, that its Banks are deck'd with Oak-Trees, Elms, Cheſnut-Trees, Walnut-Trees, Apple-Trees, Plum-Trees, and Vines which bear their fine cluſters up to the very top of the Trees, upon a ſort of ground that lies as ſmooth as one's Hand. Such Ornaments as theſe, are ſuffi-

---

[1] See p. 143, *ante*. The islands were probably those now known as the Charity group. — ED.

cient to give riſe to the moſt agreeable *Idea* of a Landskip in the World. I cannot expreſs what vaſt quantities of Deer and Turkeys are to be found in theſe Woods, and in the vaſt Meads that lye upon the South ſide of the Lake. At the bottom of the Lake, we find wild Beeves upon the Banks of two pleaſant Rivers that diſembogue into it, without Cataracts or rapid Currents. It abounds with Sturgeon and white Fiſh; but Trouts are very ſcarce in it, as well as the other Fiſh that we take in the Lakes of *Hurons* and *Ilineſe*. 'Tis clear of Shelves, Rocks, and Banks of Sand; and has fourteen or fifteen fathom Water. The Savages aſſure us, that 'tis never diſturb'd with high Winds, but in the Months of *December*, *January*, and *February*, and even then but ſeldom, which indeed I am very apt to believe, for we had but very few Storms, when I winter'd in my Fort in 1688, though the Fort lay open to the Lake of *Hurons*. The Banks of this Lake are commonly frequented by none but Warriours, whether the *Iroqueſe*, the *Ilineſe*, the *Oumamis*, *&c.* and 'tis very dangerous to ſtop there. By this means it comes to paſs, that the Stags, Roe-Bucks and Turkeys, run in great Bodies up and down the ſhoar, all round the Lake. In former times the *Errieronons*, [218] and the *Andaſtogueronons*, liv'd upon the Confines of this Lake, but they were extirpated by the *Iroqueſe*, as well as the other Nations mark'd in the Map.[1]

[1] The identity of the Erie nation is much in doubt—see *Jesuit Relations*, xxi, pp. 313–315; but their habitat was originally south of Lake Erie, named for them. Andastes was a generic term by which the French designated a congeries of tribes in Pennsylvania, among whom were those known to the Dutch as Minquas, and to the

Upon the North ſide of the Lake we deſcry a point of Land, that ſhoots fifteen Leagues into the Main[1]; and about thirty Leagues beyond that to the Eaſtward, we meet with a ſmall River that takes its riſe near the Bay of *Ganaraske*, in the Lake of *Frontenac;* and would afford a ſhort paſſage from the one Lake to the other, if 'twere not incumber'd with Cataracts.[2] From thence to the Streight or Mouth of the Lake, you have thirty Leagues; the Streight being a League over, and fourteen Leagues long. Upon this Streight you ſee *Fort Suppoſè* mark'd in the Map, which is one of the Forts that I mention'd in my 23*d* Letter. From that imaginary Fort to the River of *Condè*, we have twenty Leagues.

The River of *Condè* runs ſixty Leagues in length without Cataracts, if we may credit the Savages, who aſſur'd me, that one may go from its ſource to another River that falls into the Sea, without any other Land-carriage than one of a League in length, between the [one] River and the other.[3] I ſaw only the Mouth of the firſt River, where our *Outaouas* tried their Limbs, as I told you in my fifteenth Letter. The Iſlands that you ſee mark'd in the Map at the bottom of the Lake *Erriè*,

English as Susquehannocks, or Conestogas. All these tribes were of Huron-Iroquois stock, but at war with the Five Nations. The suffix *ronons* (roanu) signified people, or tribe. — ED.

[1] For Long Point, Lake Erie, see p. 138, *ante*. — ED.

[2] The bay which Lahontan calls "Ganaraské," is usually designated upon maps of the period as Ganadoké, and is the present Hamilton Bay, or rather all the western end of Lake Ontario. It seems likely that the river must be the present Grand, which, as Lahontan indicates, was too rugged for a trade route. — ED.

[3] For the River of Condé, see p. 155, note 1, *ante*. Lahontan has here a confused notion of the Ohio, probably taken from Indian descriptions. — ED.

are repleniſh'd with Roe-Bucks, and with Fruit-Trees, which nature has generouſly provided, in order to entertain the Turkeys, Feaſants and Deer with their Fruit. In fine, if there were a clear and free paſſage for Veſſels, from *Quebec* to this Lake, it might be made the fineſt, the richeſt, and the moſt fertile Kingdom in the World: For over and above all the beauties I have mention'd, there are excellent Silver Mines about twenty Leagues up the Country, upon a certain Hill, from whence the Savages brought [219] us great lumps, that have yielded that precious Metal with little waſte.

From the Lake *Erriè*, I ſteer my courſe to that of *Frontenac*, which I could not forbear to ſpeak of in my ſeventh and ſeventeenth Letters. This Lake (as I intimated above) is 180 Leagues in Circumference, its figure is Oval, and its depth runs between twenty and twenty five Fathom. On the South ſide it receives ſeveral little Rivers, particularly thoſe of the *Tſonontouans*, of the *Onnontagues*, and of the *Famine*[1]; on the North ſide 'tis joyn'd by the Rivers of *Ganaraske*, and of *Teonontatè*. Its ſides are deck'd with tall Trees, and the ground is indifferent even and level, for it has no ſteep Coaſts. On the North ſide we meet with ſeveral little Gulfs. You may go from this Lake to that of *Hurons*, by going up the River *Tanaouate*, from whence you have a Land-carriage of ſix or eight Leagues to the River of *Toronto*, which falls into it. You may likewiſe have a paſſage from the Lake of *Frontenac*, to that of *Erriè*, through the Bay of *Ganaraskè*, by making a

[1] The Genessee, Oswego, and Salmon Rivers, New York. See p. 72, note 1, *ante*. — Ed.

Land-carriage from thence to a little River that's full of Cataracts. The Villages of the *Onnontagues*, *Tsonontouans*, *Goyogouans*, and *Onnoyoutes*, are not far diſtant from the Lake of *Frontenac.*[1] Theſe *Iroqueſe* Nations are very advantageouſly ſeated. They have a pleaſant and fertile Country; but they want Roe-Bucks and Turkeys, as well as Fiſh, of which their Rivers are altogether deſtitute, inſomuch that they are forc'd to fiſh in the Lake, and to broil or dry their Fiſh with a Fire, in order to keep 'em and tranſport 'em to their Villages. They are in like manner forc'd to range out of their own Territories, in queſt of Beavers in the Winter time, either towards *Ganaraskè*, or to the ſides of the Lake of *Toronto*, or elſe towards the great River of the *Outaouas;* where 'twould be an eaſie matter to cut all their Throats, by purſuing the courſe I laid down in my [220] Letters. I have already touch'd upon the Forts of *Frontenac* and *Niagara;* as well as upon the River of St. *Laurence*, which here takes leave of the Lakes, and purſues a compacter courſe to *Monreal* and *Quebec*, where its waters mingling with thoſe of the Sea, become ſo brackiſh, that they are not drinkable.

It remains only to give you a Deſcription of *Acadia*, and the Iſland of *Newfound-Land*, which are two Countries that differ widely from one another. The Coaſt of *Acadia* extends from *Kenebeki*, one of the Frontiers of *New-England*, to *l'Iſle Percèe*, near the Mouth of the River of St. *Laurence.* This Sea-Coaſt runs almoſt three hundred Leagues in length, and

[1] For the names of the Iroquois tribes, see p. 58, *ante*. — ED.

has upon it two great Navigable Bays, namely, the Bay call'd *Françoiſe*, and the Bay *des Chaleurs.*[1] It has a great many little Rivers, the Mouths of which are deep, and clean enough for the greateſt Ships. Theſe Rivers would afford a plentiful Salmon-fiſhery, if there were any body to undertake it; and moſt of 'em as well as the Gulfs that lies before 'em, furniſh ſuch Cods as we take at the *Iſle Percèe.* For in the Summer time, that ſort of Fiſh make in to the Coaſt in Shoals, eſpecially about the Iſlands of Cape *Breton*, and of St. *John.*[2] 'Tis true, the latter has no Harbours, and the former has none that receive any Veſſel above the burthen of a Barque; but if theſe two Iſlands were peopled, the Inhabitants might fit out Sloops to manage the Fiſhery; and towards the latter end of *Auguſt*, when the Fiſh are cur'd and ready, the Ships might come to an Anchor near the Land, and ſo take 'em in. Two Gentlemen of the name of *Amour* of *Quebec*[3], have a Settlement

[1] Bay Française was the early name for the Bay of Fundy, which was first adequately explored by Champlain (1604-08). The tercentenary of Champlain's landfall on the shores of the Bay of Fundy was appropriately celebrated in June, 1904: at Annapolis Royal (old Port Royal), the 21st and 22d, by the Nova Scotia Historical Society; at St. John, the 23d and 24th, by the New Brunswick Historical Society; at Isle St. Croix, at the head of Passamaquoddy Bay, the 25th, by the Maine Historical Society.

The Bay of Chaleurs was so named by Cartier, who (1534) experienced great heat therein. — Ed.

[2] St. John (St. Jean) was the present Prince Edward's Island. Harisse has shown (*Découverte de Terre-Neuve*) that the former name was first (1505) applied to the northeastern portion of Cape Breton Island, and afterwards by a misconception given to the smaller island in the Gulf of St. Lawrence. Cape Breton was the name used first for the southeast extremity of the island, now known by that name, because it was the haunt of certain fishers from Brittany. Later, the term was extended to the entire island, thus succeeding the name St. John. — Ed.

[3] Three sons of Mathieu d'Amours, councillor of the King at Quebec, received

for Beaver-hunting upon the River of St. *John;* which is a very pleaſant River, and adorn'd with Fields that are very fertile in Grain. 'Tis Navigable for twelve Leagues up, from its Mouth. Between the point of *Acadia*, and the Iſland [221] of Cape *Breton*, there is a Channel or Streight about two Leagues in breadth, which is deep enough to carry the greateſt Ships in *France*. 'Tis call'd the paſs *des Canſeaux*,[1] and would be much more frequented than it is, if the Merchant-men bound to *Canada*, would ſet out from *France* about the 15*th* of *March;* for then they might paſs that way, being aſſur'd of a clear paſſage at all ſeaſons of the year, whereas the Channel of Cape *de Raye*, is oftentimes cover'd with Ice in *April:* And by this contrivance, the Ships would arrive at *Quebec* in the beginning of *May*.

Moſt of the Countries of *Acadia* abound with Corn, Peaſe, Fruit, and Pulſe; and have a plain diſtinction of the four Seaſons of the year, nothwithſtanding that 'tis extream cold for three Months in Winter. Several places of *Acadia*, afford Maſts as ſtrong as thoſe we have from *Norway;* and if there were occaſion, all ſorts of Ships might be built there: For if you'll believe the Carpenters, the Oak of that Country is

---

grants on St. John River in 1684, and established what was known as "seigneuries sauvages" — stations for trade, hunting, and fishing — and a kind of pre-eminence over the neighboring Indians. Two of this family, Réné and Mathieu, aided (1696) in the defense of the St. John against the English. — ED.

[1] The strait of Canso (Campceaux, Canseaux) lies between Nova Scotia and Cape Breton Island. The word is undoubtedly of Indian origin, and was first applied to the point at the southeastern extremity of the mainland. On his map of 1612 Champlain called the strait "Le Passage Courant"; but by 1632 it appears as that of Campseau. — ED.

better than ours in *Europe.* In a word, 'tis a very fine Country; the Climate is indifferent temperate, the Air is pure and wholeſom, the Waters clear and light, and there's good accommodation for Hunting, Shooting, and Fiſhing. The Animals that we meet with there moſt commonly, are Beavers, Otters, and Sea-Calves, all of 'em being very numerous. Thoſe who love Meat are indebted to the Doctors, who perſwaded the Popes to Metamorphoſe theſe terreſtrial Animals into Fiſh; for they are allow'd to eat of 'em without ſcruple in the time of *Lent.* To be plain, the knowledge I have of that Country, makes me foreſee that the *Engliſh* will be maſters of it ſome time or other. I could give very plauſible reaſons for the Prophecy. They have already begun to ruine the Commerce that the *French* had with the Savages, and in a ſhort time, they'll compaſs its intire Deſtruction. The [222] *French* they will prize their Goods too high, though they are not ſo good as thoſe of the *Engliſh;* and yet the *Engliſh* ſell their Commodities cheaper. 'Twere a pity that we ſhould tamely leave to the *Engliſh* a Country, the Conqueſt of which they have attempted ſo often, in conſideration of our Fur-trade and Cod-fiſhing. 'Tis impoſſible to hinder 'em to poſſeſs themſelves of the Settlements upon the Coaſt of *Acadia*, by reaſon that they lye at ſuch a diſtance from one another; ſo that they'll certainly ſucceed in ſuch Enterpriſes, as indeed they have done already. The *French* Governours, they act with the ſame view, as many of thoſe who are imploy'd in Poſts beyond Sea. They look upon their place as a Gold Mine given 'em, in order to enrich themſelves; ſo that the publick Good, muſt always march behind private Intereſt. Mr. *de Meneval* ſuffer'd the *Engliſh* to poſſeſs themſelves of *Port Royal*, becauſe that place was cover'd with nothing but ſingle Paliſſado's. But why was it not better fortified? I can tell you the reaſon; he thought he had time enough to fill his Pockets, before the *Engliſh* would attack it. This Governour ſucceeded to Mr. *Perrot*, who was broke with Diſgrace, for having made it his chief buſineſs to enrich himſelf; and after returning to *France*, went back again with ſeveral Ships laden with Goods, in order to ſet up for a private Merchant in that Country. While Mr. *Perrot* was Governour, he ſuffer'd the *Engliſh* to poſſeſs themſelves of ſeveral advantageous Poſts, without offering to ſtir. His chief buſineſs was to go in Barques from River to River, in order to traffick with the Savages: And after he was diſgrac'd, he was not contented with a Commerce upon the Coaſts of *Acadia*, but would needs extend it to the *Engliſh* Plantations; but it coſt him dear, for ſome Pyrates fell in with him, and after ſeizing his Barques, duck'd himſelf, upon which he died immediately.[1]

[223] The three principal Savage Nations that live upon the Coaſts of *Acadia*, are the *Abenakis*, the *Mikemak*, and the *Canibas*.[2] There are ſome other erratick Nations, who go and

---

[1] For a sketch of Perrot see p. 53, note 2, *ante;* it is generally believed that Lahontan's strictures upon his rapacious conduct are justifiable. He was not killed by the pirates (1690), but rescued by a French privateer, being again in Acadia in 1691. See *N. Y. Col. Docs.*, ix, p. 475.—ED.

[2] Abenaki was a generic term for the Algonquian Indians of Maine and New Brunswick. They were a powerful but mild people, dwelling in villages when first encountered by the French; but later losing their village habit to some extent, under the influence of the French, who induced them to revert to the hunting stage, in the

come from *Acadia*, to *New-England*, and go by the names of *Mahingans*, *Soccokis*, and *Openango*.[1] The firſt three (having fix'd Habitations) are intirely in the intereſts of the *French;* and I muſt ſay, that in time of War they gall the *Engliſh* Colonies with their Incurſions, ſo much, that we ought to take care to perpetuate a good underſtanding between them and us. The Baron of Saint *Caſteins*, a Gentleman of *Oleron* in *Bearn*, having liv'd among the *Abenakis* after the Savage way, for above twenty years, is ſo much reſpected by the Savages, that they look upon him as their Tutelar God.[2] He was formerly an Officer of the *Carignan* Regiment in *Canada;* and upon the breaking of that Regiment, threw himſelf among the Savages, whoſe Language he had learn'd. He married among 'em after their faſhion, and prefer'd the Forreſts of

---

interest of the all-absorbing fur-trade. The name Abenaki is said to mean "people of the East." See Vetromile, *Abnakis and their History* (New York, 1866); Maurault, *Histoire des Abenakis* (1866). They are now represented by the Penobscot and Passamaquoddy Indians in Maine, and a few at the mission village in Canada. See p. 49, note 1, *ante*.

The Micmac were dwellers in Nova Scotia and Cape Breton — a large confederated tribe, of whom Membertou was the chief when Port Royal was founded (1605). They were frequently called Souriquois by the French, and not only were devoted to the latter's interests, but many were converted to Christianity.

The Canibas were an Abenaki tribe settled around Naroutsouat (Norridgewock), Maine. Their name was a variant of Kennebec. — Ed.

[1] See p. 90, note 1, *ante*. — Ed.

[2] Jean Vincent St. Castin, of whom Lahontan gives so succinct an account, was born about 1636, and settled in the forests of Maine in 1667. After 1676 he was commandant of Pentagoët, the French fort upon the Penobscot. For many years he traded with the English, but aided his own people in King William's War (1689–97), leading his savage allies against the English settlements. Late in the century he inherited a considerable fortune in France, whither he returned about 1700. His son Anselm succeeded to his influence among the Penobscot Indians, to whom he was allied on his mother's side. See *Maine Hist. Colls.*, vii, pp. 42–72. — Ed.

Acadia to the *Pyrenean* Mountains, that encompafs the place of his Nativity: For the firft years of his abode with the Savages, he behav'd himfelf fo, as to draw an inexpreffible efteem from 'em. They made him their Great Chief or Leader, who is in a manner the Soveraign of the Nation; and by degrees he has work'd himfelf into fuch a Fortune, which any Man but he would have made fuch ufe of, as to draw out of that Country above two or three hundred thoufand Crowns, which he has now in his Pocket in good dry Gold. But all the ufe he makes of it, is, to buy up Goods for Prefents to his Fellow-Savages, who upon their return from Hunting, prefent him with Beaver-Skins to a treble value. The Governours General of *Canada* keep in with him, and the Governours of *New-England* are afraid of him. He has feveral Daughters, who are, all of [224] 'em, married very handfomly to *Frenchmen*, and had good Dowries. He has never chang'd his Wife; by which means he mean'd to give the Savages to underftand, that God do's not love inconftant Folks. 'Tis faid, that he indeavour'd to convert thefe poor People, but his indeavours prov'd fuccefslefs; fo that 'tis in vain for the Jefuits to preach up the Truths of Chriftianity to 'em; though after all, thefe good Fathers are not difcourag'd, nay, they think that the adminiftring of Baptifm to a dying Child, is worth ten times the pains and uneafinefs of living among that People.[1]

---

[1] Lahontan here belittles the Jesuit missions, which nevertheless had a considerable success among the Acadian Indians. Druillettes began his visits to the Kennebec about 1646, and by 1680 a large number of converts had been removed to the mission

Port-Royal, the Capital or the only City of *Acadia*, is in effect no more than a little paultry Town,[1] that is somewhat inlarg'd since the War broke out in 1689. by the accession of the Inhabitants that liv'd near *Boston*, the Metropolitan of *New-England*. A great many of these People retir'd to *Port-Royal*, upon the apprehension that the *English* would pillage 'em, and carry 'em into their Country. Mr. *de Meneval* surrendred this place to the *English*, as I said before; he could not maintain such a post with the handful of Men that he had, because the Palissadoes were low, and out of order. He made a Capitulation with the Commander of the Party that made the Attack; but the *English* Officer broke his word to him, and us'd him both ignominiously and harshly.[2] *Port-Royal* is seated in the Latitude of 44 Degrees, and 40 Minutes, upon the edge of a very fine Basin,[3] which is a League

colony. See p. 49, note 1, *ante*. For a fuller account of the Acadian mission, see *Jesuit Relations*, i, Introduction. — ED.

[1] For a good summary of the history of Port Royal, the settlement at which was decided upon in 1604, but not actually undertaken until the following year, see Hannay, *History of Acadia* (St. John, N. B., 1879); Hannay, *Story of Acadia* (Kentville, N. S., 1904); *Acadiensis* (special number, June, 1904); Savary, *History of the County of Annapolis* (Toronto, 1897). The census of 1686 gave 885 persons in all Nova Scotia, of whom 592 were at Port Royal, exclusive of 30 soldiers. See Sulte, *Les Canadiens Français* (Montreal, 1882), vi, pp. 8, 9. — ED.

[2] The reference is here to the siege of Port Royal by Sir William Phips in May, 1690. Menneval, son of the Baron de Portneuf, had but recently succeeded Perrot as governor of Acadia. The fort was inefficiently garrisoned and provisioned, and was entirely unable to resist the demand for surrender made by the well-equipped English fleet. The charge that Phips broke the terms of capitulation, seems to be sustained. Menneval was carried captive to Boston, where after a short imprisonment he was sent to England, afterwards exchanged, and returned to Canada, where he was useful in affording information of New England conditions. — ED.

[3] First called Port Royal Basin, but now Annapolis Basin. Situated on the northwest coast of Nova Scotia, and pouring its enormous tide into the Bay of Fundy

broad, and two Leagues long, having at the entry about ſix-teen or eighteen fathom Water on one ſide, and ſix or ſeven on the other; for you muſt know that the Iſland call'd *l'Iſle aux Chevres* which ſtands in the middle, divides the Channel into two. There's excellent anchorage all over the Baſin; and at the bottom of it, there's a Cape or point of Land that parts two Rivers, at which the tide riſes ten or [225] twelve Foot. Theſe Rivers are bounded by pleaſant Meads, which in Spring and Autumn are cover'd with all ſorts of freſh Water-foul. In fine, *Port-Royal* is only a handful of Houſes two Story high, and has but few Inhabitants of any Note. It ſubſiſts upon the traffick of the Skins, which the Savages bring thither to truck for *European* Goods. In former times, the Farmer's Company had Magazins in this place, which were under the care of the Governours. I could

through the narrow Digby Gut, this strikingly-beautiful fjord appealed strongly to the French explorers — De Monts, Champlain, and Poutrincourt — who discovered it about the twenty-fourth of June, 1604. Poutrincourt obtained from De Monts a grant of the region, and determined to settle there; but the ill-fated winter of 1604–05 was actually spent by the party on Island St. Croix, at the mouth of St. Croix River, where it empties into Passamaquoddy Bay. The next year, the remnant of the company settled on Poutrincourt's grant, on the shores of Annapolis Basin. This first settlement of the French in Canada was on the mainland, in Lower Granville, opposite Goat Island (the "Isle aux Chevres" of our author), about seven miles below and on the opposite shore to the present Annapolis Royal, at the head of the basin — whither the colony removed in later years. Annapolis Basin was too far removed from the fur trade of the interior, also was subject to English attacks, for which reasons Champlain wisely decided to found Quebec (1608) as the capital of New France.

Along the east shore of the basin is now a continuous and prosperous farming community, chiefly the descendants of early Scotch settlers and American Loyalists, with several small towns. Digby is a considerable summer resort, chiefly for New Englanders; Annapolis Royal (1000 inhabitants) is a quiet market town. Concerning the tercentenary celebration of the landfall of the early French, see p. 324, note 1, *ante*. — Ed.

eaſily mention ſome of 'em, if I were not apprehenſive that theſe Memoirs may be ſeen by others beſides your ſelf.

The Iſland of *Newfound-Land*, is three hundred Leagues in Circumference. It lies at the diſtance of ſix hundred and fifty Leagues from *France*, and forty or fifty Leagues from the Bank of the ſame name. The South ſide of the Iſland belongs to the *French*, who have ſeveral Settlements there for the fiſhing of Cod. The Eaſt ſide is inhabited by the *Engliſh*, who are poſſeſs'd of ſeveral conſiderable Poſts, ſituated in certain Ports, Bays, and Havens, which they have taken care to fortifie. The Weſt of the Iſland is waſte, and was never yet poſſeſs'd. The Iſland is of a triangular Figure, and full of Mountains, and impracticable Forreſts. It has ſome great Meadows, or rather Heaths, which are covered with a ſort of Moſs inſtead of Graſs. The Soil of this Country is good for nothing, as being a mixture of Gravel, Sand and Stones; ſo that the Fiſhery was the only motive that induc'd the *French* and the *Engliſh* to ſettle there. It affords great ſtore of Game, for Water-fowl, Patridges and Hairs; but as for the Stags, 'tis almoſt impoſſible to come at 'em, by reaſon that the Mountains are ſo high, and the Woods ſo thick.[1] In this

[1] The area of Newfoundland, which in its extreme length from north to south is 350 miles and in its average breadth from east to west 130 miles, is 40,200 square miles. Its population in 1901 was 216,215, for the most part littoral; the interior being still a wilderness, chiefly forested, although there are several broad rocky plateaus which yield little beyond moss and low-growing shrubs. The lumbering industry is being rapidly developed, the lakes and rivers furnishing easy timber highways to mill and port; mining interests are also fast growing in importance — the present annual output of copper, pyrites, iron ore, and other products amounting to a million dollars; under recent governmental bounties, the area of cultivation has been

Iſland, as well as in that of Cape *Breton*, we find Porphyry of ſeveral colours; and care has been taken to ſend to *France* ſome pieces of it for a Pattern, which were [226] found to be very pretty, only they were hard to cut. I have ſeen ſome of 'em that were red ſtreak'd with green, and ſeem'd to be extream fine; but the miſchief is, it ſplits ſo when 'tis taken out of the Quarries, that it cannot be made uſe of, but by way of incruſtation.

This Iſland of Cape *Breton* affords likewiſe black Marble, or a ſort of *Breſche* with grey Veins, which is hard, and not

extended to upwards of 100,000 acres, largely along the coast, by fishermen; the fisheries, however, are, as in Lahontan's day, still the chief industry, employing in all branches of that pursuit nearly 60,000 of the inhabitants — while American, French, and a few Portuguese vessels are also engaged in the catch. The total annual value of the cod-fish catch in this region is $10,000,000, Newfoundland's share being $600,000; to these, may be added herring, lobsters, seal, and whale — while the interior waters abound in salmon and trout, which attract tourists from Canada, England, and the United States. The principal manufacturing establishments are in St. Johns; but factories for canning lobsters, and making seal and cod-liver oil, and guano, are numerous along the coast. The island is for the most part a plateau, creased by numerous river gorges and lake basins, and capped by a few mountains of not more than 2000 feet above sea-level, with a deeply-indented, fjord-like coast — more rugged on the west, north, and east sides than on the south. The numerous fjords are valuable to fishermen as land-locked harbors, and the population, as in Norway, clings closely to the ragged fringe of shore. For a century and a half, French fishermen have controlled the west and north coasts, from Cape Ray to Notre Dame Bay; but a recent treaty between England and France (1904) has effectively disposed of this long-pending source of discontent on the part of the English residents, and England now dominates (or will, when the stipulation is formally confirmed by both parliaments) the entire island. Newfoundland is not a part of the Dominion of Canada, preferring to remain a separate colony of the British Empire. Reid's Transinsular Railroad (narrow gauge), built in 1893–98, now runs from Port-au-Basques to St. Johns, but thus far has had but slight effect in developing the island, for the cheaper water carriage is still quite generally preferred. Labrador is owned by Newfoundland, and many of the tourists who now flock to the island for fishing and hunting, take pleasure trips on Newfoundland steamers as far north as Nain. — Ed.

eafily polifh'd.[1] This Stone is apt to fplit, for 'tis not equally hard, and it has knots in it. There are no fetled Savages in the Ifland of *Newfound-Land.*[2] 'Tis true, the *Eskimaux* do fometimes crofs over to it at the Streight of *Belle Ifle* in great Sloops, with intent to furprife the Crew of the Fifhermen upon the Coaft call'd *Petit Nord.* Our Settlements are at *Placentia*, at the Ifland of St. *Peter*, and in the Bay of *Trepaffez.*[3] From Cape *Rafe* to *Chapeau Rouge*, the Coaft is very clean, but from *Chapeau Rouge* to Cape *Rafe*, the Rocks render it dangerous.[4] There are two confiderable Inconveniences, that attend the landing upon this Ifland. In the firft place, the Fogs are here fo thick in the Summer, for twenty Leagues off into the Main, that the ableft and moft expert Sailor dare not ftand into the Land while they laft: So that all Ships are oblig'd to lye bye for a clear day, in order to make the Land.

[1] The author probably means breccia, a conglomerate of angular fragments. — Ed.

[2] The aborigines of Newfoundland were few in number, and occupied chiefly the northern portion. They were known to the early French as Beothics, and exhibited an ineradicable hatred of the whites. After an act of treachery on their part, in 1810, they were nearly all exterminated. — Ed.

[3] For Placentia, see p. 275, note 1, *ante*. The little island of St. Pierre was one of the earliest visited by French fishers in the sixteenth century, and by 1670 became a permanent French settlement, with slight fortifications. After the Treaty of Utrecht (1713), all French inhabitants were expelled; but in 1763, the islands of St. Pierre and Miquelon were retroceded to France, as a refuge for fishermen; the sovereignty is still in her hands, these now being, after the Newfoundland French Shore treaty (1904), her only possessions in North America, save those in the West Indies.

Trepassey Bay is the first large indentation southwest of Cape Race. The permanent French settlement here was broken up in 1713. See Prowse, *History of Newfoundland* (London, 1895), p. 542. — Ed.

[4] The first should be Cape Ray, not Race. Chapeau Rouge is the extremity of the great peninsula between Fortune and Placentia Bays. Eastward from this point, the coast is more wild and rocky than that to the west. — Ed.

The ſecond Inconveniency, which is yet greater, proceeds from the Currents which run to and again, without any perceivable variation, by which means the Ships are ſometimes drove in upon the Coaſt, when they reckon upon ten Leagues offing. But, which is worſt of all, the inſenſible motion of the rowling Waves, throw's 'em inſenſibly upon the Rocks, which they cannot poſſibly avoid, for want of ground to anchor upon. 'Twas by this means that the King's Ship the *Pretty* was loſt in 1692, as well as a great many others upon ſeveral occaſions.[1]

[227] Of all our Settlements in North-*America*, *Placentia* is the Poſt of the greateſt Importance and Service to the King, in regard that 'tis a place of refuge to the Ships that are oblig'd to put into a Harbour, when they go or come from *Canada*, and even to thoſe which come from South-*America*, when they want to take in freſh Water or Proviſions, and have ſprung their Maſt, or been dammag'd in a Storm. This place is ſituated in the Latitude of 47 Degrees, and ſome Minutes, almoſt at the bottom of the Bay that goes by the ſame name. The Bay is ten or twelve Leagues broad, and twenty odd Leagues long. The Fort ſtands upon the ſide of a Neck or narrow Streight, which is ſixty Paces over, and ſix Fathoms water deep. The Ships that enter into the Port, are oblig'd to graze, (ſo to ſpeak) upon the angle of the Baſtions. The Port or Harbour is a League long, and a

[1] This was probably the ship "Joli," which under command of Monsieur Beaujeu conveyed La Salle's ill-fated colony to the Gulf of Mexico (1684). See Thwaites, *Hennepin's New Discovery* (Chicago, 1903), pp. 388–392, where in the original text of the reprint (London, 1698) it is misprinted "Toby." — Ed.

quarter of a League over: Before the Port there's a large, fine road, which is a League and a half wide; but lies ſo bleak to the North-Weſt, and Weſt-North-Weſt Winds, the ſtrongeſt and moſt boiſterous Winds that are, that neither Cables nor Anchors, nor large ſtout Ships can withſtand their furious ſhocks; tho' indeed theſe violent ſtorms ſeldom happen but in the latter end of Autumn. The ſame year that the *Pretty* was loſt, the King loſt another of 69 Guns call'd *the Good*, in this Road; and if the four or five other Ships that belong'd to the ſame Squadron, had not took the precaution of ſteering into the Port, they had certainly underwent the ſame fate. This Road then which is only expos'd to the North-Weſt, and Weſt-North-Weſt Winds, has ſome hidden Rocks on the North ſide, beſides thoſe at *Pointe Verte*, where ſeveral of the Inhabitants are wont to fiſh. All theſe things you may ſee plainly upon the Plan that I ſent you along with my 23*d* Letter.

[228] Commonly, there comes thirty or forty Ships from *France* to *Placentia* every year, and ſometimes ſixty. Some come with intent to fiſh, and others have no other deſign than to truck with the Inhabitants, who live in the Summer time on the other ſide of the Fort. The ground upon which their Houſes ſtand, is call'd *La grand Grave*, for in effect, they have nothing but Gravel to ſpread their Cod-fiſh upon, in order to have 'em dry'd by the Sun after they are ſalted. The Inhabitants and the *French* Fiſhermen, ſend their Sloops every day two Leagues off the Port to purſue the Fiſhery; and ſome-

times the Sloops return ſo over-loaded, that they are in a manner bury'd in the Water. You cannot imagine how deep they ſink, and 'tis impoſſible you ſhould believe it, unleſs you ſaw it. The Fiſhery commences in the beginning of *June*, and is at an end about the middle of *Auguſt*. In the Harbour they catch a little ſort of a fiſh, which they put upon their Hooks as a bait for the Cod.

Placentia is in great want of Gravel, which occaſions the thinneſs of the Inhabitants. If the Governours prefer'd the King's Service to Avarice, they might make it a conſiderable Poſt, and a great many would make gravel Walks at their own charge; but as long as the Governours prey upon the fortunes of private Men, under the fair pretence of the King's Service, which is always in their Mouths, I can't ſee that this Settlement will ever be inlarg'd or improv'd. Do's not the Governour diſgrace his Prince, and ſink the character of his Poſt, in turning Fiſherman, Merchant, Vintner, and acting in the way of a thouſand meaner and more Mechanical Trades? Is not this a piece of Tyranny? To force the Inhabitants to buy what Goods they want, out of ſuch and ſuch a Ship, and to ſell their Cod to ſuch other Ships as the Governour is intereſs'd in, and that as a principal Owner: To [229] appropriate to himſelf the Rigging and Tackle of the Ships that are caſt away upon the Coaſt, to ſtop the Crew of Merchantmen for his own Fiſhery, to ſell Habitations or Settlements, to ſtifle the bidding up for Effects ſold by way of Auction that he may ingroſs them by his ſole Authority, to change the Provifions laid up in Magazines for his Majefty's Troops, to carry off the good Biskuit and put bad in the room of it, to make fo much Beef and Bacon for the fubfiftance of the Garrifon, to force the Inhabitants to fend their Servants and Carpenters to fome work, in which his Majefty's Service is lefs concern'd than his own Pocket: Thefe, I fay, are things that I take to be plain infractions of the Orders iffued forth by *Lewis* the XIV. Thefe are abufes that muft be redrefs'd, if we would have the King to be well ferv'd: And yet there's nothing done in it. For my part, I am unacquainted with the reafon of the delay; thofe that have a mind to know, had beft ask the Deputies of Monfieur *de P* * * *. I am fully perfwaded, that all thefe Pyracies do not come to the King's Ear, for he's too juft to fuffer 'em.

To conclude; *Placentia* bears neither Corn, nor Rie, nor Peafe, for the Soil is good for nothing; not to mention, that if it were as good and as fertile as any in *Canada*, yet no body would give themfelves the trouble to cultivate it; for one Man earns more in Cod-fifhing in one Summer, than ten would do in the way of Agriculture. In the great Bay of *Placentia*, there are fome little Harbours, (befides that of the Fort) which the *Bifcay* Fifhermen refort to. Such are the little and the great *Burin*, St. *Laurence*, *Martir*, *Chapeau Rouge*,[1] &c.

---

[1] The inlets here mentioned are all upon the western coast of Placentia Bay, and still retain practically their old names. Burin Inlet has at its entrance an island of the same name. "Martir" is the present Mortier Bay, being thus named for two well-known cartographers of the seventeenth century, Corneille and Pierre Mortier. Burin and St. Lawrence were early seats of shipbuilding. — Ed.

[230] *A Liſt of the Savage Nations of* Canada.

Thoſe in Acadia.

The *Abenakis*.
The *Micmac*.
The *Canibas*.
The *Mahingans*.
The *Openangos*.
The *Soccokis*.
The *Etechemins*.

} Theſe are all of 'em good Warriours; they are more active and leſs cruel than the *Iroqueſe*. Their Language differs a little from that of the *Algonkins*.[1]

The Nations that lye upon the River of St. Laurence, *from the Sea to* Monreal.

The *Papinachois*.
The *Mountaneers*.
The *Gaſpeſians*.

} Theſe ſpeak the *Algonkin* Language.

The *Hurons* of *Loreto*, the *Iroqueſe* Tongue.

The *Abenakis* of *Scilleri*.
The *Algonkins*.

} The *Algonkin* Language.

The *Agnies* of the Fall call'd *Saut St. Louis;* they ſpeak the *Iroqueſe* Language, and are good Warriours.

The *Iroqueſe* of the Mountain of *Monreal;* they ſpeak the *Iroqueſe* Language, and are a brave People.[2]

---

[1] For these tribes see pp. 90, 327, 328, *ante*. The Etechemins — nomads, whom the French found it difficult to convert — occupied the region from the Penobscot east to beyond St. John River, and in 1677 numbered from four to five hundred. The remnants of one Etechemin tribe are the so-called Quoddy Indians of to-day. — Ed.

[2] For the Papinachois, see p. 261, note 2, *ante*. They were one of the tribe of the Montagnais (Mountaineers), by which term the French designated the wander-

Those upon the Lake of Hurons.

The *Hurons*, the *Iroquese* Language.

The *Outaouas.* The *Nockes.* The *Missisagues.* The *Attikamek.*	The *Algonkin* Language.

The *Outehipoues*, alias *Sauteurs*, good Warriours.[1]

ing Algonquian bands north of the St. Lawrence, among whom they had missions.

As the name indicates, the Gaspesiens were the aborigines of Gaspé, extending from the territory of the Etechemins northeast to the St. Lawrence. In 1677 there were from four to five hundred of these savages, whom the Jesuits found gentle and tractable.

The other tribes mentioned in this division are the Indians of the mission colonies. For Lorette, see p. 48, note 1, *ante;* for Sillery, p. 49, note 1; for the mission of Sault St. Louis to the Agnies (Mohawks), p. 56, note 1; for that of La Montagne, p. 55, note 2. — ED.

[1] The Huron confederacy was one of the largest and most enlightened bodies of North American Indians. When first encountered by the French they numbered about 16,000, and had agricultural villages in the region between Lake Simcoe and Georgian Bay — see p. 154, note 2, *ante*. An important Jesuit mission was founded in the Huron country (Huronia, in Jesuit annals), but was destroyed and the Hurons dispersed by Iroquois war-raids (1648–49) — see *Jesuit Relations*, i, pp. 21–27.

Ottawa (Outaouat) was the name applied by the early French to the Northwestern Algonquians. When first encountered, they dwelt chiefly upon Manitoulin Island, in Lake Huron, whither they had sought an asylum from the Iroquois — see p. 153, note 2, *ante*. Later, their chief habitat was about Mackinac. They were especially faithful to French interests, and Pontiac was an Ottawa chief. The remnants of this tribe were removed to Indian Territory.

For the Nockés and Mississagues, see p. 317, note 1, *ante*.

The Attikamek (Attikamègues) were a Montagnais tribe dwelling chiefly upon the upper St. Maurice River, and trading with the Western Indians. They were destroyed by the ravages of the Iroquois, and an epidemic of small-pox.

For the Saulteurs (men of the Sault), by which term the French designated the entire Chippewa (Ojibwa) nation, whether living at Sault Ste. Marie or elsewhere, see p. 149, note 1, *ante*. — ED.

[231] *Upon the* Ilineſe *Lake, and the adjacent Country.*

Some *Ilineſe* at *Chegakou.* The *Oumamis*, good Warriours. The *Maskoutens.* The *Kikapous*, good Warriours. The *Outagamis*, good Warriours. The *Malomimis.* The *Pouteouatamis.* The *Ojatinons*, good Warriours. The *Sakis.*	They ſpeak the *Algonkin* Language, and are a ſprightly active ſort of People.[1]

In the Neighbourhood of the Lake of Frontenac.

The *Tſonontouans.* The *Goyoguans.* The *Onnotagues.*	Theſe ſpeak a different Language from the *Algonkin.*

The *Onnoyoutes* and *Agnies*, at a ſmall diſtance.[2]

---

[1] For the Illinois (Ilinese) and Miami (Oumamis), see p. 77, note 1, *ante*. The Ouiatonon (Ojatinons) were a Miami tribe, later settled in western Indiana, and known to the English as Weas.

For the Mascouten and Kickapoo, see p. 174, note 2; for the Outagami (Fox) and Sauk (Sakis), p. 175, note 2; for the Menominee (Malomimis) and Potawatomi (Pouteouatamis), p. 168, note 2. These dwelt for the most part in Wisconsin, which was more densely populated with aborigines than any other Northwestern state. — ED.

[2] These were the Iroquois, for whom see p. 58, note 1, *ante*. — ED.

Near the River of the Outaouas.

The *Tabitibi.* The *Monzoni.* The *Machakandibi.* The *Nopemen d'Achirini.* The *Nepisirini.* The *Temiskamink.*	They speak the *Algonkin* Language, and all of 'em are very cowardly.[1]

To the North of Missisipi, *and upon the Confines of the Upper Lake, and* Hudson's *Bay.*

The *Nadouessis.* The *Assimpouals.* The *Sonkaskitons.* The *Ouadbatons.* The *Atintons.* The *Clistinos* brave Warriour's and active brisk Men. The *Ekimaux.*	These speak *Algonkin.*[2]

[1] The Abittibi (Tabitibi) were the Indians of the lake and river of that name, tributary of the Moose. In 1760 the French maintained a post upon Abittibi Lake. The Monsoni lived in the eastern part of Rupert Land, but wandered widely, some of that nation being present at Sault Ste. Marie when St. Lusson took possession of the Northwest (1671).

For the identification of Machakandibi, see p. 315, note 1, *ante.*

The Achirigouans (Nopemen d'Achirini) and Nipissing (Nepisirini) were kindred tribes, living north of the lake named for the latter. Charlevoix says that they were the original Algonquians, and spoke the language in its purity. There are now about two hundred of the tribe on their reservation on Lake Nipissing.

The Temiscaming (Temiskamink) Indians took their name from that of the lake, which signified "deep." About two hundred still frequent the agency on Lake Temiscaming in northern Ontario. — Ed.

[2] Lahontan is mistaken in stating that these tribes spoke the Algonquian language

[232] *A List of the Animals of the South Countries of* Canada.

Wild Beeves.
Little Stags or Harts.
Roebucks of three different Species.
Wolves, ſuch as we have in *Europe.*
Lynx's, ſuch as we have in *Europe.*
Michibichi, a ſort of baſtard Tygre.
Ferrets } ſuch as we have in *Europe.*
Weeſels. }
Aſh-colour'd Squirrels.
Hares. } ſuch as we have in *Europe.*
Rabbets. }
Badgers, ſuch as we have in *Europe.*
White Beavers, but very ſcarce.
Reddiſh Bears.
Musk Rats.
Reddiſh Foxes, as in *Europe.*
Crocodiles in the *Miſſiſipi.*
Oſſa, an Animal like a Hare, upon the *Miſſiſipi.*

— another evidence of his lack of knowledge of the Siouan country. Of all the tribes enumerated, the Cristinaux (Clistini, Cree) were the only members of that stock, although intimately associated with the Assinboin (Assimpouals) — see p. 309, note 1, *ante*.

With the exception of the Eskimo (Ekimaux), the other tribes are all Siouan (Dakotan) — see p. 175, note 3, *ante*. The Assiniboin separated from the Yankton tribe of Dakota, moved north and west, and are still one of the strongest bands of the Northwest. The Chonkasketons (Sonkaskitons) were "people of the fortified village"; the Wahpetons (Ouadebatons), a branch of the Issati (Santee); the Tetons (Atintons) a fierce tribe of western Sioux, whose later habitat was the Upper Missouri River. See Thwaites (ed.), *Original Journals of Lewis and Clark Expedition* (New York, 1904), index; also *Wis. Hist. Colls.*, xvi, pp. 193, 194. — ED.

A Lift of the Animals of the North Countries of Canada.

Orignals or Elks.

Caribous or wild Affes.

Black Foxes.

Silver colour'd Foxes.

A fort of wild Cats, call'd *Enfans du Diable*, or the Devil's Children.

Carcaious, an Animal not unlike a Badger.

Porcupines.

Fontereaux, an Amphibious fort of little Pole-Cats.

Martins.

Pole-Cats, fuch as we have in *Europe*.

Black Bears.

[233] White Bears.

Siffleurs, an Animal that makes a whizzing noife.

Flying Squirrels.

White Hares.

Beavers.

Otters.

Musk-Rats.

Suiffe Squirrels, or a fort of Squirrels, whofe Hair refembles a *Suiffe*'s Doublet.

Great Harts.

Sea-Wolves or Calves.

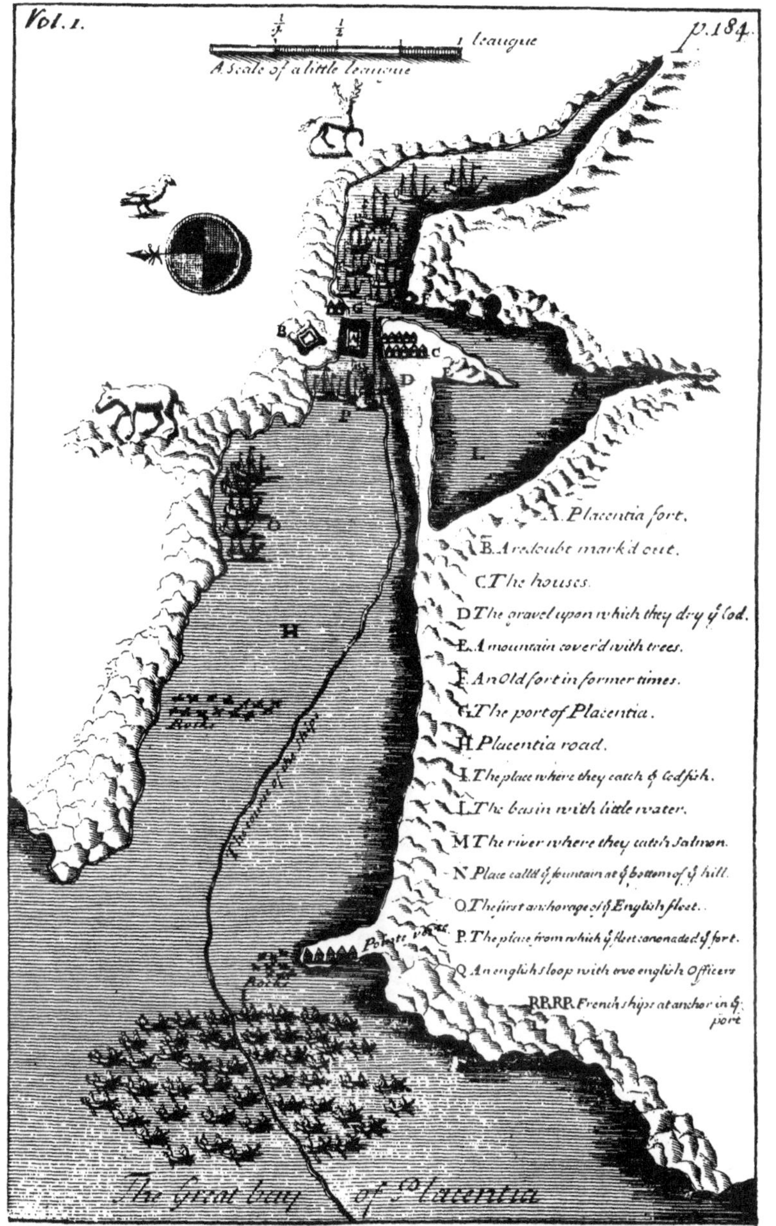

Vol. 1.
p. 184.
1/4
1/2
1 leaugue
A Scale of a little leaugue
A. Placentia fort.
B. A redoubt mark'd out.
C. The houses.
D The gravel upon which they dry ye Cod.
E. A mountain cover'd with trees.
F. An Old fort in former times.
G. The port of Placentia.
H. Placentia road.
I. The place where they catch ye Codfish.
L. The basin with little water.
M The river where they catch Salmon.
N. Place call'd ye fountain at ye bottom of ye hill.
O. The first anchorage of ye English fleet.
P. The place from which ye fleet canonaded ye fort.
Q. An english sloop with two english Officers
RRRR. French ships at anchor in ye port
Rocks
Rocks
The Great bay of Placentia

A Deſcription of ſuch Animals or Beaſts, as are not mention'd in the Letters.

The Animals of the South Countries.

THE *Michibichi* is a ſort of Tyger, only 'tis leſs than the common Tyger, and not ſo much ſpeckl'd. As ſoon as it deſcries a Man, it runs away, and climbs up the firſt Tree it meets with. It attacks all brute Animals whatſoever, and conquers 'em with eaſe; and, which is very ſingular and peculiar to it above all other Animals, it runs in to the aſſiſtance of the Savages, when they purſue Bears and wild Beeves; upon ſuch occaſions it makes as if 'twere affraid of no body, and ſally's out with fury upon the hunted Animal. The Savages call theſe Animals a ſort of *Manitous*, that is, Spirits that love Men; and 'tis upon that ſcore they eſteem and reſpect 'em to ſuch a degree, that they would chooſe rather to die, than to kill one of 'em.[1]

The *white Beavers* are much valued, upon the account of their being uncommon, though at the ſame time, their Hair is neither ſo large nor ſo fine as that of the common Beavers. As there are but few of theſe white Beavers, ſo thoſe which are quite black are very ſcarce.[2]

---

[1] The animal here described as "Michibichi" is undoubtedly the puma or American tiger-cat (*Felis concolor*). Marquette describes one that he saw swimming a river, and one of the Jesuit missionaries gives this title to a manitou. Consult *Jesuit Relations*, lix, p. 109; lxvii, pp. 159, 161. — ED.

[2] The white beaver is an albino of the ordinary *Castor canadensis*, and is very

[234] The *Reddiſh Bears* are miſchievous Creatures, for they fall fiercely upon the Huntſmen, whereas the black ones fly from 'em. The former ſort are leſs, and more nimble than the latter.[1]

The *Crocodiles* of *Miſſiſipi*, are exactly the ſame with thoſe of the *Nile* and other places. I have ſeen that *Crocodile* that is at *Engoliſma* in *Aquitaine*, and find that it has the ſame figure with theſe, only 'tis ſomewhat leſs. The moſt uſual method that the Savages have for taking 'em alive, is to throw great Wreaths or Cords made of the barks of Trees with a running knot, upon their Neck, the middle of their Body, their Paws, *&c.* After they are thus ſiez'd, they ſhut 'em up between ten or twelve Stakes, and there tie 'em after their Belly is turn'd upwards. While they lie in this poſture, they flea 'em without touching their Head or their Tail, and give 'em a Coat of Fir-bark, to which they ſet fire, having cut the Ropes that keep'd 'em faſt. Upon ſuch occaſions, theſe Animals make a fearful houling and crying. To conclude, the Savages are frequently ſwallow'd up by theſe Creatures, whether in ſwimming over a River, or in ſleeping upon its Banks. *Arioſte* in the 68 Diapaſon of his *15th* Song, gives this Deſcription of a *Crocodile.*

Vive ſub lito è dentro a la Riviera,
Ei Corpi Umani ſon le ſue Vivande,
De le Perſone miſere è incaute,
Di Viandanti è d'infelice naute.

---

rare. The black beaver is less unusual, but only about one in ten thousand is found of this color. See Martin, *Castorologia*, p. 39. — Ed.

[1] It is still a question among naturalists whether the cinnamon bear and the ordi-

That is, it lives both in the River, and upon its Banks; it ſquaſhes People with its murdering Tooth; it feeds upon the Bodies of poor Travellers, of unfortunate Paſſengers, and Sailours.[1]

The *Oſſa*, are little Animals like Hares, and reſemble 'em in every thing, excepting the Ears and Hind-feet. They run, and cannot climb. Their [235] Females have a Bag under their Belly, where their young ones enter upon a purſuit, in order to ſave themſelves along with the Mother, who immediately betakes her ſelf to flight.[2]

The Animals or Beaſts of the North Countries.

The Silver-colour'd *Foxes* are of the ſame ſhape with thoſe of *Europe*, as well as the black ones. The black ones are very ſcarce, and whoſoever catches one, is ſure to ſell it for its weight in Gold. This ſpecies is met with only in the coldeſt Countries.

The *White Bears* are a monſtrous Animal, and extraordinary long; their Head has a formidable Aſpect, and their Hair is very large and thick; they are ſo fierce, that they'll come and attack a Sloop in the Sea, with ſeven or eight Men in it. 'Tis ſaid, that they'll ſwim ſix or ſeven Leagues without being tyr'd. They live upon Fiſh and Shells upon the Sea-

nary black bear (*Ursus americanus*) are two species or one. Huntsmen, however, usually discriminate, as Lahontan does. — ED.

[1] It is possible that Lahontan received his description of the crocodile (*Alligator mississippiensis*) from some members of La Salle's ill-fated colony, whose survivors he met at Mackinac. See p. 145, *ante*. — ED.

[2] The ordinary opossum of North America (*Didelphys virginiana*). — ED.

ſhoar, from whence they ſeldom ſtraggle far. I never ſaw but one of 'em in my Life-time, which had certainly tore me to pieces, if I had not ſpy'd it at a diſtance, and ſo had time to run back for ſhelter to Fort *Louis* at *Placentia.*[1]

The *Flying Squirrels* are as big as a large Rat, and of a greyiſh white colour. They are as drouſie, as thoſe of the other Species are watchful. They are call'd *Flying Squirrels*, in regard that they fly from one Tree to another, by the means of a certain Skin which ſtretches it ſelf out in the form of a Wing, when they make theſe little Flights.

The *White Hares* are only ſuch in Winter, for as ſoon as the Spring comes on, they begin to turn grayiſh, and by degrees recover the ſame colour as our Hares have in *France*, which they hold till the end of Autumn.

The *Suiſſe Squirrels* are little Animals, reſembling little Rats.[2] The Epithet of *Suiſſe* is beſtow'd upon 'em, in regard that the Hair which covers their Body, [236] is ſtreak'd with black and white, and reſembles a *Suiſſe*'s Doublet; and that theſe ſtreaks make a ring on each Thigh, which bears a great deal of reſemblance to a *Suiſſe*'s Cap.

The large *Stags* are neither higher nor thicker, than thoſe we have in *Europe;* but they are call'd large in proportion

---

[1] Lahontan must refer here to the polar bear (*Thallassartos maritimus*), which occasionally ventures as far as the southern coast of Newfoundland. — ED.

[2] The well-known flying squirrel (*Sciuropterus volucella*) is well described. Several of the North American hares change color as thus noted; probably Lahontan means *Lepus timidus*, *var. arcticus*. The Swiss squirrel is either a chipmunk (*Tamias striatus*) or a ground-squirrel (*Spermophile tridecemlineatus*). See *Jesuit Relations*, vi, p. 315. — ED.

to two other Species of Harts that frequent the Southern Countries. The leſſer ſort affords the moſt delicious Meat.

The *Sea-Wolves*, which ſome call *Sea-Calves*, are as big as Maſtiffs. They are almoſt always in the Water, or at leaſt they never go far from the Sea ſide. Theſe Animals do not walk ſo much as they crawl, for when they raiſe themſelves out of the Water, they only creep upon the Sand or Clay. Their Head has the form of an Otter's Head, and their Feet, which have no Legs, reſemble thoſe of a Gooſe. The Female kind bring forth their young ones upon the Rocks, or upon ſome little Iſlands, juſt by the Sea. The *Sea-Wolves* live upon Fiſh, and reſort to cold Countries. There's a prodigious number of 'em about the Mouth of the River of St. *Laurence*.[1]

As for the remaining Animals of *Canada*, I gave you an account of 'em in my Letters. I will not offer to ſhew you what methods the Savages take to catch or kill all theſe Animals, for ſuch an undertaking would be endleſs. This I can aſſure you of in the general, that they rarely go a Hunting to no purpoſe, and that they make no uſe of their Dogs, but in the Hunting of Elks, and ſometimes in Hunting of Beavers, as you ſhall ſee under the Head of the Diverſions of Hunting and Shooting among the Savages.

---

[1] The ordinary seal (*Phoca vitulina*), often called sea-calf, from the sound it emits. — Ed.

[237] *A Lift of the Fowl or Birds that frequent the South Countries of* Canada.

Vultures.
Huards, a River-fowl as big as a Goofe.
Swans.
Black Geefe.
Black Ducks.
Plungeons.
Coots.
} fuch as we have in *Europe*.
Rayles.
Turkeys.
Red Partridges.
Pheafants.
Large Eagles.
Cranes.
Blackbirds.
Thrufhes.
} fuch as we have in *Europe*.
Wood-Pigeons.
Parrots.
Ravens.
Swallows.
} fuch as we have in *Europe*.
Several forts of Birds of Prey that are not known in *Europe*.
Nightingales unknown in *Europe*, as well as feveral other little Birds of different colours, particularly that call'd *Oifeau Mouche*, a very little Bird refembling a Fly; and great quantities of Pelicans.

The Birds of the North Countries of Canada.

Buſtards. White Geeſe.	ſuch as we have in *Europe*.

Ducks of ten or twelve ſorts.
Teals.
Sea-Mews.
Grelans.
Sterlets.
[238] Sea-Parrots.
Moyacks.

Cormorants. Heath-Cocks. Snipes. Plungeons. Plovers. Lapwings. Herns. Courbeious. The Water-Fowl call'd *Chevalier*.	ſuch as we have in *Europe*.

Beateurs de Faux, a Fowl as big as a Quail.
White Partridges.
Large black Partridges.
Reddiſh Partridges.
Woodhens.
Turtledoves.

White Ortolans, a Bird no bigger than a Lark.

Sterlings. } ſuch as we have in *Europe.*
Ravens.

Vultures.

Spar-Hawks. } like ours in *Europe.*
Merlins.
Swallows.

Becs De ſcie, a ſort of a Duck.

A Table of the Insects that are found in Canada.

Adders.

Aſps.

Rattle-Snakes.

Lowing Frogs.

Gnats or Midges.

Gad-Bees.

Brulots or burning Handworms.

[239] *A Defcription of fuch Birds as are not accounted for in my Letters.*

The Fowl or Birds of the Southern Countries.

THE *Huards* are a Frefhwater-Fowl, as big as a Goofe, and as dull and heavy as an Afs. They have black and white Feathers, a pointed Beak, and a very fhort Neck. They only duck or dive in the Summer, for they cannot ufe their Wings; and in that Seafon, the Savages take the Diverfion of furrounding 'em with feven or eight Canows, difpers'd here and there, and fo obliging 'em to dive down, when they offer to come up to take breath. The Savages have Entertain'd me feveral times with this agreeable Amufement, during the courfe of the Voyages I made with them.

The *Red Partridges* are wild and little, and much different from the *Red Partridge* we have in *Europe*, as well as the Pheafant, whofe Feathers being of a white colour with black fpecks, make a very agreeable diverfity.[1]

The largeft *Eagles* we find in this Country, are no bigger than Swans. Their Head and their Tail is white, and they have frequent Ingagements with a fort of Vultures, that commonly have the better of it. In our Voyages we had frequent

[1] There are no true partridges in America; those so called are quail or grouse. This was probably *Ortyx virginianus*, our ordinary "bob white," which formerly was common in Canada. — Ed.

occaſions of ſeeing theſe Ingagements, which laſt as long as the Eagle can keep up the force of its Wings.

The *Parrots* are met with in the *Ilineſe* Country, and upon the River of *Miſſiſipi*. They are very ſmall, and are the ſame with thoſe that we bring from *Brazil* and *Cayenne*.[1]

That ſort of *Nightingale* that I ſaw, is of a peculiar form; for 'tis of a leſſer ſize than the *European*, and of a blewiſh colour, and its notes are more diverſified; beſides that, it lodges in the holes of Trees, and four or five of 'em do commonly keep [240] together upon the thickeſt Trees, and with joynt Notes Warble o'er their Songs.

The *Flylike Bird* is no bigger than one's Thumb, and the colour of its Feathers is ſo changeable, that 'tis hard to faſten any one colour upon it. They appear ſometimes red, ſometimes of a Gold colour, at other times they are blew and red; and properly ſpeaking, 'tis only the brightneſs of the Sun that makes us unſenſible of the change of its gold and red colours. Its beak is as ſharp as a Needle. It flies from Flower to Flower, like a Bee, and by its fluttering ſucks the flowery Sap. Sometimes about Noon it pearches upon the little branches of Plum-trees or Cherry-trees. I have ſent ſome of 'em dead to *France*, it being impoſſible to keep 'em alive, and they were look'd upon as a great Curioſity.[2]

There are ten or twelve ſorts of Ducks in this Country.

---

[1] All the early travellers speak of paroquets in the Ohio valley. They were the Carolina parakeets (*Conurus carolinensis*), now restricted to Florida and some Southwestern States. — Ed.

[2] The humming bird is peculiar to America; the ordinary variety in the Eastern States and Canada is the ruby-throat (*Trochilus colubris*). — Ed.

Thoſe call'd *Branchus*, are the smalleſt indeed, but they are much the prettyeſt. The Feathers upon their Neck looks ſo bright, by vertue of the variety and livelineſs of their colours, that a Fur of that nature would be invaluable in *Muſcovy* or *Turky*. They owe the name of *Branchus*, to their reſting upon the branches of Trees. There's another Species of Ducks in this Country, that are as black as Jackdaws, only their Beak and the circle of their Eyes are red.

The Birds of the Northern Countries.

The *Seamews*, *Grelans* and *Sterlets*, are Fowls that fly inceſſantly over Seas, Lakes, and Rivers, in order to catch little Fiſh. Their Fleſh is good for nothing, beſides that, they have no ſubſtance of Body, though they ſeem to be as big as Pigeons.

The *Sea-Parrots* bear the name of *Parrots*, upon the account that their Beak is of the ſame form with that of the Land *Parrot*. They never quit the Sea or the Shoar; and are always flying upon the ſurface of the Water, in queſt of little Fiſh. Their [241] colour is black, and their ſize is much the ſame with that of a Pullet. There are great numbers of 'em upon the bank of *Newfound-Land*, and near the Coaſt of the Iſland, which the Seamen catch with Hooks cover'd with a Cod's Roe, and hung over the Prow of the Ship.

The *Moyacks* are a ſort of Fowl, as big as a Gooſe, having a ſhort Neck, and a broad Foot; and which is very ſtrange, their Eggs are half as big again as a Swan's, and yet they are all Yelk, and that ſo thick, that they muſt be diluted with Water, before they can be us'd in Pancakes.

The *White Partridges*, are as big as our *red Partridges*.

Their Feet are cover'd with ſuch a thick down, that they reſemble thoſe of a young Rabbet. They are only ſeen in the Winter time, and ſome years they are ſcarce ſeen at all, though on the other hand, in other years they are ſo plentiful, that you may buy a dozen for Nine pence. This is the moſt ſtupid Animal in the World; it ſits upon the Snow, and ſuffers it ſelf to be knock'd on the head with a pole without offering to ſtir. I am of the opinion, that this unaccountable numbneſs is occaſion'd by its long flight from *Greenland* to *Canada*. This conjecture is not altogether groundleſs, for 'tis obſerv'd, that they never come in flocks to *Canada*, but after the long continuance of a North or a North-Eaſt Wind.

The *Black Partridges* are truly very pretty. They are bigger than ours; and their beak together with the circle of the Eyes, and the Feet are red; their plumage being of a ſhining black colour. Theſe Animals are very proud, and ſeem to have a ſenſe of their beauty as they walk. They are but very uncommon, as well as the reddiſh *Partridges*, which reſemble Quails in their bulk and briskneſs.

The *White Ortolans* are only met with in Winter; but I am of the opinion, that their Feathers are naturally [242] of a white colour, and that they retrieve their natural colour in the places they retire to, when they diſappear in *Canada*. They are indifferent good to eat when they are fat, but that they ſeldom are. In the Winter great quantities of 'em are catch'd about the Barns, with Nets ſtretch'd out upon the Straw.[1]

[1] For the birds of Canada, see Macoun, *Catalogue of Canadian Birds* (Ottawa, 1900–03). — Ed.

A Defcription of the Infects of Canada.

THE *Adders* of *Canada* do no harm at all. The *Afps* indeed are very dangerous, when the People bathe in the ftagnating Water towards the South Countries. The *Rattle-Snake* or *Sounding Serpent* is fo call'd, in regard that at the extremity of its Tail, it has a fort of a Cafe, containing certain bones which make fuch a noife when the Serpent creeps along, that 'tis heard thirty Paces off. Thefe Serpents betake themfelves to flight when they hear the found of Mens Feet, and commonly fleep in the Sun either in green Fields, or open Woods. They never fting but when they are trod upon.[1]

The *Lowing Frogs* are fo call'd with refpect to their croaking, which founds like the lowing of an Oxe. Thefe *Frogs* are twice as large as thofe we have in *Europe*. The *Canada Gad-Bees* are a fort of Flies about twice as big as Bees; but of the fame form with a common Fly. They fting only between Noon, and three a Clock in the Afternoon; but then they do it fo violently, that they fetch Blood. However, 'tis only upon certain Rivers that they are met with.

The *Brulots* are a fort of Hand-worms, which cleave fo hard to the Skin, that their pricking occafions the fame fenfe,

---

[1] Bain says (Alexander Henry, p. 168, note 2) that there is no true rattlesnake (*Crotalus horridus*) in Canada; the variety found there is the *Caudisona tirguemina*. — ED.

as if 'twere a burning Coal, or a ſpark of Fire. Theſe little Animals are unperceivable, though at the ſame time they are pretty numerous.

[243] *The Names of the Fiſh in the River of St.* Laurence, *from its Mouth to the Lakes of* Canada.

Balenots or little Whales.
A Fiſh almoſt as big as a Whale, call'd *Souffleur.*
White Porpoiſes.
Salmon, ſuch as we have in *Europe.*
Eels.
Maycrel, as in *Europe.*
Herrings.
Gaſperots, a ſmall Fiſh like a Herring.
Baſes.
Shad-fiſh.
Cod-fiſh.
Plaices.
Smelts.
Turbots.
Pikes.
The Gold-colour'd Fiſh.
Roaches.
Lampreys.
Merles or Sea-Tench.
Thornbacks.
Cungars.
Sea-Cows, a kind of Porpoiſes.

The Shell-Fiſh.

Little Lobſters.
Crab-fiſh.
Cockles.
Muſcles.

The Fiſh that are found in the Lakes of Canada, *and in the Rivers that fall into 'em.*

Sturgeons.
The Armed Fiſh.
[244] Trouts.
White-Fiſh.
A ſort of Herrings.
Eels.
Mullets
Carp.
Gull-Fiſh.
Gudgeons.

The Fiſh found in the River of Miſſiſipi.

Pikes, ſuch as we have in *Europe*.
Carps.
Tench.
Perches.
Dabs, and ſeveral others that are not known in *Europe*.

A Deſcription of the Fiſh that are not mention'd in the Letters.

Thoſe between the Mouth of the River, and the Lakes.

THE *Balenot* is a ſort of a Whale, only 'tis leſs and more fleſhy, and does not yield Oil in proportion to the Northern Whales. This Fiſh goes fifty or ſixty Leagues up the River.

The *Souffleurs* are much of the ſame ſize, only they are ſhorter and blacker. When they mean to take breath after diving, they ſquirt out the Water through a hole behind their Head, after the ſame manner with the Whales. Commonly, they dog the Ships in the River of St. *Laurence.*

The *White Porpoiſes* are as big as Oxen. They always go along with the Current; and go up with the tide till they come at freſh Water, upon which they retire with the ebb Water. They are a ghaſtly ſort of Animals, and are frequently taken before *Quebec.*

[245] The *Gaſperots* are a ſmall Fiſh, not unlike a Herring. In the Summer time they make in to the ſhoar in ſuch ſhoals, that the Cod-fiſhers take as many of 'em as ſerves for Bait for that Fiſhery. Theſe Fiſhermen do likewiſe make uſe of Herrings, when the ſeaſon obliges them to put into the ſhoar to Spawn. In a word, all the Fiſh that are made uſe of for a Bait

to make the Codfiſh bite at the Hook, are call'd *Boete* in the Fiſhermens Dialect.

The *Gold-colour'd Fish* are nice Food. They are about fifteen Inches long; their Scales are yellow, and they are valued very high.

The *Sea-Cows*, which are a ſort of Porpoiſes, are bigger than the *Normandy* Beeves. They have a ſort of Paws cut like a Gooſe's Foot, their Head reſembles that of an Otter; and their Teeth, which are two Inches thick, and nine Inches long, are reckon'd the fineſt Ivory that is. 'Tis ſaid that they range wide of the ſhoar, towards Sandy and Marſhy places.

The *Lobſters* of this River ſeem to be exactly the ſame with thoſe we have in *Europe*.

The *Cockles* are of a piece, with thoſe we have upon the coaſt of *France*, excepting that they are larger, and have a more agreeable taſte, though their Fleſh ſeems to partake more of crudity and indigeſtion.

The *Muſcles* of this River are prodigious large, and taſte very well; but 'tis next to an impoſſibility to eat 'em without breaking one's Teeth, by reaſon of their being ſtuff'd with *Pearl;* I call it *Pearl*, tho' the name of Gravel or Sand may be more proper, with reſpect to its value, for I brought to *Paris* fifty or ſixty of the largeſt and fineſt, which were rated only at a penny a piece; notwithſtanding that we had broke above two thouſand Muſcles to make up that number.

[246] The *Lake-Sturgeons* are commonly five or ſix Foot

long: But I once ſaw one of ten Foot, and another of twelve in length. The Savages catch 'em with Nets in the Winter, and Grapples in the Summer. 'Tis ſaid, they have a certain ſort of Fleſh about their Head, that taſts like Beef, Mutton, and Veal; but I have eat of it ſeveral times, and never could obſerve any ſuch thing, which makes me look upon the allegation as chimerical.

The *Fiſh in Armour*, is about three Foot and a half long. 'Tis defended by ſuch ſtrong and hard Scales, that 'tis impoſſible for any other Fiſh to hurt it. Its Enemies are Trouts and Roaches, but 'tis admirably well provided for the repulſing of their Attacks, by vertue of its pointed Snout, which is a Foot long, and as hard as its Skin. It eats very well, and its Fleſh or Subſtance is as firm as 'tis white.

The *Lake Dabs* or *Sandings* are not above a Foot long, but they are very thick all over. They are call'd *Barbues* in *French*, with alluſion to a certain ſort of Beards that hang down from the ſide of their Muzzle, and are as big as ears of Corn. Thoſe which we find in the River of *Miſſiſipi*, are of a monſtrous ſize. Both the one and the other are catch'd with a Hook, as well as with a Net; and make very good Victuals.

The *Miſſiſipi Carps* are likewiſe of an extraordinary ſize, and admirably well taſted. They are of the ſame form with ours. In the Autumn they put in towards the ſhoar, and are eaſily catch'd with a Net.

The largeſt *Trouts* we meet with in the Lakes, are five Foot and a half long, and of one Foot Diameter. Their flefh is red, and they are catch'd with great Hooks made faft to pieces of Wire.

The Fifh catch'd in the Lakes, are better than thofe we take at Sea, or in the Rivers, particularly [247] the white Fifh, which for goodnefs and nice Eating, are far beyond all the other Species. The Savages that live upon the fides of thofe little frefh-water Seas, prefer the Broth of Fifh, to Meat-broth, when they are indifpos'd. This choice they ground upon experience; whereas the *French* on the other hand find that Venifon Broth is at once more fubftantial and reftorative.

The Rivers of *Canada* are replenifh'd with an infinity of other fifhes, that are not known in *Europe*. The Fifh catch'd in the North-Country Rivers, are different from thofe of the South; and thofe taken in the *Long River*, which difimbogues into the River of *Miffifipi*, favour fo rank of Mud and Clay, that 'tis impoffible to eat of 'em; abating for a fort of little Trouts that the Savages take in the adjacent Lakes, which make a tolerable Mefs.

The Rivers of the *Otentats*, and the *Miffouris*, produce fuch odd fhap'd fifhes, that 'tis impoffible to defcribe 'em without they were drawn upon Paper. Thefe Fifhes tafts but forrily, and yet the Savages love it mightily, which I take to proceed from their knowing no better.

The Trees and Fruits of the South Countries of Canada.

Beech-Trees. }
Red Oak. } ſuch as we have in *Europe.*

Bitter Cherry-trees.

Maple-trees.

Aſh-trees.

Elms. }
Linden-trees. } ſuch as we have in *Europe.*

Nut-trees of two ſorts.

Cheſnut-trees.

Apple-trees.

[248] Pear-trees.

Plum-trees.

Cherry-trees.

Hazel-trees, ſuch as we have in *Europe*

Vines.

A ſort of Citrons.

Water Melons.

Sweet Citruls.

Wild Gooſeberries.

Pine-apples.

Tobacco, ſuch as our *Spaniſh* Tobacco.

The Trees and Fruits of the North Countries of Canada.

White Oak.

Red Oak.

Birch-trees.

Bitter Cherry-trees.
Mapple-trees.
Pine-trees.
Epinettes.
Fir-trees of three ſorts.
Peruſſes.
Cedar-trees.
Aſpin-trees.
White Wood.
Alder-trees.
Maiden Hair.
Strawberries.
Rasberries.
Gooſeberries.
Bluets.

A Deſcription of the above-mention'd Trees and Fruits.

YOU muſt remark, that all the Wood of *Canada* is good of its kind. The Trees that ſtand expos'd to the North-Winds are apt [249] to be influenc'd by the Froſt, as it appears from the chops and chinks that it occaſions.

The *Bitter Cherry-tree*, has a hard and whitiſh Wood, with a grey Bark. Some of 'em are as tall as the loftyeſt Oaks, and as big as a Hogſhead. This Tree grows ſtreight; it has an oval Leaf, and is made uſe of in Beams, Rafters, and other Carpenter's work.

The *Mapple-tree* is much of the ſame height and bulk; but it has a brown Bark, and the Wood is reddiſh. It bears no reſemblance to that ſort we have in *Europe.* It yields a Sap, which has a much pleaſanter taſte than the beſt Limonade or Cherry-water, and makes the wholſomeſt drink in the World. This Liquor is drawn by cutting the Tree two Inches deep in the Wood, the cut being run ſloping to the length of ten or twelve Inches. At the lower end of this gaſh, a Knife is thruſt into the Tree ſlopingly, ſo that the water running along the Cut or Gaſh, as through a Gutter, and falling upon the Knife that lies acroſs the Channel, runs out upon the Knife, which has Veſſels plac'd underneath to receive it. Some Trees will yield five or ſix Bottles of this water a Day; and ſome Inhabitants of *Canada*, might draw twenty Hogſheads of it in one day, if they would thus cut and notch all the *Mapples* of their reſpective Plantations. The gaſh do's no harm to the Tree. Of this Sap they make Sugar and Syrup, which is ſo valuable, that there can't be a better remedy for fortifying the Stomach. 'Tis but few of the Inhabitants that have the patience to make *Mapple-Water*, for as common and uſual things are always ſlighted, ſo there's ſcarce any body but Children that give themſelves the trouble of gaſhing theſe Trees. To conclude, the North-Country *Mapples* have more Sap than thoſe of the South Countries; but at the ſame time the Sap is not ſo ſweet.

[250] There are two ſorts of Nut-trees in this Country. The one bears round, and the other long, Nuts; but neither of 'em is good for any thing, no more than the wild Cheſnuts that grow in the *Ilineſe* Country.

The Apples that grow upon ſome of their Apple-trees, eat well when they are Codled, but they are good for nothing when they're Raw. Upon the *Miſſiſipi* indeed, there's a ſort of Apples that have a taſte not unlike that of ſome *European* Apples. The Pears are good, but very ſcarce.

The Cherries are ſmall, and extream red; and though their taſte is not good, yet the Roe-bucks like 'em ſo well, that in the Summer time they ſcarce ever miſs to lye under the Cherry-trees all Night long, eſpecially if it blows hard.

This Country affords three ſorts of excellent Plums, which bear no reſemblance to ours either in figure or colour. Some are long and ſmall, ſome are round and thick, and ſome very little.

The Vines twine round the Trees to the very top; and the Branches of thoſe Trees are ſo cover'd with Grapes, that one would take the Grape to be the fruit of the Tree. In ſome Countries of North-*America*, the Grape is little, but very well taſted; but towards the *Miſſiſipi*, 'tis long and thick, and ſo is the cluſter. There has been ſome Wine preſs'd from the Grapes of that Country, which after long ſtanding became as ſweet as Canary, and as black as Ink.

The Citrons of North-*America* are ſo call'd, only becauſe their form reſembles that of our Citron. Inſtead of a Rind, they have only a ſingle Skin. They grow upon a Plant that riſes three Foot high, and do's not bear above three or four at a time. This Fruit is as wholſom as its Root is dangerous; for the one is very Healthy, and the juice of the other is a mortal ſubtile Poyſon.[1] While I ſtay'd at Fort *Frontenac*, [251] in the year 1684, I ſaw an *Iroqueſe* Woman take down this fatal Potion, with a deſign to follow her deceas'd Husband; after ſhe had took leave of her Friends, and ſung the Death Song, with the Formalities that are uſual among theſe blind Wretches. The Poiſon quickly work'd the deſir'd effect; for this Widdow, who in *Europe* would be juſtly look'd upon as a miracle of Conſtancy and Fidelity, had no ſooner ſwallowed the murdering Juice, than ſhe fell into two or three ſhivering Fits, and ſo expir'd.

The *Water-Melons*, call'd by the *Spaniards Algiers Melons*,

[1] Doubtless Lahontan here refers to the may apple or mandrake (*Podophyllum peltatum*), from whose root a poison may be extracted. The Jesuit missionaries called this fruit citron. — Ed.

are round and thick like a Ball; ſome are red, and ſome white, and the kernels, which are very large, are ſometimes black, ſometimes red. As for their taſte, 'tis exactly the ſame with that of the *Spaniſh* or *Portugueze Melons.*

The *Citruls* of this Country are ſweet, and of a different nature from thoſe of *Europe;* and I'm inform'd, that the *American Citruls* will not grow in *Europe.* They are as big as our *Melons;* and their Pulp is as yellow as Saffron. Commonly they are bak'd in Ovens, but the better way is to roaſt 'em under the Embers, as the Savages do. Their taſte is much the ſame with that of the Marmelade of Apples, only they are ſweeter. One may eat as much of 'em as he pleaſes, without fearing any diſorder from 'em.[1]

The wild Gooſeberries are good for nothing, but for Confits: But that ſort of Confits are ſeldom made, for Sugar is too dear in *Canada*, to be imploy'd for ſuch uſes.

---

[1] For the citrul (citrouille), see p. 148, note 2, *ante.* — ED.

[252] *A Defcription of the Trees and Fruits of the Northern Countries.*

THE *Canada* Birch-trees are much different from thofe we have in fome Provinces of *France;* both for bulk and quality. The Savages make Canows of their Bark, fome of which is red, and fome white; but both are equally proper for that ufe. That which has the feweft Veins and Chops, is the beft; but the red bark makes the fineft fhow. There are fome little Baskets made of the young Birches, that are much efteem'd in *France;* and Books may be made of 'em, the Leaves of which will be as fine as Paper. This I can fpeak by experience, for I have frequently made ufe of 'em for want of Paper, in writing the Journal of my Voyages. Nay, I remember I have feen in a certain Library in *France*, a Manufcript of the Gofpel of St. *Matthew*, written in *Greek* upon this fort of Bark; and, which is yet more furprifing, I was then told, that it had been written above a thoufand years; and at the fame time I dare fwear, that 'twas the Genuine Birch-bark of New-*France*, which in all appearance was not then difcover'd.

The *Pine-trees* are very tall, ftraight, and thick; and are made ufe of for Mafts, which the King's Pinks do oftentimes tranfport to *France*. 'Tis faid, that fome of thefe Trees are big enough, to ferve for a Maft to a Firft-rate Ship.

The *Epinette* is a ſort of a Pine, with a ſharper and thicker Leaf. 'Tis made uſe of in Carpenters work, and the matter which drains from it, ſmells as ſweet as Incenſe.[1]

There are three ſorts of *Firs* in this Country, which are ſaw'd into Dales [deals] by certain Mills, that the *Quebec* Merchants have caus'd to be built in ſome places.

[253] The *Peruſſe* is the propereſt of all green Woods for the building of Ships, upon the conſideration that 'tis compacter, and has cloſer Pores, ſo that it do's not ſoak or drink in the moiſture as much as others.

Here are two ſorts of *Cedar*, namely, the white and the red; but one muſt view 'em narrowly before he can diſtinguiſh 'em, by reaſon that both of 'em have much the ſame ſort of Bark. Theſe Trees are low, buſhy, and full of Branches and little Leaves, reſembling the tag of a Lace. The Wood of this Tree, is almoſt as light as Cork; and the Savages make uſe of it in the Wreaths and Ribs of their Canows. The red ſort looks admirably well, and may be made into Houſhold-Goods, which will retain an agreeable ſmell for ever.

The *Aſps* are little Shrubs, which grow upon the ſides of Pools or Rivers; and in a word, in moiſt and marſhy Countries. This Wood is the common food of the Beavers, who, in imitation of the Ants, take care to make a collection of it round their Hutts in the Autumn, which ſerves 'em for ſuſtenance when the Ice impriſons 'em in Winter.

The *White Wood* is a midling ſort of Tree, that's neither too

[1] The "epinette" has been identified as the hemlock spruce (*Abies canadensis*). — Ed.

big nor too little. 'Tis almoſt as light as Cedar, and as eaſily work'd upon. The Inhabitants of *Canada* make little Canows of it, for fiſhing and croſſing the Rivers.

Maidenhair is as common in the Forreſts of *Canada*, as Fern is in thoſe of *France*, and is eſteem'd beyond that of other Countries; inſomuch, that the Inhabitants of *Quebec* prepare great quantities of its Syrup, which they ſend to *Paris*, *Nants*, *Rouan*, and ſeveral other Cities in *France*.

Strawberries and *Rasberries*, are wonderfully plentiful in *Canada*, and taſte extream well. We meet likewiſe with ſome white Gooſeberries in this Country; but they ſerve for no uſe, unleſs it be to make a ſort of Vinegar of 'em, that is very ſtrong.

The *Bluets* are certain little Berries, not unlike ſmall Cherries, only they are black, and perfectly round. The Plant upon which they grow, is as big as a Rasberry-buſh. Theſe Berries ſerve for ſeveral uſes, after they are dry'd in the Sun, or in an Oven; for then they make Confits of 'em, or put 'em into Pyes, or infuſe 'em in Brandy. The North-Country Savages make a Crop of 'em in the Summer, which affords 'em very ſeaſonable relief, eſpecially when their hunting comes ſhort.[1]

[1] "Bluet" is the term still used by Canadians for the blueberry (*Vaccinium canadense*). — Ed.

A General View of the Commerce of Canada.

I COME now to give a brief and general account of the Commerce of *Canada*, which I have already touch'd upon in my Letters. The *Normans* were the firft that fęt up this trade, and ufually they fet out from *Havre de Grace*, or *Dieppe;* but the *Rochellers* have now work'd 'em out of it, for as much as the *Rochel* Ships furnifh the Inhabitants of that Continent with the neceffary Commodities. There are likewife fome Ships fent to *Canada* from *Bourdeaux* and *Bayonne*, with Wines, Brandy, Tobacco, and Iron.

The Ships bound from *France* to that Country, pay no Cuftom for their Cargo, whether in clearing in *France*, or in their entries at *Quebec;* abating for the *Brazil* Tobacco which pays five *Sols* a pound; that is to fay, a Roll of 400 pound weight, pays a hundred Livres by way of Entry, to the Office of the Farmers-General.[1]

Moft of the Ships go laden to *Canada*, and return light or empty. Some indeed bring home Peafe when they are good cheap in the Colony, and others take in a Cargo of Planks

[1] In addition to large quantities of tobacco raised in New France, much was imported, this being preferred by both Indians and habitants. As early as 1676 an impost of ten per cent advalorem was laid upon Brazil tobacco; five sols being equivalent to about nineteen cents in the American money of to-day, the retail price of imported tobacco must, at that rate, have reached nearly two dollars per pound. — ED.

and Boards: Others again go to the Iſland of Cape *Breton*, and there [255] take in a Cargoe of Pit-Coal, which they carry to the Iſlands of *Martinico* or *Guardaloupa*, where the refining of Sugars occaſions a great conſumption of Coals. But thoſe Ships which either belong, or are recommended to the topping Merchants of the Colony, are fraughted with Skins, which turns to a great account. I have ſeen ſome Ships unload at *Quebec*, and then ſteer to *Placentia*, to take in Cod-fiſh which they purchas'd with ready Mony; but generally ſpeaking, there's more loſt than got by that way of trading. The Merchant that has carried on the greateſt trade in *Canada*, is the Sieur *Samuel Bernon* of *Rochel*, who has great Ware-Houſes at *Quebec*, from which the Inhabitants of the other Towns are ſupplied with ſuch Commodities as they want.[1] 'Tis true, there are ſome Merchants at *Quebec*, who are indifferent rich, and fit out Ships upon their own bottom, that ply to and again between *France* and *Canada;* and theſe Merchants have their Correſpondents at *Rochel*, who ſend out and take in every year the Cargoes of their Ships.

There's no difference between the Pyrates that ſcowr the Seas, and the *Canada* Merchants; unleſs it be this, that the former ſometimes inrich 'emſelves all of a ſudden by a good Prize; and that the latter can't make their fortune without trading for five or ſix years, and that without running the hazard of their Lives. I have known twenty little Pedlars that had not above a thouſand Crowns ſtock when I arriv'd at

[1] Bernon was a Huguenot, whom the bishop required the governor to order out of his domain. See Parkman, *Old Regime*, pp. 291, 292. — Ed.

Quebec, in the year 1683; and when I left that place, had got to the tune of twelve thoufand Crowns. 'Tis an unqueftion'd truth, that they get fifty *per Cent* upon all the Goods they deal in, whether they buy 'em up upon the arrival of the Ships at *Quebec*, or have 'em from *France* by way of Commiffion; but over and above that, there are fome little gaudy Trinkets, fuch as Ribbands, Laces, Embroideries, Tobacco-Boxes, Watches, [256] and an infinity of other baubles of Iron Ware, upon which they get a hundred and fifty *per Cent*, all Cofts clear.

In this Country a Hogfhead of *Bourdeaux* Wine, which contains 250 Bottles, is worth about forty *French* Livres, in time of Peace, and fixty in time of War. A Hogfhead of *Nants* or *Bayonne* Brandy, will fetch 80 or a 100 Livres. In the Taverns a Bottle of Wine cofts fix *French* Sous, and a Bottle of Brandy is fold for twenty. As for dry Commodities, their price rifes and falls upon occafion. *Brazil* Tobacco is worth 40 Sous a pound by way of Retail, and 35 by Wholefale. Sugar will fetch at leaft 20 Sous a pound, and fometimes 25 or 30.

The earlieft Ships that come from *France*, fet out commonly in the latter end of *April*, or the beginning of *May;* but to my mind, they might fhorten their Voyage by one half, if they put to Sea about the middle of *March*, and then fweep'd along the North Coaft of the *Azores* Iflands; for in thofe Seas the South and South-Eaft Winds commonly blow from the beginning of *April*, to the end of *May*. I have mention'd this feveral times to the moft expert Pilots; but they ſtill put me off with the plea, that they dare not ſteer that Courſe for fear of ſome Rocks: And yet theſe Rocks are not to be met with but in their Charts. I have read ſome Deſcriptions of the Ports, Roads, and Coaſts of theſe Iſlands, and of the adjacent Seas, done by the *Portugueze*, which make no mention of the Shelves that are chalk'd down in all our Charts: On the contrary, they affirm that the Coaſt of theſe Iſlands is altogether clear, and that for twenty Leagues off into the Main, theſe imaginary Rocks were never met with.

As ſoon as the *French* Ships arrive at *Quebec*, the Merchants of that City who have their Factours in the other Towns, load their Barques with Goods in [257] order to tranſport 'em to theſe other Towns. Such Merchants as act for themſelves at *Trois Rivieres*, or *Monreal*, they come down in Perſon to *Quebec* to Market for themſelves, and then put their Effects on board of Barques, to be convey'd home. If they pay for their Goods in Skins, they buy cheaper than if they made their payments in Money or Letters of Exchange; by reaſon that the Seller gets conſiderably by the Skins when he returns to *France*. Now, you muſt take notice, that all theſe Skins are bought up from the Inhabitants, or from the Savages, upon which the Merchants are conſiderable Gainers. To give you an inſtance of this matter. A Perſon that lives in the Neighbourhood of *Quebec*, carries a dozen of Martins Skins, five or ſix Foxes Skins, and as many Skins of wild Cats, to a Merchants Houſe, in order to ſell 'em for Woollen Cloth, Linnen, Arms, Ammunition, *&c.* In the truck of theſe Skins, the Merchant draws a double profit, one upon the ſcore of his paying no more for the Skins, than one half of what he afterwards ſells 'em for in the lump to the Factours for the *Rochel* Ships; and the other by the exorbitant rate he puts upon the Goods that the poor Planter takes in exchange for his Skins. If this be duly weigh'd, we will not think it ſtrange that theſe Merchants have a more beneficial Trade, than a great many other Tradeſmen in the World. In my ſeventh and eighth Letter, I related the particulars of the Commerce of this Country, eſpecially that which the Inhabitants carry on with the Savages, who ſupply 'em with the Skins of Beavers, and other Animals. So that now it remains only to give you an Inventory of the Goods that are proper for the Savages, and of the Skins which they give in exchange, together with their neat [net] Prices.

[258] Short and light Fuſees.
Powder.
Ball and cut Lead, or Small-ſhot.
Axes both great and ſmall.
Knives with their Sheaths.
Sword-blades to make Darts of.
Kettles of all ſizes.
Shoomakers Awls.
Fiſh-hooks, of all ſizes.
Flint Stones.
Caps of blew Serge.
Shirts made of the common *Brittany* Linnen.
Woolſted Stockins, ſhort and coarſe.
Braſil Tobacco.

Coarſe white Thread for Nets.
Sewing Thread of ſeveral colours.
Pack-thread.
Vermillion.
Needles, both large and ſmall.
Venice Beads.
Some Iron Heads for Arrows, but few of 'em.
A ſmall quantity of Soap.
A few Sabres or Cutlaſſes.

Brandy goes off incomparably well.

The Names of the Skins given in exchange, with their Rates.

THE Skins of Winter Beavers, *alias Mufcovy* Beavers, are worth *per pound* in the Farmer Generals Warehoufe. — — — — 4 *Livres.* 10 *Sous.*

The Skins of fat Beavers, the Hair of which falls off, while the Savages make ufe of 'em, *per pound*,[1]	5 *L.*	0 *S.*
Of Beavers taken in Autumn, *per pound* — —	3	10
[259] Of dry or common Beavers, *per pound* —	3	0
Of Summer Beavers, *per pound.* — — —	3	0

The Skin of a white Beaver is not to be valued, no more than that of a Fox that's quite black.

The Skins of Silver-colour'd Foxes a piece. —	4	0
Of common Foxes, in good order, — — —	2	0
Of the common Martins. — — — —	1	0
Of the prettyeft fort of Martins. — — —	4	0
Of red and fmooth Otters. — — — —	2	0
Of the Winter and brown Otters. — — — or more.	4	10

[1] The skins of beavers most valued by the French were those known as *castor gras d'hiver* (fat winter beaver); that is, skins killed in the winter, then made by the savages into robes, and worn long enough to be thoroughly greased by contact with their bodies. See Perrot, *Mémoire sur les Mœurs, Coustumes et Relligion des Sauvages de l'Amèrique Septentrionale* (Paris, 1864), p. 317.—ED.

	Livres.	Sous.
Of the fineſt black Bears. — — — —	7	0
The Skins of Elks before they're dreſs'd, are worth *per pound* about. — — — — —	0	12
The Skins of Stags are worth *per pound* about —	0	8
The wild Cats or *Enfans de Diable*, a piece —	1	15
Sea Wolves — a piece. — — — — or more.	1	15
Pole-Cats, and Weaſels — — — —	0	10
Musk Rats. — — — — — —	0	6
Their Teſticles. — — — — —	0	5
Wolves. — — — — — —	2	10
The white Elk-skins, *i. e.* thoſe dreſs'd by the Savages a piece — — — — — —	8 or m.	
A dreſs'd Harts Skin is worth — — —	5 or m.	
A Caribous — — — — — —	6	
A Roe-buck's — — — — — —	3	

To conclude, you muſt take notice that theſe Skins are upon ſome particular occaſions dearer than I rate 'em, but the difference is but very ſmall, whether under or over.[1]

[1] For comparison with this interesting table of prices, see that given for 1713 in Martin, *Castorologia*, pp. 110, 111; those for about 1750, in *Jesuit Relations*, lxiv, p. 127; and those at the beginning of the English regime, in Henry, *Travels*, pp. 55, 56. — Ed.

[260] *An Account of the Government of* Canada *in General.*

IN *Canada* the Politick, Civil, Ecclefiaftical and Military Government, are all in a manner one thing, in regard, that the wifeft Governours have fubjected their Authority to that of the *Ecclefiafticks;* and fuch Governours as would not imbarque in that intereft, have found their Poft fo uneafie, that they have been recall'd with difgrace. I could inftance in feveral, who for not adhering to the Sentiments of the Bifhop and the Jefuits, and for refufing to lodge their Power in the hands of thefe infallible Gentlemen, have been turn'd out, and treated at Court like hot-headed Incendiaries. Mr. *de Frontenac* was one of this number, who made fuch an unhappy exit; for he fell out with Mr. *Duchefnau*, Intendant of that Country, who finding himfelf protected by the Clergy, induftrioufly infulted that illuftrious General; and the General was forc'd to give way, under the weight of an Ecclefiaftical League, by reafon of the Springs they fet at work againft him, in oppofition to all the principles of Honour and Confcience.[1]

The Governour General that means to neglect no opportunity of advancing or inriching themfelves, do commonly

[1] Lahontan, as a partisan of Frontenac, presents his side of the disagreements with Duchesneau. For an account of their petty quarrels, which led to the recall (1682) of both governor and intendant, see Parkman, *Frontenac*, pp. 44–71. — ED.

hear two Maſſes a Day, and are oblig'd to confeſs once in four and twenty hours. He has always Clergy-men hanging about him where-ever he goes, and indeed properly ſpeaking, they are his Counſellours. When a Governour is thus back'd by the Clergy; the Intendants, the Under-Governours, and the Sovereign Council, dare's not cenſure his Conduct, let it be never ſo faulty; ſor the protection of the Eccleſiaſticks, ſhelters him from all the charges that can be laid againſt him.

The Governour General of *Quebec*, has twenty thouſand Crowns a year, including the pay of his [261] Company of Guards, and the particular Government of the Fort. Over and above this Income, the Farmers of the Beaver-Skins make him a Preſent of a thouſand Crowns a year; his Wines and all his other Proviſions imported from *France* pay no Fraight; not to mention that by certain ways and means he ſucks as much Money out of the Country, as all the above mention'd Articles amount to. The Intendant has eighteen thouſand Livres a year; but the Lord knows what he makes otherwiſe: I have no mind to touch there, for fear of being rank'd among thoſe Detractors, who ſpeak the truth too ſincerely.[1] The Biſhops Incomes are ſo ſmall, that if the King were not graciouſly pleas'd to add to his Biſhoprick ſome other Benefices in *France*, that Reverend Prelate would be reduc'd to as ſhort

[1] The office of intendant was established in New France when the King took over the colony from the hands of the commercial company (1663). It was analagous to the intendancy in France, and created substantially a second head to the colony, causing much friction with the governor general. The duties of the intendant were numerous, and the powers vague and far-reaching; he was especially charged with the administration of finance and justice. For a list of both governors and intendants in New France, see *Jesuit Relations*, lxxii, pp. 116–118. — ED.

Commons, as a hundred of his Character are in the Kingdom of *Naples*.[1] The Major of *Quebec* has fix hundred Crowns a year, the Governour of *Trois Rivieres* has a thoufand; and the Governour of *Monreal* is allow'd two thoufand.[2] A Captain has a hundred and twenty Livres a Month, a Lieutenant ninety Livres, a reform'd Lieutenant is allow'd but forty, and a common Soldier's pay is fix *Sous* a Day, of the current Money of the Country.

The People repofe a great deal of confidence in the Clergy in this Country as well as elfewhere. Here the outward fhew of Devotion is ftrictly obferv'd, for the People dare not abfent from the great Maffes and Sermons, without a lawful Excufe. But after all, 'tis at the time of Divine Service, that the married Women and Maids give their humours a full loofe, as being affur'd that their Husbands and Mothers are bufie at Church. The Priefts call People by their names in the Pulpit; they prohibit under the pain of Excommunication, the reading of Romances and Plays, as well as the ufe of Masks, and playing at Ombre or Lanfquenet. The Jefuits [262] and the Recollets agree as ill as the Molinifts and the Janfenifts.[3]

---

[1] Laval, first bishop of Quebec, was titular bishop of Petræa, and had a large private fortune; see p. 43, note 2, *ante*. St. Vallier, the second bishop, was abbé of a rich monastery of that name in France. — ED.

[2] The three local divisions of New France. In 1722 the government of Quebec comprised forty-one parishes, Three Rivers thirteen, and Montreal twenty-eight. Frontenac attempted to establish a rudimentary type of self-government, by permitting the inhabitants to elect their local officials; but the autocratic paternalism of the French court reversed these plans, and all officials were thereafter appointed by the King. — ED.

[3] The Molinists and Jansenists were two schools of theologians, the former followers of the Jesuit Molina (1535–1600), the latter those of the Dutch scholar Jansen

The former pretend that the latter have no right to confefs. Do but look back to my eighth Letter, and there you'll fee fome inftances of the indifcreet zeal of the Ecclefiafticks.

The Governour General has the difpofal of all Military Pofts; He beftows Companies, Lieutenancies, and Under-Lieutenancies, upon who he pleafes, with his Majefty's gracious Approbation; but he is not allow'd to difpofe of particular Governourfhips, or of the place of a Lord Lieutenant of a Province, or of the Major of any Town. He is impower'd to grant to the Gentry and the other Inhabitants, Lands and Settlements all over *Canada;* but thefe Grants muft be given in concert with the Intendant. He is likewife authoris'd to give five and twenty Licences a year to whom he thinks fit, for trading with the Savage Nations of that vaft Continent. He is invefted with the power of fufpending the execution of Sentences againft Criminals; and by vertue of this Reprieve, can eafily procure 'em a Pardon, if he has a mind to favour 'em. But he can't difpofe of the King's Money, without the confent of the Intendant, who is the only Man that can call it out of the hands of the Treafurer of the Navy.[1]

(1585–1638). The controversy agitated Western Europe throughout the seventeenth century, involved courts and society, and had a profound influence upon French literature. In his later years, Louis XIV, prompted by the Jesuits, persecuted the party of the Jansenists, and finally broke up their retreat at Port Royal. — ED.

[1] The governor-general of Canada, usually a military noble, was commandant of the army, leader of military expeditions, supreme arbiter of life and death in criminal justice — in short, representative of the king and of paternal government in the colony. For his commissions, see *Edits et Ordonnances* (Quebec, 1856), iii, pp. 5–81. On the subject of licenses (*congés*), see p. 99, note 1, *ante*. The "Treasurer of the Navy" is the English translator's rendition of the Department of the Marine, which had the colonies in charge. — ED.

H. Moll Fecit.

Vol. I. p. 225.

Straits of Belle Isle

0. 10. 20. 30. 60.

English Miles

ST. LAURENS BAY.

THE MAIN SEA.

NEW FOUND LAND.

This Coast is Call'd Petit Nord.

Great Bay

P. St. Iulian

Passage of y Savages

Haver Deep

Foggs Bay

Gory

Penguin I.

Norterdam

St. Paul

C. Frals

Gull

Flower B.

Indian Bay

Greenpond

Deadman

Bloody Bay

Cople I.

Friswater Bay

C. Bonavista

Salvaye

Flowers

North head

Kiels Bay

Black head Bay

Ragged harb.

South head

Trinity harbour

Bonaventure head

Smits Sound

Trinity Bay

R. Random

Breakheart P.

Platforme

Bacolai I.

Bay of Isles

C. Anguille

St. George Bay

C. Ray

Bulls

Conception Bay

Verte

Lompa

Martir

Burin R.

Platinel

I. Rua

C. Francis

Torbay

I. Disper

Saguanon

Brutt

Kirk Sound

St. Laurence Bay

Chapeau Rouge

Placentia

St. Iohns

Fortune

Grand Duns

P. Dauns

Lasne

C. Iulie

Placentia Bay

Petty harb.

Maynelon

Bay

C. St. Maria

Bull Bay

Fortune

Dunes

C. May

Baline H.

Gose I.

St. Marys Bay

Fermowes

Feryland head

I. St. Peter

Trepassez Bay

Freshwater Bay

Banck of the Islands

C. Pine

C. Race

Criple Cove

Verte Banck

Main Banck

52 51 50 49 47

20 45 40 70 80 60 28 28 28 30 38 30 70 70 75 60

321 Degrees from Ferro Isle E. 324 325 326

The Governour General can't be without the ſervice of the Jeſuits, in making Treaties with the Governours of *New-England*, and *New-York*, as well as with the *Iroqueſe*. I am at a loſs to know, whether theſe good Fathers are imploy'd in ſuch Services, upon the ſcore of their judicious Counſels, and their being perfectly well acquainted with the Country, and the King's true intereſts; or upon the conſideration of their ſpeaking to a Miracle, the Languages of ſo many different Nations, whoſe intereſt are quite oppoſite; or out of a ſenſe of that condeſcenſion and ſubmiſſion, that is due to theſe worthy Companions of our Saviour.[1]

[263] The Members of the ſupreme Council of *Canada*, can't ſell or convey their Places to their Heirs, or to any body elſe without the King's approbation; though at the ſame time their places may be worth not ſo much as the place of a Lieutenant to a Company of Foot.[2] When they have nice points under their conſideration, they uſually conſult the Prieſts or Jeſuits: And if any cauſe comes before 'em, in which theſe good Fathers are intereſs'd, they are ſure not to be caſt, unleſs it be ſo very black, that the cunningeſt Lawyer can't give it a plauſible turn. I've been inform'd by ſeveral Perſons, that the Jeſuits drive a great trade in *European* Com-

[1] The employment of the Jesuit missionaries as envoys and interpreters was not only due to their skill in languages, but to their large acquaintance with the habits and customs of the Indians, and a certain degree of ascendancy which they had acquired over the latter's minds. The negotiations with New England and New York dealt almost entirely with Indian relations. — ED.

[2] For the sovereign council of New France, see p. 41, note 3, *ante*. In 1703 the title was changed to superior council. In a few cases, the king permitted a son to succeed his father in this office. See Parkman, *Old Regime*, pp. 274, 275. — ED.

modities, and *Canada* Skins; but I can ſcarce believe it, or at leaſt if it be ſo, they muſt have Correſpondents and Factors that are as cloſe and cunning as themſelves; which can never be.[1]

The Gentlemen of that Country, are oblig'd to be very cautious in carrying even with the *Eccleſiaſticks*, in reſpect of the good or harm that the good Fathers can indirectly throw in their way. The Biſhop and the Jeſuits have ſuch an influence over the Governours General, as is ſufficient to procure places to the Children of the Noblemen or Gentlemen that are devoted to their Service, or to obtain the Licences that I ſpoke of in my eighth Letter. 'Tis likewiſe in their power to ſerve the Daughters of ſuch Gentlemen, by finding 'em agreeable and rich Husbands. The meaneſt Curates muſt be manag'd cautiouſly, for they can either ſerve or diſſerve the Gentlemen, in whoſe Seignories they are no more than Miſſionaries, there being no fix'd Cures in *Canada*, which indeed is a grievance that ought to be redreſs'd.[2] The Officers of the Army are likewiſe oblig'd to keep up a good correſpondence with the *Eccleſiaſticks*, for without that 'tis impoſſible for 'em to keep their ground. They muſt not only take care that their own conduct be regular; but likewiſe [264] look

[1] The charge was often made that the missionaries participated in the advantages of the fur-trade. There is evidence that this was sometimes true before 1642; but there was passed about that time a stringent order against it, and they thenceforth almost wholly refrained, except in the case of lay brothers, and an occasional transgressor who was speedily punished. See *Jesuit Relations*, index. — Ed.

[2] Lahontan probably means that all the parish priests (curés) were affiliated with the seminary which Bishop Laval had established; see p. 42, note 1, *ante*. St. Vallier attempted to break up the system, and it was probably in the interest of this movement that Lahontan wrote as above. — Ed.

after that of the Soldiers, by preventing the Diſorders they might commit in their Quarters.

Commonly the Troops are quarter'd upon the Inhabitants of the *Cotes*, or Seignories of *Canada*, from *October* to *May*. The Maſter of the Houſe furniſhes his Military Gueſts only with Utenſils, and imploys him all the while at the rate of ten *Sous* a Day beſides his Victuals, in the cutting of Wood, grubbing up of Grounds, rooting out Stumps, or the threſhing of Corn in a Barn. The Captain gets likewiſe by their work; for to make 'em diſcount the half of their pay to him, he orders 'em to come thrice a Week to exerciſe their Arms at his Quarters. Now, their Habitations being diſtant four or five *Arpents* from one another, and one *Cote* or Seignory being two or three Leagues in Front, the Soldiers chooſe rather to give the Captain a ſpill, than to walk ſo far in the Snow and the Dirt: And the Captain takes it very conſcientiouſly, upon the plea that *Volenti non fit injuria*. As for ſuch Soldiers as are good Tradeſmen, he's ſure of putting their whole pay in his Pocket, by vertue of a Licence that he gives 'em to work in the Towns, or any where elſe. In fine, moſt of the Officers marry in this Country, but God knows what ſort of Marriages they make, in taking Girls with a Dowry, conſiſting of eleven Crowns, a Cock, a Hen, an Ox, a Cow, and ſometimes a Calf. I knew ſeveral young Women, whoſe Lovers, after denying the Fact, and proving before the Judges the ſcandalous Converſation of their Miſtreſſes, were forc'd upon the perſwaſion of the *Eccleſiaſticks* to ſwallow the bitter Pill, and take the very ſame Girls in Marriage. Some Officers indeed marry well, but there are few ſuch. The occaſion of their marrying ſo readily in that Country, proceeds from the difficulty of converſing with the ſoft Sex. After a Man has made four Viſits to a young Woman, he is oblig'd to unfold his Mind to her Father and Mother; [265] he muſt then either talk of Marriage, or break off all Correſpondence; or if he do's not, both he and ſhe lies under a Scandal. In this Country a Man can't viſit another Man's Wife, without being cenſur'd, as if her Husband was a Cuckold. In fine, a Man can meet with no diverſion here, but that of reading, or eating, or drinking. Though after all, there are ſome Intrigues carry'd on, but with the ſame caution as in *Spain*, where the vertue of the Ladies conſiſts only in diſguiſing the matter handſomly.

Now, that I am upon the Subject of Marriage, I can't forbear to acquaint you with a comical Adventure that happen'd to a young Captain, who was preſs'd to marry againſt his will, becauſe all his Companions and Acquaintances were already buckled. This young Officer having made ſome Viſits to a Counſellor's Daughter, he was deſir'd to tell what Errand he came upon; and Mr. *de Frontenac* himſelf, being related to the young Lady, who is certainly one of the moſt accompliſh'd Ladies of this Age, us'd his utmoſt efforts to ingage the Captain to marry her. The Captain being equally well pleas'd with a free acceſs to the Governour's Table, and the company of the Lady whom he met there not unfrequently; the Captain, I ſay, being equally fond of theſe two Advantages, endeavour'd to ward off the deſign, by asking ſome time to conſider of it. Accordingly, two Months were granted him; and after that time was expir'd, he had ftill a mind to let out his Traces, and fo defir'd two Months more, which were granted him by the Bifhop's interceffion. When the laft of thefe two was at an end, the Cavalier began to be apprehenfive that he was in danger of lofing both his good Cheer, and the agreeable company of the Lady. However, he was oblig'd to be prefent at a Treat that Mr. *Nelfon* (the *Englifh* Gentleman I [266] fpoke of in my 23*d* Letter) gave to the two Lovers, as well as the Governour, the Intendant, the Bifhop, and fome other Perfons of Note: And this generous *Englifh* Gentleman, having a kindnefs for the young Ladies Father, and her Brethren, upon the fcore of their trading with one another, made an offer of a thoufand Crowns to be paid on the Wedding Day, which added to a thoufand that the Bifhop offer'd, and a thoufand more which fhe had of her own, befides feven or eight thoufand that Mr. *de Frontenac* offer'd in Licences, not to mention the certain profpect of Preferment; all thefe Items, I fay, made the Marriage very advantageous to the Captain. After they had done eating, he was prefs'd to fign the Contract, but made anfwer, that he had drunk fome bumpers of heady Wine, and his Head was not clear enough for weighing the conditions of the Contract; fo that they were forc'd to put off the matter till the next day. Upon this delay he kept his Chamber till Mr. *de Frontenac*, at whofe Table he us'd to eat, fent for him in order to know his Mind immediately. Then there was no room left for fhuffling; there was a neceffity of giving a pofitive anfwer to the Governour, who fpoke to him in plain and precife terms, and at the fame time reminded him of the favour they had fhewn him, in allowing him fo much time to confider of the propos'd Marriage. The young Officer reply'd very fairly, that any Man that was capable of Marrying after four Months deliberation, was a fool in buckling to. 'I now fee, 'fays he, what I am; the eager defire I had of going to Church 'with Mademoifelle *D*.... has now convinc'd me of my folly; 'if you have a refpect for the Lady, pray do not fuffer her to 'marry a young Spark, that is fo apt to take up with extrava-'gant and foolifh things. As for my own part, Sir, I proteft 'fincerely, that the little reafon and free [267] judgment that 'is left me, will ferve to comfort me upon the lofs of her, and 'to teach me to repent of having defir'd to make her as 'unhappy as my felf. This Difcourfe furpris'd the Bifhop, the Governour, the Intendant, and in general, all the other Married Officers, who defir'd nothing more than that he fhould be catch'd in the noofe as well as they; fo true it is, that *Solamen miferis focios habuiffe doloris*. As they were far from expecting any fuch retractation; fo the poor reform'd Captain fuffer'd for't; for fome time after Mr. *de Frontenac* did him a piece of Injuftice, in beftowing a vacant Company over his Head, upon Madam *de Ponchartrain*'s Nephew, notwithftanding that the Court had fent orders on his behalf; and this oblig'd him to go for *France* along with me in the year 1692.[1]

[1] Under this thin disguise, Lahontan here relates an episode in his own career. The lady in question was doubtless Geneviève, daughter of Mathieu d'Amours of the sovereign council, whose brothers traded with Nelson, the English merchant — see

To refume the thread of my Difcourfe: You muft know that the *Canadefe* or *Creoles*, are a robuft brawny well made People; they are ftrong, vigorous, active, brave and indefatigable; in a word, they want nothing but the knowledge of polite Letters. They are prefumptuous, and very full of themfelves; they value themfelves beyond all the Nations of the Earth, and, which is to be regrated, they have not that veneration for their Parents that is due. Their Complexion is wonderfully pretty. The Women are generally handfom; few of them are brown, but many of 'em are at once wife and lazy. They love Luxury to the laft degree, and ftrive to outdo one another in catching Husbands in the trap.

There's an infinity of diforders in *Canada*, that want to be reform'd. The firft ftep of a true Reformation, muft be that of hindring the Ecclefiafticks to vifit the Inhabitants fo often, and to pry with fuch impertinence into the minuteft affairs of the Family; for fuch practices are frequently contrary to the good of the Society, and that for reafons [268] that you are not ignorant of. The next thing to be done, is to prohibit the Officers to ftop the Soldiers pay, and to injoyn 'em to Difcipline their Men every Holy-day, and every Sunday. In the third place, the Commodities ought to be rated at a reafonable price, fo that the Merchant may have his profit, without exacting upon the Inhabitants and the Savages. A fourth Article of Reformation, would confift in prohibiting the exporting from *France* to *Canada*, of Brocado's, Gold and

---

pp. 265, 311, *ante*. Mademoiselle d'Amours married (1703) Jean Baptiste Céloron de Blainville. For further details, see Roy, *Lahontan*, pp. 92, 93. — ED.

Silver Galloons or Ribbands, and rich Laces. In a fifth place, the Governour General ought not to ſell Licences for trading with the Savages of the great Lakes. Sixthly, there ought to be fix'd Courts.[1] In the ſeventh place, they want to have their Militia modell'd and diſciplin'd, that upon occaſion, they may be as ſerviceable as the Regular Troops.[2] For an eighth Article, the ſetting up Manufactories for Linnen, Stuffs, *&c.* would be very uſeful.[3] But the moſt important alteration would conſiſt in keeping the Governours, the Intendants, the ſupreme Council, the Biſhops and the Jeſuits, from ſplitting into Factions, and making Clubs one againſt another; for the conſequences of ſuch Diviſions can't but thwart his Majeſty's Service, and the Peace of the Publick. Were this but happily effected, that Country would be as rich again as 'tis now.

I wonder that inſtead of baniſhing the Proteſtants out of *France*, who in removing to the Countries of our Enemies,

---

[1] It is difficult to know what Lahontan means by "fixed courts," since justice in New France was well administered by a series of such. The sovereign council was the court of appeal; judges held sessions in the three towns of Montreal, Three Rivers, and Quebec; the seigneurs administered justice in petty disputes; and above all was the jurisdiction of the governor and intendant, the latter holding a special court in his palace, which was known therefrom as the Palace of Justice. — ED.

[2] Canadians had served as militia from the foundation of the colony, no regular troops coming out until 1665. In time of war all the male population between the ages of fifteen and sixty was enrolled in the militia, and officers were appointed from each parish, besides general officers for especially exposed localities. In 1691, 1313 Canadians received pay as soldiers — Sulte, *Canadiens français*, vi, 46; vii, 47. — ED.

[3] Unlike the English government, the French authorities stimulated and protected colonial manufactures. But the population was too sparse to accomplish much in this direction. Some cloth had been woven and articles in iron produced, and ship-building had been inaugurated early in the eighteenth century. — ED.

have done ſo much damage to the Kingdom, by carrying their Money along with 'em, and ſetting up Manufacturies in thoſe Countries; I wonder, I ſay, that the Court did not think it more proper to tranſport 'em to *Canada.* I'm convinc'd, that if they had receiv'd poſitive aſſurances of injoying a liberty of Conſcience, a great many of 'em would have made no ſcruple [269] to go thither. Some have reply'd upon this Head, that the Remedy had been worſe than the Diſeaſe; in regard that ſome time or other they would not have fail'd to expel the *Catholicks* by the aſſiſtance of the *Engliſh:* But I repreſented to 'em, that the *Greeks* and *Armenians*, who are ſubject to the Grand *Seignior*, and at the ſame time are of a Nation and Religion that's different from that of the *Turks;* I repreſented, I ſay, that theſe diſſenting Subjects did ſcarce ever implore the aid of foreign Powers, in order to rebel and ſhake off the Yoak. In fine, we have more reaſon to believe, that if the *Huguenots* had been tranſported to *Canada*, they had never departed from the fealty they ow'd to their natural Soveraign. But, let that be as it will; I do but ſpeak as that King of *Arragon* did, who boaſted, that if God had daign'd to conſult him, he could have given him ſeaſonable advice with reference to the ſymmetry and the courſes of the Stars: For in like manner, I do affirm, that if the Council of State had follow'd my Scheme, in the ſpace of thirty or forty years, *New-France* would have become a finer and more flouriſhing Kingdom, than ſeveral others in *Europe.*

A Discourse of the Interest of the French, *and of the* English, *in North*-America.

SINCE *New-France* and *New-England* subsist only upon the Cod-Fishery, and the Fur-trade, 'tis the interest of these two Colonies to inlarge the number of the Ships imploy'd in the Fishery, and to incourage the Savages to hunt and shoot Beavers, by furnishing them with what Arms and Ammunition they have occasion for. 'Tis well known, that there's a great consumption of Codfish in the [270] Southern Countries of *Europe*, and that few Commodities meet with a better and readier Market, especially if they are good and well cur'd.

Those who alledge that the destruction of the *Iroquese*, would promote the interest of the Colonies of *New-France*, are strangers to the true interest of that Country; for if that were once accomplish'd, the Savages who are now the *French* Allies, would turn their greatest Enemies, as being then rid of their other fears. They would not fail to call in the *English*, by reason that their Commodities are at once cheaper, and more esteem'd than ours; and by that means the whole Commerce of that wide Country, would be wrested out of our hands.

I conclude therefore, that 'tis the interest of the *French* to weaken the *Iroquese*, but not to see 'em intirely defeated. I own, that at this day they are too strong, insomuch that they cut the Throats of the Savages our Allies every day. They have nothing lefs in view, than to cut off all the Nations they know, let their Situation be never fo remote from their Country. 'Tis our bufinefs to reduce 'em to one half of the power they are now poffefs'd of, if 'twere poffible; but we do not go the right way to work. Above thefe thirty years, their ancient Counfellors have ftill remonftrated to the Warriours of the five Nations, that 'twas expedient to cut off all the Savage Nations of *Canada*, in order to ruine the Commerce of the *French*, and after that to diflodge 'em of the Continent. With this view they have carry'd the War above four or five hundred Leagues off their Country, after the deftroying of feveral different Nations in feveral places, as I fhew'd you before.

'Twould be no difficult matter for the *French* to draw the *Iroquefe* over to their fide, to keep 'em from plaguing the *French* Allies, and at the fame time to ingrofs all the Commerce with the five *Iroquefe* [271] Nations, that is now in the hands of the *Englifh* in *New-York*. This might be eafily put in execution, provided the King would allow ten thoufand Crowns a year, for that end. The method of effecting it is this. In the firft place, the Barques that were formerly made ufe of about Fort *Frontenac*, muft be rebuilt, in order to convey to the Rivers of the *Tfonontouans* and the *Onontagues*, fuch Commodities as are proper for 'em, and to fell 'em for the prime coft in *France*.[1] Now this would put the King to the

[1] By 1677 La Salle had four vessels upon Lake Ontario, with a capacity of twenty-five to forty tons each. These were all destroyed when Fort Frontenac was abandoned (1689). — ED.

charge of about ten thoufand Crowns for fraight; and I'm perfwaded, that upon that foot the *Iroquefe* would not be fuch fools as to carry fo much as one Beaver to the *Englifh* Colonies, and that for four Reafons. The firft is, that, whereas they muft tranfport 'em fixty or eighty Leagues upon their backs to *New-York*, they have not above feven or eight Leagues travelling from their own Villages, to the banks of the Lake of *Frontenac*. For a fecond reafon, 'tis manifeft that the *Englifh* can't poffibly let 'em have their Commodities fo cheap, without being confiderable lofers, and that thereupon every Merchant would drop that fort of Trade. The third is drawn from the difficulty of having Subfiftance upon the Road between the *Iroquefe* Villages and *New-York*; for the *Iroquefe* go thither in great Bodies, for fear of being furpris'd, and I acquainted you before feveral times, that there's no Venifon in that fide of the Country. The fourth reafon is this. In marching fo far from their Villages, they expofe their Wives, their Children, and their fuperannuated Men, for a prey to their Enemies, who upon that occafion may either kill 'em, or carry 'em off; and of this we have two Inftances already. Over and above the cheapnefs of our Commodities, 'twould likewife be requifite that we made 'em Prefents every year, and at the fame time intreated 'em not to difturb the repofe of our [272] Confederate Savages, who are fuch fools, as to wage War one with another, inftead of entring into a joint League in oppofition to the *Iroquefe*, the moft redoubted of their Enemies, and thofe whom they have moft reafon to fear. In a word, if we would manage our affairs with the *Iroquefe* to the beſt advantage, we ought to put in execution that Project that I mention'd in my 23*d* Letter.

To alledge that theſe *Barbarians* have a dependance upon the *Engliſh*, is a fooliſh Plea: For they are ſo far from owning any dependance, that when they go to *New-York* to truck their Skins, they have the confidence to put rates upon the Goods they have occaſion for, when the Merchants offer to raiſe their price. I have intimated already ſeveral times, that their reſpect for the *Engliſh*, is tack'd to the occaſion they have to make uſe of 'em; that this is the only motive which induces 'em to treat the *Engliſh* as their Brethren, and their Friends; and that if the *French* would ſell 'em the Neceſſaries of Life, as well as Arms and Ammunition, at eaſier rates, they would not make many journeys to the *Engliſh* Colonies. This is a conſideration that ought to be chiefly in our view; for if we minded it to the purpoſe, they would be cautious of inſulting our Savage Confederates, as well as our ſelves. The Governours General of *Canada* would do well to imploy the ſenſible Men of the Country that are acquainted with our Confederates, in preſſing 'em to live in a good correſpondence with one another, without waging War among themſelves; for moſt of the Southern Nations worm out one another inſenſibly, which affords matter of joy to the *Iroqueſe*. Now, 'twere an eaſie matter to prevent this fatal mouldering, by threatning to give 'em no further ſupplies of Commodities in their Villages. To this precaution, we ought to add that of indeavouring to ingage two or three Nations to live together; [273] the *Outaouas*, for inſtance, with the *Hurons;* the *Sakis* with the

Pouteouatamis, aliàs *Puants*.[1] If all thofe Nations who are imbarqued in a Confederacy with us, would but agree one with another, and put up their quarrels, they would give themfelves wholly to the hunting of Beavers, which would tend to the inlarging of our Commerce; and befides, they would be in a condition of making one joint Body, when the *Iroquefe* offer'd to attack either one or t'other.

'Tis the intereft of the *Englifh* to perfwade thefe Nations, that the *French* have nothing lefs in view, than to deftroy them as foon as they meet with an opportunity; that the growing populoufnefs of *Canada*, is a fufficient ground of alarm; that they ought to avoid all Commerce with the *French*, for fear of being betray'd in any way whatfoever; that to hinder the repairing of Fort *Frontenac*, and the rebuilding of Barques for that Lake, is to them a thing of the laft Importance, by reafon that the *French* might in four and twenty hours, make a Defcent from thence to their Villages, and carry off their ancient Men, their Women and their Children, at a time when the Warriours might be ingag'd in the hunting of Beavers; That they would promote their own intereft by waging War with the *French* from time to time, by ravaging the Seignories and Settlements in the upper part of the Country, in order to oblige the Inhabitants to abdicate the Colony, and to difcourage thofe who would otherwife remove out of *France*, and fettle in *Canada;* and in fine,

[1] Lahontan here confuses two entirely different, though neighbouring, Wisconsin tribes; the Potawatomi were of Algonquian, the Puants (Winnebago) of Siouan stock. — Ed.

That in time of Peace 'twould be very proper to ſtop the *Coureurs de Bois* at the Cataracts of the *Outaouas* River, and to ſeize the Arms and Ammunition that they carry to the Savages upon the Lakes.

Farther, if the *Engliſh* would purſue their meaſures to the beſt advantage, they ought to ingage the *Tſonontouans* or the *Goyoguans* to go and ſettle upon the Banks of the Lake *Erriè*, near the Mouth [274] of the River of *Condè;* and at the ſame time they ought to build a Fort there, with ſome long Barques or Brigantines: For this is the moſt convenient and advantageous Poſt of all that Country, and that for an infinity of Reaſons which I am oblig'd to conceal. Beſides this Fort, they ſhould build another at the Mouth of the River *des François;* and then 'twould be abſolutely impoſſible for the *Coureurs de Bois* to reach the Lakes.

They ought likewiſe to ingage the Savages of *Acadia* in their intereſt; which they may do with little charge. The Planters of *New-England* ſhould mind this, as well as the fortifying of the Ports in which they fiſh their Cod. As for the fitting out of Fleets to deſtroy the Colony, I would not adviſe the *Engliſh* to give themſelves that trouble; for ſuppoſing they were aſſur'd of Succeſs, 'tis but ſome places that can be reckon'd worth the while.

To conclude; I muſt ſay the *Engliſh* in theſe Colonies are too careleſs and lazy: The *French Coureurs de Bois*, are much readier for Enterpriſes, and the *Canadeſe* are certainly more vigilant and more active. It behoves the Inhabitants of *New-York* to inlarge their Fur-trade by well concerted Enterpriſes;

and thoſe of *New-England*, to render the Cod-fiſhing more beneficial to the Colony, by taking ſuch meaſures as many other People would, if they were as advangeouſly ſeated. I do not intend to ſpeak of the limits of *New-France*, and *New-England*, for they were never well adjuſted; though indeed 'twould ſeem that in ſeveral Treaties of Peace between theſe two Kingdoms, the Boundaries were in a manner mark'd out in ſome places. Whatever is in that matter, the deciſion of it is too nice a point for one that can't open his mind without pulling an old Houſe upon his Head.

The End of the Firſt Volume.

[275] A TABLE explaining ſome Terms made uſe of in both Volumes.

A.

ASTROLABE *is a Mathematical Inſtrument that can ſcarce be uſed in the Ocean by reaſon of the Waves. There are two ſorts of them. The firſt are made uſe of by* Eaſt-India *Maſters, at a time when the Sea is as ſmooth as the face of a Looking-glaſs. This ſort are ſerviceable in taking the heighth of the Sun, by the means of two little Pins, which are bor'd ſo as to have two dioptrick Perforations, that ſerve to conduct the rays of light to that Luminary. The latter are ſuch as the Mathematicians commonly make uſe of for Aſtronomical Obſervations, and are furbiſh'd with Azimuths, Almucantara's, Loxodromick Tables, and the Concentrick and Excentrick Tables of the Sphere.*

B.

Bank *of* New-found-land, *or* Bank *in general, is a riſing Ground in the Sea, which ſhoots like a Hat beyond the other brims. The Bank of* New-found-land *has thirty or forty Fathom Water, and is pav'd with Cod fiſh.*

Baſin, *is a head of ſtagnating Water, not unlike a Pool or Lake.*

Bouteux *ſignifies little Nets belag'd to the end of a Stick. The Fiſhermen make uſe of them to catch Fiſh upon a ſandy Ground, and eſpecially Eels, upon the ſide of St.* Laurence *River.*

Bouts de Quievres, *are Nets not unlike* Bouteux, *which ſerve for the ſame uſe.*

Breaking ground *ſignifies the weighing Anchor and putting to Sea.*

Brigantine, *a ſmall Veſſel one Deck, built of light* [276] *Wood, which plies both with Oars and Sails. 'Tis equally ſharp at Prow and Poop, and is built for a quick Sailer.*

C.

Calumet *in general ſignifies a Pipe, being a* Norman *Word, deriv'd from* Chalumeau. *The Savages do not underſtand this Word, for 'twas introduc'd to* Canada *by the* Normans *when they firſt ſettled there; and has ſtill continued in uſe amongſt the* French *Planters.*[1] *The* Calumet *or Pipe is call'd in the* Iroqueſe *Language* Ganondaoe, *and by the other Savage Nations* Poagan.

Canadeſe *or* Canadans, *are the Natives of* Canada *ſprung from a* French *Father and Mother. In the Iſlands of* South-America *the Natives born of* French *Parents are called* Creoles.

Capa y d'eſpada, *A* Gaſcogne *Title which the People of that Province gave in former times by way of Irony, to the Members of the ſupreme Council of* Canada, *becauſe the firſt Counſellors wore neither Robe nor Sword, but walk'd very gravely with a Cane in their Hands, both in the City of* Quebeck, *and in the Hall.*

Caſſe-tête *ſignifies a Club, or a Head-breaker.*[2] *The Savages call it* Aſſan Ouſtick, Ouſtick *ſignifying the* Head, *and* Aſſan, *to* break.

---

[1] Strictly speaking, the word calumet (chalumeau) referred only to the reed or stem of the pipe. — Ed.

[2] The word casse-tête is usually rendered by the Indian term tomahawk, although more properly a war-club than a hatchet. — Ed.

Channel *is a ſpace of pretty deep Water between two Banks, or between two Shoars. Commonly the Channels are incloſed by Flats, and for that reaſon* Bouys *or Maſts are fixt upon 'em, in order to direct the Pilots, who ſteer either by theſe Marks, or by ſounding, for they would run the riſque of looſing their Ships, if they did not keep exactly to the Channel.*

Coaſt along, *ſee* Sweep.

Compaſs of Variation. *'Tis larger than the ordinary Compaſſes, and ſerves to point out the inequal Motions of the Needle, which leans always to the North-Eaſt in the other Hemiſphere, whereas it ſtill plies to the North-Weſt; in this, I mean on this ſide the Equinoctial line: The* [277] *Needle touch'd with the Loadſtone departs from the true North a certain number of Degrees to the right and left; and Mariners compute the Degrees of its departure by the means of an Albidada, and a thread which divides the Glaſs of the Compaſs into two equal parts, and ſo ſhews the Variation of the Needle at Sun-ſet, that being the true proper time for making the Obſervation; for at Sun-riſing, and at Noon, one may be deceiv'd by Refractions,* &c.

Coureurs de Bois, *i. e. Foreſt Rangers, are* French *or* Canadeſe, *ſo call'd from employing their whole Life in the rough Exerciſe of tranſporting Merchandize Goods to the Lakes of* Canada, *and to all the other Countries of that Continent, in order to Trade with the Savages: And in regard that they run in Canows a thouſand Leagues up the Country, notwithſtanding the danger of the Sea and Enemies, I take it, they ſhould rather be called* Coureurs de Riſques, *than* Coureurs de Bois.

E.

Eddy, *or boyling Water, is little Watery Mountains that riſe at the foot of Water-falls or Cataracts, juſt as we ſee the Water plays in the Ciſterns of Water-works.*

Edge *of a Bank, is the ſhelving part of it that runs ſteep like a Wall.*

F.

Fathom, *among the* French *is the meaſure of ſix foot.*

Feaſt of Union, *a Term us'd by the* Iroqueſe *to ſignify the renewing of the Alliance between the five* Iroqueſe *Nations.*

Flats *are a ridge of Rocks running under Water from one Station to another, and riſing within five or ſix foot at leaſt of the Surface of that Element, ſo as to hinder Ships, Barques,* &c. *to float upon 'em.*

Fraight, *ſignifies in this Book the Cargo, tho' in other Caſes it ſignifies likewiſe the Hire or Fare.*

Furl the Sails, *ſignifies the drawing them up to a heap* [278] *towards the Top-maſt, not long ways as we do the Curtains of a Bed, but from below upwards. This is done by two Ropes, that draw up the Sail as a String does a Purſe.*

H.

Head-Bars *are two round pieces of Wood, reaching on each ſide from one end of a Canow to the other. Theſe are the Supporters of the Canow, for the Ribs and Spars are made faſt upon them.*

K.

Keel *of a Ship, is a long piece of the ſtrongeſt Wood, or at leaſt ſeveral pieces joyn'd together, to bear the great weight of all the other Timber.*

Kitchi Okima, *is the general Name for the Governour General of* Canada *among all the Savages, whose Languages approach to that of the* Algonkins. Kitchi *signifies* Great, *and* Okima, Captain. *The* Iroquese *and* Hurons *call the Governor General* Onnontio.

L.

Latitude. *Every Body knows that it imports the Elevation of the Pole, or the distance from a fix'd Point of the Æquator.*

Land-carriage *signifies the transporting of Canows by Land from the Foot to the Head of a Cataract, or from one River to another.*

Light *Ships are such as are empty, without any Cargo.*

P.

Poop *is the Stern or After-part of the Ship in which the Rudder is fix'd.*

Precipice *of a Bank, see* Edge.

Prow *is the Head or Fore-part of a Ship, which cuts the Water first.*

Q.

Quarter. *Tho' the Word Quarter in a Maritime Sense, is not well explain'd; I put the meaning of it to be this.* [279] *The North Quarter comprehends the space that lies between North-West and North-East. The East Quarter runs from North-East to South-East. The South Quarter comprehends that part of the Heavens that falls between South-East and South-West: And the West Quarter extends from South-West to North-West.*

R.

Refitting *of a Ship, ſignifies the repairing and dreſſing of it, and putting it into a Condition to ſail, by putting in new Planks, caulking the Seams,* &c.

Ribs *of a Canow, are much like thoſe of a Pink, only there's this difference, that they line the Canow only on the in-ſide from one Head Bar to another, upon which they are inchas'd. They have the thickneſs of three Crowns, and the breadth of four Inches.*

Ruche, *an Inſtrument for fiſhing, reſembling a Bee-hive.*

S.

Scurvy, *is a Corruption of the Maſs of Blood. There are two ſorts of it; one call'd the Land Scurvy, which loads a Man with Infirmities that gradually bring him to his Grave; the other is the Sea Scurvy, which infallibly kills a Man in* 8 *days unleſs he gets a-ſhoar.*

Shieve, i. e. *Row the wrong way, in order to aſſiſt the Steerſman to ſteer the Boat, and to keep the Boat in the Channel.*

Shoot. *To ſhoot a Water-fall or Cataract, implies the running a Boat down theſe dangerous Precipices, following the ſtream of the Water, and ſteering very nicely.*

Sledges *are a Conveniency for travelling, built in an oblong quadrangular form, upon two pieces of Wood, which are* 4 *foot long, and* 6 *foot broad; upon the Wood there are ſeveral pieces of Cloath or Hide nail'd to keep the Wind off. Theſe two pieces of Wood are very hard, and well ſmooth'd, that they may ſlide the better on Snow or Ice. Such are the Horſe Sledges. But thoſe drawn by Dogs are open, and made of two little pieces of hard ſmooth, and ſhining Wood, which are half an Inch thick,* 5 *foot long, and a foot and a half broad.*

[280] Spars *are little pieces of* Cedar *Wood, of the thickneſs of a Crown, and the breadth of* 3 *Inches, and as long as they can be made. They do the ſame Service to a Canow, that a good lining does to a Coat.*

Stand *in for Land, ſignifies to ſail directly towards it.*

Steer a Ship, *imports the managing of a Ship by the means of a Rudder, (as we do a Horſe with a Bridle) when there's Wind enough to work her; but if there be no Wind, a Ship is more unmoveable than a Gouty Perſon in an Elbow Chair.*

Stem *a Tide or the Current of a River*, i. e. *to ſail againſt the Current, or to ſteer for the place from whence the Tides or Currents come.*

Strike, *to ſtrike the Sails or Flag ſignifies the lowering of 'em, whether it be to ſubmit to an Enemy, or by reaſon of high Winds.*

Sweep *a Coaſt, ſignifies to ſail along the Coaſt ſide at a reaſonable diſtance.*

T.

Top-gallant-Maſts *are two little Maſts ſet upon the two Top-Maſts, and have two Sails fitted for 'em.*

Top-Sails *are two Sails fitted for the two Top-Maſts, which ſtand directly above the two great Maſts.*

Traverſe. *To traverſe ſignifies ſailing* Zigzag, *or from ſide to ſide as a drunken Man reels, when the Wind is contrary, for then they are oblig'd to tack ſometimes to the right, and ſometimes to the left, keeping as near to the Wind as they can, in order to make what way they can, or at leaſt to prevent their loſing Ground.*

Tree *of Peace, a Symbolick Metaphor for Peace it ſelf.*

[End of Volume I.]

www.ingramcontent.com/pod-product-compliance
Lightning Source LLC
LaVergne TN
LVHW011255110826
845149LV00001B/137

* 9 7 8 1 4 1 8 1 8 8 8 6 3 *